全国14家国家特色服务出口基地（语言服务）联合推荐
新文科语言服务学术文库

众包与在线协作翻译
拓宽翻译学的边界

Crowdsourcing and Online Collaborative Translations

Expanding the Limits of Translation Studies

Miguel A. Jiménez-Crespo ● 著

韩林涛 ● 导读

上海外语教育出版社
外教社 SHANGHAI FOREIGN LANGUAGE EDUCATION PRESS

图书在版编目（CIP）数据

众包与在线协作翻译：拓宽翻译学的边界：汉文、
英文 / 米格尔·希门尼斯-克雷斯波著；韩林涛导
读. —上海：上海外语教育出版社，2024
（新文科语言服务学术文库 / 王立非总主编）
ISBN 978-7-5446-8084-4

Ⅰ.①众…　Ⅱ.①米…②韩…　Ⅲ.①翻译—研究—
汉、英　Ⅳ.①H059

中国国家版本馆CIP数据核字（2024）第068874号

Original edition *Crowdsourcing and Online Collaborative Translations: Expanding the limits of Translation Studies* by Miguel A. Jiménez-Crespo.
© 2017 John Benjamins Publishing Company, Amsterdam/Philadelphia
Reprinted by permission for distribution in the People's Republic of China only.
本书由约翰·本杰明出版社授权上海外语教育出版社有限公司出版。
仅供在中华人民共和国境内销售。
图字：09-2022-0943号

出版发行：上海外语教育出版社
（上海外国语大学内）　邮编：200083
电　　话：021-65425300（总机）
电子邮箱：bookinfo@sflep.com.cn
网　　址：http://www.sflep.com
责任编辑：王晓宇

印　　刷：上海宝山译文印刷厂有限公司
开　　本：635×965　1/16　印张21　字数403千字
版　　次：2024年2月第1版　2024年2月第1次印刷

书　　号：ISBN 978-7-5446-8084-4
定　　价：68.00元

本版图书如有印装质量问题，可向本社调换
质量服务热线：4008-213-263

"新文科语言服务学术文库"专家委员会

顾问：
李宇明（北京语言大学）
王继辉（北京大学）

主任：
王立非（北京语言大学）

委员：（姓氏笔画为序）
王传英（南开大学）
王华树（北京外国语大学）
王宗琥（首都师范大学）
王铭玉（天津外国语大学）
文　军（北京航空航天大学）
艾　斌（上海财经大学）
冯光武（广东外语外贸大学）
司显柱（北京第二外国语学院）
吕世生（北京语言大学）
任虎林（北京科技大学）
刘　宏（大连外国语大学）
刘和平（北京语言大学）
孙　玉（上海外语教育出版社）
李　梅（同济大学）
杨明星（郑州大学）
张　政（北京师范大学）

张天伟（北京外国语大学）

张法连（中国政法大学）

张慧玉（浙江大学）

罗慧芳（当代中国与世界研究院）

屈哨兵（广州大学）

赵蓉晖（上海外国语大学）

胡开宝（上海外国语大学）

俞敬松（北京大学）

祝朝伟（四川外国语大学）

贺永中（美国蒙特雷高等国际研究院）

高明乐（北京语言大学）

高　霄（华北电力大学）

郭英剑（中国人民大学）

黄立波（西安外国语大学）

曹　进（西北师范大学）

崔启亮（对外经济贸易大学）

蒙永业（北京悦尔信息技术有限公司）

蔡基刚（复旦大学）

穆　雷（广东外语外贸大学）

Arle Lommel（美国 CSA 咨询公司）

前　言

　　语言服务兴起于 20 世纪 90 年代的欧美。2010 年，中国翻译协会首次正式在我国提出"语言服务"的概念。语言服务指以语言能力为核心，以促进跨语言、跨文化交流为目标，提供语际信息转化服务和产品，以及相关研究咨询、技术研发、工具应用、资产管理、教育培训等专业化服务的现代服务业。

　　根据统计，尽管全球经济不断受到挑战，但语言服务行业依然保持增长，2022 年，全球语言服务产值突破 600 亿美元。我国对外开放、中外人文交流和"一带一路"建设不断促进我国的语言服务市场增长。2022 年，我国的翻译公司和各类型的语言服务企业总计超过 42 万家，总产值突破 554 亿元人民币。语言服务发展的同时也带来巨大的人才需求。

　　语言服务教育在我国是一个新生事物，目标是培养行业需要的口笔译、语言技术和项目管理人才。2007 年，我国开办翻译硕士专业学位教育，为语言服务行业培养翻译人才。近年来，部分高校通过开设研究方向或独立设置二级学科点等方式，招收本地化管理、技术传播、翻译项目管理、医学语言服务、国际语言服务研究生，培养"语言 + 技术""语言 + 专业"和"语言 + 管理"的复合型和应用型人才。部分高校成立了语言服务研究院所、应急语言服务基地（中心），召开语言服务论坛，编写语言服务研究报告等。2020 年，中国英汉语比较研究会批准成立语言服务研究专业委员会，出版《语言服务研究》集刊。2022 年，商务部、教育部、中国外文局等部委批准成立特色语言服务出口基地，国家发改委和商务部批准语言服务进入鼓励外商投资产业目录。以上举措有力地促进了语言服务的发展。

　　为了帮助广大师生了解国外语言服务领域学术研究和行业发展动态，满足高校语言服务学科建设、人才培养、教学科研的需要，上海外语教育出版社组织专家精心策划了"新文科语言服务学术文库"，从国外原版引进多种语言服务学术著作。本文库涵盖翻译及语言服务的职业技能和企业管理两个方面，包括翻译教学、技术文档写作、本地化技术、质量管理、服务管理、众包翻译管理等，体系完整，内容丰富，值得推荐。同时，为了方便读者理解重点，文库各书还专门配有中文导读和推荐阅读书目。

　　本文库可用作研究生教材，也适合语言服务行业人士和对语言服务感兴趣的广大社会读者作为参考书使用。希望文库的出版能为我国的语言服务发展贡献一份力量。

专家委员会主任

王立非

2023 年 12 月

导　读

一、本领域概述

"众包"一词，起源于英语 crowdsourcing，由美国《连线》杂志记者 Jeff Howe 于 2006 年创造。这一术语融合了 crowd（人群）和 outsourcing（外包）的概念，描述了一种创新的工作模式：企业或机构将传统上由内部员工完成的任务，基于自愿原则委托给广泛、不特定的公众参与者。2006 年，网络世界见证了几个重要的里程碑事件：实时通信工具 Skype 的用户数突破一亿，维基百科的志愿者编撰的文章数量超过一百万篇；同年，《时代》杂志将"你"（You）评为年度人物。这些事件彰显了互联网时代一个重要现象——全球范围内，越来越多的网站内容由用户自行创造。正是在这样的背景下，"众包"这一概念应运而生，标志着越来越多的互联网用户开始自发参与各类商业和公益项目。

翻译领域一直是新技术的试验田，从 20 世纪 50 年代机器翻译技术在军事领域的早期应用，到个人计算机和互联网在 20 世纪 70 年代的兴起，技术革新不断推动翻译行业的演变。互联网的普及让全球的普通用户得以通过个人计算机访问世界各地的信息，并参与跨文化沟通。正是在这个基础上，众包翻译——一种充分利用互联网群体智慧的翻译模式，应运而生。通过这种模式，无论是专业翻译人员还是业余翻译人员，都可以为不同语言间的信息交流贡献自己的力量。这不仅加速了翻译过程，也极大地丰富了翻译内容的多样性和质量。

信息技术行业跨国贸易对翻译的需求催生了计算机辅助翻译工具和本地化行业，为众包翻译模式的繁荣提供了先进的技术支持和良性的行业环境。1990 年本地化行业标准协会在瑞士成立，标志着国际本地化行业初步成形，本地化行业从业者逐步开始使用 Trados 等商业计算机辅助翻译工具完成 Windows 操作系统等信息技术产品的本地化工作。

本地化行业的迅猛发展极大加速了互联网企业的国际化进程。在 2000 年前后，谷歌、腾讯、阿里巴巴等知名互联网企业相继成立，标志着新时代的开始。自 2006 年以来，智能手机、云计算、大数据技术得到普及，以机器翻译为代表的人工智能技术实现了突破，这些技术领域经历了长达 15 年的快速发展。这一时期为 21 世纪 30 年代强人工智能技术的崛起奠定了坚实的算法、技术和数据基础，预示着一个全新的、由智能技术驱动的时代的到来。这些技术进步不仅改变了我们日常生活的方方面面，也为全球互联网企业的国际化和跨文化交流带来了前所未有的机遇。

在这个由信息技术、互联网和人工智能技术主导的时代，翻译行业正面临着前所未有的融合与变革机遇。作为这一变革的关键环节，众包翻译不仅依托先进技术，同时也积极参与并推动它们的发展。这一过程始于专业译者和业余译者自愿地参与维基百科等平台的国际化工作，随后迅速扩展到更广泛的领域。众包翻译的兴起和发展，不仅体现了翻译行业和本地化行业对新技术的快速适应能力，也展现了它在推动全球跨语言和跨文化交流中不断变革的潜力。

二、作者简介

本书作者 Miguel A. Jiménez-Crespo 是美国新泽西州立罗格斯大学教授，他的主要研究领域是：翻译技术、本地化、语料库翻译学、认知翻译学、翻译理论和翻译教学法。除本书外，他还著有《翻译和网站本地化》（*Translation and Web Localization*）及数十篇与翻译学、翻译技术、翻译教学相关的学术论文。

三、内容概要

（一）本书概况

本书主要讨论了众包翻译与在线协作翻译的兴起及其对翻译学和语言服务行业的深远影响。本书以众包和协作作为切入点，从翻译学的角度对众包翻译和在线协作翻译进行了深入研究，对 2018 年及之前的相关文献进行了系统梳理，对翻译的跨学科趋势进行了细致分析。

众包与协作翻译的兴起离不开技术的发展。在过去的二十年里，技术的进步极大地影响了翻译学的多个领域，如计算机辅助翻译、机器翻译、机器翻译译后编辑、语料库研究、翻译教育以及软件本地化等。在这些领域中，众包翻译与在线协作翻译作为较新的现象，不仅是计算机技术和互联网技术不断进步的产物，更成为推动翻译领域新兴形态出现的重要力量。正是由于这些技术的发展，我们见证了翻译技术产品的快速涌现，如云端计算机辅助翻译工具、在线机器翻译译后编辑平台等。这些产品通过技术创新，不仅挑战了翻译学科中的许多传统观念，还拓展了翻译学的边界，促使研究者深入探讨它们对当前和未来翻译理论及实践的影响。

本书精心剖析了众包翻译和在线协作翻译的本质，探讨了它们如何与不同领域融合，并预测了这种融合可能对未来造成的影响。本书采用丰富的实践案例和深入的学术观点，对这些新兴翻译实践进行了详尽的描述和分析，覆盖了翻译学及其多个分支学科，包括认知翻译学、社会学、翻译教学和文本语言学等领域。随着增强现实、神经机器翻译和大数据分析等新技术的涌现，翻译研究和实践经历了巨大的变革，不仅催生了创新的技术应用和产品，还重塑了人们对翻译过程和功能的理解。这些变革和创新在翻译领域引发了深刻的思考，赋予翻译学科更广阔的视野和更深刻的洞见。

（二）本书结构

本书正文共分为引言及十个章节：第一章对众包和在线协作翻译进行定义和分类；第二章梳理了众包和在线协作翻译的出现背景和发展过程；第三章展示了众包翻译的专业工作流程和案例，将其与传统翻译流程进行了区分；第四章从认知翻译学视角切入，分析在众包翻译过程中人是如何完成众包工作的；第五章探讨了众包翻译质量评估；第六章从文本、话语和语言学的视角探讨了众包翻译如何突破传统的文本定义方法；第七章引入字幕翻译案例探讨视听翻译的规范和挑战；第八章从社会学视角探讨众包翻译如何将翻译学从社会学转向引入技术转向；第九章从翻译人才培养的角度探讨如何为众包翻译模式建构更合理的翻译能力模型；第十章对全书的研究问题进行总结，指出众包翻译对语言服务行业翻译研究的重要影响。

（三）各章概要

引言部分简明扼要展示了众包和在线协作翻译的发展背景，以及这类新兴实践模式对翻译学的重要意义，并指出应深入研究众包和在线协作翻译对当前乃至未来翻译理论及翻译实践的影响。

第一章　众包与协作翻译在翻译学中的定义和类型

本章从翻译学的视角对众包（crowdsourcing）和在线协作翻译（online collaborative translation）进行了定义和类型划分。众包和在线协作翻译作为两个随着技术发展而不断变化的概念，既有共通之处，又各有不同。本章首先回顾了文献中有关众包的最具影响力的定义，详细梳理了众包的来源、特征和类型，然后从狭义和广义两个维度分析了协作翻译的本质，并据此将协作翻译划分为众包翻译和在线协作翻译，探讨了二者的共同点和不同点。对翻译学领域中与协作翻译相关的不同概念进行分析后，本章给出了众包翻译和在线协作翻译的具体定义，随后将众包翻译与翻译学中既有的相关概念进行对比分析，并详细分析了在线协作翻译的诸多类型。本章最后探讨了容易吸引志愿者参与众包翻译的各类文本，为后续研究奠定了基础。

第二章　众包与在线协作翻译的兴起

本章重点探讨众包和在线协作翻译出现的历史背景和发展历程，通过对翻译研究文献记录的早期协作翻译现象的历时概述，追溯了众包翻译和在线协作翻译的起源，据此认为其与早期依托网络开展的语言任务外包有根本性的不同。本章还回顾了协作翻译的类型和所涉领域，分析了互联网和 Web 2.0 如何影响协作翻译范式的转变、如何推动了众包翻译的发展，并根据众包翻译历史发展进程将其划分为五个不同的阶段，分别是：

第一阶段：个人计算机和互联网出现之前的合作翻译，如《圣经》和佛经的翻译等；

第二阶段：依托互联网迅速发展起来的粉丝社区积极主动地开展协作翻译；

第三阶段：志愿者通过机器翻译译后编辑的形式开展众包翻译，相关的众包翻译平台相继出现；

第四阶段：社交类互联网公司开始借助免费的众包翻译迅速扩张；

第五阶段：有偿众包翻译成为一种商业模式。

本章以互联网的出现作为分水岭，详尽分析互联网时代之前（1980 年之前）的协作翻译发展历史，以及个人计算机、互联网、万维网出现后（1980—1995 年）协作翻译发生的根本性变化；介绍了互联网出现后参与式文化（participatory culture）的发展背景，将该文化视为协作翻译的基础。本章还分析了 20 世纪最后 20 年在线协作翻译的具体实践（如字幕组、开源软件本地化等），以及 21 世纪初期社交网站、维基百科、非营利组织的众包翻译案例。

本章最后介绍了有偿众包。随着众包翻译逐渐成为主流模式，商业市场也开始探索有偿众包。在商业资本的介入下，有偿众包场景不断丰富和完善，众包流程变得更为专业。

第三章　众包与语言服务行业

本章从语言服务行业视角分析了与众包相关的专业工作流程和技术解决方案等。正是由于众包翻译模式被商业市场接受，包括翻译记忆、机器翻译在内的传统翻译技术与众包翻译模式相结合，传统翻译流程才发生了变化，众包翻译也得到了革新。本章展示了传统翻译流程如何发生彻底改变，详细分析了众包翻译的专业工作流程，并用描述性方法分析了大量语言服务行业中的众包技术应用实例，如Facebook、Kiva、Trommons、Asia Online、Crowdin、TED 等产品，介绍了不同类型的众包翻译平台，分析了机器翻译译后编辑模式在众包翻译中的应用研究。

本章最后将重点放在志愿者动机上，认为语言服务行业重在技术研究和推进，翻译学科则主要关注众包现象和最佳实践，但行业研究和学术研究应当互为补充，共同完善，可以将参与众包翻译的志愿者动机作为二者开展联合研究的切入点。

第四章　众包与认知翻译学

本章围绕认知翻译学展开。作为翻译学的重要分支，认知翻译学试图揭示译者在翻译过程中的认知原理。虽然其研究重点并非翻译志愿者或业余翻译人员，但对众包翻译中非专业翻译人员的认知过程研究也同样重要。本章指出，众包翻译和在线协作翻译需要与认知翻译学密切融合，从而更好地研究众包翻译过程，通过分析专业翻译人员和业余翻译人员的认知过程差异，可以判断在众包翻译中哪些任务可以交给专业翻译人员，哪些可以交给业余翻译人员。

本章首先探讨了众包翻译时代的分布式认知和延展认知。在探讨分布式认知时，本章基于译者借助翻译记忆库提升翻译效率和质量等具体的协作翻译和众包翻译案例，认为协作翻译的分布式认知体现在认知任务会分配到众包翻译软件和众包社区中。此外，本章还分析了译者在网络辅助下所处的不断变化的工作环境，认为认知不仅仅发生在译者的大脑中，还发生在复杂的真实网络环境中，所以认知翻译研究还应关注具身认知、情境认知和延展认知，去真正的众包翻译实境中研究译者的认知行为。

针对众包翻译场景的认知翻译学也引出了一个新的问题：如何定义专业翻译？本章就此问题从专业知识和翻译能力的角度详细分析了专业翻译和业余翻译的区别。

技术的出现改变了翻译流程，改变了译者的认知过程，也影响了译者的心理。本章简要探讨了众包翻译中的翻译动机和翻译过程中志愿者收到的反馈对译者心理的影响。

本章最后探讨了认知翻译学的新方法，认为可以依托互联网扩大科学实验的参与者规模，将有声思维法（Think Aloud Techniques, TAPs）与协作翻译相结合，并将这些研究方法引入翻译教育过程中。

第五章　众包与翻译质量

本章审视了众包翻译和在线协作翻译中的质量评估问题。质量是翻译研究中极具争议的问题之一，语言服务行业已不再完全基于翻译理论来评估翻译质量，而是由翻译活动的参与各方共同定义何为符合需求的质量、何为足够好的质量。本章试图重新定义众包翻译和在线协作翻译中的翻译质量，探讨学界和业界如何通过协作来评估翻译质量。

本章首先对"翻译质量"这个重要概念进行了系统分析，认为它不再是静态的，而取决于用户和环境，由用户和应用场景确定什么是好的翻译并判断翻译结果是否达到预期目标。

随后本章引入动态翻译质量评估模型，认为这类动态且可定制的评估框架是行业对动态质量问题带来的挑战的回应，并探讨了针对众包翻译和协作翻译应选择怎样的动态质量模型，如何针对有偿众包任务的实际需求定制翻译质量标准，如何针对众包翻译开展质量保障工作。

由于动态翻译质量评估模型来源于行业实践，所以本章还探讨了这类源自行业的研究成果如何影响翻译学领域的质量评估理论，梳理了翻译学领域里与翻译质量相关的前沿研究，如以 Facebook、Twitter

等产品为代表的众包翻译实践中出现的迭代翻译模型和通过用户投票来提升翻译质量的方法，以及众包翻译质量实证研究。

第六章　文本与众包

本章主要探讨众包翻译对翻译学中文本、话语和语言学方法的影响。现代翻译理论将文本视为稳定且完整的单元，但众包翻译和新兴技术（如翻译记忆和本地化等）挑战了这一观念。在众包翻译和协作翻译中，源文本的拆分、分发和重整问题对翻译单位、连贯性和一致性等原则构成挑战。随着翻译技术的发展，稳定文本的基本前提逐渐受到削弱，源文本在句子级别被分割成文本单元，这导致了众包翻译中的非沟通现象，挑战了传统翻译理论中文本的核心地位。本章对众包翻译时代的文本和语言学方法进行了深入探讨，以期为翻译学提供新的视角。

本章首先定义了在协作翻译中动态产生的"文本"，指出众包翻译和协作翻译中的文本与传统翻译理论中定义的文本有所不同。随后，本章深入分析了在翻译记忆技术和本地化技术影响下出现的文本分割成句段的现象，并从语言学和翻译学的角度审视众包时代文本的关键特征。在传统翻译学中，我们强调翻译前要通读全文；然而，在众包翻译过程中，文本被切割成片段，这促使我们重新思考"全文"概念的含义。本章从众包的角度出发，探讨了"全文"和"翻译单元"的定义。基于以上讨论，本章最终重新定义了众包之后产生的文本，将其视为一种新型的翻译产品。

第七章　字幕组与视听翻译规范

本章主要关注视听翻译领域字幕组提供的译文如何挑战专业翻译规范。字幕组的诞生源于观众对专业翻译质量的不满，他们在众包翻译中尤为活跃，敢于挑战既定的翻译规范和标准，从自身需求出发提供视听产品的字幕译本。

本章首先分析了视听翻译中的滥用字幕问题，该问题促使专业字幕团队重塑视听规范，推动字幕组社区不断应用和完善专业的工作流程。随后，本章介绍了字幕组所使用的翻译规范和字幕制作规范。字幕组提供的字幕翻译服务和专业团队提供的翻译服务往往针对不同的受众，视频的粉丝和普通观众对字幕的需求是不一样的，字幕组往往更具有自由度和创造力，这也导致字幕组所遵循的规范对专业视听翻译规范产生了挑战。本章对这种挑战进行了详细分析，其中有关字幕组的研究也为传统翻译学提供了新的视角。

第八章　翻译社会学视角下的众包

本章主要探讨众包翻译研究中社会学方法的应用及其与技术转向的结合，分析这些方法在众包和在线协作翻译研究中的重要性。

本章首先重点分析翻译学中的社会学转向现象。社会学方法自 20 世纪 90 年代末起逐渐受到关注，将焦点从语言问题转向译者及其所处的社会文化和社会经济背景。本章结合布尔迪厄的场域理论和拉图尔的行动者网络理论这两种社会学方法的主要理论框架，分别分析了译者的惯习和协作翻译。

本章随后将关注点放在技术转向。20 世纪末出现的技术转向推动翻译技术与翻译学相整合，本章以此为出发点分析了众包与经济转向的关系、协作翻译与行为主义转向的关系。当社会学转向和技术转向相结合，不断影响众包翻译和协作翻译后，数字化世界中的翻译实践人人皆可参与，因此产生的伦理问题也成为本章探讨的重点。本章分别分析了翻译学中的众包伦理和字幕组遇到的版权问题。

本章最后系统梳理了众包和协作翻译中的社会学研究方法，总结了众包研究中与动机相关的成果和与参与众包的志愿者群体有关的研究成果。

第九章　众包与翻译培训

本章围绕众包翻译培训展开，探讨了在线协作平台如何成为翻译教学采用社会建构主义方法的理想环境。

众包和在线协作翻译社区已然成为联系和培养翻译能力及特定子能力的理想平台。为此，本章讨论了在众包和协作翻译中如何将参与翻译的志愿者培养为专业翻译，并指出对于传统的翻译教学而言，在线协作翻译实践也可以成为其培养人才的重要途径。本章分析了在线协作翻译实践是否可以融入翻译教学，讨论了如何将志愿者社群整合到教学环境中。

本章随后围绕社会建构主义方法展开，探讨了在线协作翻译项目如何将社会建构主义方法应用于在线翻译培训，以及学生如何在这种建构主义方法和情境学习方法中不断获得建设性的反馈以提升翻译能力。翻译能力的提升不是模糊判定的，而是基于科学的翻译能力模型。本章从认知翻译学的角度分析了何为翻译能力、如何使用 PACTE 和 TRANSCOMP 等翻译能力模型来系统描述翻译能力、译者如何获得翻译能力等话题。

基于上述翻译能力的讨论，本章最后结合 PACTE 模型，探讨了可以通过参与在线协作翻译实践而获得的各项翻译子能力，以此强调众包和在线协作翻译在翻译教育中的重要性。

第十章　结论

本章对全书内容进行总结。本书旨在深入研究众包翻译和在线协作翻译，关注四个相互关联的目标：1）以跨学科的方法描述语言服务行业快速发展的现象；2）对现有文献和研究趋势进行批判性研究；3）确定翻译学未来应关注的领域；4）从这些新兴实践的角度对翻译学及其诸多子领域进行分析。为此，本书详细研究了语言服务行业、在线翻译社区、翻译学及其子领域和其他相关学科的历史和现状。技术和需求的变化可能导致人们在众包翻译和在线协作翻译方面的合作更加灵活，虽然这些合作在某种程度上是不可预测的，但它们仍将在未来几年持续引起翻译研究学者的关注。如今，许多语言服务供应商同时提供专业翻译和众包翻译，翻译研究者将会持续关注二者未来的发展。

韩林涛

参考文献

Jiménez-Crespo, Miguel A. 2013. *Translation and Web Localization*. London and New York: Routledge.

Hutchins, W. John. 2014. "Machine Translation: History and Applications." In *The Routledge Encyclopedia of Translation Technology* (1st Edition), Chan Sin-wai (ed.), 120–135. London and New York: Routledge.

O'Brien, Sharon. 2011. "Collaborative Translation." In *Handbook of Translation Studies*, Vol.2, Yves Gambier and Luc van Doorslaer (eds.), 17–20. Amsterdam and Philadelphia: John Benjamins.

推荐阅读

Millán, Carmen and Francesca Bartrina (eds.). 2013. *The Routledge Handbook of Translation Studies*. London and New York: Routledge.

Chan Sin-wai. 2023. *The Routledge Encyclopedia of Translation Technology* (2nd Edition). London and New York: Routledge.

Cronin, Michael. 2013. *Translation in the Digital Age*. London and New York: Routledge.

管新潮、徐军. 2019. 翻译技术. 上海：上海交通大学出版社.

陆艳. 2014. 网络众包翻译模式研究. 北京：世界图书出版公司.

王华树. 2020. 人工智能时代翻译技术研究. 北京：知识产权出版社.

Crowdsourcing and Online Collaborative Translations

Expanding the limits of Translation Studies

Miguel A. Jiménez-Crespo
Rutgers University

Table of contents

Acknowledgements   IX

List of figures and tables   XI

Abbreviations   XIII

Introduction   1

CHAPTER 1
Crowdsourcing and collaborative translation in Translation Studies:
Definitions and types   11
1.1   Introduction   11
1.2   The wider context: The crowdsourcing paradigm   11
      1.2.1   Definitions of crowdsourcing   12
      1.2.2   Typologies of crowdsourcing   15
              1.2.2.1   Estellés and González (2012b) typology
                        of crowdsourcing   15
              1.2.2.2   Brabham's (2008, 2013) typology of crowdsourcing   16
1.3   Collaboration in translation   17
      1.3.1   Translation crowdsourcing   18
      1.3.2   Online collaborative translations   19
      1.3.3   Common features of crowdsourcing and online
              collaborative translations   19
      1.3.4   Distinguishing features of crowdsourcing
              and online collaborative translations   21
1.4   Definitions of translation crowdsourcing and types of collaborative
      practices in TS   23
1.5   Mapping crowdsourcing into related TS concepts   26
1.6   Classifications of online collaborative translations   30
1.7   Which translations are outsourced? Of preferred genres
      and translation types   33

CHAPTER 2
The emergence of crowdsourcing and online collaborative translations   37
2.1   Introduction   37
2.2   Collaborative translations: A brief historical overview
       until the Internet era (until 1980)   38
2.3   The emergence of personal computing, the Internet
       and the WWW (1980–1995)   42
2.4   Participatory cultures on the Internet as a foundation
       for collaborative translations (1980s)   45
2.5   The development of collaborative translations on the web
       (1995–2005)   48
       2.5.1   The emergence of fansubbing   48
       2.5.2   The early days of videogame "rom hacking"
                and open software localization   49
       2.5.3   The emergence of crowdsourcing and collaborative
                translation technological platforms (2000–2005)   50
2.6   Crowdsourcing translation goes mainstream (2005–2010):
       From social networking sites to Wikipedia and non-profit initiatives   52
2.7   A continuing evolution: Paid crowdsourcing and the exploration
       of the limits of crowdsourcing (2010–20xx)   57

CHAPTER 3
**Crowdsourcing and the industry: From workflows
to prescriptive approaches**   61
3.1   Introduction   61
3.2   Revolutionizing traditional professional translation processes   62
3.3   Crowdsourcing processes from a workflow perspective   64
3.4   Workflows and novel approaches to translation   73
       3.4.1   Social networking sites: Facebook   73
       3.4.2   Non-Profits: Kiva and Trommons   76
       3.4.3   MT post-editing: Asia Online and Crowdin   78
       3.4.4   Audiovisual translation: TED and Amara   79
       3.4.5   The fansubbing process   81
3.5   Crowdsourcing platforms: An overview   82
3.6   Post-editing MT and crowdsourcing   86
3.7   Crowdsourcing and prescription: Industry and the case of motivation   91

CHAPTER 4
Crowdsourcing and Cognitive Translation Studies:
Moving beyond the individual's mind   97
4.1 Introduction   97
4.2 Distributed and extended cognition in the age
     of translation crowdsourcing   100
     4.2.1 The introduction of embodied, situated and extended
            cognition approaches to translation   103
4.3 But what is an expert anyhow? Insights from Cognitive Translatology   109
     4.3.1 Expertise in translation and non-professionals: Findings   113
4.4 Other significant issues in CT: Cognition, technology and emotions   117
4.5 Reflections on new methodologies: Internet-mediated methods
     and collaborative translation protocols   118

CHAPTER 5
Crowdsourcing: Challenges to translation quality   121
5.1 Introduction   121
5.2 Translation quality: A multifractal notion in constant evolution   122
5.3 Dynamicity in models of translation quality: Towards adaptable models
     of quality   124
     5.3.1 Quality tiers in MT: Towards a model for crowdsourcing
            and collaborative models   126
     5.3.2 Paid crowdsourcing and the customization
            of translation quality   129
5.4 Guaranteeing quality in crowdsourcing   131
5.5 Crowdsourcing, quality and challenges to TS   136
     5.5.1 Translation theory: A prerequisite for quality evaluation?   137
     5.5.2 The minimal unit to evaluate quality: Between internal
            and external quality   140
     5.5.3 Is translation quality always improving through the process?   141
     5.5.4 Crowdsourcing and different assessment types   144
     5.5.5 Translation quality in MT   145
5.6 A critical review of the iterative translate/vote crowdsourcing
     approaches in the light of Translation Studies   146
     5.6.1 The Facebook model and reader-response approaches   147
     5.6.2 The iterative quality models and functionalist approaches   149
     5.6.3 Corpus-assisted approaches   151
5.7 Empirical studies on crowdsourcing translation quality in TS   154

CHAPTER 6
Texts and crowdsourcing: Perspectives from textual,
discursive and linguistic approaches   157
6.1   Introduction   157
6.2   Defining texts in an era of dynamic texts produced in collaboration   158
6.3   The atomization of texts in TS: From TM to localization   160
        6.3.1   Textual segmentation and TM   160
        6.3.2   Textual segmentation and localization   163
6.4   Texts in a crowdsourcing era: Insights from linguistics and TS   165
6.5   "Entire texts" as the unit of translation:
        The crowdsourcing perspective   169
6.6   The "unit of translation" and crowdsourcing   172
6.7   Redefining crowdsourced "texts" as a translation product   175

CHAPTER 7
Fansubs and AVT norms   179
7.1   Introduction   179
7.2   From professional norms to "abusive subtitling" … and back   180
7.3   Translation and subtitling norms in fansubbing research   182
7.4   Fansubbing or how collaboration can challenge translation norms   185
        7.4.1   Challenges to professional audiovisual norms from fansubbing   186
7.5   Challenges to subtitling norms: A summary   188

CHAPTER 8
Crowdsourcing: Insights from the sociology of translation   195
8.1   Introduction   195
8.2   The "sociological turn" in TS   196
        8.2.1   Bourdieu's theory of fields and the translator's "habitus"   197
        8.2.2   Latour's Actor-Network theory and collaborative translations   199
8.3   Overlapping turns: When the sociological and the technological
        turns collide   200
        8.3.1   Crowdsourcing and the "economic turn"   201
        8.3.2   The "activist turn" and collaborative practices   203
8.4   Ethics of translation in a participatory digital world   204
        8.4.1   TS research into the ethics of crowdsourcing   209
        8.4.2   Copyright infringement and fansubbing   213
8.5   Methodologies from the social sciences in research
        into collaborative practices   216
        8.5.1   Questionnaire and survey methodologies in the study
                of crowdsourcing   217
        8.5.2   Netnographic approaches and mixed methods   218

8.6   Motivation to participate in online collaborative initiatives:
      A summary   **219**
8.7   Volunteer profiles: A summary   **223**

CHAPTER 9
Crowdsourcing and translation training   **227**
9.1   Introduction   **227**
9.2   Crowdsourcing and collaborative translation in training:
      The path from volunteer to professional   **228**
9.3   Are online collaborative practices "accidental training" environments?   **230**
9.4   Socio-constructivist approaches and crowdsourcing   **233**
      9.4.1   The development of online collaborative training models   **234**
9.5   The search for constructive feedback: On the identification
      of initiatives that can enhance student's learning   **235**
      9.5.1   Neunzig and Tanqueiro's (2005) classification
              of online translation feedback   **236**
      9.5.2   A classification of collaborative initiatives on the basis
              of feedback   **238**
9.6   Translation competence models in Cognitive Translatology,
      the development of translation competence and collaborative
      voluntarism   **241**
      9.6.1   Translation competence in TS   **241**
      9.6.2   The PACTE and TRANSCOMP translation
              competence models   **243**
      9.6.3   The acquisition of translation competence   **248**
9.7   Componential translation competence models from the perspective
      of collaborative voluntarism   **251**

CHAPTER 10
Conclusions   **255**
10.1 Introduction   **255**
10.2 Language industry perspectives and impact on the profession   **258**
10.3 Impact on Translation Studies   **261**

References   **265**

Index   **301**

Acknowledgements

I would like to thank Dr. Stephen Doherty and Professor Sandra Hale, as well as the entire faculty of Interpreting and Translation Studies at the University of New South Wales, Australia, for the invitation as Senior Visiting Fellow in 2015 where most of this monograph was written. This monograph would have not been possible without the support and the oustanding intellectual environment they provided for the writing process.

I would also like to thank Rutgers University and the Université Paris 8 for awarding me the visiting professorship in 2014 with the project on translation collaboration in a digital world. The initial idea for this book germinated during these months in Paris. My thanks go to Anthony Cordingley and Céline Frigau-Manning for their support and the organization of the IATIS 2014 conference entitled "Collaborative Translation: From Antiquity to the Internet" in which an initial summary for the first part of this book proposal was delivered as a keynote.

My thanks go to my family in Spain for their unconditional love and support: Miguel J., Juani M. C., Tomi J., Fernando J., Yolanda M., Nani J., Yolandita J. and Juan de la Cruz P. My thanks also go to my amazing and supporting family in Sydney, Alan D., Alan C., Haris K., Cath M., Matt O., Allan J., Gordy T. and many others. This book project owes a lot to your love and support.

Last but not least, many thanks to the anonymous peer-reviewers and Yves Gambier for their invaluable feedback and comments on the initial manuscript and its subsequent revisions.

List of figures and tables

Figure 1.1 Mapping concepts related to "crowdsourcing" prior
            to the emergence of the WWW in Translation Studies.   28

Figure 1.2 Translation crowdsourcing subtypes.   31

Figure 3.1 High-level representation of a localization workflow proposal
            in comparison with TEP processes by DePalma and Kelly.   63

Figure 3.2 Example of translation segment in Facebook with feedback
            for grammatical issues with programming variables.   75

Figure 3.3 Translate Facebook workflow model at the string level.   76

Figure 3.4 Representation of the subtitling workflow and process of TED
            in their description webpage.   80

Figure 3.5 Workflow structure of the ArgenTeam subtitling community.   81

Figure 4.1 Schematic representation of an online amateur complete network.   106

Figure 4.2 Network complexity in the study of a client/author process
            of a freelance translator.   107

Figure 5.1 Translation quality cline in terms of human to MT including
            crowdsourcing.   128

Figure 5.2 Microsoft Language Portal request for translation improvement
            by the crowd.   143

Figure 6.1 Access to the text during collaborative translation processes.   171

Figure 6.2 Expanding the notion of "translated text".   176

Table 8.1   Summary of initiatives and participants in studies into motivation.   220

Figure 9.1 Classification of online translation feedback
            by Neunzig and Tanqueiro.   238

Figure 9.2 Classification of crowdsourcing and collaborative initiatives
            based on feedback received.   240

Figure 9.3 PACTE group translation competence model.   244

Figure 9.4 TRANSCOMP translation competence model.   246

Figure 9.5 PACTE translation acquisition model.   250

Abbreviations

AVT	Audio Visual Translation Studies
ACG	Anime, Comics and Games
CAT	Computer-Assisted Translation
CPE	Crowd Post-Editing
CT	Cognitive Translatology
CT3	Community, Crowdsourced, and Collaborative Translation
FOMT	Free and Open Machine Translation
HAMT	Human Aided Machine Translation
MT	Machine Translation
RBMT	Rule-Based Machine Translation
ROI	Return on Investment
SMT	Statistical Machine Translation
TEP	Translate/Edit/Publish
TM	Translation Memory
TS	Translation Studies
UGT	User-Generated Translation
YAWL	Yet Another Workflow Language
CBTS	Corpus-Based Translation Studies

Introduction

> We control the world basically because we are the only animals
> that can cooperate flexibly in very large numbers [...] This is something
> very unique to us, perhaps the most unique feature of our species.
>
> Interview in National Public Radio by Yuval Hariri,
> author of *Sapiens: a Brief History of Humankind* (2015)[1]

The rise of crowdsourcing and online collaborative translation

The advent of new technologies has had profound impact on translation practices, giving rise to a wide range of fascinating phenomena that are reshaping translation practices and public perceptions. During the last two decades, an increasing number of researchers have been exploring the impact of technological advances in Translation Studies (TS) (i.e., Pym 2004; Dunne 2006; Quah 2006; Alcina 2008; O'Brien 2012b; Cronin 2013; O'Hagan 2013; Jiménez-Crespo 2013a; Chan 2014; Alonso and Calvo 2015; Bowker and Corpas 215). The wide range of technology-dependent phenomena that have attracted the attention of TS scholars encompasses a wide range of topics, such as, to name a representative few, translators' workstations (Hutchins 1998), translation tools (i.e., Austermühl 2000; Bowker 2002; Chan 2014), machine translation (MT) (i.e., Hutchins 2014), MT post-editing (i.e., Guerberof 2009; O'Brien 2006; O'Brien et al. 2011b; Mitchell 2015), computerized corpora (Laviosa 2002; Olohan 2004), translation e-learning (i.e., Massey 2005; Olvera-Lobo et al. 2005, 2009; Jiménez-Crespo 2015b), software localization (Dunne 2006; Roturier 2015), web localization (Jiménez-Crespo 2013a), or videogame localization (O'Hagan and Mangiron 2014). One of the latest phenomena that has risen to the forefront of the discipline is the emergence of a cluster of collaborative translation practices enabled by the open, participatory, and interactive nature of the Web 2.0. These sets of dynamic and rapidly evolving practices, fueled by technological innovation, hold the potential to challenge many traditional axioms in the discipline. They are expanding limits of TS, demanding an in-depth examination of how they might impact its current and future theorizations and

---

1. http://www.npr.org/2015/02/07/383276672/from-hunter-gatherers-to-space-explorers-a-70-000-year-story

research. They also raise questions of interest that require careful consideration due to its novel, unique, and fast evolving nature. This monograph attempts to provide a descriptive account of existing practices and, at the same time, critically analyze and distill their implications for TS and its many subdisciplines or branches, such as cognitive translatology (CT), sociological approaches, translation training, text linguistic approaches, corpus-based TS (CBTS) or translation criticism, and quality to name a few. In doing so, intradisciplinary connections will be fostered and strengthened.

No current estimations exist on the extent of crowdsourcing and collaborative practices worldwide. While no clear figures exist of the number of professional translators around the world, it is safe to assume that possibly many more might consistently engage in voluntary translation activities, such as fansubbing, post-editing the free output of Google Translate, or translating social networking sites. In July 2016, the Internet has approximately 3.611 billion users (Internetwoldstats 2016), with over 47.7 billion webpages indexed by Google (WorldWideWebSize 2016). Out of these pages, not even 0.1% of the new content is professionally translated (DePalma et al. 2013), while Google Translate can produce in a day 10 times more translated words than the entire volume of professional translators in the world (Van de Meer 2010). Google Translate, at the same time, always offers end users the possibility of collaborating in the post-editing of the output, both through the Google Translate website and directly on the output of MT translations of web content. The potential to engage millions of volunteer users is staggering.

Even though English used to be the dominant language on the web, nowadays it accounts for only 53.2% of web content (W3tech.com 2016),[2] while languages such as Russian (6.1%), German (5.7%), Japanese (5%), Spanish (4.8), French (4.1%), Portuguese (2.6%), or Chinese (2.1%) keep increasing their share (ibid). Literally, there is a funnel effect by which a negligible amount of emerging content can be translated professionally (Gambier 2012). Now more than ever, the interconnectedness and immediacy afforded by the WWW is increasing the access to content in different languages that users would like to understand. Free and open machine translation (FOMT) (Gaspari 2014), post-editing of MT by users (Mitchell 2015), crowdsourcing translation in social networking sites (Jiménez-Crespo 2011, 2013b, 2016), or even "paid translation crowdsourcing," initiatives in which participants are normally paid below market rates (García 2015), are expanding the possibilities of access through translation of this immense "embodiment of human knowledge," in the words of the creator of the WWW (Berners-Lee et al. 1992: 52). Users

---

2. https://w3techs.com/technologies/overview/content_language/all

are now taking part in the translation of the content they create or that they would like their peers or language communities to access, producing a diverse patchwork of quality, adequacy, or usability.

Not all languages, genres, and modalities can be equally served in this wide range of translation possibilities. For example, FOMT systems work better in some languages than others, since statistical machine translation systems (STM) depend on the prior existence of massive parallel corpora of translated text (Zaidan and Calliston-Burch 2011; Moorkens, Doherty, Kenny and O'Brien 2013). They also depend on the learning process and fine-tuning carried out by experts and even by user post-editing. Another factor to consider is that not all language communities have the same rate of participation or success in crowdsourcing or volunteer initiatives. For example, Munro (2013) published online a study on the language diversity of English-speaking crowdsourcing workers, and it was found that the main second languages of these workers were Hindi, Tamil, Malayalam, Spanish, French, Telugu and German.[3] Similarly, the industry has recently realized that not all language combinations are equally successful in "paid crowdsourcing" that offers low rates; while companies might have relative success in crowdsourcing Chinese – English content, the same cannot be said of other language combinations such as German or Norwegian – English.

What is true is that "world of translation" has been definitely and irrevocably changed, with the industry introducing new business models due to the impact of the combined effect of MT and crowdsourcing. An example of this impact is the implementation of content prioritization to assign translations to different translation processes and subsequent quality levels based on different criteria, such as type of genre, potential impact of low translation quality on businesses, and expectations of users (see 5.2.1 and 5.2.2). All types of volunteer and collaborative translations represent an additional and quite necessary process to pick up what professional markets cannot fulfill on a strict business sense. The results of the process are also quite varied, from high-quality crowdsourcing through crowd expert selection, all the way to fansubs that can result, depending on the initiatives, in either poor quality (Bogucki 2009) or subtitled TV series close to professional levels (Orrego-Carmona 2015). In the words of Gambier: "translation volume clearly surpasses the total work capacities of professionals who have received appropriate training in the field" (Gambier 2012: 27). This is precisely the point of departure of this monograph: an exploration of a new and necessary option to cover the translation gap in our globalized participatory world.

---

3.   http://idibon.com/crowdsourcing-and-worker-diversity/

Why crowdsourcing matters to Translation Studies

Technologies have opened up a wide range of research trends and directions, re-quiring an in-depth examination of the merging of translation and technology. In the 21st century, the "interrelationship between translation and technology is only deepening" (O'Hagan 2013: 503), and consequently, the "widespread technologi-cal impact on translation" and obviously, on TS, "is only likely to increase" (ibid: 514). Technology keeps developing at a quantum speed, and the demands made on the professional translator do not show any signs of abating, quite the oppo-site: "in today's market, the use of technology by translators is no longer a luxury but a necessity if they are to meet rising market demands for the quick delivery of high-quality texts" (Bowker and Corpas 2015: np). The need to study in depth the impact of technologies has been widely shared by TS scholars. Munday, for example, points to the "exciting re-evaluation of translation practice and theory" (Munday 2008: 194) that can potentially emerge from the analysis of the conflu-ence of translation activity, technologies, digital societies, and the changes in the translation as a profession. Mossop (2005: 26–27) also calls for the examination of technological phenomena and the potential they open for new theory building. In hindsight, he predicted that if web localization would become a new profes-sion, or if enough translators would specialize in this modality, then "a theory of web translation will arise" (2005: 27). Years later, this prediction came true with new approaches in this area (Jiménez-Crespo 2013a). Many scholars have already pointed out the revolutionary implications of crowdsourcing for translation theory (i.e., Cronin 2010, 2013; Gambier 2012, 2014; O'Hagan 2013, 2016). The volume of research on crowdsourcing and online collaborative practices has kept steadily increasing with special issues in journals (O'Hagan 2011), monographs on specific topics such as fansubbing (Massidda 2015), innumerable journal articles, a vast and comprehensive selection of which will be reviewed throughout this book (i.e., O'Hagan 2016; Jiménez-Crespo 2016, 2014; Flanagan 2016), an ever-growing list of PhD (i.e., Dombek 2013; Morera-Mesa 2014; Tesseur 2014b; Orrego-Carmona 2015; Mitchell 2015), and MA theses (i.e., Verbruggen 2010; Garcia-Manchón 2014; De Wille 2014; Liu 2014; Hsiao 2014; Deriemaeker 2014; Rossum 2014; Wilcox 2014), and a frequent presence in general TS conferences and those dedicated to translation technologies or non-professional translation in the second decade of the 20th century.

TS has been increasingly adapting and evolving since the irruption of technol-ogies and new practices and business models. Highly interdisciplinary in nature (Snell-Hornby 1988, 2010), TS has nurtured a number of successive paradigms, theories, and models that have been fostering its development and widening the potential avenues for research. It has been enriched by means of importing and merging current paradigms, theoretical models, and methods from diverse disciplines, from Applied Linguistics to Sociology, from Internet Studies to Computational Linguistics. The emergence of crowdsourcing and collaborative translations has made true both the evolutionary and interdisciplinary nature of the discipline: the existing literature has been merging research inspired by the "technological turn" (Cronin 2010; O'Hagan 2013), the "sociological turn" (Wolf 2007; Angelelli 2012), and the "audiovisual turn" (Remael 2010) (see 8.1 and 8.2). Studies on this area have continued the TS tradition of importing theories and paradigms to provide a different lens on existing phenomena under focus, from critical theory of technology (i.e., O'Hagan 2016) to crisis communication management (i.e., O'Brien 2016). Crowdsourcing and collaborative translations can, and already have, open up new directions, models, and practices that did not exist before:

> Massive online collaboration might change the rules of the game for translation, by sometimes introducing new problems, sometimes enabling new and better solutions to existing problems, and sometimes introducing exciting new opportunities that simply were not on our minds before.   (Desilets 2007: np)

The author was referring here to the language industry in his publication, but the statement also holds true for TS: these novel practices can allow the observation of translation and all related phenomena from a vantage point introducing new, exciting opportunities that simply were not on our minds before, to paraphrase this quote. For example, translation theory has often been grounded on an individualistic perspective, while scholars from different perspectives have started to point out that group processes are under-represented and under-theorized in Western TS (i.e., Tymoczko 2007: 18). Crowdsourcing reverses this classic foundation upside down: collaboration in translation becomes the rule rather than the exception. Cronin, for example, already pointed out this issue when he indicated that crowdsourcing brings "a move away from the monadic subject of traditional agency – Saint Jerome alone in the desert – to a plurisubjectivity of interactions" (2013: 102). It also possibly brings us back to the origins of translation: "historically speaking, translation has often been a collaborative act" (St. Andre 2010: 72).

The impact of crowdsourcing and collaborative practices can be explored both in the macro and micro levels similar to O'Hagan's (2013) proposal for the general impact of technologies on translation practices and translation research. O'Hagan indicates that in TS, the micro level refers to the impact of technologies on the translator's immediate work, such as CAT tools, cloud technologies, post-editing MT, or online search databases. It can be argued that crowdsourcing and online collaborative translations offers new workflows or environments in which participants develop their translation tasks (see Chapter 3), with new professional platforms emerging both in computers (i.e., Translate.com, GetLocalization, Transifex) and smartphones (i.e., Unbabel or Stepes). The impact also encompasses the socio-professional environment, with new career profiles being created, such as the management of volunteer communities, the selection and evaluation of candidates, or the professional post-edition of crowdsourced translations. These novel practices are creating new translation processes that impact cognitive processing (see Chapter 4), and at the same time, lead to the emergence of new digital genres and varieties of translated texts that will eventually require further study (Jiménez-Crespo 2015a). The second impact the O'Hagan brings to the surface is the impact at macro level. This refers to the global changes that affect the wider translation environment, such as the impact of crowdsourcing on reshaping business practices, public views on translation, or the professional context (see Chapter 8). It is of interest how the diversification of translation business models can impact the overall translation industry, with crowdsourcing appearing at the core of what scholars have started to refer to as the "economic turn" (Gambier 2012, 2014) (see 8.2.1). Additionally, collaborative practices online have opened up new, distinct translation business segments with different models and theoretical implications. According to Gouadec (2007: 312):

> the industrialisation of translation tools and procedures is largely responsible for the appearance and the development of the rift between three separate translation worlds, i.e. "industrial" translation, "craft" translation and "amateur" translation.

It goes without saying that both the "industrial or professional world" and the "craft" or "literary" world have been extensively researched in the discipline, while the "amateur" world is still in dire need of further research and a comprehensive and global analysis beyond specific cases and some areas of interest, such as non-professional community interpreting (i.e., Martínez-Gomez 2015). With this overall focus in mind, it is necessary to establish how these novel practices can help redefine, reposition, or enlarge a number of tenets in translation theory, such as the notions of text, translation professionalism or expertise, quality, agency, and translation training through deliberate practice. Ultimately, this monograph attempts to establish why crowdsourcing and online collaborative translations matters to TS, mirroring previous debates in the discipline (Gile, Hansen and Pokorn 2010).

Summary of chapters

This book covers from an interdisciplinary perspective the most significant areas in which crowdsourcing can have an impact on TS as a whole, and also on its different subdisciplines, such as technological, linguistic, cognitive, sociological, pedagogical, audiovisual, or industry-oriented approaches. In doing so, it provides a global multiperspective approach that can enrich the existing body of knowledge and help foster new research. It critically overviews existing research trends in crowdsourcing and online collaborative translations from a multidisciplinary approach. It is intended to allow an in-depth exploration of this phenomenon from the main research directions in TS, and at the same time, allow specialists from different subfields interested in these sets of phenomena to gain a wider perspective, creating cross-disciplinary and cross-subdisciplinary connections. This exercise is very much due to the necessity to continue exploring how translation technologies impact translation practices, as well as the potential of crowdsourcing to provide a novel perspective on translational phenomena and the many subdisciplines and research directions in TS. It has also been developed with an eye on novel or established researchers interested in gaining a comprehensive and complete crowdsourcing and collaborative translation phenomena from a TS lens and its main directions and current research trends.

Chapter 1 delves into epistemological and terminological problems, attempting to critically analyze and consolidate the terminological confusion reflected in most publications (i.e., Pym 2011a; Bold 2011: 4–6; Jiménez-Crespo 2015a). It starts with the general crowdsourcing paradigm and it then centers on current epistemological and terminological debates on TS. Chapter 2 traces the evolution and different avenues for collaboration from antiquity to contextualize current practices following renewed interest in this area (i.e., Cordingley and Frigau Manning 2016). In order to provide a global understanding of this set of phenomena, Chapter 3 descriptively analyzes from an industry perspective the different approaches, workflows, technological solutions, and prescriptive publications. Its goal is to provide a clear understanding of the existing phenomenon in its real habitat.

This is followed by six chapters that encompass the distinct areas and subdisciplines within TS that can benefit from the new perspectives and vantage points these practices can provide. It starts with insights from Cognitive TS in Chapter 4, exploring notions such as expertise and translation competence. It also analyzes the potential of crowdsourcing to be analyzed from a distributed, situated, and embodied cognition perspective. Quality in translation is also one of the most controversial issues when these novel practices are discussed. Chapter 5 reviews how crowdsourcing has continued to expand the notion of "fit for purpose" or "good enough" that initially emerged from MT approaches and that now is commonplace in current quality evaluation proposals (Lommel et al. 2014; Göröj 2014a). While companies and professionals have for decades strived to raise compensation for translation tasks, offering a fuzzy "high-quality" translation (Drugan 2013), the irruption of these novel practices have meant that companies such as Gengo offer as part of the new market strategies and dynamics different tiers of quality for different contents. Quality in this new paradigm involves customers becoming requesters of a degree of quality at the moment of commission, even when they might not be knowledgeable of what exactly they are getting in terms of target text features. New labels for quality tiers have appeared and are now common in the language industry, such as "machine," "standard," "business," and "ultra," with different processes requested to achieve that goal, such as high-quality human, human post-edited, crowdsourced, human crowdsourced post-edited, and raw machine translation. Nevertheless, the same puzzling questions still remain: customers are already unable to identify clearly what a "high-quality" translation is or to know the specifics of the "translation brief". How are they supposed to be able to diligently discern between different types of quality provided, including the possibility of crowdsourcing their translation for lower rates? In light of a move from a static notion of translational quality to a dynamic paradigm (O'Brien 2012a; Jiménez-Crespo 2013a; Göröj 2014a), can TS provide the tools for this new enlargement of the notion of quality in a moment when there is not even any consensus in the discipline as to what "quality" is (Colina 2009; Jiménez-Crespo 2013a)?

The next issue of interest is text linguistics and discourse approaches. Chapter 6 explores how the notion of text, a key construct of TS in text linguistics and discourse contexts in the discipline, finds new threats in how industry and communities conceptualize and handle texts that are crowdsourced through micro task approaches common in the industry. The notion of translation norms and the challenges brought by fansubs and other forms of audiovisual translation are the next objective of analysis in Chapter 7. The interest on this issue lies in the fact that the free and open nature of collaborative audiovisual practices has allowed participants to be extremely creative and playful with existing norms, subsequently resulting in a reconceptualization of professional AVT norms. The chapter overviews the wide range of studies on this area, an area initially "under-represented in audiovisual translation scholarship" (Peréz-González 2007: 276). Nevertheless, today, it can be argued that it has emerged as one of the most popular research areas within online collaborative translation.

Chapter 8 starts with the intersection of the "technological turn" with the "sociological turn" since research into crowdsourcing and collaborative translation has found an ideal meeting point in this intersection. In fact, research into translation crowdsourcing has mainly focused in researching social issues, such as the profile and motivation of participants in these volunteer initiatives. Other issues of interest for scholars in the sociological turn, such as translator ethics, are also analyzed in this chapter. Finally, Chapter 9 is grounded from the premise that translation education requires extensive guided and structured practice, while scholars have started to research whether volunteer initiatives represent ideal "accidental training environments" to complement institutionalized learning

(O'Hagan 2008; Orrego-Carmona 2014b). The chapter offers an analysis and classification of the potential of volunteer initiatives to contribute to the acquisition of translation competence within the framework provided by competence models, such as PACTE and expertise studies (Shreve 2006a). It also overviews how componential competence models, such as PACTE or TRANSCOMP (Göpferich 2009), provide a reliable foundation to operationalize the introduction of these volunteer practices in translation education programs. Chapter 10 includes the conclusions and perspectives on the evolution of this unpredictable phenomena and the impact on TS and its many subdisciplines.

Crowdsourcing and collaborative translation in Translation Studies
Definitions and types

> Translation volume clearly surpasses the total work capacities
> of professionals who have received appropriate training in the field.
>
> (Gambier 2012:27)

1.1 Introduction

This first chapter addresses the delimitation and definition of crowdsourcing and online collaborative translations, a dynamic and fast-evolving object of study in constant evolution. It serves as an introduction that covers the epistemological and conceptual level, a much-needed step given the multitude of perspectives both outside and within Translation Studies (TS). It starts with a review of the most influential definitions of crowdsourcing from different disciplines in the extensive literature on this topic during the last decade. It then moves on to identify the specific nature of translation crowdsourcing and online collaborative practices within the wider paradigm of translation. It analyzes the wide range of existing attempts in TS to define and delimit this set of phenomena, and clarifies its relation to a number of existing notions within the discipline, such as volunteer, "collaborative," "social" or "non-professional," or "community" translation. It also offers an overview of proposed typologies of general crowdsourcing and proposes a typology that can serve as a foundation for further research.

1.2 The wider context: The crowdsourcing paradigm

In order to address the multitude of perspectives that have attempted to define "crowdsourcing" over the last decade, several highly cited review studies have compiled and critically analyzed existing definitions in different disciplines (Estellés et al. 2015; Yin et al. 2014; Estellés and González 2012a). As the next section will elucidate, these review studies conclude that definitions tend to be fuzzy and are quite different depending on the perspective of study. This is in part due to the fact that different crowdsourcing types continue to emerge and it is applied to new tasks across a wide spectrum, bearing witness to the dynamic and creative nature of these relatively new sets of technology-dependent phenomena that are still "in [their] infancy" (Estellés and González 2012a: 198). Similarly, if an initial approach to the definition of "translation crowdsourcing" is attempted, it should be mentioned that TS does not have a common definition for "translation" itself, as described in entries in encyclopedias and handbooks in the discipline (i.e., Halverson 2010; Hermans 2013a). For example, Halverson indicates in her chapter on the *Handbook of Translation Studies Vol. 1*, that the discipline has moved beyond "the ideal of a definitive Translation to the exploration of multiple Translations" (Halverson 2010: 378).[1] It is thus common to agree to disagree in the quest for a one-size-fits-all definition of the main object of study, translational phenomena. According to Hermans, efforts to define translation in the discipline have failed due to the myriad of definitions and the diverse angles they bring to this issue, suggesting "that translation is a complex thing and that a comprehensive and clear-cut view of it is hard to obtain" (Hermans 2013a: 45). In this complex setting, and before delving into epistemological discussions on "translation crowdsourcing" *per se*, the following section focuses on the existing definitions and typologies of general crowdsourcing. This will help set the stage for an analysis of the different types of collaborative practices of sociocultural and linguistic mediation.

1.2.1   Definitions of crowdsourcing

During the last decade, crowdsourcing has been growing and evolving in a multitude of domains and tasks parallel to the continued growth of the Internet. It has been applied to a wide range of "collective intelligence" tasks, from drafting the Icelandic constitution (Siddique 2011) to creating computer operating systems (Arjona Reina et al. 2013); from providing solutions to scientific problems with Innocentive, to identifying stars and galaxies with GalaxyZoo or even collaboratively translating its spinoff website Zoouniverse (Michalak 2015). The broad range of initiatives has continually challenged researchers who have attempted to provide a comprehensive and multidisciplinary definition of crowdsourcing (Estellés et al. 2015).

---

1.   Halverson (2010) includes different perspectives on the definition and conceptualization of the term "translation" over the years, such as the "prototype approach" of Halverson (1998), the "cluster" approach of Tymoczko (2007), or the "thick translation" approach by Hermans (2007) based on Appiah (1993).

Generally, the term crowdsourcing is attributed to Howe (2006) who created this compound term by joining the words "crowd" and "outsourcing." This American journalist first defined it in his seminal article in *Wired* Magazine as:

> [T]he act of taking a job traditionally performed by a designated agent [...] and outsourcing it to an undefined, generally large group of people in the form of an open call. This can take the form of peer-production, but it is also often undertaken by a sole individual.   (2006:np)

Crowdsourcing represents a practice firmly grounded in the participatory nature of the Web 2.0, and it has been used by businesses, organizations, institutions, or collectives to harness the wisdom of the crowd, be it a large group of amateurs, experts, volunteers, professionals, fans, or citizens, to accomplish any given task. The crowd is rewarded in a variety of ways, mostly through intrinsic rewards, such as recognition, satisfaction, entertainment, prestige, as well as extrinsic ones related to money, prices, presents, job experience, or merchandise. Howe stressed that crowdsourcing affects many professional domains, such as photography, design, or public policy. MIT scholar Brabham (2013:xix) also provided another seminal definition that stresses "problem solving" and "production models" as the origins of crowdsourcing:

> [A]n online, distributed problem-solving and production model that leverages the collective intelligence of online communities to serve specific organizational goals. Online communities, also known as the crowds, are given the opportunity to respond to crowdsourcing activities promoted by the organization, and they are motivated to respond for a variety of reasons

It can be argued that these practices originally emerged in certain business contexts, such as the seminal cases of Threadless, iStockphoto, or Amazon Mechanical Turks (Howe 2006), and quickly evolved and spread to other realms (Estellés et al. 2015), such as translation or computational linguistic tasks.

The crowdsourcing revolution quickly spreads across potential tasks that could be assigned to be completed by crowds. Soon, many areas of scholarly inquiry experienced a radical impact. This meant that a large number of researchers from numerous disciplines quickly drew their attention to this phenomenon since 2007. The volume of research from a multitude of disciplines and perspectives literally exploded. This increased attention, combined with the dynamic nature of this emerging practice, resulted in wide differences in how scholars approached its definition. Estellés and González (2012a) addressed this initial confusion in their seminal and much cited paper *Towards an integrated crowdsourcing definition*. This study identified and synthesized shared elements in forty existing definitions from different perspectives. As a result, the paper proposed one of the most widely used definitions in the research community:

> [T]ype of participative online activity in which an individual, an institution, a non-profit organization, or company proposes to a group of individuals of varying knowledge, heterogeneity, and number, via a flexible open call, the voluntary undertaking of a task. The undertaking of the task, of variable complexity and modularity, and in which the crowd should participate bringing their work, money, knowledge and/or experience, always entails mutual benefit. The user will receive the satisfaction of a given type of need, be it economic, social recognition, self-esteem, or the development of individual skills, while the crowdsourcer will obtain and utilize to their advantage what the user has brought to the venture, whose form will depend on the type of activity undertaken.
>
> (Estellés and González 2012a: 198)

This definition reflects the synthesis of definitions that primarily share the following common traits according to this study:

1. There is a clearly defined crowd.
2. There is task at hand with a clearly stated goal.
3. The participants receive some type of recompense.
4. The crowdsourcer or initiator of the crowdsourcing activity is clearly identified in the open call.
5. Participants are clearly aware of the compensation obtained by them.
6. The type of process is online based.
7. There is a call to participate that is more or less open.
8. The Internet is the medium for participation.

A later 2015 review of this same study identified that the scientific production on crowdsourcing had grown exponentially in the three-year period in a wide range of fields (Estellés et al. 2015). Nevertheless, it shows that the majority of publications used one of the three previous definitions mentioned in this section, Howe's (2006), Brabham's (2008, 2013), or Estellés and González's (2012a). The authors argue that towards the middle of the 2010s, a consolidation of research has started to occur, with new publications focusing on the applications of crowdsourcing to specific areas rather than attempting to linger in definitional efforts. The increase in collaborative initiatives that attempt to explore the "wisdom of the crowd" has nevertheless continued to defy what is and what is not crowdsourcing: "sometimes the boundaries of what is and what is not crowdsourcing are not completely clear" (Estellés et al. 2015: 34). For example, the authors point to cases such as Wikipedia, a typical case of the use of "collective intelligence" that is organized and self-managed by the community. Researchers often argue that this case cannot be considered as crowdsourcing as such (Brabham 2013; Estellés and González 2012a), since crowdsourcing necessarily entails top-down efforts from an organization with leverage from the collective intelligence of the crowd. Crowdsourcing requires thus that the locus of control resides firmly within the initiating organization. The case of Wikipedia is what is known as commons-based peer production of knowledge (Benkler 2006) and the locus of control resides within the community, therefore not qualifying strictly as "crowdsourcing."

1.2.2 Typologies of crowdsourcing

General typologies produced outside TS are of interest to the study of translation crowdsourcing since they help in locating translation-related phenomena in the wider context of the crowdsourcing macrocosm. Scholars have proposed several general crowdsourcing typologies to account for the wide range of applications to harness the problem-solving capacity, the wisdom or creativity of the crowd. Nevertheless, the number of typologies in the literature is extremely limited when compared with the proposals to define crowdsourcing (Estellés et al. 2015). The two most widely accepted and cited typologies have been again presented by the leading scholars in the study of crowdsourcing, Brabham (2013) and Estellés and González (2012b). The following two sections describe them and locate translation-related activities in their typologies.

1.2.2.1 *Estellés and González (2012b) typology of crowdsourcing*
The proposed typology of crowdsourcing by Estellés and González (2012b) includes five different categories as follows:

1. Crowdcasting. This process entails organizing contests in order for a problem or task to be solved by the crowd. The first person to find the solution or do it better will receive a prize. Cases of this category are Threadless for t-shirt designs or Innocentive to solve scientific problems.
2. Crowdcollaboration. This category refers to instances in which individuals communicate freely with the crowd without the participation of the initiator. The authors subdivide crowdcollaboration further into two subtypes, "crowdstorming" and "crowdsupport." The first one refers to massive online brainstorming sessions in which the crowd can support ideas with their votes. The latter, crowdsupport, refers to cases in which the customers themselves help other customers with issues and problems that might arise. In this last type, the company is not contacted for product support, such as Getsatisfaction or the user-based Apple or Adobe products forums.
3. Crowdcontent is defined as cases in which the crowd uses their labor and knowledge to create different types of content. This category does not involve competition among peers, such as the case of crowdcasting. This category is further subdivided into "crowdproduction," "crowdsearching," or

"crowdanalyzing." It is within this category that Estellés and González locate translation. They categorize it as a case of "crowdproduction" in which the participants are responsible for the production of content, that is, translation.
4. Crowdfunding. In "crowdfunding," individuals or organizations request funding in exchange for a reward. Prime examples would be Kickstarter, Indigogo, or Gofundme. The non-profit organization Kiva (see 3.3.2) can be considered mainly a crowdfunding organization that uses both translation "crowdproduction" in order to mediate between the requesters of the micro-loans in developing countries and the "crowdfunders" who help finance them.
5. Crowdopinion. This type has as a goal to delve into the opinions of the crowd regarding specific issues or products through votes, comments, tags, etc. A myriad of websites nowadays request voting and opinions from the crowds, from books such as Goodreads, to businesses with Yelp or even the Blue Board on Proz.com in which translation and interpreting agencies are rated by freelancers.

1.2.2.2   *Brabham's (2008, 2013) typology of crowdsourcing*
The other often-cited proposal in literature was offered by Brabham (2008, 2013), who subdivides crowdsourcing into the following types:

1. Knowledge discovery and management
2. Broadcast search
3. Peer-vetted creative production
4. Distributed-human-intelligence tasks

The first type, "knowledge discovery and management," refers to cases in which the organizations challenge existing communities to discover knowledge, multiplying the possibilities of organizations with limited capabilities. The geolocation platform Ushaidi or Peer to Patent are examples of this approach. This last initiative was created by the United States Patent and Trademark Office to open to the community the process of patent application examination. Anyone in the community can provide information in order for the organization to assess the claims of patent applications, thus linking the community to the legal process of adjudicating patent cases. Ushaidi was created to monitor the ethnic violence in the Kenyan elections of 2007. It used Google Maps to allow volunteers to geolocate and tag in a map eyewitness reports of violence and violations of the rights of voters. This system has subsequently been applied to a variety of humanitarian causes, such as the integration with the system created by Munro in the aftermath of the Haiti earthquake in which volunteers would both translate SMS from Creole and locate on the map the emergency (Meier and Munro 2010) (see 2.5).

"Broadcast-search" approaches intend to find a solution to a problem by means of finding a single specialist in a specific field to adapt previous work and find a suitable solution to a problem. Oftentimes, the expertise of the participant is from outside the specific area of the problem, and this is often argued to be a positive contribution since outsiders can often find new and innovative solutions that experts in a field cannot. The problems in this case are normally scientific in nature, and Innocentive and the Goldcorp Challenge are presented as examples of this category.

"Peer-vetted creative production" addresses the creation and design of products through an open call to a network of users. The proposals are later voted on in order to select the ones preferred by the crowd. This subtype is related to cases in which taste, market, or user preferences are the main problem to solve. The T-shirt design website Threadless could be considered a prime example.

The fourth and last type is "distributed-human intelligence," and it has as a goal the processing of any type of data by means of decomposing data problems into small tasks that require human intelligence and cannot be processed by computers. Brabham argues that this type is less creative and less intellectually stimulating than the other three. Consequently, the tasks in this type are often carried out through paid crowdsourcing models using platforms such as Amazon's Mechanical Turks or Crowdflower. Translation is considered as a case of distributed-human intelligence. It is of interest that the recent rise of "paid translation crowdsourcing" might attest to the fact that many translation tasks, as Gambier indicates, "[do] not generate the same enthusiasm" (2012: 16) as photography, cinema or journalism in the web. This is also related to higher volunteer motivation in creative subtypes such as fansubs or journalism, as well as non-profit causes.

1.3   Collaboration in translation

Collaboration, despite the historical individualistic character of translation in TS literature, is "evident in all types of translation scenarios and across the whole process of translation, from authors, publishers, to translation agencies and to translators" (O'Brien 2011a: 17). According to O'Brien (ibid), collaborative translation as such has generally been understood in TS as two broad notions; in a narrow sense, it means the actual collaboration between two or more translation agents to produce a single translation, the final product being the result of more than one subject. Technology has helped to multiply and facilitate this type of collaboration, such as in the case of members of a large community or crowd in a crowdsourcing initiative online working in the same document, or professional translators working in the same document through the cloud using, for example, Google Docs or networked CAT tools. It also includes the type of collaboration between translation and reviewers, opening also the possibility of revision in a single document by several agents. This type of collaboration between translators is precisely the objective for the purposes of the study of crowdsourcing and online collaborative translations.

In a broader sense, it also means collaboration between a number of translating and non-translating agents, one or more of which might not be a translator. This is often the sense in which a number of previous translation theories have approached collaboration, such as functionalism (Nord 1997), action theory (Holz Mänttäri 1984), situated and extended cognition (Risku 2014; Risku and Windhager 2013) (see 4.1.1), Latour actor – network application to literary translation (see 8.1.2), as well as professional approaches (Gouadec 2007). It has therefore been common to explore the wide range of interactions and connections that occur before, in the course of and after any single translation project (see 4.1.1). The new emergent collaborative practices mediated through the web are highly diverse and vibrant in nature. This cluster of collaborative practices can be broadly divided into two closely related subtypes, henceforth referred to as (1) crowdsourcing and (2) online collaborative translations.

1.3.1   Translation crowdsourcing

The first type, "translation crowdsourcing," is defined primarily by the existence of a call by an organization, institution, or collective to a large undefined community in the web to perform a translation task in a collaborative manner (Estellés and González 2012a; Brabham 2008, 2013). It therefore represents a directed and organized top-down effort leveraged by the bottom-up contribution from the crowd with the objective of harnessing the "wisdom of the crowds" (Surowiecki 2004). It can be contextualized within the surge of interest in the wider business community in crowdsourcing and the exploration of the "collective intelligence" towards the middle of the 2000s (Levy 1997). In this decade, companies and organizations started to harness the collective intelligence of web users to serve "business goals, improve public participation in governance, design products, and solve problems" (Brabham 2013: xv). This included translation and other linguistic-related tasks. In translation, classic examples of this type of approach could be translations in Facebook or Twitter (see 3.3.1), community translations of software products and websites, such as those of Skype or Adobe products, as well as initiatives put forth by non-profit organizations, such as Kiva, Amnesty International, or Translate America (see 3.3.2).

1.3.2   Online collaborative translations

The second notion, "online collaborative translations," could be in principle considered a hypernym of the former, since all "crowdsourcing" efforts are basically a collaborative venture. Nevertheless, for the purposes of clarity in this monograph, it will refer to horizontal bottom-up efforts by self-organized communities to complete translation tasks collaboratively. This type of translational activity has a wide range of constellations, such as the subtitling of audiovisual products, the collaborative translation of literary works by fans, or the localization of open-source software. Collaborative translations can be traced back to the rise of "participatory cultures" that expanded thanks to new technologies (Jenkins et al. 2006), and the influence of fan subcultures that celebrated a do-it-yourself ethic (Delwiche and Henderson 2012) (see 2.3). In this context, participatory cultures started to blur the lines between consumers, users, and fans, giving rise to what was also known as the "prosumer" (Toffler 1980), a type of participatory user that both uses and creates the content he/she enjoys online. In certain cases, this prosumer has also been referred to as the "playbor" (Scholz 2013), the intersection of work and play in which certain tasks associated with professional fields are performed in a gamified way, such as translation tasks in the language learning platform Duolingo. Examples of this approach are the subtitling of movies by fans (see Chapter 7), wiki initiatives (McDonough-Dolmaya 2012, 2015; Michalak 2015), as well as the localization of open-source software or videogames (Muñoz Sánchez 2009; O'Hagan and Mangiron 2013).

1.3.3   Common features of crowdsourcing and online collaborative translations

Both collaborative translation models share several basic features. The most significant one is that they are mainly carried out on a volunteer or pro-bono basis and, in some cases, for extremely low compensation. In a discipline that prototypically conceptualizes translation as a deliberately acquired skill, mainly associated with professional (i.e., Gouadec 2007) or expert approaches (Shreve 2006a), the widespread presence of what is known as non-professional or unprofessional translation (Antonini 2011), raises interesting challenges that have started to be explored by recent trends in TS (i.e., Pérez-González and Sebnem-Saraeva 2012; O'Hagan 2011).[2] Nevertheless, collaborative translations in the web are not solely the realm

---

2.   It is also one of the main foci of conference series such as the Non-Professional Translation and Interpreter Conferences (NPIT) (https://www.zhaw.ch/en/linguistics/institutes-centres/iued/research/npit3/?pk_campaign=shortlink&pk_kwd=www.zhaw.ch%2Flinguistics%2Fnpit3%2F).

of non-professionals, since they also attract professional or trained translators to participate, depending usually on the prestige or the symbolic value of the initiative (i.e., McDonough-Dolmaya 2012; Camara 2015).

In addition to participation without monetary compensation, these two activities have developed and grown on the shoulders of the communicative and participatory revolution brought by the Web 2.0. Even though collaborative translations have existed since antiquity (see 2.2), their current explosion would have never occurred without the widespread global penetration rates of the Internet and the WWW (see Internetwoldstats 2015), the interconnectivity and immediacy they provide, and the development of dedicated technological platforms on the cloud to mediate and manage collaboration.

This dependence of the technological and digital revolution brought by the Internet and the WWW means that these novel approaches to collaboration in translation represent distinct phenomena in a similar fashion to what happens in general crowdsourcing. According to Brabham:

> Although the underlying concepts of crowdsourcing have existed for centuries, what we today know as crowdsourcing and what we enjoy as the fruits of crowdsourcing did not truly come into being until the widespread adoption of the Internet in the late 1990's and the spread of high-speed connectivity and the cultivation of online participatory culture in the 2000s.   (Brabham 2013:xxii)

The author offers as historical examples of what cannot be considered as crowdsourcing: the Alkali price, a call for participation by King Louis XVI of France who offered an award in 1778 to whomever could make alkali by decomposing sea salt by the simplest and most economical method. Another example would be the publication of the Oxford English dictionary in the 1800s with the help of 800 volunteers. The same can be said of online collaborative translations: these novel practices are the result of profound changes in digital infrastructure and the subsequent development of participatory cultures and networks. Eminent sociologist and information society scholar Manuel Castells (1996, 2003) argued that the emergence of the "internet galaxy" and the "network society" of decentralized participatory networks was due to rapid changes in the digital infrastructure, radically transforming the ways in which societies learn, work, and play. Obviously, it has also radically transformed how people translate, from participation in professional production networks (Abdallah 2014; Abdallah and Koskinen 2007) to participation in volunteer translation communities.

1.3.4 Distinguishing features of crowdsourcing and online collaborative translations

The main differences between both polarities of practice reside in the agent(s) who initiate the translation process and where the locus of control resides, whether in the self-organized community or in a company or organization. According to Estellés et al., crowdsourcing is defined by the fact that "the crowdsourcer is clearly identified" (2015: 35), and the crowdsourcer can therefore be either an organization that could have potentially carried out the translation with in-house or freelance translators but decided to crowdsource the work for a variety of reasons, or a self-organized collective with a common interest in translating and distributing any type of content. Both cases can involve casting a call for participation, but obviously the reasons behind them are quite different. This distinction was initially put forward by O'Hagan (2009) who distinguished between "solicited" and "non-solicited" models of online volunteer collaboration. The former refers to cases in which a company, institution, or non-profit purposefully puts out a call to the community to complete a specific translation task, such as Facebook, Skype, Adobe, and Twitter, or NGOs such as the Rosetta Foundation (Anastasiou and Schäler 2009; De Wille 2014) or Kotoba no Volunteer [Volunteers of words] (Kagueura et al. 2011). Strictly speaking, only solicited models should be considered instances of crowdsourcing, since this model entails an initiator or commissioner that "outsources" to the "crowd" the cognitive work normally done by a professional or in-house employee (Brabham 2013). The non-solicited model refers to cases in which self-organized collectives of users undertake specific translation tasks. These translations are later distributed to potential users through the WWW, such as in the case of websites, blogs, subtitling by amateurs, tweets, the translation of videogames or comic books by fans, or any type of digital texts. In the case of self-organized communities, the initiator of the effort represents an entity of variable nature, and there is not the possibility of performing the translation by in-house or freelance employees. In non-profit settings, translation crowdsourcing shares the basic trait in the locus of the control of the translation process and community. For example, Kiva represents a non-profit organization that clearly sets up admission procedures for volunteer translators and that requires a standard of quality and a minimum time commitment on a monthly basis for participation.

Other scholars in TS have also previously acknowledged the need to differentiate between these two distinct types. Costales (2012: 96), for example, also argues that:

> A difference must be established between collaborative translation and crowd-sourcing. While the former is based on the relationship between supporters of a certain field or volunteers in particular settings and scenarios, the latter cannot be included in the same category [...] In other words, we have a relation among equals on the one hand and a hierarchical structure on the other.

It can be argued that the main distinction should not be established between hierarchical structures or horizontal organizations, since self-organized communities also tend to establish highly hierarchical structures once well established (i.e., Orrego-Carmona 2012). Fernandez-Costales (2013), nevertheless, settles the difference from a different perspective when the business nature of translation crowdsourcing is highlighted; in other words, crowdsourcing is "a market driven phenomenon," while collaborative translation on the web is "a user-centered process" (ibid: 98). Other scholars have separated existing practices according to whether they fall within or without the scope of the business-oriented language industry and professional contexts. Gambier (2012) separates these phenomena according to whether they fall within or without the translation industry or whether they depend or not on market forces. Translations are thus divided between "amateur translations," which encompasses both "translations by fans" such as fansubs, fandubbing, and scanlations, and "participatory or collective translations," that is, the translation crowdsourcing in this monograph. In professional settings, distinctions are made between "collaborative translations" done by professionals enabled by modern networking translation technologies and "volunteered networked translations," in cases of professional participation in non-profit initiatives such as ECOs, Babels, or Translators without Borders. This distinction based on socio-professional issues can be of interest in the theoretical analysis of these novel practices but many of these practices entail the collaboration of professionals and non-professionals hand in hand, both in "translations by fans" and "crowdsourcing." Additionally, translations in the non-profit arena represent a fluid and dynamic area in which professionals and amateurs collaborate to different degrees – from initiatives exclusively open to professionals such as the above-mentioned Babels or Translators without Borders, to other open ones such as Rosetta Foundations, Trial Internationals, or Kiva.

Another difference between both types is the use of technology in these two types (see 3.4 for a categorization of technology platforms for translation crowdsourcing). Crowdsourcing heavily depends on custom-made (Facebook, Twitter, Hootsuite) or off-the-shelf collaborative translation platforms in order to produce and manage the collaborative translations. These web platforms or translation management systems both manage the componential process and potentially structure different steps, roles, and responsibilities (i.e., manager, editor, translator, bilingual participant, etc.). Nevertheless, in self-organized horizontal initiatives, the use (or not) of cloud collaborative solutions varies widely and only some off-the-shelf solutions are used. Some use platforms developed for this purpose, such as Trommons and Kanjingo by the Rosetta Foundation, Transbey, Transifex, or Amara for video subtitling, but this mostly depends on the size of the organization. In some communities, such management can take the form of a forum or a simple excel spreadsheet shared in a cloud environment in which volunteers note the work they did, the deadlines, and the role they took (Baker 2015, 2016).

1.4   Definitions of translation crowdsourcing and types of collaborative practices in TS

Translation Studies has not been immune to this initial terminological and conceptual confusion surrounding collaborative practices and crowdsourcing (Pym 2011a; Gambier 2014; Jiménez-Crespo 2015a; Horvath 2016). This is partly due to the novelty of these phenomena and their constant evolution. Over the years, a wide range of terms have been proposed in TS literature to refer to the umbrella of phenomena that emerged with the participatory revolution brought by the Web 2.0, creating a terminological confusion that this section attempts to clarify. Gambier already indicated that "the terminology used in English is both redundant and vague" (2012:16), while Pym (2011a) also delves in the existing terminological fuzziness in TS. Different umbrella terms have been used to refer to crowdsourcing, modifying "translation" with qualifiers such as "crowd" (Kageura et al. 2011), "user-generated" (O'Hagan, 2013; Perrino, 2009), "open" (Cronin 2010), "community," or "volunteer" (Pym 2011a).[3] Terminological complexity has only increased with the introduction of new acronyms, such as "CT[3]" – meaning community, crowdsourced, and collaborative translation (Ray and Kelly 2011) – while many other TS concepts often appear in publications as synonyms for crowdsourcing, including "collaborative translation," "community translation," "social translation," "non-professional translation," and "volunteer translation" (McDonough-Dolmaya 2012; Pym 2011a). These later terms are often used in conjunction with the former as some sort of explicitation or explanation. The use of these terms shift the foci of attention either to the contrast between individual/community practices, the fact that they emerged parallel to the rise of social networking sites, or that translation tasks are performed without monetary compensation, respectively. Generally, all of them are often used to refer to general crowdsourcing as well as to

---

3.   Industry publications have also proposed a range of alternative denominations such as "accidental translation," a term mentioned by Perrino (2009) that the researcher attributes to McConnell (2008) in reference to the crowdsourcing tool Der Mundo.

other collaborative phenomena mediated through the web. These latter concepts can only be considered as superterms or "umbrella" terms (Vandepitte 2008: 578): their superordinate nature is due to the fact that they describe translation practices that exist with and without web mediation.

It is acknowledged that definitions "change overtime as [...] realities change. In other words, definitions are — by definition – dynamic in nature" (Chesterman et al. 2003: 197). Nevertheless, working definitions are necessary for research purposes since they are not "ends in themselves; they are only means, tools which enable us to formulate claims and arguments, or to set up useful classifications" (Chesterman 2005: 28). This need to provide terminological tools to establish classifications has led a number of TS scholars to propose definitions from different perspectives, sometimes not clearly defining the scope of the definiendum. For example, O'Hagan (2011: 14) defines crowdsourcing as volunteer or community translations produced through some form of collaboration by a group of Internet users forming an online community. This definition contains the basic keywords that define novel participatory practices; "volunteer," "translation," "collaboration," "internet," and "community." A similar generic approach is taken by Declercq (2014: 46) who indicates that crowdsourcing is "the outsourcing of a task (or several tasks at the same time) to an undefined, generally large, group of people or community, mutually connected through an e-medium." The volunteer nature of translation crowdsourcing and collaborative translation is also stressed by Gambier (2012: 17) who defines it as a "translation task offered to an undefined group of volunteer translators." Gambier also added the significance of the social network society to the emergence of these practices when he defined it as "using the huge reach of Social Media to encourage voluntary participatory or collective translation" (Gambier and Munday 2014: 24). Meanwhile, some definitions stress the potential of amateurs and professionals to participate, such as McDonough-Dolmaya (2012: 169), who defines it as "collaborative efforts to translate content [...] either by enthusiastic amateurs [...] or by professional translators." Similarly, Perrino (2009:62) includes the possibility of experts to participate in what she refers to as "user-generated translations." Departing from the notion of user-generated content by Flew (2008: 35–36), this process intends:

> to harness the Web 2.0 services and tools to make online content – be it written, audio or video – accessible in a variety of languages. It differentiates from automatic translation for it requires human expertise and implies the collaboration between users – be they amateurs or experts.

Some of the definitions stress the fact that crowdsourcing entails outsourcing work previously done by professionals, "crowdsourcing, roughly meaning the delegation to (unpaid) volunteers of tasks previously reserved for professionals"

(García 2010: 1). Gough indicates that crowdsourcing means that "the skill of a few professionals is being replaced by the power of potentially unlimited numbers of volunteers, professionals and amateurs" (2010: 18). Related to the professional considerations are issues in relation to whether participants in crowdsourcing tasks receive compensation. Only one definition found in the literature review stresses that crowdsourcing can appear in paid contexts where "the existence of a platform and a volunteer community/crowd willing to translate with low payment (if any) content which is submitted online" (Anastasiou and Gupta, 2011: 638). Finally, Cronin contextualizes the crowdsourcing within the ubiquitous presence of Internet connections and defines it as translations that are "personalized, user-driven and integrated into dynamic systems of ubiquitous delivery" (2010:4).

These definitions shed light on the main aspects that, from a TS perspective, scholars highlight as specific traits; mainly that translations are collaborative in nature, that the community is made up of volunteers or professionals, that the Internet is necessary for participation, that payments might be received as compensations, or that the reach of technologies has allowed translation to be ubiquitous. Nevertheless, a close analysis of these definitions shows that some are generic in nature but only refer to "translation crowdsourcing" initiated mainly by companies (García 2010; Gambier 2012; Declerq 2014), while some others include or refer to both "online collaborative translations" and to "crowdsourcing." As mentioned previously, scholars have stressed the fact that crowdsourcing only refers to top-down vertical initiatives in which the locus of control resides in the initiator of the activity. Several of the definitions surveyed above (Perrino 2009; Cronin 2010; McDonough-Dolmaya 2012; O'Hagan 2013) apply to both initiatives in which the locus of controls is within the community of translators and in the organization casting the call for participation. Following the existing literature on crowdsourcing (Brabham 2013), a difference should be made between top-down initiatives and horizontal bottom-up ones, hence the distinction proposed in this monograph between "crowdsourcing" and "online collaborative translations."

In the light of this review and the specific characteristics of these two interrelated practices, translation crowdsourcing could be defined as:

> Collaborative translation processes performed through dedicated web platforms that are initiated by companies or organizations and in which participants collaborate with motivations other than strictly monetary.

Similarly, the notion of "online collaborative translations" can be defined as:

> Collaborative translation processes in the web initiated by self-organized online communities in which participants collaborate with motivations other than monetary.

1.5   Mapping crowdsourcing into related TS concepts

From an epistemological point of view, it is necessary to map notions that refer to practices that pre-dated the emergence of the WWW and those that depend on this new medium for its existence. "Collaborative translation" could be considered a hypernym that would include collaboration in a wide range of settings. Some of them existed prior to the emergence of the WWW (see Chapter 2), such as collaboration between translators working in the same source text into different languages, between author and translators in literary contexts and between translator(s) and the number of agents in the overall translation event (Risku and Windhager 2013). As mentioned previously, the term "online collaborative translations" is the first term identified to refer to this novel model of production of harnessing the power of the Internet and the existing communities (Shimohata et al. 2001).[4] This groundbreaking project was a research initiative and was not driven by market forces, but rather a way of "distributing human intelligence tasks" (Brabham 2013) to achieve higher quality MT output (see 3.5).

"Community translation" has been generally associated with "community interpreting" or "public service interpreting," a field that has produced a considerable amount of research in recent years (i.e., Mikkelson 2013; Hertog 2010). If definitions, such as Hertog's (2010: 49), are adapted from interpreting, it could be argued that "community translation" is a practice that "takes place to enable individuals or groups in society who do not speak the official or dominant language of the services provided by central or local governments to access these services and to communicate with the service providers." This same notion is also found in the literature under the term "social translation," as it is in the case of the positioning paper of the European Network of Public Service Translation and Interpreting (2013) that defines it as:

> a form of translation: (1) in which the written message is faithfully and fully translated from a source language to a target language (2) to provide everyone with access to high-quality, regular social and public service provision and assistance so that everyone is able to guarantee their rights and fulfill their obligations.

This type of community translation occurs mostly due to migration flows and it has emerged as a topic of research in some geographic areas such as Australia (i.e., Kim 2008; Taibi and Ozolin 2016). In a narrow sense, Pym defines "community

---

4.   These efforts were meant to improve MT quality through a combination of collaborative translation, dictionaries, term extractors, and a dedicated community management system (Shimohata et al. 2001).

translation" as "a term used for the practice whereby non-professionals translate software or websites that they actually use" (2011a: 78). This definition focuses exclusively on digital genres (even though other genres such as apps or videogames are not mentioned), but it also misses the social aspect of translation in intranational settings. Scholars such as Pym also differentiate between the fact that crowdsourcing can be accomplished by a community either by translating directly or by post-editing MT output. This is also known as "crowd post-editing" (Tatsumi et al. 2012). This process is used by the main web-based MT engines such as Google Translate or the Microsoft Translator API, and also by crowdsourcing platforms such as Asia Online. Mitchell, Roturier, and O'Brien have defined this practice as cases in which "community members post-edit MT content rather than translating it directly" (2014: 238) (see 3.5).

"Social translation" is often used in order to refer to translations that occur within any given society. However, if the literature in TS is analyzed, this type of translation is also used with two differentiated meanings: some scholars place social translation closer to activist approaches to translation (Newmark 2003; O'Hagan 2011; Baker 2014), while in the context of technology scholars have again used it as a synonym for crowdsourcing (Austermühl 2011; O'Brien 2011a; Wasala et al. 2013). The use of social translation as a synonym of crowdsourcing can probably be traced back to the fact that it was widely popularized by the rise of social networking sites such as Facebook, Twitter, or Path.

The fact that translations are not remunerated is behind the introduction of "volunteer translations," defined as those "conducted by people exercising their free will to perform translation work which is not remunerated, which is formally organized and for the benefit of others" (Olohan 2014: 19). This term appeared in TS literature hand in hand with the rise of web-mediated practices, as witnessed by the lack of references prior to the year in which the Translate Facebook phenomenon started, 2007. This term does not fully overlap with "collaborative translation," since volunteer work does not necessarily entail collaborative translation, as in cases in which crowdsourcing participants can translate an entire text from beginning to end. Similarly, collaborative translations appear in a wide constellation of practices and not all of them are pro-bono or on a volunteer basis. This would be the case of paid crowdsourcing, or many of the collaborative models that existed prior to the emergence of the WWW mentioned previously. Pym (2011a: 91) also suggests using the term "volunteer translation" rather than collaborative or community translations. Yet the ambits covered by collaborative and volunteer translation do not fully overlap as mentioned above. Collaborative translation, as much as crowdsourcing, may be paid or unpaid, and occur with or without the Internet or dedicated web platforms.

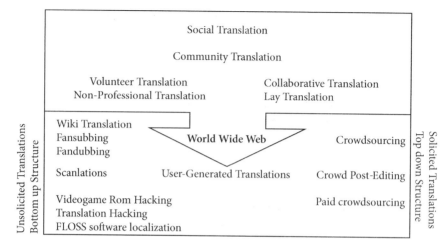

Figure 1.1 Mapping concepts related to "crowdsourcing" prior to the emergence of the WWW in Translation Studies.

Figure 1.1 shows the conceptual overlap and mapping of terms related to crowdsourcing. In this map, phenomena related to translational practices that occur both with and without web-mediation are placed as superterms. In the center of the chart appear concepts that pertain to translation contexts, practices, and phenomena that emerged with the advent of the Web 2.0. The medium, the Internet, and the WWW, therefore, represent the main difference between general practices and those below, as indicated by Brabham (2013). The most generic term is "user-generated translations," that Perrino identifies as the "umbrella term used to define translation practices made possible by various online services" (Perrino 2009:55). It therefore covers most, but not all, novel collaborative practices on the web. This is due to the fact that in cases such as activist or non-profit approaches, translations are not performed by users, but rather by mediators to facilitate the communication between organizations, donors, and recipients of whichever type of assistance. For O'Hagan (2009), "user-generated translation" emerges as a hypernym that encompasses crowdsourcing and online collaborative translations:

> a wide range of Translation, carried out based on free user participation in digital media spaces where Translation is undertaken by unspecified self-selected individuals. The user in UGT therefore is somebody who voluntarily acts as a remediator of linguistically inaccessible products and direct producer of Translation on the basis of their knowledge of the given language as well as that of particular media content or genre, spurred by their substantial interest in the topic.
>
> (O'Hagan 2009: 101)

Audiovisual collaborative practices of different types represent some of the most productive areas of volunteer translation online, such as fansubbing, fandubbing, scanlations, or videogame romhacking. They are related to subcultures that, for example, are known in China as ACG, or anime, comic, and videogame. Fansubbing has been defined initially as "a fan-produced, translated, subtitled version of a Japanese anime program" (Díaz Cintas and Muñoz Sánchez 2006: 37), even when today it encompasses any type of audiovisual product, from movies to TV series or video clip subtitling. It also includes dubbing by amateurs, the so-called "fandubbing." When the objects of translation are comic books, the process is known as "scanlation," or "a streamlined manga fan translation practice where officially published pages of manga are first scanned, translated and distributed by fans" (O'Hagan 2008: 162). The process of hacking videogames to localize their content is known as romhacking (Muñoz Sánchez 2009). It can be described as:

> the process of modifying the ROM data (Read-Only Memory) therefore not meant to be changed by the user of a video game to alter various aspects of the game, including the game's language and in the process of fan translation.
>
> (O'Hagan and Mangiron 2013: 10)

When romhacking focuses exclusively on the linguistic aspects of the game, it can be referred to as "translation hacking" (O'Hagan 2009: 94) in order to differentiate these earlier precursors from the widespread romhacking practices carried out through emulators in modern-day personal computers. Translation hacking involves a hacker and a translator working together to extract the relevant text from the ROM and to replace it with a translated script. It can therefore be distinguished from romhacking in that the latter can potentially include any aspect of the videogame, such as graphics, addition of levels, and changing the events. These practices are related to what is referred to as "modding," the illegal modification of the videogames to customize them to users' preferences or creativity (O'Hagan and Mangiron 2013: 296).

A last concept to clarify is that of "mobile translation." (Jiménez-Crespo 2017). This phenomenon is related to "mobile crowdsourcing" that, in general terms, involves leveraging the wide distribution and use of mobile phones to crowdsource small micro tasks, such as translation, transcription, surveys, and news reporting (Gonçalves et al. 2015). In this context, the term "mobile translation" has emerged in the language industry. According to Armstrong (2016) in the blog from the translation crowdsourcing app Stepes, "mobile translation" is often understood as three distinct and interrelated phenomena: (1) localization of apps, (2) the use of MT smartphone apps, and (3) the use of apps inspired in crowdsourcing workflows to carry out human translation either through post-editing MT or through direct human translation. Examples of this phenomenon are the mobile translation companies Stepes or Unbabel (see 2.6)

1.6   Classifications of online collaborative translations

In addition to the subdivision mentioned before between the crowdsourcing and the online collaborative translation, different scholars have proposed a range of potential classifications of collaborative practices based on a range of parameters. Subdivisions have thus been marked according to the objectives of the process (i.e., DePalma and Kelly 2011; Bey, Kageura and Boitet 2006b), the type of community involvement (Mesipuu 2012), or the workflows established (Morera-Mesa 2014; Morera-Mesa, Collins and Filip 2014). The openness of the call to participate defines whether translation crowdsourcing is characterized as an "open" or "closed" model (Mesipuu 2012). In the open model, any member of a community, i.e., Facebook or Twitter users, can openly participate, while, in a closed model, only the pre-selected or invited members by a company or organization can participate, i.e., Kiva, TED talks, or Skype. This implies that organizations or self-organized collectives might impose hierarchical structures within the community, selecting, depending on the task at hand, participants with different skill levels or characteristics. For example, a study by Camara (2015) reported that professional translators in TED talks were often assigned to higher responsibility jobs, such as reviewers or translation managers in the community. Other self-organized communities also impose strict evaluation criteria that determine how members move up the organization ladder, as is the case with the aRGENTeaM subtitle community in Argentina (Orrego-Carmona 2012). Thus, the term online "community" cannot be loosely understood as an anonymous collective of users, but rather as a group of people subject to varying degrees of internal or external organization, control and limitations to access, skills, participation, etc.[5]

DePalma and Kelly (2011) proposed to divide crowdsourcing processes into cause-, product-, or outsource-driven models. Cause-driven processes are those in which a collective is motivated to produce collaborative translation for a specific common goal, such as helping with translation in disasters as in the case of the Haiti earthquake (Munro 2010). Volunteers work without any monetary compensation and they translate at their own convenience. Product-driven efforts represent those in which a company would not normally localize a product due to return on investment (ROI) issues, but, with the help of crowdsourcing, it might become a reality. It is also the case in the development of open software or the emergent case of localizing smartphone apps. This is what happens with software such as OpenOffice, Mozilla, and Flock Lion browsers or other products partially

---

5.   For example, any volunteer participating in Facebook should have an account, but they need to be members for at least a month to participate.

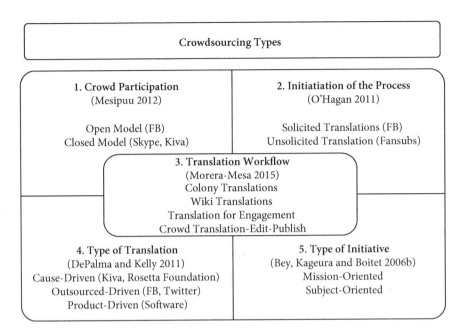

Figure 1.2 Translation crowdsourcing subtypes.

crowdsourced such as Adobe, Symantec, or Sun software products. Finally, outsourced crowdsourcing is represented by portals in which crowdsourced translations are offered sometimes in combination with professional translation and/ or MT. The number of portals offering these services is steadily growing, with services such as Duolingo, Getlocalization, Cucumis, Smartling, Lingotek, Tolingo, Transifex, or MNH (García 2015). Therefore, the notion of "paid crowdsourcing" would be included in this term. Participants are sometimes anonymous users or translators approved by the provider, and some of them offer different tiers of translation services based on the level of expertise of the participants involved. For example, in the crowdsourcing platform Cucumis, translations are paid by means of credits earned while translating for others. After receiving quality ratings over 70% in translations, members can move up to "expert" levels. When requesting a translation, an "expert" translation costs more translation credits than a general one.

A very similar proposal was put forth by Bey, Kageura and Boitet (2006b). Their proposal refers only to collaborative translations and not crowdsourcing as such. It proposes a distinction between "mission-oriented translator communities," that is, tightly coordinated collectives of volunteer translators who focus on specific sets of content, such as technical documentation, and "subject-oriented translator network communities," individual translators who focus on online documents such as news and reports, and who make their translations available on personal or group websites.

Morera-Mesa (2014) reviewed previous typologies of general crowdsourcing and translation crowdsourcing in his doctoral dissertation and developed a crowdsourcing typology based on an analysis of workflows implemented. His typology includes "colony translations," "wiki translations," "translation for engagement," and "crowd translation-edit-publish." Colony translation is defined by the request of multiple translations for the same translation unit, followed by a selection through an automatic or human process. Volunteers are often unaware of the fact that multiple translations are requested for the same segment. The selected contributions are later integrated into the final texts, a process somewhat similar to the MT approach applied by Zaidan and Calliston-Burch (2011). Wiki translation is an open model that is defined by the fact that volunteers can add contributions that can be subsequently edited either by other members or by the participant. These contributions are later integrated to form the final text. Amara, Wikipedia, or Transifex are examples of this wiki translations model. Translation for engagement is characterized by the fact that the open crowd can translate and vote/select segments at the translation unit level, that letters are integrated to form the complete text. Facebook, Twitter, CrowdIn, or Pootle are examples of this approach. In crowd translation-edit-publish, single translators translate entire texts from beginning to end and the integration of all translations in the community only occurs at the website level, when all translations are added. Translators are normally pre-selected and screened. Examples of this approach would be Kiva or Verbalizelt.

These typologies of translation crowdsourcing offer different perspectives on the classification of collaborative initiatives, and they categorize practices from different perspectives. Some of them can be complementary, such as the distinction between open and closed communities, that can at the same time be solicited and non-solicited. At the same time, all these categories could also be mission or subject oriented. In addition, the only empirical categorization (Morera-Mesa 2014) can also benefit from the fine-grained descriptive power of the other categorizations in order to describe initiatives. In this sense, these categorizations can be complementary rather than exclusive.

1.7 Which translations are outsourced? Of preferred genres and translation types

Nowadays, virtually any type of text can be crowdsourced, from literary texts to medical educational videos to be used by NGOs in Africa. The emergence of open crowdsourcing platforms designed for crowdsourcing, such as Transifex, those focused on learning languages – Duolingo and Looha – or translation bartering cases, such as Cucumis, means that anything can be forwarded to online translation communities. The Traduwiki community indicates in its description:

> What kind of documents could be submitted?
> Pretty much all regular texts. Magazine stories, academic textbooks, essays, poetry, novels, technical papers and more. Documents containing formulas are trickier; they will be integrated later. So will be video subtitles.[6]
>
> (Traduwiki 2015)

The only limits to the type of content are participants' interest, given that "volunteers are in control of what they will give and this is determined to some extent by the cause" (O'Brien and Schäler 2010: 10). This emphasis on volunteer motivation and interest brings about one of the most intriguing aspects of crowdsourcing and collaborative translations: the fact that since volunteers are in control outside the business cycle, motivations, and the "desire to translate" (Gambier 2012) might gravitate towards specific textual genres, translation types, or translation modalities, such as fan-related audiovisual genres or web localization of social networking sites that empower users.

In order to delve into the myriad of content that might be the focus of these efforts, the notions of "text type" and "textual genre," as well as "translation types" should be first clarified. Following Hurtado Albir (2000), "translation types" represent a classification tool related to socio-professional activities such as medical, legal, or religious translation. If crowdsourcing efforts are analyzed from the point of view of translation types, specialized translation types are less prominent in crowdsourcing than general types, such as the translation of journalistic texts (i.e., The Guardian July 23rd, 2014). Specialized translations often appear in cases such as technical manuals for open software (Arjona Reina et al. 2013) and software help forums (Mitchell 2015) to medical information translated by non-profits (Lyons 2014). For example, in the realm of medical translation, the organization Translators without Borders initiated a wide campaign to recruit volunteers and funds in order to help translate medical information materials during the 2014 Ebola or the 2015 Zika crises in Africa. This organization also initiated the

---

6. http://traduwiki.org/Faq

100x100 campaign, an effort to translate into 100 languages the top one hundred most read medical-related articles in Wikipedia, the so-called Wiki Project Med Foundation.[7] Nevertheless, this organization only recruits professional translators with several years of experience or college degrees in the field. A recognition of the expertise of professionals is sometimes perceived in these models, with crowd-sourcing companies such as Speaklike offering "specialized translation" services by professionals as opposed to "basic" ones, or others such as Gengo specifically excluding medical or legal translations from the services they offer.

Educational translation is another field in which crowdsourcing has found a niche. The desire to access knowledge to learn from communities all over the world has sprung initiatives to translate MOOC courses in Asia (Lee, Meng-Feng and Bonk 2007; Beaven et al. 2013; Cao 2015) or all the Coursera materials into Russian. Similarly, initiatives such as the website Khan Academy[8] have opened up the possibility of crowdsourcing any type of educational genre online. Education is also behind the drive to learn foreign languages and the initiatives to combine users' yearning for acquiring foreign languages with the crowdsourcing of texts, such as the cases of Duolingo or Looha. Among the learning materials and types could be included the translation from French to English of the Encyclopedia of Diderot and D'Alembert from the 19th Century in the University of Michigan. Similarly, a number of initiatives have also focused on the translation of research articles.

On the other hand, "textual genres" represent prototypes of conventionalized forms of texts that help achieve a communicative purpose in recurring social occasions (Hatim and Mason 1990). "Textual genres" help reduce the cognitive load and uncertainty in the communicative interactions as they represent frames that can be followed in the production and comprehension of repetitive communicative situations (Jiménez-Crespo 2013a). This notion is often confused with that of "text type" in TS (García Izquierdo 2005). The main difference between them is that genres are defined by extratextual factors, such as sociocultural, communicative, and cognitive features, while text types are conventionalized in respect to their intratextual or linguistic configuration (Trosborg 1997). Genres are more concrete than textual types, such as a poem, a personal blog, or a tweet, while text types represent more abstract categories with closed limited categories, such as exhortative, expositive, and argumentative types (Hatim and Mason 1990). Both are culture dependent as they depend on a recurring social or communicative occasion in a specific sociocultural context to exist, such as a business letter, a social networking site for professional goals, or the need to persuade someone to buy your product online.

---

7.   https://meta.wikimedia.org/wiki/WPMED

8.   https://khanacademy.zendesk.com/hc/en-us/categories/200186020-Translators

For the purpose of classifying and identifying types of texts that interest volunteers, the theoretical framework offered by the notion of "textual genres" can be highly useful. For example, digital genres such as corporate websites are less amenable to crowdsourcing when compared with social networking sites, wiki sites, or websites of non-profit organizations. In the latter cases, user-centered participation is essential to motivate the "prosumer," "fan," or "volunteer." Genre-based approaches to the study of crowdsourcing can also provide interesting insights such as in cases of "hybrid" or "complex" genres, such as websites. Australian genre theoretician Martin (1995) defined "complex" genres as those that can include instances of other genres in their structures, such as a privacy policy within a social networking site (Jiménez-Crespo 2013a). Martin (1995:24) and Bhatia (1997) refer to this relation between primary and secondary genres as "genre embedding." The fact that websites can include different genres within their structure is of interest since experiences such as Facebook have shown that volunteers are mostly motivated to translate small segments in the user interface and interactive contexts, but not so much in specialized legal texts or other longer chunks (Jiménez-Crespo 2011). These more complex texts are often handled by in-house translators.

In the realm of audiovisual translation, initiatives have been mostly focused on a handful of genres that spark the fandom phenomenon, such as all types of TV series (Orrego-Carmona 2012), movies, different genres of Japanese manga and anime (O'Hagan 2006; Pérez-González 2006, 2007), or even music video clips or songs (Hernandez Gerrero 2014). Journalistic videos have also attracted the interest of volunteers, such as the crowdsourcing effort by the USA channel PBS to translate important broadcasts such as presidential speeches. "Edutainment" genres, a combination of learning and entertainment (Santini 2015), have also attracted a large number of volunteers, such as the popular case of the TED Open Translation initiative. Other cases with lower volumes of translation can be found in the subtitling of videos for specific purposes, such as medical information videos (Ludewid 2014) or user-generated videos in activist circles (Baker 2015). The emergence of user-based subtitling platforms such as Amara or Viki has also meant that any type of audiovisual genre, from music video clips to Korean soap operas or user-generated videos of sneezing pandas, can be potentially subtitled. This is what can be considered "commons-based peer production" videos (Benkler 2006), such as any type of videos uploaded by users in video sharing platforms such as YouTube or Vimeo.

Digital genres that emerged with the advent of digital technologies, such as smartphone apps, web genres, software applications, and videogame genres, have been similarly widely translated by the crowd, both in solicited and non-solicited models. Crowdsourcing efforts can be said to have started in technology-related domains, such as the translation of open software in the pre-web era (Arjona Reina et al. 2013) or assisting in the development of MT systems to translate webpages (i.e., Shimohata et al. 2001). These efforts in the realm of MT have continued to date, such as the post-editing MT to train MT engines (Zaidan and Calliston-Burch 2011). The translation of any type of user-generated content by the crowd has also found a niche in certain digital genres, such as all types of wikisites (McDonough Dolmaya 2015), blogs (Grunwald 2011), or tweets (Arend 2012; Šubert and Bojar 2014). In the case of videogames, volunteers have shown a preference for classic arcade and console games (Sánchez 2008, 2009), as well as RPGs or Role Playing Games with a high volume of text (Mangiron 2013). Many of these digital genres are often translated with either full human translation or the post-editing of MT. Taking a wide perspective, the post-editing done by users in the output of FOMT engines such as Google Translate implies that virtually any textual genre can potentially be the object of crowdsourcing practices.

The wide constellation of textual genres surrounding non-profit organizations is also of interest (i.e., Anastasiou and Schäler 2009; Petras 2011; Tesseur 2014a; O'Brien 2016), from websites to press releases, all types of educational brochures and materials, SMSs in times of crises (Munro 2010), or microloan applications in Kiva. As an example, the web-based platform offered by the Rosetta Foundation, called Translation Commons (Trommons), can be used by non-profit communities and language volunteers to translate any textual genre in the wide constellation of potential texts used in these communities (De Wille 2014).

As indicated previously, both crowdsourcing and online collaborative translations depend on the motivation and interest of a collective of volunteers to make whichever instance of text available in any targeted language(s). This review has highlighted the preference for specific "textual genres" and certain "translation types" in crowdsourcing and collaborative translation efforts. It was also indicated that potentially any text could be translated due to the existence of platforms that can help any initiator to request a crowdsourcing project. Nevertheless, the resistance of the crowd to participate has been eased in cases of translation bartering such as Cucumis, Linqapp, or Hellotalk, or the emergence of paid crowdsourcing in the late 2000s. In paid crowdsourcing efforts, language service providers test the initial resistance of volunteers to engaging in difficult, lengthy, or uninteresting content by means of offering small compensation. In these cases, there is a shift of responsibility to some extent from the company and translator to the customer since they are in charge of requesting "crowdsourced" translation quality in lieu of "expert" or "professional" translation that is considerably more expensive. This opens up the potential of any textual genre to be translated as far as the initiator or commissioner is comfortable with the potential quality of the product (also see 5.2.1 and 5.2.2).

CHAPTER 2

The emergence of crowdsourcing and online collaborative translations

> [Historically] speaking, translation has often been a collaborative act.
> (St. Andre 2010:72)

2.1   Introduction

This chapter traces the origins of crowdsourcing and online collaborative translation through a historical overview from the earlier known collaborative translation phenomena as documented in TS literature, to their consolidation in the second decade of the 20th century. The need for this overview lies in the fact that novel types of online collaborative translation are different from pre-Internet activities following established principles in crowdsourcing research. As described in Section 1.2.3, Brabham (2013) argues that crowdsourcing is radically different from historical examples in which cognitive tasks were outsourced to volunteers, such as the 1980's Oxford dictionary or the Alkali price. Consequently, a historical overview of collaboration in translation, its types and main areas, is necessary to contextualize current practices and understand how digital technologies have influenced their evolution. This chapter thus serves as a general overview, though brief given the inherent limitations, of how new translational phenomena emerged and the possible influence of preceding practices, as well as how they transitioned and distinctly evolved into a new paradigm thanks to the affordances provided by Internet and the Web 2.0. This review of the evolution of collaborative translation throughout history is divided here into five distinct stages. It starts with a brief overview of collaboration in translation since antiquity to the consolidation of the personal computers and the Internet in the 1980s and 1990s. This stage centers in the constant practice throughout history of collaboration in sacred texts, such as Bible translations or Buddhist texts in China, as well as the different types of collaboration in literary and scientific translations. The second stage involves the emergence of "participatory cultures" and the "fandom movement" (Jenkins 1992, 2006b; Delwiche and Henderson 2012), since, in these contexts, communities quickly took advantage of the networking and collaborative possibilities brought by the Internet to adapt and expand their translation initiatives. The next phase revolves around the origins of online crowdsourcing with the first attempts in MT using volunteer translators on the web (Shimohata et al. 2001; Utiyama and

Isahara 2003), as well as the emergence of collaborative translation platforms to harness the wisdom of the crowd. This is followed by the fourth stage in which collaborative practices grew exponentially when social networking sites, such as Facebook, resorted to crowdsourcing to translate their websites. These initiatives by widely popular social networking sites represented a quantum leap towards the consolidation of collaboration and the rise of public awareness in the second half of the 2000s. The chapter ends with an analysis of both the explosion and the exploration of the limitations of crowdsourcing and volunteer initiatives in the 2010s, including the emergence of new models such as "paid crowdsourcing" (García 2015), as well as a wider diversification of workflows, models, and initiatives.

2.2   Collaborative translations: A brief historical overview until the Internet era (until 1980)

In general, it could be argued that collaboration had been present since the first documented instances of translated text (Cordingley and Frigau Manning 2016). Without any doubt, sacred texts in different geographical areas are of special interest in the study of the evolution of collaboration in translation. They have been throughout history the object of collaborative ventures in their quest of religions to expand since antiquity (Long 2013). A complete review of collaboration in sacred text would require a monograph of its own, because as Long indicates "[s]acred texts, particularly the Bible in the Western communities, provide a wealth of material for the translation studies researcher" (Long 2013: 472). This section merely highlights the most representative examples of collaboration with the objective of exemplifying instances of mass collaboration in this domain throughout the centuries.

The earliest historically documented instance of collaborative processes is the translation of the Septuagint Bible translation from Hebrew into Koine Greek in the 3rd century BC. This translation process is mentioned several times in the New Testament, and it was orally transmitted for generations. According to documentary sources, this translation was reputedly undertaken by seventy-two translators who were locked up separately in different rooms. During the extended period of isolation, they all produced identical versions of the translated texts – a unique version that was supposedly inspired by the grace of God. Recent research, however, has pointed out the unreliable nature of this translation myth, since it has been argued that each book of the Bible has a translator who identifies himself as a real individual (Baslez 2014a, 2014b).

In the following centuries, the translation of the Bible has provided throughout centuries a fertile ground for collaborative translation, such as the King James

Bible. This version, for example, was produced through committees that were established with a minimum of six specialists from different areas, such as Hebrew, Greek, linguistics, theology, English language, poetry, and other disciplines (Burke 2013). The process to carry out the translation of this canonical version, a case of the wider collaboration paradigm according to O'Brien's (2011a) proposal, provided a process model for later collaborative translations of Christian sacred texts. This translation model thus had a tremendous impact on all substantive translation of the Bible into English and other languages. Other Bible translations, such as St Jerome vulgate Latin translation in the 5th century, included, for example, consultation and collaboration with rabbis as linguistic informants (Rogers 2015). The Wycliffe translation of the Bible in Middle Age England is also renowned as a collaborative venture, with a range of names associated with his production and two different versions from the 1370s and the 1380s (Ellis and Oakley-Brown 2009). The first translation version is more literal than the second one, witness to the potential interaction and collaboration between authors. Examples of collaborative translations of the Bible also abound since the foundation of the American Bible Association in 1816, bearing witness to their efforts to make this sacred text available in all possible existing languages. Collaboration has continued until recent years with examples such as the 2001 translation version of the Bible into French coordinated by Frédéric Boyer (Gambier 2012). Not only the Bible has been the object of collaborative translation processes, translations of other Christian sacred texts have also been produced by teams. Venuti (2009), for example, mentions the case of the "Whole Booke of Psalmes Faithfully Translated into English Metre" (Venuti 2009), the first written and printed book in North America in 1640.

Non-Western sacred texts have also been the object of collaborative processes throughout history. While discussing the history of translation in China, St Andre argues that "historically speaking, translation has often been a collaborative act" (2010: 72). This means that, historically, translation needs to be explored from the lens of different agents and cultural traditions and it also means that collaboration can have different purposes depending on the translation cultures, agents involved, etc. In general, research has explored, for example, the translation of the Buddhist sutras from Sanskrit into Chinese in the late Qing dynasty (1890–1911) (Hung 1999; Hung 2006). In these processes, it has been argued that collaboration was often the norm rather than the exception, with anywhere from two to 1000 translators working as a team to translate one single text. Translation was thus a communal act, typically performed by monks who resided in a monastery. According to Hung (2006), the translation process could be summarized as follows. The first step was for the oral recitation in the source language of one sutra followed by any pertinent clarifications or commentaries on the meaning. The text would then be recited in Chinese followed by a discussion by all present on the different possibilities of translation. This discussion was followed by the recording of the final version of the agreed-upon target text. After the recording, commentaries, revisions, and discussions would ensue, including the possibility of comparisons with older translations of the same sutras. The process required at least an interpreter and audience. The latter could include monks and laymen, as well as at least one scribe. This process could sometimes last years and involve as many as 1000 people. This model of translation based on Buddhist principles has reached the modern age and current volunteer translator groups in Buddhist circles follow a similar process (Neather 2015). Collaboration in sacred texts also extended to translation in the Ming and Qing dynasties by the Jesuits from and into Latin and Chinese (Hung and Pollard 1997; Hung 1999).

Not only sacred texts were collaboratively translated in the Chinese context. The tradition of collaboration applied to sacred texts was also adopted to the translation from English and French in the Qing Court after the defeat in the Second Opium War (1860). This defeat meant that a range of letters and diplomatic documents needed to be translated, with translators working in collaboration. Without any doubt, one of the most puzzling cases of collaborative translation in China is represented by the famous and influential translator Lin Shu, the most influential translator in his era, who "translated" over 150 literary works even when he did not know any foreign language (Zhang 2014). Lin Shu was an eminent writer and poet who would have "interpreters" read the source texts in Chinese while he would be writing. In his original writings, he indicated that it was a sort of automatic process; when the interpreter would stop speaking he would write the translation inspired by the interpreting. By means of this process, he translated and popularized in China Western classics such as Dickens, Haggard, Dumas, or Stowe. Collaborative translation in Eastern contexts thus represents a fascinating topic that deserves a much-detailed treatment than the brief overview in this chapter.

In Western Europe, examples of collaborative translation also took place during the Medieval and Renaissance ages, such as the processes found in the so-called School of Toledo of King Alphonse the 10th of Castile, in which Hebrews, Arabs, and Christians would collaborate in translations of different nature (Gargatagli 1999). Similarly, during the Renaissance, there was a surge in the collaborative translation of texts in Europe (Bestué 2013).

In the Western context, the translation of all sorts of literary works has been, after the Bible, the most productive context for collaboration in translation (Cordingley and Frigau 2016). The model here is understood both in the general and in the narrow sense proposed by O'Brien (2011a). As far as collaboration between translators, it has occurred between groups of translators working on translations into different languages between translators working on the same literary text. One example of the former is the case of collaboration between translators of the works of Japanese author Haruki Murakami (Kaminka and Zelinska-Elliot 2014). The former case, collaboration between translators to work on the same literary text, offers a large number of instances (Wittman 2013: 443–444), such as the 2007 translation of the Ulysses by James Joyce (Gambier 2012). This type of collaboration has also extended to the volunteer translation of popular fiction by fan communities (i.e., Guerrero 2016), such as the case of the volunteer translation of a Harry Potter installment in China that was produced in 48 hours (Munday 2008). Collaboration in these cases often occurs with different participants working on segments or chunks of the literary work, and recent research based on stylometry in the field of computational linguistics has been able to identify, for example, the points in the works in which translators change (i.e., Heydel and Rybicki 2012).

Some of the most interesting cases of collaboration are those in which translators are invited to collaborate with authors in the translation of their literary works, bringing out their visibility in the process. Classical examples are those of the processes set up by Borges, a case in which scholars have delved into the difficulties this type of author/translator collaboration entails (Fraser 2004). Other authors who have collaborated with translators are Umberto Eco, Milan Kundera (Wittman 2013) or the case of James Joyce collaborating with translators of his works (Costanzo 1972, apud O'Brien 2011a). Gunter Grass has also been convening with his translators since 1978 on each book to discuss with them the difficulties they encountered in the translation (Letawe 2014). In many instances, research has explored and described the translation of literature in workshops and training settings (Maher 2014).

Stage translation also represents a case in which collaboration often takes place between authors and translators (Bassnet 1998; Zatlin 2005; Espasa 2013), and it also extends to musical theatre in which the translation of dialogue and musical librettos is combined (Sorby 2015). In poetry translation, the most common collaboration is between translators and authors (Raffel 1988: 129–137), while the popular poetry translation workshops often focus collaboration between translators. Recent research in literary translation has focused on collaboration with external agents in translation following Latour's actor – network theory, such as the case of Spies and Feinauer (2014) or Buzelin (2005, 2006). This last researcher, in her study of literary translators in Canada, demonstrates that – in addition to the translators – managing directors, editors-in-chief, revisers, press officers, and representatives of the publishing houses can all be involved in the process and, thus, also contribute to co-creating the translation.

2.3   The emergence of personal computing, the Internet and the WWW (1980–1995)

Collaborative practices entered a new era once digital technologies arrived in the world of translation since the 1980s, radically transforming how translations were processed. The first consequence of the "technologization" in translation was the emergence of the use of "translation workstations" or "workbenches" (Sommers 2003), the intersection of technology and the profession (Austermühl 2001). These workstations can to date be defined as "personal computers [...] [where] the translator [is] provided with software and other computer-based facilities to assist in the tasks of translation" (Sommers 2003:7). Translation memory systems represented the core of these workstations. They were initially sketched in the 1970s by scholars such as Kay (1980) or Melby (1981, 1995), and they started to be widely implemented from the mid-1990s (2003: 31–33). These technologies quickly became the norm in the industry, radically changing how translators, language providers, and clients collaborated in the translation cycle, a process that facilitated the language industry globalization. Nowadays, the dependence of professional translation of translation technologies is only deepening, and translation needs to be irrevocably conceptualized as "human – computer interaction" (O'Brien 2012b). Collaboration in both professional and volunteer settings cannot be separated from the existence of these computer workstations, with the Internet and the WWW being key components (Chan 2014). The constant evolution of these workstations or workbenches continues to date, with the WWW prompting a shift towards a "cloud" paradigm. In this context, TM or management tools do not reside any more in translators' workstations, but rather they are accessed remotely via web connections and browsers and reside on online servers. Translation tasks are increasingly processed through computers, tablets, or even smartphones connected to servers via cloud TM systems, such as Wordfast Anywhere or MateCat, or even all collaborative micro-crowdsourcing platforms, such as Transifex or Acuna. This transition to a cloud paradigm has been instrumental in the development of all types of crowdsourcing and collaborative online platforms that mediate and manage the many types of translation collaboration (see 3.4).

Two indispensable components of the 21st-century workstation are the WWW and the Internet. These two terms are often confused and interchanged, even when the WWW is merely one of the many communicative situations enabled by the Internet (O'Hagan and Ashworth 2003), such as chats, videoconferencing, and new online SMS apps in smartphones. The Internet quickly emerged as a paradigm-changing medium, impacting all areas of modern lives and creating vast areas for research and scientific inquiry (Consalvo and Ess 2011; Dutton 2013). Its history began in the 1960s when researchers in the USA developed protocols to connect computers remotely. It was not until 1982 when the current TCP/IP protocols were standardized that the Internet as we know it was born. The Internet emerged as a powerful communication tool, allowing for email, instant messaging, Voice over Internet calling, video conferencing, discussion forums, blogs, social networks, etc. The seeds of online collaboration in translation were planted. In the 1996 book *The Coming of Age of Teletranslation*, O'Hagan reports the quantum jump from 213 computers that participated in the Internet network in 1981 to 1.776.000 computers in 1994, with a total of 25 million users that was doubling each year. Nowadays, InternetStats (2015) reports 3.3 billion users worldwide, with a 753% growth in the 2000–2015 period. Historically, its radical impact is such that it is often compared to the invention of the printing press by Guttenberg in the 15th century. The language industry and translators quickly took advantage of this initial communication revolution (O'Hagan 1996; O'Hagan and Ashworth 2003). New translation processes mediated through technology-enabled forms of communications emerged. The delocalization and fragmentation of translation professionals soon became the norm rather than the exception. A language provider could work on a multilingual project employing translators all over the world, as long as they had an Internet connection and a computer. The foundation of collaborative translation processes with participants simultaneously collaborating in a single translation process around the world was set in place.

At the end of the 1980s, Tim Berners-Lee created in the European Center for Nuclear Research (CERN) what we refer to today as the World Wide Web, when he hosted in his own computer, called the NeXT, a website with the basic information about the web, how to upload and access other people's pages, and how to set up web servers. In 1991, he created the Hypertext Markup Language (HTML), and this same year the WWW was also made available to the wider public using the existing Internet connection in personal computers. Berners-Lee himself defined the WWW as "the universe of network-accessible information, an embodiment of human knowledge" (Berners-Lee et al. 1992: 52). This emerging embodiment of human knowledge entailed a revolution for translation and interpreting professionals, due both to the availability to communicate with clients and other translators through web platforms, but also as a documentation source. In addition to the communication revolution that the Internet provided (O'Hagan 1996), the possibilities of immediate access to a massive repository of information, both general and translation-interpreting related (i.e., terminology databases or online parallel corpora), meant that professionals no longer needed massive amounts of paper-based documentation. In a profession in which documentation is a key component (Massey and Ehrengsberger-Dow 2011), the world library was accessible anywhere, with clear implications for the work of translators worldwide.

The WWW has transitioned through several stages that have had significant implications for its impact on translation. The initial Web 0.1 represented a static model in which webpages and websites were consulted with minimal user intervention. Forums and discussion boards were popular, and they also existed prior to the emergence of the WWW. It was not until the deployment of the Web 2.0 at the beginning of the 2000s that users became active participants in the creation and distribution of content. The term Web 2.0 was popularized by Tim O'Reilly and Dale Dougherty in 2005 to describe a number of services that enable today's Internet users to interact and share information efficiently (O'Reilly 2005).[1] This represented a change of paradigm from the static notion of the web to an open and participatory platform in which social participation was a key in the form of mixing production and consumption of content. Berners-Lee himself coined the term "ReadWriteWeb" in a clear recognition of its interactive nature. He also anticipated the massive impact on social practices and the rise of social networks when he indicated that "the web is more a social creation than a technical one" (Berners-Lee 2000: 113). The previous one-way street where content was somewhat controlled by the producers of information gave way to a model in which anyone could potentially create and distribute content, empowering users and communities worldwide. The most significant examples of the power of the Web 2.0 to impact modern societies were social networking sites or other web genres that facilitated producing and distributing all types of content, from videos to photos to personal information. These platforms gave a certain amount of control to users over the type of content that was produced, distributed, and, in many cases, translated. Some of the most visited websites worldwide, such as Facebook, Twitter, YouTube, Wikipedia, Reddit, LinkedIn, or even translation sites such as Proz.com, represent instances of web initiatives of users consuming and producing what is known as "user-generated content," and all of them include "user-translated" content. The most recent developments in web technologies represent a move towards the Web 3.0 or the semantic web, in which users can customize and personalize their digital life through the convergence of media, platform, and content (Metz 2007). It hinges around the complete integration of web, social media, apps, widgets, etc., and the accumulation of knowledge and personalization of each user's experience. In this context, the WWW is also adjusting to the explosion in mobile technologies that are slowly replacing desktop computers in the daily lives of millions.

---

1.   The term "Web 2.0" was initially coined by Darcy DiNucci in 1999 in an article in Print magazine (DiNucci 1999).

Over the years, the wide reach of the WWW has prompted continuous new developments in translation practices and the translation microcosm. Examples of these advances are the widespread adoption of FOMT practices around the world, the subsequent adoption of web-mediated MT post-editing practices (Aikawa, Yamamoto and Isahara 2012; Mitchell, O'Brien and Roturier 2014; Mitchell 2015), and the impact of online collaborative translation and crowdsourcing. In this area, examples of disruptions can be seen both in the business models and in the professional arena: the professional community was shaken in 2007 after the outrage caused by LinkedIn requesting only professional translators to crowdsource the website (Kelly 2009; American Translators Association 2009). A myriad of discussions erupted on the potential negative implications of large corporations crowdsourcing their translation tasks. Professional associations, such as the International Federation of Translators (FIT), released statements on their position regarding these novel practices and warning about the different dangers associated with them (FIT 2015). Institutions such as the European Union produced extensive publications analyzing this phenomenon (European Union 2011), while industry think tanks such as Common Sense Advisory attempted to shed light on the potential benefits for the industry of this new model through a number of reports (i.e., DePalma and Kelly 2008; Ray and Kelly 2011).

2.4 Participatory cultures on the Internet as a foundation for collaborative translations (1980s)

The most prominent instances of collaborative translation communities that existed prior to the Internet and the WWW consisted of audiovisual fan communities within the context of what Media Studies refers to as "participatory cultures" (Jenkins 2006b: 137). This term was coined by Jenkins (1992) in his seminal study of Star Trek fan communities entitled *Textual Poachers: Television Fans and Participatory Cultures*. One of the main contributions of this study consisted of an epistemological distinction between classic "viewers" of audiovisual content and dedicated "fans." Viewers were defined as those immersed in a passive and isolated model of consumption of media, similar to the more static user interaction in the Web 1.0 paradigm. Meanwhile, "fans" are deeply involved in interaction with others through discussions, forums, or events to reflect on their experiences with the audiovisual product. In 2006, Jenkins et al. traced the evolution of participatory cultures in modern societies (Jenkins et al. 2006: 7), proposing the classic definition in the literature. They are defined as those with:

1. Relatively low barriers to artistic expression and civic engagement.
2. Strong support for creating and sharing one's creations with others.
3. Some type of informal mentorship whereby what is known by the most experienced is passed along to novices.
4. Members who believe that their contributions matter.
5. Members who feel some degree of social connection with one another (at the least they care what other people think about what they have created).

The rise of the Internet allowed the current explosion in participatory cultures to move beyond the "fandom" phenomenon centered around audiovisual products, as witnessed by the multiplication of websites in which collectives share and create content. Currently, participation is prompted and structured by a large number of specialized interests and activities, such as strengthening friendships, gaming, creative production, or work among others (Ito et al. 2009). This surge in collaboration occurred through bottom-up horizontal initiatives self-organized by web users in domains, such as political and civic activism, fandom, creative collaboration to produce fiction, poetry or comics, scientific research, civic engagement, or education and learning (Delwiche and Henderson 2012). In modern societies, all these cultures are part of the daily lives of billions, to the extent that:

> knowledge cultures have become an integral part of our lives, they function as prosthetic extensions of our nervous system and we often feel crippled when our access to these networks is curtailed.   (Delwiche and Henderson 2012:4)

The Web and related technologies have afforded not only the exponential growth of these communities, but also a reconfiguration of how they are structured and how they function (Hills 2002). They empowered users to move beyond the passive consumption of all types of content mediated through the web, turning them into co-creators of media that is distributed through the web and that even media companies routinely incorporate, moving to what Banks (2009) defines as the "co-creative user" and others define as the "prosumer" (Toffler 1980) in the fansubbing phenomenon. Since the early 2000s, not only did fans create and participate in digital networks creating and distributing content, but also the social networking era made every user of the Internet both a creator and a user, from postings in Facebook to tweets or photos in Instagram. The rise of the social network society has meant that the multiplication of users in Internet-based activities has moved the fandom phenomenon "from cult status to cultural mainstream" (Jenkins 2002:161).

All these types of collaboration are based on the principle of "collective intelligence," defined as "a form of universally distributed intelligence, constantly enhanced, coordinated in real time, and resulting in the effective mobilization of tasks" (Levy 1997: 13). This "universally distributed intelligence" results in the ability of a collective to solve more problems and/or solve them more efficiently than any single person or expert. It is easy to identify how translation crowdsourcing by companies such as Facebook or Twitter fits within this notion in which the final translation of a website is produced by a massive number of unidentified participants (Jiménez-Crespo 2011). The evolution of participatory cultures has clear parallels with the evolution of collaborative translation. According to Delwiche and Henderson, the evolution of participatory cultures can be traced in the following four stages:

1. Emergence (1985–1993). The early instances of fansubbing of Japanese manga and anime that used analog video technologies represent the first cases of translation in participatory cultures.
2. Waking up to the Web (1994–1998). This stage was also mostly dominated by the "fandom phenomenon," with fansubbing, scanlations, and videogame romhacking being the main practices.
3. Push button publishing (1999–2004). In this stage, collaboration exploded, from comic scanlation (Ferrer-Simó 2005), to all types of audiovisual texts.
4. Ubiquitous connections (2005-now). Volunteer translation appears here in most areas of participatory cultures, from the explosion of fansubbing around the world (see Chapter 7) to the translation of fiction such as Harry Potter (Munday 2008) or civic engagement as seen in recent uprising in Middle Eastern countries (Baker 2015, 2016).

In this last stage, a special mention should be made of activist approaches for social and civic engagement (i.e., Brough and Shresthrova 2012; Delwiche 2012), creating the phenomenon of "fan activism" or "citizen translation" in the context of civic and political scenarios. This fan activism represents a combination of "activism" (Baker 2006, 2015) and "fandom," impacting activist translation collaborations in cases such as the Egyptian revolution (Baker 2015, 2016) or even the emergence of activist translation networks such as Babel (Boeri 2008), Translators without Borders, Translators for Progress, Permondo, Translate America, EngageMedia, or Global Voices. Collaborative practices online are being currently used in this context as "instrument[s] of human political intervention" (Cronin 2010: 102), in a way that the combination of technologies and activism can be used to "to further human concerns or agendas" (ibid). The interest in the discipline has led scholars to coin a term to refer to this phenomenon as the "activist turn" (Wolf 2012) (see 8.2.2).

2.5   The development of collaborative translations on the web (1995–2005)

The mainstream expansion of collaborative practices can be traced to the first decade of the 2000s, parallel to the emergence of the Web 2.0 and the ever-increasing Internet usage rates in modern societies. The objective of this section is to trace origins of web-mediated collaborative practices in the last two decades of the 20th century such as fansubs, romhacking, and the localization of open-source software, ending with a review of the earliest known instances of translation crowdsourcing found in the development of machine translation in Japan (Shimohata et al. 2001; Sukehiro et al. 2001; Murata et al. 2003) and in the Google in Your Language campaign in 2001 (Google 2008).

2.5.1   The emergence of fansubbing

The fansubbing phenomenon, without any doubt, represents one of the most prolific avenues for collaborative translation in the context of "participatory cultures" (Jenkins 1992, 2006a, 2006b) that quickly profited from the communicative affordances provided by the WWW. It can be considered as the most productive precursor of current practices (Díaz Cintas and Muñoz Sánchez 2006), as well as one of the most widely researched phenomena in Audiovisual TS (see Chapter 7). Anime started to be distributed in the United States in the 1960s (Leonard 2005), while the first fan clubs started to emerge in the 1970s. It has been argued that the fansub networks flourished as a reaction to the ban or heavy censorship of these Japanese audiovisual products in the US market in 1982 due to their inappropriate content (Massidda 2015). The early days of anime fansubbing were characterized by the use analog video technology using VHS tapes that were mailed to fans as means of distribution. This was a very expensive and labor-intensive process that attests to the motivation and sense of identity and community of the early "fan-subbers." Fansubbing communities used self-addressed stamped envelopes, the so-called "SASE system," in order to distribute their products. This self-addressed system meant that the distribution was primarily free of charge to dedicated fans. A similar system was employed for the translations of Japanese manga, "scanlations," that would be scanned and subsequently the translation would be inserted in the original comic (O'Hagan 2013). The earliest recorded instance of fansubbing in the USA is said to be the version of Lupin III in VHS format in the mid-1980s (O'Hagan 2008: 161), where the actual history of fansubbing starts. These types of communities took advantage of the digital revolution of the Internet using RC chats and forums, later expanding exponentially with the advent of the WWW and the emergence of dedicated subtitling management platforms online.

Two main factors contributed to the emergence of fansubbing communities in this decade: on the one hand, the already mentioned lack of distribution of the audiovisual product in a pre-Internet era, and on the other hand, the language barrier (Díaz Cintas and Muñoz Sánchez 2006). Debates in the discipline on the legality and the ethics of this phenomenon (see 8.3.2) usually point at the apparent mutual benefit from fansubs since they helped popularize and promote audiovisual products that would have not been otherwise consumed in the receiving cultures (Massidda 2015). Witness to this fact is the lack of legal actions against translation fan communities in the early days by the rightful holders of the copyright (Diaz Cintas and Muñoz Sánchez 2006). Quickly, fan communities adopted the common practices of including a disclaimer, indicating that distribution of subtitled versions would be stopped as soon as the product would be commercially available in the target country (O'Hagan 2009).

2.5.2 The early days of videogame "rom hacking" and open software localization

In the realm of videogames, the process of producing volunteer "unofficial" localizations is commonly known as "rom hacking." The actual unofficial collaborative translation of videogames can be traced back to 1996/1997 when the first groups of fans started to organize themselves following the lead of several hackers to localize a number of videogames, mostly attempting to work on the console games such as the installments of the role-playing game *Final Fantasy*. Its origins can thus be traced back to the wide popularity of these types of role-playing games (RPG) in the mid-1990s that required the translation of vast quantities of text (O'Hagan and Mangiron 2013). These vast amounts of texts in videogames, up to 100 hours of video and dialogue, entailed a considerable investment to produce localized versions, and thus localization was subject to stringent ROI considerations. When the localization process was reduced to textual aspects, the process was considered as "translation hacking" (O'Hagan 2009: 94), defined as the sole translation of the textual component of the game without programming modifications. Rom hacking a videogame required highly skilled programmers, reducing the potential for expansion in the early years when compared with fansubbing. This higher technical competence was highlighted by O'Hagan (2009: 19): "[i]t is this technical knowledge and intensive interest in the game development process by some gamers that characterize the unique nature of fan translation of games." Fan participation in these initiatives increased thanks to the development of emulators in PCs in the 1990s that allowed fans to play classic games that had not been previously localized from different types of consoles and formats. This made the classic PC into a virtual console gaming machine (Muñoz Sánchez 2008). Another interesting phenomenon, parallel to what happened with fansubs and scanlations, is that, in the 1990s, the directionality of translation switched from Japanese to English, to mainly localizations from English into other languages independent of the country of origin, witness to the status of English as the international lingua franca.

A less researched topic in TS is the collaborative effort to translate open software such as Linux, Open Office, or Mozilla, even when its application to the profession and to training has been the objective of a number of publications (i.e., Diaz Fouçes and García Gonzalez 2009; Sandrini and García Gonzalez 2015). According to García (2015), this movement began in the early 1980s when open-source communities started organizing themselves in order to provide localized versions of open software. One of the earliest documented examples of translation communities was Traduc.org, an organization that was set up in France in 1992 in order to tackle the localization of Linux in the 1990s, moving later to other developments in the 2000s such as Mozilla or Ubuntu. Nowadays, the open translation of software continues (Sandrini and García Gonzalez 2015), with an expansion beyond software to all types of apps (Roturier 2015: 121–123).

2.5.3 The emergence of crowdsourcing and collaborative translation technological platforms (2000–2005)

The rise and expansion of collaborative translations on the web would not have occurred without the development of web-based platforms to organize the workflow of participants' efforts and coordinate and manage community projects. In the earlier stages of collaborative translation, communities would collaborate through forums and IRCs mediated through the Internet. They later moved to web hubs that facilitated the collaboration and distribution of materials. However, collaborative translations were still performed following to some extent regular processes set up by the language industry. Collaboration took place primarily through forums, sharing sites or chats. It was not until the late 1990s that the first online platforms to facilitate collaborative translation practices emerged in Japan. The earlier examples, such as Yakushite.net (Shimohata et al. 2001; Utiyama and Isahara 2003), initially attempted to harvest the collective intelligence of crowds in order to assist in a blended model with MT tasks. The earlier prototypes were intended for efforts that the developers called "collaborative translation on the web" or "network translations," and it entailed the crowdsourcing of dictionaries as well as post-editing of MT output that would assist in the translation of web pages. This represented a case of interest since it involved human – machine collaboration with volunteers post-editing and helping translate webpages or any document uploaded. The MT system used a pattern-based approach, a less common model nowadays after the explosion of rule-based and statistical MT systems.

The system also included a forum in which volunteers could collaborate in order to discuss any potential issues. The development of this project over the following two years continued, focusing on specialized dictionaries to tackle specialized domains (Utiyama and Isahara 2003). Despite the fact that the researchers suggested the inclusion of a TM functionality, a precursor of the now common MT-TM hybrid systems, it was not implemented in the earlier prototypes.

It can be argued that the first large technology company to set up a collaborative platform to crowdsource the translation of its website was Google. In 2001, it launched Google in Your Language (Google Blogs 2008), a campaign to let users collaborate in the localization of this search engine. In over a decade, 118 language versions were produced. The system allowed the user, once an available language was selected, to choose between translating and editing existing translations, and all languages displayed a discussion forum. Recent initiatives have continually expanded the language range for Google such as the 2007 initiative that included languages such as Maori or Navajo (Google Blog 2008).[2] Google opened up not only the Search engine to community localization but also other popular functionalities such as Google Maps (Google Blogs 2009).[3]

Some other similar systems were also developed in the framework of the Worldwide Lexicon project, in which a combination of MT and volunteer translation would be used to translate webpages, such as the GNUTrans project (Perrino 2009). Nevertheless, the efforts never led to a commercial or open release of the system. The same research group attempted to develop a volunteer-based system of IM communication using the translator as a pivot in a three-way communication system, what O'Hagan and Ashworth (2003) referred to as "chat translation." This prototype dating to 2004 was called MIMS (Multilingual Instant Messaging System) and was also never used commercially, but the seed of the digital revolution in translation and the possibility of using volunteer communities in the translation of web-mediated texts was put in place.

It was not until 2004 that translation memory function started to be present in collaborative crowdsourcing platforms, such as the earlier prototypes of the TransBey project (Bey, Kageura and Boitiet 2005). The earlier system, known as Qrlex, was presented at the 19th Asia-Pacific Conference on Language, Information and Computation. It departed from the premise that the automatization of the translation workflow was needed since the Linux translation communities were more static and therefore "[a]lmost all linguistic tools are not maintained and updated; this due to the lack of automatic tools that coordinate and make tasks easier." (2005: np). Their research efforts were supported by interviews with

---

2.   https://googleblog.blogspot.com.au/2008/08/google-in-your-language.html

3.   http://google-latlong.blogspot.com.au/2009/02/map-making-in-your-language-on-your.html

volunteer translators. In their survey studies, participants weighed the necessity of including a TM functionality in the system: "integrated computer-aided translation environment is the more important aspect that volunteer translator communities ask for" (ibid). In 2006, the first actual prototype of a collaborative wiki environment for volunteer translators, known as the TransBey prototype, was presented (Bey, Boitiet and Kageura 2006a, 2006b). At this point, TS was still focused on the development and assessment of translation technologies and the potential application of computerized corpus-methodologies to the translation process (i.e., Bowker 2002). No documented research attempted to analyze or foresaw the impending revolution that made crowdsourcing go mainstream. The cloud revolution was not yet underway and CAT tools started to allow collaboration in the production of any single document through the use of existing TMs or through networked TMs within a company (see also 6.2.1). Nevertheless, the potential to tap into large communities in the Web using translation platforms was still unexplored. Publications in translation technology such as Chan's 2005 Dictionary of Translation Technology did not include entries for "collaborative translation," "volunteer translation," or "crowdsourcing," a term introduced in the discipline around 2007–2008 (Desilets 2007; O'Hagan 2009). In the late 2000s, crowdsourcing started to become part of the mainstream discourse in TS, mainly due to the overpowering influence of the Facebook initiative and the initial interest by the translation industry in exploring the wisdom of the crowd (i.e., DePalma and Kelly 2008).

2.6 Crowdsourcing translation goes mainstream (2005–2010): From social networking sites to Wikipedia and non-profit initiatives

In the second part of the 2000s, the best-known examples of online collaborative translations emerged. These years were precisely the time when Howe (2006) coined the term "crowdsourcing" in his seminal article in *Wired* magazine. By the mid-2000s, the Web 2.0 was flourishing and user involvement was booming, with ever-growing penetration rates of the Internet all over the world and the wider availability of fast Internet connections. The stage was set for the explosion of collaborative translation initiatives that gave wide popularity and visibility to translation in the digital world. These years witnessed the emergence of iconic success stories in crowdsourcing and collaborative practices, such as Wikipedia, Facebook, Kiva, or TED Talks Open Translation Initiative.

Wikipedia emerged in 2001 in English. It soon overpassed and eclipsed Nupedia, the encyclopedia intended to be edited by experts only, leading to its closing in 2003. Wikipedia users soon started to create other language versions, such as German and Japanese within the first months. Towards the end of 2001, there was a clear push for multilingualism and the first push for translation was recorded. According to the Wikipedia History page:

> [i]n September 2001, an announcement pledged commitment to the multilingual provision of Wikipedia, notifying users of an upcoming roll-out of Wikipedia for all major languages, the establishment of core standards, and a push for the translation of core pages for the new wikis.   (Wikipedia 2016)

Wikipedia involves the continued and open initiation and edition of articles in all languages. The initial English dominance was soon eclipsed when already in 2004, less than 50% of content was in English, and in 2014 over 85% of Wikipedia content was in a language other than English. Currently, Wikipedia represents an interesting case in which articles can not only be the product of innumerable original writers and editors, but also be a large number of translators and editors who can openly at any time add or change previous translations or even add the original content. In this vibrant community, writing and translation into other languages represents a parallel process in which the edition of source texts and translation can occur almost simultaneously. All Wikipedia pages incorporate an open and searchable web history that allows the user to identify whether the page is an original creation or a translation from other page, as well as the complete collaborative translation history for that page. Nevertheless, despite recent studies into the collaborative translation of Wikipedia articles (McDonough-Dolmaya 2015), no studies in TS have delved into the role of translation in the early stages of the Wikipedia expansion.

Without any doubt, Facebook represents the most successful initiative in crowdsourcing due to both the approach (see 3.3 for a description of the crowdsourcing workflow and process), and the impact that the fastest growing social networking site had in modern digital societies. Facebook implemented its crowdsourcing model in order to produce language versions of his English website in 2007, when it premiered its Translate Facebook app. Spanish was the first language into which FB was successfully translated, and the strategy was later deployed in French and German. The crowdsourcing translation application was initially advertised to foreign students at Stanford University, and the Spanish version took less than a week to be completed. French and German came next and each version was produced in less than a day. The initial success of this initiative was soon advertised in technology blogs and soon the IT world started to look at this initiative as a model to follow. The expansion in the number of potential languages has been continually growing, reaching 135 in 2016. The success was such that many language versions originally appeared due to the request of language communities around the world, such as Basque in Spain. Even when industry experts indicate that crowdsourcing can cost anywhere from 20% of similar professional approaches (Munro 2013) to the same, the motivation of Facebook was not economic but rather participatory (Mesipuu 20012), since large companies that crowdsource their own websites end up spending a similar amount of money in producing their crowdsourced versions (DePalma and Kelly 2011). This is due to the costs involved in creating and managing the platform and communities.

The approach taken by Facebook can be described as crowdsourced translations in which a company or collective (such as a non-profit) requests users to translate certain content, that is, "solicited translations" (O'Hagan 2009). It should also be mentioned that the Facebook approach is nevertheless a hybrid one, with users producing and voting on translations, while professional translators are hired to supervise and address potential issues throughout the entire process. In this sense, it can be argued that this hybrid model intends to extract the subconscious framework of expectations of users, while at the same time maintaining a professional overview of the entire cycle (Jiménez-Crespo 2011, 2013b). Therefore, despite its many revolutionary components, it cannot be considered a fully volunteer model such as the Wikipedia one. Generally, the model mainly operates at the segmental or microtextual level, while the macrotextual level is mostly controlled by experts. This is of great importance in TS literature, given that errors or inadequacies at the macrotextual level, such as terminological inconsistencies in a text or website, are considered more important than errors at the microtextual level (Nord 1997; Larose 1998; Williams 2003), i.e., a typographical error in a single segment. The successful implementation by Facebook was followed by a large number of companies, with the large majority of social networking sites currently requesting the involvement of communities in their translation processes, such as Twitter. This last company started with a professional approach and incorporated crowdsourcing towards 2011, with Dutch and Indonesian being the first languages that were open to community translation. The success of Twitter in this domain was clear when the simplified Chinese version of the website was translated and moderated in 4 days (Kelly and Zetzsche 2012).

To some extent, the success by Facebook brought to the fore in the industry the possibilities that crowdsourcing opened up for companies, and this impact was reflected in the presence of crowdsourcing in international industry conferences. In 2007 crowdsourcing first appeared in two of the main industry conferences related to localization, the Internationalization and Unicode Conference 31 and Localization World Seattle. Initially, discussions encompassed not only the impact on companies but also the potential of social media to revolutionize the way professionals worked. By 2008, the main localization conferences already included crowdsourcing and user-generated translations among the topics of discussions. This year also saw the publication of the first Common Sense Advisory report on the area, *Translation of, for, and by the People: How User-Translated Content Projects Work in Real Life* (DePalma and Kelly 2008), pointing at the interest in the industry to attempt to incorporate crowdsourcing in their business models. A wide range of web-based companies started to implement collaborative platforms to translate their websites, such as Hootsuite, Hi5, or FourSquare.

The late 2000s witnessed a continued stream of software companies that started to crowdsource their localization processes. Some examples are Adobe, Norton, Avast, Microsoft, Skype, or open-source project such as Audacity. Companies tended to rely to a greater extent on "close models" (Mesipuu 2012): the call for collaboration was open, but the participants were selected to participate. In some cases, such as Soft Interface, only professionals were invited to participate and they got a free license for the software. Users with high literacy in computing and programming with multilingual skills were obviously the early adopters of volunteer practices, not only in the localization of software, websites, and help documentation, but also in the collaborative translation of learning materials and courses for software packages and certifications, such as the setup of a website to translate the Cisco Networking Academy learning courses (Jakab et al. 2008).

Non-profit organizations also quickly adopted crowdsourcing models, such as Kiva, Translators without Borders (O'Brien 2016), or Amnesty International (Tesseur 2014a) (see 3.3.2). One of the most widely discussed cases is that of the non-profit Kiva, and the organization that provides microloans to initiatives and individuals and developing countries. It is self-described as a person-to-person microloan website, in which individuals can choose to lend money to any existing application. The organization was founded in 2006 and it was recognized in that year as one of the top ideas of the year by the *New York Times* magazine. The team includes over 300 translators and it contains differentiated profiles such as translators and revisers. The structuring of the translation process is to some extent similar to professional practices: translators need to undergo an admission process with a translation exam, and each translator works on a minimum number of microloans per week to remain active. It also involves the edition of each translation by a senior translator who provides feedback to the original translator (see also 3.4.3).

Another much discussed case is that of the crowdsourcing of translation during the times of disasters, such as the January 2010 Earthquake in Haiti (Munro 2010; Meier and Munro 2010; Gao, Barbier and Goolsby 2011). In this situation, all infrastructure in the country was disrupted except for the SMS system. The local phone company Digicel made a free phone number available to groups of organizations that set up an information-sharing platform, in which victims of the Earthquake could send emergency text messages. Non-profits who rushed to help in the scene did not possess the linguistic ability to understand these calls for help. This prompted Rob Munro, a linguist and graduate fellow at Stanford, to create a project entitled 4636, the toll free number for emergencies in that country. Munro had been developing methods for processing large volumes of SMS text messages, as well as working on crowdsourcing projects, and his project entailed creating a workflow to crowdsource the translation of text messages to bilingual speakers of Haitian Creole all over the world. This helped agencies identify and assist in these emergencies. His system relied on the previously developed free and open-source mapping tool Ushaidi, a platform initially developed to document human rights violations during the 2007/2008 post-election violence in Kenya. Using this platform, volunteers could at the same time translate and locate the emergencies on the map (Meier and Munro 2010). In six weeks, more than forty thousand text messages were received, translated, and sent back, witness to the power of the crowd in this type of situation. This platform has been used in many other crises around the world, such as the Egyptian uprising, the Ebola crisis, or the Syrian conflict and it has been used by non-profit volunteer communities such as Translators without Borders.

The translation of journalistic texts by self-organized communities is also a common phenomenon globally, such as the collective ECOS in China, the PBS TV station volunteer initiative, or the website Translate America. The now disappeared ECOS group was founded in 2006 in China in order to translate each issues of The Economist into Chinese. Every issue was on average translated by 40 volunteers who underwent an admission process where only after they had successfully translated 8 articles were they fully incorporated into the initiative. This effort was originally funded by donations, and currently over 240 volunteers translate all the issues. This is one of the cases in which volunteer efforts are beneficial to the source organization as they publicize and drive new customers to the original source initiative. This was proven by the fact that the Economist even granted them approval to continue with their work (Ray and Kelly 2011).

Audiovisual translation also saw the rapid emergence of platform to facilitate the formerly difficult process of subtitling videos and distributing them on the web. The more complex process using different software tools since the emergence of the WWW, called "digisubbing" (Leonard 2005), transitioned to web platforms that facilitated and streamlined the work of users and allowed collaborative subtitling processes to thrive. Platform such as Amara, formerly known as Universal Subtitles, Dotsub or Viki, Yyets or Schooter.cn in Asia emerged. Amara is the platform used in one of the most popular crowdsourcing initiatives in the realm to date, the TED translation talk project. TED Talks is a non-profit initiative in which expert and non-experts provide short talks in different venues around the USA and the UK that are recorded and made available on their website. According to the organization, the talks involve "ideas that inspire" and in 2009 the organization deployed the TED translation project in which talks are translated by volunteers in 113 languages (Olohan 2014). Witness to the expansion of collaborative practices is the fact that, according to their website, in summer 2016 more than 98 thousand translations have been published and over 24 thousand volunteer translators collaborate in the process (see also 3.4.2).

2.7 A continuing evolution: Paid crowdsourcing and the exploration of the limits of crowdsourcing (2010–20xx)

A race to incorporate crowdsourcing in language industry workflows and business models ensued, testing not the limits only of the "wisdom of the crowd" but also the "limits of the crowd." The language industry quickly identified that the potential feared impact on the profession and the industry was much smaller or negligible than initially anticipated (DePalma and Kelly 2011). It was quickly acknowledged that unpaid crowdsourcing could only be employed "in very narrowly defined contexts" (Kelly, Rey and DePalma 2011: 92). This seems to be a constant to date. For example, the 2016 European Language Industry Survey of 445 language service providers (LSPs) from 35 countries showed that in 2016 the interest in incorporating crowdsourcing decreased in LSPs for the first time in four years: "Although much hyped across the industry, crowdsourcing [...] simply [doesn't] seem to be taking off. Only 11% of the LSPs are considering trying or further developing crowdsourcing of linguistic tasks" (Elia 2016: 7). Similarly, in a 2015 TAUS industry conference with representatives from some of the largest language industry players, Valli indicated that no company showed any interest in using crowdsourcing for translation purposes because "as a lesson learned from other companies, crowdsourcing requires significant efforts in terms of internal infrastructure to coordinate and manage the crowd" (Valli 2015: 51). This is also argued by Muzii who indicates (2013: 12):

> Crowdsourcing is not free [...] It costs money to manage work, whether workers are volunteer or paid, and build a collaborative translation capability.[...] a specialized back-end infrastructure is needed to bolster the productivity of the community.   (Muzii 2013: 12)

The smaller than anticipated impact of crowdsourcing in the translation industry has also been recognized by translation scholars such as Gambier (2012: 17):

> The impact of crowdsourcing on the translation industry will be limited, despite the current euphoria of the discourse, and it will be most evident in only very visible instances.

It is nowadays widely recognized that the potential of volunteer crowdsourcing is quite limited, and it is mostly likely that the language industry will only feel the effect of a downward pull on translation prices. Volunteers are in control and they will only translate that content that appeals to them:

> Unsurprisingly, unpaid collaborators would invariably go for the visual, exciting things and skip uninteresting content – and not only in commercial projects, but also in highly altruistic ones.
> (García 2015: np)

These potential limitations also call for further research into the "limits of the crowds."

The industry, on its part, has already reacted through a number of initiatives and business ventures that explore "paid crowdsourcing" models that range from extremely low compensation, all the way to higher per-word rates to professionals who participate through crowdsourcing workflows. According to García, this phenomenon represents:

> an entirely new way of doing businesses. It emerged around 2008, pioneered by Gengo, One Hour Translations, SpeakLike and Tolingo, and fueled by the sheer reach of cloud computing itself.
> (García 2015: 18)

This development was also due to the early realization in the industry that there were clear limits to the potential expansion of volunteer translation in for-profit business due to issues related to community recruiting and motivation. They exploited the fuzzy boundaries between professional and non-professional translation and the possibility of achieving "fit-for-purpose" quality levels using the "wisdom of the crowd" (Surowiecki 2004). These new ventures were inspired by the desire to reduce costs to customers, speed up the process, and explore new language industry niches. They initially attempted to provide faster services at considerably lower rates than professional translation. The technological solutions developed are modeled according to earlier online platforms that managed collaborative processes in volunteer translation.

In addition to a number of web cloud services that will be described in detail in Section 3.3, the ongoing evolution of crowdsourcing also involves the introduction of professional translation to mobile smartphones, such as the apps developed by the language industry innovators Stepes or Unbabel. Here lie possibly two of the main impacts of years of volunteer crowdsourcing innovations on the professional area for the coming years: (1) companies are now offering professional translation services using crowdsourcing workflows (see also 5.2.2) and (2) innovations will also come from the expansion of services that offer professional translation through smartphone apps (Jiménez-Crespo 2017).

Stepes and Unbabel are two examples of this new frontier. Stepes emerged in 2015. Its workflow revolves around a process that resembles mobile text messaging to translate text by "professional" or "specialized" selected crowds, the so-called "chat-based translation."[4] This company offers a technology referred to as "swish" that replicates messaging apps in order to translate from anywhere and anytime. This term refers to the fact that translators can "swish" left or right to see the source text or target text, respectively (DePalma 2015). Translators, once approved, download the Stepes app in their smartphones. In the process, the company uses Termwiki, also developed by the same people responsible for the app, to harness the translations' database and the extensive terminology resources. Once the project is leveraged with existing TMs and terminology databases, the project is ready to be sent to translators through a micro task approach. Selected translators immediately receive a message on their cellphones, indicating that a suitable project is ready for them. If accepted, they can start translating immediately in a segmental approach that displays one segment at a time in a UI that replicates smartphone messaging. The translator has the available number of total segments and the remaining ones. Stepes, according to their website, uses "translation memory, spell checker and voice dictation [...] to improve the quality and increase translation productivity." The company stresses the fast turnaround that this new approach through smartphone apps and a massive crowd can provide, what the company refers to as "hyper fast translation turnaround times." This means that it specifically targets social media platforms such as Facebook and Twitter translation where speed is of essence. Nevertheless, it also offers regular services for fields such as legal or medical. This model has been referred to as the "Uber for translation" including peer rating of translators in order to provide clients an indication of participant trustworthiness.

Unbabel, on the other side, was created in 2013 and it was the first company to introduce professional translation to the smartphone through MT post-editing processes. Approved participants have the option of participating in both free and paid translation tasks. Given the post-editing model, the company compensates professional translators through hourly rates rather than the per-word classic approach. Translators-editors are therefore paid for their time spent performing post-editing tasks. In summer 2016, rates started at 8$ and with the possibility of achieving 18$ per hour maximum rate, depending on the quality and efficiency of the time spent post-editing. Unbabel stresses that the translation community includes "professional translators and native speakers," supposedly including as

---

4. This should not be confused with the notion of "chat translation" in O'Hagan and Ashworth's (2003) work that refers to the translation of actual chat exchanges.

professionals those who excel in their reviews and performance at the tasks offered by the company. The potential to be selected as an editor for paid tasks therefore depends on the testing results and the performance, including a review trustworthiness business model through peer and client task reviews.

A last issue of interest in terms of the evolution of crowdsourcing is that the ability to recruit and motivate a community of volunteer or below-market-rate translators varies widely between language combinations and geographical areas. Languages such as German and French are much more difficult to crowdsource in for-profit scenarios. This is now reflected in existing industry practices. For example, the company OneHourTranslations offers almost double the rates for combinations between Norwegian, French Canadian, Icelandic, Irish, Japanese, Swiss (DE, IT, FR), Flemish, Hebrew to German and French. Paid crowdsourcing merely represents another flexible approach from the industry to providing fast and efficient content to customers that might value lower rates or speed over quality. It also opens up the business range to offer translations from the free options all the way to different price points until professional rates, whichever they might be, are reached. What these paid crowdsourcing companies offer is to monetize the "wisdom of the crowd" or the "collective intelligence," setting up workflows and mechanisms that somewhat guarantee a sufficient degree of quality through different mechanisms that will be explored in Chapters 3 and 5.

CHAPTER 3

Crowdsourcing and the industry
From workflows to prescriptive approaches

> Fifteen years ago, translation buyers – corporations, institutions
> and individuals – had a somewhat restricted choice. [...]
> Nowadays [...], what were once resorts against shortfalls of professional
> translation are emerging as valid options in their own right:
> raw MT, by far the cheapest and fastest; and crowdsourcing among
> bilinguals, conveniently situated between MT
> and expert human output in terms of speed and cost.
>
> (García 2015: 18)

3.1 Introduction

In order to delve into crowdsourcing from a TS perspective, a descriptive analysis of industrial approaches is necessary in order to uncover specific practices and innovative models that can provide clues into unexplored phenomena and practices. It is no secret that the language industry has not relied on the body of knowledge of TS to develop workflows and models. This is not anything new; the same happened with other technology-related advances (O'Hagan 2013), such as MT or localization (Dunne 2006; Jiménez-Crespo 2013a). Nevertheless, to some extent this freedom and ingenuity has led to a wide range of creative solutions that could expand the discipline as a whole by directing scholars to areas that are in constant dynamic flux, such as the nature of translation, the role of textual aspects in the process, quality, technologies, agency, ethics or the role of the translator and the audience. In doing so, the limits of what the discipline understands as translation can be further expanded (Hermans 2013a), both in the "translation" and "translator" approaches advocated by Chesterman (2009).

The point of departure is the evolution of collaboration in translation explored in Chapter 2 and the ever-growing collaboration functionalities present in all TM systems. Nowadays, translation technologies allow several agents to collaborate synchronously or asynchronously in the same document, while different people (or the same) can collaborate in the pre-translation stage through the development of terminology databases or source text editing and in the post-translation stage through revision. New workflows, inspired by existing micro-task crowdsourcing approaches and TM/MT technologies, have further reshaped how texts are segmented, translated, edited, verified, approved, reassembled and published in a search for maximum efficiency and acceptable quality, while at the same time accounting for the potential lack of professional skills in participants. The revolution is coming full circle with some mainstream professional translation solutions implementing principles inspired by micro-task crowdsourcing approaches. It seems like the revolution has been set in motion.

This chapter thus reviews from a descriptive perspective industry approaches, presenting an overview of implemented practices in this free and dynamic world. This comprehensive review by no means can encompass all the developments in the industry. It has been developed with the objective of identifying the most interesting developments from a TS perspective. It also cannot include the very latest developments, since new initiatives will emerge from the time this monograph was finished in mid 2016. What the analysis attempts to uncover and highlight are unexplored practices and phenomena in TS such as, for example, the implications of mechanisms to roll back translations when volunteers compromise quality, requesting multiple translations that can be discarded for each segment from the crowd (Zaidan and Calliston-Burch 2011) or attempting to produce translations using only a crowd of "monolinguals" (i.e., Hu et al. 2011). In the description of actual implemented crowdsourcing workflows, the chapter reviews the findings in publications from research groups in the University of Limerick (Morera-Mesa, Aoudad and Collins 2012; Morera-Mesa, Filip and Collins 2014; Morera-Mesa 2014). It also offers a descriptive overview of the main case studies in social networking sites, non-profits, MT post-editing or audiovisual translation. Since collaboration is made possible by advances in crowdsourcing platforms and technologies, a categorization of crowdsourcing technological solutions is offered. Finally, the chapter ends with a review of prescriptive approaches by industry key players (i.e., Ray and DePalma 2011).

3.2   Revolutionizing traditional professional translation processes

Established models in the language service industry tend to follow the so-called Translate-Edit-Publish model (TEP) in the industry (Kelly, Ray and DePalma 2011). In more complex processes it is also referred to as the "waterfall" approach (Dunne 2011), in which each stage is completed before moving to the next one. Pre-translation and project preparation is followed by the translation itself, followed by the revision and delivery/publishing. The reviewing and editing stage of the entire, or chunked, portion of a project does not start until the translation is finished. This can be considered the main approach in most professional approaches (i.e. Gouadec 2007), and it is also reflected in quality norms such as the European

EN15038 or the Canadian CAN/CGSB-131.10–2008. Already in the late 1990's, the impact of technologies and new flexible models of production, translation, localization and distribution started to bring to the surface certain shortcomings of TEP models (Jiménez-Crespo 2013a). For example, websites are dynamic in nature, with constant addition, changes and updates to source texts that require timely and efficient localization workflows. Content Management Systems emerged as the solution to these challenges, handling in a dynamic, flexible and innovative manner source text segmentation, processing, translation, revision integration and publishing. Crowdsourcing technologies and models can be said to have emerged in this context, merging features of CMS, TM solutions, MT, natural language processing, and micro-task crowdsourcing platforms in other domains.

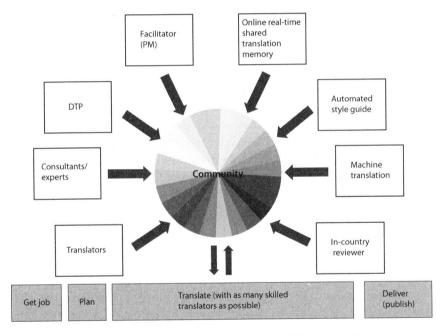

Figure 3.1 High-level representation of a localization workflow proposal in comparison with TEP processes by DePalma and Kelly (2011: 380).

A number of challenges have been posed by the irruption of crowdsourcing that workflow models have been attempting to address, such as the relative lack of trust or authority in the agents, the different types of crowd participation or the targeted quality of the final output. In this new paradigm, the responsibility for the successful completion of a translation process does not fall on the shoulders of professional translators and revisers in collaboration. It shifts towards developers and managers who need to prepare successful workflows, management procedures, community building and the different levels of authority and participation. The careful preparation of the crowdsourcing initiatives becomes essential to the achievement of whichever objectives are established. In this sense, crowdsourcing requires a powerful "pre-translation" stage, a notion that can be defined as, "all the operations carried out prior to the translation proper" (Gouadec 2007: 379). It also requires extensive involvement of managers and/or "pre translators", or, "the operator[s] responsible for all the operations carried out prior to the transfer phase (i.e. analysis, documentation, terminology, etc.)" (ibid). In this pre-translation stage, the selection and development of a crowdsourcing platform represents an essential phase: it has been shown that the shortcomings of some platforms can be detrimental to the engagement and motivation of volunteers (Dombek 2013). The success of the initiative does not stop in the selection of the workflow solution; the industry has also provided exhaustive lists of "best practices" (DePalma and Kelly 2008, 2011; Desilets and van de Meer 2011; Collaborative Translation Patterns 2011), describing from an anecdotal and experiential perspective how to handle aspects related to the crowdsourcing process. Desilets and van de Meer indicated, in their analysis of best practices in crowdsourcing, that "most practices [...] are not that different from best-practices which are being used for crowdsourcing in other domains" (2011: 41). They then questioned whether translation required a distinctive set of best-practices. Nevertheless, as this chapter will show, translation crowdsourcing has developed some distinct procedures and models that do not exist in other domains and a workflow perspective can point to these specific areas in which translation crowdsourcing is radically different.

3.3 Crowdsourcing processes from a workflow perspective

In recent years, researchers have proposed a wide range of proposals for translation crowdsourcing workflows (Exton, Wasala, Buckley and Schäler 2009; Filip and Ó Conchuir 2011; DePalma and Kelly 2011), as well as models that combine crowdsourcing with MT (i.e., Carson-Berndsen, Somers and Vogel 2009: 60; Hu et al. 2011; Ambati et al. 2012; Mitchell et al. 2014; Mitchell 2015). However, the description of existing workflow patterns in community crowdsourcing has been mainly addressed by scholars at the University of Limerick (Morera-Mesa, Aoudad and Collins 2012; Morera-Mesa, Filip and Collins 2014; Morera-Mesa 2014). The publications resulting from research efforts by these research groups have delved into workflows or the "description of sequences of interactions between the system and its users" (Morera-Mesa, Aoudad and Collins 2012: np). This notion is defined as "the automation of a business process, in whole or part, during which documents, information or tasks are passed from one participant to another for action, according to a set of procedural rules" (WfMC 1999). Control flow perspective is the main approach taken, since the way crowdsourcing processes are handled and how textual segments move through the process embody some of the main differences between traditional professional workflows and novel collaborative ones. From the several existing business-modeling languages, Morera-Mesa and colleagues have relied on the Yet Another Workflow Language (YAWL) to represent the workflows under scrutiny. Their analysis of descriptive accounts provides invaluable insights as to distinctive procedural aspects of collaborative practices that are relatively different or nonexistent in professional practices. They also provide a glimpse into how translation, translation processes or the role of the agents are differently conceptualized.

In the publications of Morera-Mesa, Collins and Filip and Collins (2013) and Morera-Mesa (2014: 131–132) a total of sixteen recurring patterns were identified through the analysis of the workflow models of different collaborative and crowdsourcing initiatives up until 2014, such as Crowdin, Facebook, Asia Online, Wikipedia translation project, Dotsub, Amara, Launchpad's Rosetta and Pootle. These patterns were subject to refinement through subsequent interviews with experts responsible for the main initiatives in this field. The patterns identified are:

1. *Content selection.* The first pattern is the selection of content that has the potential to be successfully crowdsourced, a key issue in the industry (see also 1.7). This is due to the fact that not all content will be equally amenable to being submitted to the crowd since volunteers are in control (O'Brien and Schäler 2010). The analysis of content selection in the industry does not stop at the potential motivation (or lack thereof) of volunteers. Many other considerations need to be taken into account, such as the potential legal consequences for the initiator or promoter of the process. As a result, legal, confidential or critical content is often not crowdsourced. The company Gengo, for example, excludes legal, medical or marketing content from their crowdsourcing model. One of the potential solutions is content prioritization and selection, sometimes closing the gap between fully free professional models through paid-crowdsourcing in both professional and non-professional varieties. Micro-task crowdsourcing to professional or carefully selected and vetted communities, can also address the confidential and sensitive nature of some materials. For example, many crowdsourcing companies such as Getlocalization or Speaklike offer professional or "specialist" crowdsourcing (see 5.2.2), while audiovisual platforms such as Amara now offer professional subtitling services. Types of content that are highly amenable to crowdsourcing are those with embedded communities, such as software or social networking sites.

2. *Unit Granularity selection.* Crowdsourcing implies the chunking of tasks and the distribution to different participants in the crowd and therefore, the selection of the type of translation unit emerges as a basic consideration. It is widely recognized that sentence-level segmentation is the most successful approach. Texts of limited dimensions, such as the 250-word Kiva microloans or short videos, are also widely successful, but in this case it is mostly due to the attachment of certain communities to the values or the philosophy behind certain initiatives. It is widely acknowledged that paragraph or longer translation units are associated with a higher risk of volunteers dropping the task or reducing their engagement. Longer segments are also problematic in MT-related initiatives that attempt to collect several translation alternatives for a same segment. In certain cases such as software or apps, the sentence level processing is due to programming and how the developers handled textual content.

3. *Leveraging translation memory.* Crowdsourcing platforms were inspired by existing translation memory solutions whose workflows were adapted to collaborative translations. Nowadays, almost all of them incorporate TM leveraging functionalities and leverage translation memories in their process. While some of these platforms simulate translation memory offering different types of full or fuzzy matches, some can directly approve leveraged full matches or even pipeline them to crowd voting, such as Crowdin. Despite some platforms using TM principles, one of the issues becomes how to train the crowd or participants to understand the principles of TM technologies. Sometimes, TM matches and MT output are offered indistinctively for participants to post edit without any indication of the percentage of the TM match.

4. *Leveraging MT* (see also Section 3.5). A wide range of platforms incorporate MT engines in their workflows, both from Google Translation or Microsoft Bing Translator, such as Crowdin or Unbabel. Other initiatives incorporate custom-made statistical machine engines, such as Asia Online or ACCEPT (Mitchell 2015). The output can be directly post-edited by the crowd, or in some cases it can be either directly voted on through alternatives or through correct/incorrect choices.

5. *Leveraging Terminology.* Some initiative leverage terminology either automatically or through glossaries. Translate Facebook for example currently offers terminology matches under the translation window when a match is identified in the source segment. In some cases the terminology is collaboratively produced prior to the start of the translation stage in open source initiatives or in specific forums such as the case of Symantec software. Terminology can also be collected from the crowd in order to improve MT systems (Shimohata et al. 2001).

6. *Translation without redundancy.* This practice entails replicating the professional Translation-Edit-Publish process. In this model the translation unit is normally a complete text that is claimed or assigned to one translator. Once the translation is finished, it is subsequently sent for revision. This is one of the most common processes in some non-profit, activist, political and journalistic initiatives. The project is subsequently closed by the reviser or a community manager, and approved for publication. Assigning text-length translations to individuals often requires testing procedures for admission to the initiative, either before they are admitted (Kiva, TED, Translate America) or during the first translations (Ecos translation in China of the Economist). This process allows crediting the translation work to a single translator and reviser, such as the case of the Open Translation initiative in TED, potentially increasing the motivation of some participants to translate. This practice has some benefits if compared with sentence-based crowdsourcing: assigning an entire text to a single translator increases the cohesion, coherence and homogeneity of style. Additionally, in cases of confidential or sensitive nature, this practice is easier to carry out since seeking confidentiality agreements from limited number of volunteers is less complex. Nevertheless, if compared with processes that allow for parallelization of tasks within a single document, this practice entails higher probabilities of deadlines not being met. If this occurs, the task needs to be assigned to a different participant, potentially wasting the work that was already completed by the first volunteer.

7. *Open Alternative Translations.* This practice entails collecting multiple renditions of the same translation unit from different participants, often small segments, while the rest of participants can publicly see the collaborations of others. It is implemented in most social networking site initiatives such as Translate Facebook and Twitter Translation Center, Crowdin and LaunchPad's Rosetta. While in some cases participants can see the entire corpus of alternatives for any source segment such as Twitter Translation Center (Arend 2012), in others the number is limited. For example, Translate Facebook initially displays three options, and it is necessary to activate the option to see all existing proposals. This practice can generally produce lots of data in terms of variants that is often wasted, although in some cases it is used to train statistical MT engines. Despite the potential waste of effort in this model, research in TS has shown that the open alternative patterns with voting mechanisms can lead to translations that resemble naturally produced texts in the target language (Jiménez-Crespo 2013b).

8. *Hidden Redundant Translation.* This pattern is often related to MT approaches. It refers to collecting multiple translations for the same segment from different volunteers without letting them see renditions submitted by others. This

approach represents to some extent a new concept in professional translation since collecting multiple translations for the same source text is often not feasible in a for-profit context.[1] In the industry this pattern has been used by TxtEagle, Crowdflower (Eagle 2009) or Asia Online Wikipedia initiative (Vashee 2009), while it has also been in MT research (Zaidan and Calliston-Burch 2011; Bentivogli et al. 2011). The benefits of this approach appear in models that implement automatic selection among several renderings based on frequency, metadata or expertise of participants. For example, in the Asia Online Wikipedia initiative each MT segment was offered to three volunteers for post-editing. When two contributions out of three were similar, that translation suggestion was automatically approved and inserted in the target text. A benefit identified in this pattern is that since participants are not primed with previous proposals, initiatives using alternatives to train MT engines can potentially obtain higher degrees of variation. As indicated by Morera-Mesa (2014), this approach could eliminate the so-called "social influence" effect (Lorenz et al. 2011) by which participants in collaborative decision-making tend to agree with the most voted or agreed upon solution. One of the drawbacks of this pattern, from an ethical perspective, is the potential waste of volunteer effort when their proposals are hidden and potentially discarded. Another drawback of this pattern is the multiplication of effort and the subsequent need for higher participation levels. As a consequence, this approach is often combined with a paid crowdsourcing model to encourage members of the crowd.

9. *Super Iterative Translation.* This process allows multiple participants to propose translation suggestions through different workflows and the accumulated effort of a participating crowd shapes the final outcome. Different models exist, such as the Translate Facebook approach with a translation and a voting stage, as well as other open translation paradigms, such as wiki translation, in which participants directly edit the translation. In Facebook, for example, in some languages a translation can be changed if and when a different alternative translation collects more votes than the existing one. This results in a dynamic and ever-changing translation process in which the direct participation from users dynamically shapes the translation throughout time. The translation process can therefore be conceptualized as a constant lively process in which the target product is not fixed but rather the result of an ever-changing cycle

1. Corpus-based research, for example, has delved into the difficulty in finding multiple translations for the same source text (Mamlkjaer 1998), while statistical MT training requires this type of input. It is therefore not surprising that most approaches implementing this pattern are associated to developers or researchers of MT.

subject to crowd participation. Facebook does implement a "freezing" of translation in different languages and closes the process for some segments, but not for others or when new source segments are added. Facebook is a classic case of initiatives with an embedded community of motivated participants. In these cases, it has been argued that in the initial stages publishing lower quality translations can be related to higher motivation of participants, since they can perceive that a possible improvement in quality is in their hands. The drawbacks of this pattern can also be numerous. Often translators can see that their contributions have been changed or reviewed without an established feedback loop or possibility of discussion, igniting potential conflicts or discontent. Also, the dynamicity and openness can be problematic if no freezing point through any sort of authoritative review is established. This can lead to reductions of quality overtime, though if the Wikipedia and the "collective intelligence" principles are applied, it could be assumed that with high-enough collaboration the worsening in quality might be temporary. Additionally, it is often necessary to set in place mechanisms to control malicious activity, and examples of implemented practices are user or IP blocking or the protection of content that is controversial in nature.

10. *Freeze.* While freezing or closing a translation is a normal step in professional practices, in open crowdsourcing projects this pattern responds to the need to protect the translation and avoid vandalism. Several prototypical examples of crowdsourcing allow to freeze their translations such as Facebook, Dotsub and Amara,[2] or Crowdin. Morera-Mesa (2014) points at Wikipedia as an example of the successful implementation of freezing practices in order to control vandalism or as a "defense mechanisms" (Warren et al. 2008). Freezing a translation requires the intervention of an authoritative agent that can identify loss of quality or vandalism, a procedure that goes against the open nature of the Wikipedia and wiki translation approaches. Nevertheless, sometimes the freezing stage is required due to the nature of the project, for example in cases with time sensitive materials, the existence of release dates or legal reasons. Once closed, some initiatives also allow for an "unfreezing" mechanism, since sections might need to be corrected in any frozen document. In addition to these to patterns, several sub classifications exist, such as "pseudo freeze" or "natural freeze". In the former the translation is still open for participation but end users have available a frozen or closed translation. A "natural freeze" appears when a project is nearing completion or when in iterative models after

---

2. Nevertheless, many initiatives that use these platforms prefer to include reviewing stages and freezing of translations, such as TED Open Translations or the Osho Talks Translation Initiative.

a period of time, though contributions might continue, no change is perceived in the translation.

11. *Version Rollback.* Sometimes, worsening in quality over time requires rolling back a previous translation version. This is often associated with workflows that are open and continually open to volunteer participation to control malicious activity, such as Dotsub, Amara or Wikipedia. Version rollbacks offer a glimpse into two interesting issues: the fact that translation quality is conceptualized in a continuum always moving towards more positive results (see 5.4.3) and assuming that the "wisdom of the crowd" or the "collective intelligence" will always produce acceptable results without supervision. Research into FLOSS communities and Wikipedia has delved into the work of malicious participants or those unaware of low performance, creating mechanisms to control it manually or automatically (Geiger and Ribes 2010; Müller-Birn et al. 2015), a paradigm also adopted in MT crowdsourcing research (Yan et al. 2015). This practice in open initiatives also goes against the open nature of these projects, since it requires hierarchization of collaborative structures and the assignment of trust to agents to perform this rollback. For example, in the case of in Amara the agent in charge of the change can be the owner of the video, the person that uploaded it. In other cases managers or higher status volunteers can be assigned this task (Jansen, Alcala and Guzman 2014).

12. *Deadlines.* Deadlines are critical in professional approaches (Gouadec 2007; Rodriguez-Castro 2015), and one of the most significant issues in translation management (Dunne and Dunne 2011). Collaboration in professional translation is an established practice to deal with deadlines in professional approaches: "a high volume of translation and/or a tight deadline mean that the work can only be done by a team of translators" (Gouadec 2007: 104). Nevertheless, the time pressure associated with deadlines is often seen as a potential demotivating factor for professionals, with "deadlines getting tighter in the industry. Thus, deadlines are expected to be contributors to translator dissatisfaction" (Rodriguez-Castro 2015:37). Volunteer translation without monetary compensation offers new challenges to the timely completion of translation projects. This is why initially it was claimed that deadlines in crowdsourcing are impossible to implement (Desilets 2007). Nowadays, they are common practice but depend on whether the process is free, paid lower or higher, whether it is a collaborative or individual process, as well as whether the content is time sensitive in nature. Stepes for example offers crowdsourced tweets within an hour, using mobile translation and crowdsourcing in order to accomplish this goal. Deadlines appear in processes such as TED Talks, Skype (Mesipuu 2012) or Adobe TV. Time also appears as a main factor in journalistic initiatives such as the PBS project to crowdsource US presidential speeches.

The presence of deadlines depends of many factors, but in general they tend to be more frequent in higher prestige initiatives, such as edutainment or non-profits, than in lower status ones. This fact is reflected on participation agreement and terms: while sanctions for non-compliance with deadlines tend to be explicit in certain high status initiatives, in the later deadlines they can be a demotivating factor. In these last cases, some initiatives have established automatized practices to deal with non-compliance, such as automatically de-assigning projects, opening them for translation to the community, or other management solutions such as showing the percentage of completion for each locale version.

13. *Open Redundant Assessment.* This pattern refers to users voting up or down any other proposed translations through Open Alternative Translations. Most social networking initiatives implement this type of voting mechanisms, as well as smartphone-based ones such as Unbabel. There are other types of open assessment such as ranking of alternatives (Zaidan and Calliston-Burch 2011), but this has only been implemented in hidden assessment models. In some cases users can see the total number of votes, such as Twitter, while in others the ongoing results are hidden, such as Facebook. This process is not suitable for longer translation units as Facebook quickly discovered as the crowd was mainly attracted to voting sentence level units. Morera-Mesa, Filip and Collins (2013) cite the experiment of Muchnik, Aral and Taylor (2013), when discussing that the visibility of positive votes can create bubbles, while negative votes are neutralized over time. For example, the Twitter initiative displays for voting all proposed renditions of a segment ranked according to the number of existing votes. This practice can hide more adequate translations from participants since it is widely known in usability studies that users tend not to scroll down the webpage (Nielsen 1999; Price and Price 2002: 147). However, in Twitter if a participant cannot see a rendition and decides to propose it, if it already exists, the platform offers the possibility of simply voting for it. In cases with a large number of crowd proposals, experts are called in to select a limited number of proposals that are open for voting, but this is not the case of Twitter.

14. *Hidden Redundant Assessment.* Hidden assessment is conducted when participants are evaluating a translation, either through voting or ranking (Zaidan and Calliston-Burch 2011), but they are unaware of the fact that others are also participating in the same process. This process allows for frequency assessment and automatic selection of variants once a threshold of votes for an option is reached, such as five or more. To some extent, this practice eliminates the motivational benefits of participants' feelings of belonging to a community,

but it also helps overcome other negative effects such as the "social influence" effect that can appear in open assessment processes.

15. *Expert Selection and Edition.* The involvement of an expert in the management of the crowdsourcing process appears as a common trend in the industry. New job profiles in the translation industry have emerged to fill these roles, such as "language community manager" (DePalma and Kelly 2011). These experts can help solve some of the main issues related to crowdsourcing, such as deciding when to freeze a translation, picking up untranslated portions or texts, controlling malicious activity, increasing consistency, providing a final macrostructural review, helping to motivate the community, selecting volunteers or higher skilled volunteers, etc. Experts, and not only professional translators but also programmers, specialists, etc., appear in initiatives such as Pootle, Launchpad, Crowdin, etc. as well as for languages with full support in social networking initiatives such as Facebook. It is of interest that companies are replicating models similar to the different levels of localization in software and websites (Singh and Pereira 2005; Jiménez-Crespo 2013a: 33–35). While some digital products offer full localization, second and third tier languages get different degrees of localization depending on ROI issues, while the rest might remain in English. Similarly, experts in crowdsourcing initiatives appear only in languages with full support, while many other languages do not. This distinction, made by companies that hire experts for some language versions while others are completely self managed, offers a glimpse into the continuum between professional and non-professional translation and the impact of ROI approaches in crowdsourcing.

16. *Metadata Based Selection.* In this practice, the translated segment is selected from among the several existing alternatives through different types of metadata attached to it. It can be implemented through a ranking or trust system on translators (i.e., Yan et al. 2015), time stamp, crowd assessment or frequency such as the Asia Online Wikipedia initiative. Facebook, for example, implements a selection based on crowd assessment that uses in the user interface the translation with the most votes, a process that can be dynamically changed if any other rendition accumulates more votes. While the industry considers that this is the fastest selection method, this practice has never been implemented in professional settings or even discussed in translation theory. This automation process can be reminiscent of the prediction of Cronin's of translators becoming "translational cyborgs who can no longer be conceived of independently of the technologies with which they interact" (2003: 112). In this sense, technology is further ingrained in the translation process with the automatization of quality selection in a somewhat similar principle to automatized metrics in MT.

This pattern collection has been mainly concerned with crowdsourcing from solicited models, that is, those from companies that have an interest in harnessing the knowledge or wisdom of the crowd. They do not focus on self-organized communities since often they lack the ability to develop distinct technological solutions for their collaborative efforts beyond replicating professional practices, such as using forums, email and excel spreadsheets shared on the cloud as management tools, sometimes using free technology solutions such as Dotsub or Amara for subtitles or Transifex. An analysis of workflows and typical processes in fansubs, for example, will be described in Section 7.5.

3.4   Workflows and novel approaches to translation

This section reviews from a descriptive perspective the processes in the most popular and successful initiatives, both from the translational context and the translation process itself. It includes a classic example for each practice: Facebook for social networking sites and the translation of its user interfaces, Amara and TED for audiovisual practices, Kiva and the platform Trommons from the Rosetta Foundation for non-profit initiatives and Asia Online and Crowdin for workflows that incorporate MT post-editing. The descriptions specifically focus on areas in which these workflows and processes radically depart from professional process or that help conceptualize translation under a different light.

3.4.1 Social networking sites: Facebook

Facebook represents one of the quintessential cases of translation crowdsourcing with a great influence in the development of subsequent crowdsourcing platforms. It was originally released in 2007 when the Spanish user interface was translated in a week, and subsequently opened to German and French that were completed in one day each. As of 2016, Facebook offers 135 locale versions and the possibility for communities to request opening a new locale to the community. The Translate Facebook app has changed throughout the years, an ongoing process fueled by internationalization efforts while expanding to other languages. For example, users could vote up or down any proposed changes until 2015, and from that year the platform changed to positively vote for a proposed translation, or to flag it. Flagging a proposal then opens up a dialog box with the possibility to indicate that the problem is "wrong style or wording", "grammar or spelling errors", "wrong meaning", or "abusive or offensive". This platform change to allow volunteers to qualify their negative feedback is possibly related to metadata automatic tasks, such as flagging and blocking malicious users, low performers, or simply discarding segments that are not usable as variants for MT training.

The process of crowdsourcing translations in FB can be described as follows. The first step is to create and continue adapting the translation application and the extraction of all existing and new strings from the source English version. This is an ongoing process as FB continues to add new textual material to their website and the many apps within it. The entire experience is organized around the translation community in which users can see how many of their translations get published in order to motivate them. Motivational features can be found such as the leaderboard of most successful volunteer translators, a community board or profiles and number of friends that use the social network in the locale that the user is translating into. Although users can start translating immediately, they need to be FB members for a month at least and they have to actively enable the translation application in order to participate in the platform. The platform offers supporting materials such as a glossary and style guide for each version, as well as a discussion forum where they can discuss terms, translation problems, etc. The current platform shows glossary matches when a "new translation" for a segment is activated. Users can either choose to translate or to vote for existing translations. In the translation section, users can see the different strings to translate. There is some context offered and the choice to annotate whether the gender or the prospective viewing user of the translation would pose a problem in the target language. As an example, the segment "memorize profile" includes the following contextual comment: "option for selecting a label on a contact form". If the grammatical gender or number of any word included in a programming variable is an issue, users can activate an additional window that allows the selection of the more fine-grained comment on the issue.

Since the strings to translate have increased in difficulty due to the inclusion of a large number of software variables, such as "{icon}attending {object} at {place-name} with {name1}.", the app has recently included a box with the variables that can be copied into the translation similar to the placeables options of TM programs.

Once the translations are suggested, the next option is to vote on translations by the active community of users. In previous releases of the platform, only three translation renditions were displayed to volunteers in order to limit the potential choices. Additionally, options could be voted with thumbs up or down icons to indicate approval or disapproval. The forum offers the possibility of discussing any entry if users deem it appropriate. Changes in the 2015 platform allow a limited number of variations with the possibility of expanding to see all the possible translations. Instead of the voting up or down, translations are either approved (with a check icon) or flagged (with a flag icon) as previously mentioned. Interestingly, despite the great efforts into internationalizing the platform, the change from the {icon} attending {object} at {place-name} with {name1} .

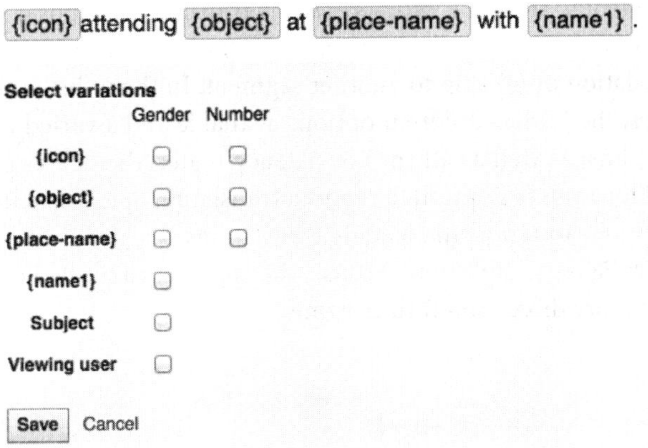

Select variations

	Gender	Number
{icon}	☐	☐
{object}	☐	☐
{place-name}	☐	☐
{name1}	☐	
Subject	☐	
Viewing user	☐	

Save Cancel

Figure 3.2 Example of translation segment in Facebook with feedback for grammatical issues with programming variables.

more internationally recognized up or down thumbs to the check and flag icons can raise issues related to the metaphorical symbolic relationship between the visual flag and the notion of flagging an incorrect entry that can turn into a "broken metaphor" for other languages (such as the relationship between the house icon and the homepage). This voting stage would be the initial step in the quality evaluation process, followed by an evaluation by professional translators that are hired for fully supported languages. During this stage, users are also encouraged to verify not just glossary items or strings, but also entire pages or messages in order to guarantee that they are consistent and accurate.

During the last stage and for most languages, a group of expert translators hired by FB checks and verifies all the translations, making sure that they are globally coherent and consistent. This allows the correction of any potential shortcomings. While literature often points out that quality in crowdsourced translations can be inconsistent (Díaz Cintas and Muñoz Sánchez 2006), a comparable corpus study by Jiménez-Crespo (2013b) identified that the translations of Facebook Spain did contain the most common terminological and syntactic features in non-translated local Spanish social networking sites. For some languages without full community manager support, the platform can automatically insert or replace the most-voted translations dynamically in the user interface. In other cases, the approval can be made by experts and certain segments are "frozen", with each language version showing the rate of completion.

It should be mentioned here that the smartphone app version of Translate Facebook offers a completely different user interface and interactivity options from the web browser version. The smartphone app, once activated, immediately displays one segment to translate with its existing translation proposal. Users can either (1) select an existing proposed translation, (2) report a translation, (3) propose a new translation or (4) skip to another segment. In the website application for web browsers, the UI has different options available and a varied number of interactivity options, as well as all the consistency materials such as glossaries, style guides and forums. The option to report a translation opens up a menu with different four options to report inadequate translations, such as "Wrong style or wording" or "Wrong meaning". In that sense, the app offers a limited experience, even when it is a more direct and intuitive one.

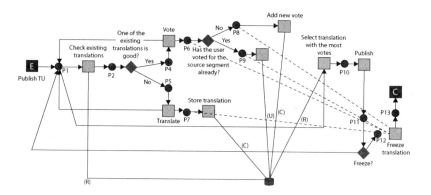

Figure 3.3 Translate Facebook workflow model at the string level (Morera-Mesa, Filip and Collins 2014: 11).

The Morera-Mesa (2014: 99) and Morera-Mesa, Filip and Collins (2013) modeled the workflow of the Translate Facebook at the string level. The annotations were done using YAWL workflow language to process each string that is submitted to translation. The model offers interesting insights such as the fact that users can continually vote on any string and change their votes in the future.

3.4.2 Non-Profits: Kiva and Trommons

The realm of volunteer translation for crowdsourcing has produced several workflow solutions that range from platforms that follow the TEP process, such as Kiva, to fully-fledged translation workflow management solutions similar to other collaborative crowdsourcing platforms such as Trommons by the Rosetta Foundation (De Wille 2014; Du et al. 2015) or MNH-TT (Utiyama et al. 2009; Kageura et al. 2011; Babych et al. 2012). These last platforms incorporate TM and terminology functionalities with an advanced translation management system with role assignment and the possibility of parallelization of translation tasks, meaning that an unlimited number of participants can simultaneously work on the same text and segment. The objective of the Trommons platform is "to connect non-profit translation projects and organizations with the skills and interests of volunteer translators" (Du et al. 2015: 57). The platform allows organizations and non-profits to register and to create translation projects open to registered volunteers. Trommons is an open platform and anyone can potentially registered without strict admission controls. These organizations can upload a project and assign three different tasks, translation, proofreading or segmentation (ibid: 59). The source text can then be translated as a whole or can be segmented and volunteers can translate these discrete segments. The project can then be assigned to different language combinations, and currently, English to and from Spanish account for almost 45% of all processes. Other common languages are French, Portuguese, Russian and Chinese. Once the translation is completed it can be assigned to proofreading and subsequently finalized. The Rosetta foundation has also developed in 2016 Kanjingo, a smartphone app to post-edit MT output to be used by non-profit organization in emergency situations.[3]

The non-profit organization Kiva offers a translation management platform but does not incorporate any translation technologies such as TM or terminology matches but rather, a simple platform to manage the volunteer translation workflow. Kiva initially provides a translation exam in what is known as a priory quality control and new translators, once they have passed the test, undergo a mentoring and training program. Once accepted, translators have access to the Kiva platform and they must commit two hours per week for a minimum of six months. The platform allows volunteers to claim one or more 200-word microloan applications in the language combination. Before the translation starts, the volunteers are also in charge of conducting a series of checks in the source text, such as checking whether the source language marked is correct, the name of the person applying for the loan is not on the actual text (for privacy reasons) or that the photo that accompanies the microloan corresponds to the applicant. Once the source text check is completed, the translator can proceed with the translation. If the translation is not completed within the deadline, an extension can be requested or it can be sent back to the pool of translators. Translators are supposed to self-revise the translation and once this initial review process is completed, it is sent for review to the reviewers or coordinators for each language combination. Translators can then receive feedback from their translations and the translation can be finally approved. This process is somewhat similar to the main organization and workflow of most fansub communities, even when these later ones can divide the text into several agents and quick and fast turnaround is essential.

---

3. http://www.therosettafoundation.org/blog/kanjingo-the-post-editing-app-for-volunteers/

3.4.3 MT post-editing: Asia Online and Crowdin

Initiatives that leverage MT and TM with crowd post-editing continue to emerge globally both in volunteer initiatives, such as the (now extinct) Asia Online Wikipedia initiative (Vashee 2009; DePalma 2011), as well as new for-profit initiatives such as Unbabel with statistical MT with built-in artificial intelligence for learning. The initiative by Asia Online to translate Wikipedia into Thai represents one of the initial large-scale initiatives that developed distinct creative workflow to leverage translation memory, post-editing and translation experts. The initiative translated 3.5 million Wikipedia articles until 2011 using a wide range of volunteers, from professionals to language students in Thailand (DePalma 2011). At the time, this was the largest scale top-down crowdsourcing effort to translate content in the world. The process was organized as follows. The articles were selected and processed, segmented and pre-translated using the Asia Online SMT engine. Each segment was subsequently post-edited by three translation volunteers. This literally means that each of those 3.5 million Wikipedia articles were post-edited in its entirety three times. If two post-edited versions of a segment would match, the segment would be automatically approved for inclusion in the translation memory and for publication. If the three post-editors would not agree, the segment would be then sent to an expert that would select one of the three variants. The expert would subsequently have the option of sending one or two of the other variants to train the SMT engine. Thus, even when most of the post-edited versions would not appear in the final translation, they would be used as "feedback translations" for MT training and not totally discarded. These as "feedback translations" are thus human post-edited MT segments that are only used to train MT engines (Volk and Harder 2007; O'Hagan 2013). Translation, therefore, is not only produced and used for final publication but also for MT training as in the Zaidan and Calliston-Burch (2011) studies. This type of workflow in which language learners, TM, MT and translation experts collaborate represents an example of interest in that the different components increasingly facilitate and speed the translation process, with more direct TM matches and domain specific training of the statistical machine engine as the project progresses.

The Crowdin platform allows for MT leveraging and at the same time for translation and voting in the community. In this process, once the text is selected by a manager, it can be assigned to different locales, and it can be marked as an open or closed project. Open projects are open to anyone in the community. Each segment is subsequently leveraged with the Crowdin TM, with Google Translate and Bing Translator. Any matches from the TM or from the MT engines are stored as pre-translations. If the voting stage is not activated, the pre-translated text can be downloaded directly with the untranslated segments included. If the voting and translation is activated, participants can, according to the settings, translate, post-edit or vote on the existing variants. The voting process leads to the selection of the translation with the most votes and the approval of the segment for inclusion in the final target text.

3.4.4 Audiovisual translation: TED and Amara

The emergence of online crowdsourcing workflow platforms such as Amara, Dotsub or Viki has simplified tremendously the technological skillset necessary for volunteers to perform subtitling tasks. These platforms thus helped expand collaborative translation of videos beyond the realms of early "digisubbing" and the complex software process involved (Massidda 2015), to the wider context such as Open Translation at TED that uses Amara and focuses on edutainment, religious/meditation initiatives such as Osho Talks Translation Initiative with Dotsub or activist and committed circles such as Txalcala. Collaboration in audiovisual translations requires a distinct process and workflow due to the different nature of this modality. This section reviews two classical interrelated cases, the collaborative platform Amara and the overall process of TED Open Translation Talks that uses a customized version of the former.

Amara is a collaborative subtitling platform formerly known before 2012 as Universal Subtitles. It is currently used in a variety of settings such as Netflix, Twitter, TED Talks, EngageMedia, Khan Academy, Coursera, Udacity, and Google use Amara's Enterprise services to build their own dedicated subtitling. Amara includes two distinct workflows at the video level and at the translation level (Morera-Mesa 2014: 106). The process at the video level starts when the video is uploaded and the captioning and timing have to be performed. Then languages can be added, and the overall text is segmented into individual subtitles. The translation subworkflow starts and subtitles can be translated by "followers" of any given video. The changes are saved and then all followers are notified of the finalized translation. Since Amara is an open platform, subtitles can be changed in the future by any participant. Video owners, nevertheless, have the option of "rolling back a translation" in order to reestablish an earlier version of the translation should any malicious activity occur or a worse translation appear in the future. The TED translation initiative offers a customization of the platform and it does include a translation freeze option in order to close a translation and stop changes from being implemented by non-authorized translators. Amara does offer the possibility of leveraging each subtitle with Bing Translator, but this option is not used in TED talks.

TED is a non-profit organization that was established in 1984 as a conference for those interested in technology, entertainment and design. The organization holds two annual conferences a year in which well-known speakers give inspirational talks following the organization motto regarding "the power of ideas to change attitudes, lives and ultimately the world" (TED np). The philosophy of TED centers around "ideas worth spreading" and the talks are short, up to 18-minute presentations of all kinds of topics. Most talks are recorded and uploaded to the website where presentations are disseminated globally. The popularity of the initiative led to the creation by popular demand of the TED Open Translation initiative in 2009 to make the talks accessible around the world. The TED project has expanded to other languages and countries, adding more in the way of source languages and combinations. In mid 2016, the initiative had produced over 97,834 translations in 113 languages by more than 24,175 volunteers. The interest in this initiative has expanded to the transcription and translation of TEDxTalks, TED-Ed lessons and the localization of the TED smartphone app.

For volunteers, the process to apply involves opening an account both in TED talks and in Amara. Once the application is processed and approved, volunteers need to contact the different language groups in order to be accepted by them. The organization then offers a large number of learning materials, such as all types of tutorials in text and audiovisual format on the use of Amara, basic subtitling guidelines, guidelines on collaboration, etc., including a Wiki site named OTPedia for each language. The basic process of translation in TED resembles the traditional TEP model with the addition of the transcription before the project is initiated.

Figure 3.4 Representation of the subtitling workflow and process of TED in their description webpage (https://www.ted.com/participate/translate/get-started).

The talks are uploaded to the website, and using Amara, volunteers can transcribe or translate talks. Vetted higher status participants conduct the review and approval process. These are called "language coordinators" and their tasks are to "elevate translation quality", "support collaboration", "mentor new volunteers" or "perform the final proofread of subtitles (approval step)" (TED np). Thus, participants are selected according to their abilities and those with experience or professional background can quickly move on to be reviewers or managers (Camara 2015). All translations that are revised include a feedback loop for the translators in order to improve future performance. Since talks are primarily translated by an individual or a small group of volunteers, each version includes credits to the transcription, translation and revision.

3.4.5 The fansubbing process

The typical workflow of fansub communities does not emerge from the industry, but nevertheless it is pertinent to describe it at this point to compare it and contrast it with industrial practices. This workflow has been extensively explored in different publications in Italy (Barra and Guarnaccia 2008; Massidda 2015: 41–42), Argentina and Spain (Orrego-Carmona 2013), Brazil (Bold 2011) as well as Poland and the Czech Republic among others (Luczaj and Cwiek-Rogalska 2014: 185). Most fansub groups around the world tend to posses a highly hierarchical structure in which all tasks are subdivided and teams and committees are assigned to different TV series or projects. This workflow represents a summary of a typical project in fansub groups in Italy, Poland, Spain or Argentina (Orrego-Carmona 2013; Massidda 2015; Luczaj, Holy-Luczaj and Cwiek-Rogalska 2015). Participants are normally divided between translators, junior translators, revisers, prerevisers, community managers and administrators, while other communities also include "timers" to synchronize the subtitles with the video and "encoders" in case "hard subs are produced, that is, those delivered encoded with the videofiles (Luczaj, Holy-Luczaj and Cwiek-Rogalska 2014: 185–186). Massidda also adds other participants, such as "resynchers", those "responsible for adjusting the spotting in the fansubbed version to accord, with the various versions available online" (2015: 51), as well as "synchmasters" or those in charge of training future translators how to time subtitles.

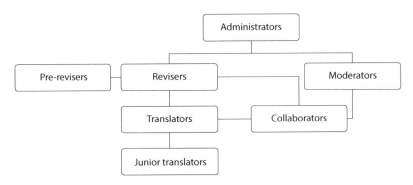

Figure 3.5 Workflow structure of the ArgenTeam subtitling community (Orrego-Carmona 2013: 9).

Orrego-Carmona offered a workflow structure from a participant perspective for the ArgenTeam subtitling community in Argentina (Orrego-Carmona 2013: 9). The process entails the participation of seven distinct profiles: junior translators undergoing their training process, translators, revisers and pre-revisers, as well as managing agents such as administrators and moderators.

Once a project is started or an individual or group decides to take up an existing series, episode or movie, the video in raw format is identified and normally downloaded from Torrent sites. Then the script or English subtitles are searched and downloaded. Usually, many Western fansub groups attempt to find transcripts made by Chinese groups, or if unsuccessful, they attempt to obtain the script via voice recognition software. They can also extract the source dialogue from the closed captions or the subtitles for the deaf and hard of hearing (Bold 2011). This step is important since transcribing the source dialogue is an extremely time consuming and error-prone process for amateurs. The English subtitle file is normally uploaded to the fansub forum and the tasks are subdivided among translators and proofreaders, setting deadlines since a quick turnaround is essential for fansubbing purposes. Subtitlers might choose to work on the .srt file, one of the most common standards for subtitles, or work with some of the freely available subtitling software, such as Visualsynchsub, Subtitle Workshop or Miyu and Jumbler. Collaboration is achieved through constant interaction in forums and IM messengers. Once the translations are finished, each member of the team sends his part to the reviser or supervisor who proofreads the work and merges the file. Then the .srt file or the "hard -sub" video file is uploaded to whichever website or database.

3.5   Crowdsourcing platforms: An overview

Over the years, a highly varied number of technological solutions have been developed to respond to harnessing the wisdom of the crowd. They were initially based on TM technologies and they have evolved to include hybrid MT- TM approaches. According to Morera-Mesa et al. (2014), two main differences exist between most professional translation memory tools and current crowdsourcing platforms in terms of workflow management. On the one hand, while TM platforms allow the inclusion in TMs of multiple versions for the same source segment, they do not allow voting processes. On the other, TM tools do not allow the parallelization of the process, that is, the possibility of different participants working on the same segment without stalling the overall process. The success of crowdsourcing, nevertheless, has meant that commercial TM tools have started to incorporate features that support crowdsourcing, such as the online documentation management by MemoQ or Lingotek, or platforms in which an indefinite number of translators can collaborate simultaneously in the same text, such as MateCat.

Crowdsourcing is reaching a maturity point that is reflected in the existing variety of technological platforms with different objectives and workflows. Categorizing them represents a difficult endeavor, but for the purposes of a description from a TS perspective, the different types of platforms and their workflow approaches have been grouped according to criteria such as the objective of the process, specialization in a certain modality or the profit vs. not profit nature.

1. *General crowdsourcing platforms.* The first group is those platforms for general micro task crowdsourcing that allow for the translation of small segments, such as TxtEagle, Mobileworks, Crowdflower, Amazon Mechanical Turks (AMT). These platforms tend to follow a business model with micropayments of different types to participants. AMT has been used mostly in machine translation training settings (Zaidan and Calliston-Burch 2011; Yan et al. 2015). TxtEagle was created in Africa in order to crowdsource micro tasks through SMSs taking advantage of the wider availability of cellphones rather than computers in some areas. Using this system, participants have translated segments into different long tail languages receiving cellphone credit airtime as compensation (Eagle 2009). The same system has been expanded to Asia with other initiatives such as Mobileworks (Narula et al. 2011) or mClerk (Gupta et al. 2012). This last initiative, for example, involved images distributed through SMS messages that users could either translate or transcribe.

2. *Crowdsourcing developed by for-profit language industry companies.* The next category includes all those platforms that been created in for-profit scenarios and that can be used to crowdsource either to professionals or to volunteers. Examples of this pool in continuous expansion are Crowdin, Smartling, Lingotek Lingohub, Crowdsight, Getlocalization, Yoosource by Synble, Transfluent, Transifex, Onesky, or Translation Workspace. Many other platforms have been developed for professional crowdsourcing, such as Verbalizit or Zanata. For example, Crowdin is a localization purpose platform that was created in 2009 in Ukraine and that was popularized when it was used to translate the popular videogame Minecraft by 4500 players. Nowadays it offers both solutions to crowdsource to professionals or to volunteers.

3. *Open source crowdsourcing platforms.* Some of the most popular platforms that allow to crowdsource to professionals or volunteers are open source, such as Pootle, Translate Wiki or Launchpad Translation for open source software.

4. *Custom-developed platforms by companies.* Many companies developed their own crowdsourcing platforms, mostly associated with social networking sites such as Facebook, Twitter (Twitter 2011; Arend 2012), PCtools Together (Rickard 2009), Hootsuite (Ray 2011), Norton Together platform, etc. They depend on the type of workflow targeted and they allow for customizations

of the platform overt time, such as the evolution of the Facebook Translate platform previously described.

5. *Audiovisual translation platforms.* Audiovisual translation platforms with established workflows have popularized collaborative subtitling that used to be the realm of dedicated fan communities with advanced subtitling software skills. Some of these platforms such as Dotsub and Amara are widely popular all over the world. Others are widely popular in Asia such as Yeeyam, Yyets or Viki. The case of Viki is an interesting one since it originated as a free collaborative platform for translation of mainly Korean dramas and it expanded to incorporate a wide range of audiovisual genres (Dwyer 2013). It was sold in 2013 and it is currently a for-profit company that benefits from the dedicated labor of volunteers.

6. *Non-profit platforms.* Several collaborative platforms have been specifically developed for non-profit or activist causes, such as Trommons and the Kanjingo smartphone app by the Rosetta Foundation, Kiva, MNT-TT, the Translators Without Borders Translate app, or the adaptation of the Ushahidi platform to add translation data to the geolocation tasks. The platform Trommons has been developed by the Rosetta Foundation (De Wille 2014) and it is an open platform in order to translate content from non-profits. Similar to MNH-TT (Babych et al. 2012), the platform can be used by different non-profits as an off-the-shelf solution.

7. *Language learning platforms.* Language learning platforms have also been used to crowdsource translation initiatives through the principle of majority voting to the crowdsourcing of translation tasks. The most famous example of this trend is Duolingo (García 2013), although other cases have emerged such as Linquap, Hellotxt or Flitto.

8. *Smartphone app solutions.* The move from desktop-based applications to cloud environments, and the gradual substitution of desktops by smartphones and tablets in many situations has meant that translation crowdsourcing has opened up to these new ubiquitous platforms. Most language learning platforms, such as Duolingo and Linqapp, also function as apps. Several platforms have been recently developed as an app, such as the MT crowd post-editing platforms Unbabel. The Unbabel app combines the free paradigm with paid crowdsourcing, offering users each time in the main menu to participate both in free or remunerated tasks. It combines crowd post-editing with artificial intelligence in a continuous process of MT system training. Other initiatives harness the power of the crowd via smartphone such as the image-based translation crowdsourcing initiative UbiAsk. In this app users can upload images containing different languages and users can translate the content. The other users that know the language will response to the image (Liu et al. 2012;

Mahmud and Aris 2015). An interesting innovation in mobile translation is brought by the company Stepes, that offers an app with user interface that simulates text messaging in order to provide fast crowd post-editing via smartphones. Smartphone apps are also in the process of development in non-profits, such as the Kajingo app previously mentioned.

9. *MT-Based crowdsourcing platforms.* MT post-editing approaches harness the power of the crowd to both post-edit output and at the same time to improve statistical machine engines, such as Google Translate and Microsoft Bing Translator. New initiatives such as Microsoft Translation Hub allow the customization of a MT engine with the potential to crowdsource the post-editing and train the system. Business initiatives such as the now extinct Asia Online are examples of the development of workflows that include post-editing in different variations in order to continue training their statistical machine engines (Vashee 2009). Other industry examples are Translate.com or Unbabel. Research-based initiatives also exist, such as the ACCEPT platform financed by the European Union for community content (Mitchell, O'Brien and Roturier 2014; Mitchell 2015), or the Kanjingo app. The collaborative translation of Wikipedia has attracted the attention of scholars working with projects that use crowd post-editing using a simple workflow that provides MT pretranslations that can be edited by users (Kumaran Saravanan and Maurie 2008; Alegria et al. 2015).

10. *Linguistic tasks to support translation.* Crowdsourcing can also be applied in different workflows to develop not only final translations, but also translation resources. For example, initiatives have focused on the crowdsourcing of terminology resources such as Termwiki, Omega Wiki or Wikitionary, while some companies have developed solutions such as Teaminology by Weblocalize. The development of translation memories is also an example at hand, with initiatives such as Mymemory or VLMT.

Crowdsourcing solutions have been expanding technological translation workflows in a dynamic and user-friendly approach. The wide range of variation between existing platforms highlights that crowdsourcing can be considered the most vibrant and dynamic translational phenomenon in this decade, having the potential to impact professional workflows and practices when approaches to collaboration, efficiency or speed are transferred to the professional world. The case of Stepes described above illustrates this point. This review highlights the diverse approaches to crowdsourcing and collaborative translations through the range of existing technological solutions. The main trend in TM systems is mainly a move to the cloud and the integration of TM and MT (i.e. Wordfast Anywhere, Casmacat, MateCat). In this last model, examples like Translate.com, Casmacat or the app localization platform El Loco have developed business models that offer free MT services, while the offer to use human translation is continuously present on the screen. Users thus can decide once the output appears whether a human translation might be better idea. In Translate.com for example, the "human translation" is subsequently through a crowd of "professional" post-editors in a fast process. These professional crowdsourced models bring to mind the prediction of García that professional translators would soon be post-editing MT in "in low-paid, call-centre conditions" (2010: 211), but it obviously might still far from becoming a reality, if ever. Numbers do not exist to date on the impact of professional crowdsourced post-editing, but the impact of crowdsourcing MT models might be still quite small. What is clear is that crowdsourcing models have already had an impact in the professional market with the adaptation of crowdsourcing models using professionals to streamline and quicken processes.

3.6   Post-editing MT and crowdsourcing

The potential combination of crowdsourcing with MT has been explored since the late 90's as a mechanism to improve MT output. Early on, as previously mentioned, researchers attempted to use crowdsourcing as an alternative solution to both improve and train MT systems (Shimohata et al. 2001; Utiyama and Isahara 2003) and to post-edit the output in diverse ways. In the industry, Google Translate and Bing Translator quickly allowed users to post-edit the resulting translations, helping both users achieve the quality levels they find acceptable, and also to continue to train the MT systems. New applications and widgets such as Google Website Translator or Microsoft Collaborative Translation Framework (Tatsumi et al. 2012), also allow users to suggest "better translations" when websites get localized, putting post-editing even further in the hands of end users and their preferences. Even in cases such as the introduction of Bing Translator to social networking apps, post-editing can be a reality. In Twitter, for example, tweets in languages other than the interface one selected by users can be translated automatically. When this is done, the user is offered to option to offer a better translation of the tweet in question by clicking on the "wrong translation?" option.[4]

This paradigm is known in the industry as Human Aided Machine Translation (HAMT), the combination of MT and TM (García 2011; Moorkens, O'Brien, Kenny and Doherty 2013; Hutchins 2014), with highly successful initiatives such as Asia Online or Unbabel, as well as three recent EU granted projects such as MateCat

---

4.   https://support.twitter.com/articles/20172132

(Federico et al. 2014), Casmacat (Alabau et al. 2014; Elming, Winther and Carl 2014) or ACCEPT (Mitchell et al. 2014). Years ago, García (2009, 2011) predicted a future in which professional translation would be bound to transition from the triple combination of management, translating textual segments with TM and quality control towards a HAMT model that primes: (1) management, (2) pre and post-editing of web texts with TM-assisted MT and (3) quality control. The transition is still in the making: post-editing, however, represents that to date less than 5% of the content in the language industry is the result of professional post-edition (Doherty 2015), even when FOMT (Free and Open Machine Translation) engines such as Google Translate and Bing Translator get billions of hits daily and can translate up to 10 times the total volume of professional translations in the world. In a sense, the initial fears that MT would take over professional translation, or that translators would quickly become post-editors, did not necessarily match the initial hype (though it will happen in the near future for some domains and text types). Similarly, no estimates exist on the volume of post-editing participation by the crowd in FOMT systems or other initiatives. This phenomenon is parallel with how crowdsourcing initially provoked some fears in the professional community, but after some years, the economic impact in the industry has been smaller than anticipated.

Post-editing in professional settings has been proven to increase the efficiency and turnaround of translation if compared to professional translation (Guerberof 2009; Plitt and Masselot 2010) and consequently, crowdsourcing post-editing has emerged as a potential solution to deal with the vast volume of user-generated content in the web. Mitchell (2015) argues that a difference needs to be made between "crowd post-editing" and "community post-editing". Crowd post-editing (CPE) represents the process of obtaining post-edited translations from MT output through crowdsourcing to a crowd, such as translation students in the case of Tatsumi et al. (2012). Research in these areas has mostly focused on the structuring of workflows and alternative processes to guarantee quality rather than examining the final quality of the output itself, a rather prolific area in MT research. Crowd post-editing also appears in three distinct varieties: free post-editing, what could be called "low-cost crowdsourced post-editing" through crowdsourcing platforms at rates much lower than the industry, as well as "professional crowdsourced post-editing", as in companies that offer professional services at higher rates such as Unbabel. "Community post-editing", on the other hand, refers to the process of having regular users of user-generated content to post-edit the output of content translated by MT systems, such as the case of the Norton Antivirus forums (Mitchell 2014). Participants did not join the initiative to translate or post-edit; they merely accessed the forum to get information about the products, problem solving, support, etc. Community members might have an interest in helping other members in the community. The fact that members are already part of the community and knowledgeable about the products is a common control mechanism, and it is often argued that frequent users might represent ideal candidates for monolingual or bilingual post-editors. The community involvement with the MT output can also appear in holistic models such as in usability or readability evaluations of the output. These are cases in which MT translated pages in support forums include the possibility of approving or not the page in terms of whether "the [MT translated] page helped solve my problem". These evaluations of usability are related to the prevailing "good enough" or "fit for purpose" models of quality in the industry and MT research (see Chapter 5). A recent newcomer to the field is what could be referred to as "professional post-editing of crowdsourcing". This model has emerged in the industry as an alternative to professional post-editing and involves the post-editing by professionals of translations produced by the crowd. Normally this process involves the comparison in terms of cost, time, efficiency and cognitive efforts with MT post-editing. This emerging trend deserves much needed attention from a research perspective in TS and it will soon emerge as another common post-editing type in the industry.

Two distinct types of MT architectures exist (Hutchins 2014): the earlier rule-based MT with services, such as Babelfish based on Systrans technology, and the later statistical MT (SMT) based on massive corpora. This latter architecture is the main approach in initiatives using crowdsourcing. Statistical MT systems are based on data provided by large corpora of parallel and monolingual texts and the translation is extracted using specific statistical methods as well as language models. Translations are produced using probabilistic models that emerge from the statistical analysis of these existing corpora. It is currently the most popular model in web-based fully automated MT systems, and its architectures are continually being improved through the feedback and intervention from users. Free Online MT (FOMT) such as Google Translate and Microsoft Translator offer communities the possibility of improving the final quality of the automatic localization of web pages (Tatsumi et al. 2012), one of the prime examples of the convergence of crowdsourcing and MT. This type of MT learning is common in recent approaches such as the MateCat or the Casmacat projects, while the ACCEPT project specifically addresses the crowdsourcing of MT post-editing of user-generated content. This project financed by a EU grant is directly related to volunteer translation since it has as an objective "aspects related to community post-editing, e.g. motivation and preferences for monolingual or bilingual post-editing environments." (Mitchell et al. 2014: 238). SMT approaches are also ideal for crowd post-editing due to the possibility of machine learning through the intervention of the crowd. As described in Section 3.4.4, in iterative systems, such as the Asia Online Wikipedia Initiative, alternative post-edited solutions to one segment can also serve as training material for SMT engines.

In professional translation, MT appears in a quite prototypical process in which, after building, training or using an off-the-shelf MT engine, post-editors can pre-edit the source text, the MT engine pretranslates the text, and the post-editor works on the output of MT systems following certain rules, such as the TAUS post-editing guidelines (TAUS 2010). The evaluation of the output can be performed using automatized metrics such as the BLEU (Papineni et al. 2002) or METEOR, as well as new human-based dynamic metrics such as QT Launchpad (Lommel et al. 2014).

The involvement of the crowd in the process, nevertheless, has followed a less predictive path with multiple approaches not only restricted to direct post-edition of the output. For example, the earliest publications attempted to develop workflows that gather terminology resources to enrich MT systems (Shimohata et al. 2001). The creation of parallel corpora for the training of statistical machine translation systems has often been crowdsourced by means of producing a corpus of source segments aligned with their translations. It has been argued that the quality output is similar to cases in which professional translators had provided the translation in the parallel corpora (Zaidan and Calliston-Burch 2011; Zbib et al. 2013; Yan et al. 2014). The direct post-editing of MT output by the crowd has also obviously been investigated using different platforms (Aikawa Yamamoto and Isahara 2012; Tatsumi et al. 2012; Mitchell, O'Brien and Roturier 2014; Mitchell 2015), as well as the crowdsourcing of quality evaluation of MT output (Bentivogli et al. 2011; Mitchell et al. 2014; Goto, Lin and Ishida 2015), or even the evaluation and comparison of MT systems performance using crowd participation (Goto, Lin and Ishida 2015).

Many of the main research questions of interest in MT and TS research are directly applicable to the analysis of whether and how to use crowd post-editing. Issues of interest are, among others, the skills or profile of the post-editor, whether post-edition is feasible both in bilingual or monolingual settings, or whether professionals, domain experts or bilinguals differ in their post-editing. In terms of how to conduct the post-editing, the issue of comparing whether bilingual or monolingual post-editing is equally effective (Koehn 2010; Hu et al. 2011; Koponen and Salmi 2015). Crowd members can contribute with their domain, genre and advanced language knowledge without being experts in translation transfer. Studies have generally identified what would be expected in this regard. If the three pillars of MT evaluation are analyzed, fluency, adequacy and fidelity (Papineni et al. 2002; Lommel et al. 2014), the first two can be similarly achieved in both monolingual and bilingual post-editing, while fidelity to the source text clearly suffers if the post-editing is conducted without the source text. This bears clear implications for volunteers that possess low language skills in one or both languages and that might be involved in post-editing. It also poses implications for those models that attempt to produce translations using monolinguals mediating through the MT system (Hu et al. 2011). Nevertheless, Yamada (2015) identified that there is no direct correlation between being an A level student in courses of the language in question and the quality of the post-editing conducted. A correlation was obviously found between having lower grades or negative attitudes towards MT and the performance in post-editing tasks, but nevertheless, certain cognitive traits were more related to less dynamic and early stages of translation competence acquisition (PACTE 2014) and better correlated to increase in quality. This might be due to the fact that post-editing guidelines focus on "good enough" quality (TAUS 2010), or what Allen (2003) calls "rapid post-editing", correcting errors but without focusing on style or fluency, rather than "full post-editing". The variation between subjects that in principle would be good candidates for crowd post-editors also matches the findings of Mitchell (2015) and Mitchell et al. (2014), in that as opposed to professionals, bilinguals exhibit a wide variation in the quality of the output that they can produce. While professional post-editors and domain experts show a more similar performance, bilingual students range from 20% to 75 % error correction rates. Another issue of interest is that bilinguals can be as rigorous in rating the quality of post-edited user-generated content as domain experts (Mitchell et al. 2014: 259). This has implications of interest since many crowdsourcing initiatives allow to set open or closed workflows and often domain specialists (and not professional translators), are invited to participate in crowdsourcing efforts. In terms of comparing bilinguals and professionals, the study by Goto, Lin and Ishida (2015) suggests that bilinguals might not be able to perform as well as professionals in evaluation tasks, but when the objective of the evaluation is the MT system, both populations lead to similar results and, therefore MT system evaluation might be a potentially successful avenue for crowdsourcing to non-professionals.

It is also of interest that two studies, Yamada (2015) and García (2010), correlate with a positive attitude of the participants towards MT post-editing with the results of their performance in the experimental tasks. This might be related to different cognitive traits in what the PACTE research group refers to as "psycho-physiological components" (2003) or Kelly (2005) refers to as the "translator's attitude". These differences and the lack of trust in the skills of bilingual post-editors have been addressed in MT publications and practices through the development of creative workflows such as those seen in Section 3.2 and 3.3., with different checks, as well as automatized and human quality measures to account for potential variations in quality. The issue of attitudes in participants and their "untrained" performance is of interest since, while translation can be considered a "natural" skill in all bilinguals (Harris and Sherwood 1974), post-editing MT in professional settings has been defined as a non-natural activity that requires careful training

(Moorkens and Doherty 2013; Doherty adn Kenny 2014). This activity requires adjusting to the post-editing guidelines that are provided, guidelines that often professional translators themselves tend not to observe (de Almeida 2013). The question of interest to research in this area would then be how volunteers adhere to post-editing guidelines, when professionals themselves tend to ignore them. The "good enough" paradigm means that issues of style, fluency or adequacy might be sidestepped in order to achieve quicker turnaround and efficiency. This requires adjusting some natural cognitive traits of professionals trained to follow certain procedures and sidestepping some acquired mechanisms.

3.7   Crowdsourcing and prescription: Industry and the case of motivation

Over the years, different stakeholders in the study of translation have followed different paths due to diverging objectives. These objectives range from the prescriptive and applied industry approaches to theoretical or empirical studies in TS. Industry research often appears in response to the rapid development of technologies and the need to quickly adapt to an ever-evolving field. In terms of crowdsourcing, the industry has tried to rapidly understand, harness and exploit the power of the crowd to produce translations, working mostly on workflow models and the development of best practices. Industry experts normally produce applied research at a much quicker rate than academic disciplines (O'Hagan 2013), while TS often trails behind industry research. In terms of technological innovations TS also tends to adopt industrial de-facto models and conceptualizations resulting from this applied and prescriptive approach (Jiménez-Crespo 2013a).

The industry has mostly produced literature in two related areas, the description of crowdsourcing phenomena (i.e. DePalma and Kelly 2011; European Union 2012), and collection of best practices (Desilets and Van de Meer 2011; DePalma and Kelly 2011). The need for best practices is often stressed since "there is a clear need for a more concise, summative body of knowledge that captures recurrent best practices" (Desilets and van de Meer 2011: 29). The same authors also mention that current practitioners are the most suitable subjects for creating them: "we advocate the building of such a compendium, [...] which could be written collectively by practitioners of collaborative translation." (ibid: 29). It should be mentioned at this point that according to the canonical map of TS as a discipline, research can fall under the Theoretical/Descriptive or the Applied branches. The latter branch focuses its attention on the work of professionals and practitioners, while the Theoretical/Descriptive branch is largely the realm of scholars and researchers. Both branches represent a global cycle in which the transfer of knowledge in both directions represents one of the main engines of evolution of the discipline and the production of knowledge about existing phenomena (Rabadán 2008). That is, both branches feed into each other and therefore help refine theories, models and applied practices. Obviously, the several stakeholders interested in the advancement of research (namely professionals and scholars), can have different objectives, tempos and research agendas, but both can and should cooperate towards a common goal.

The case of volunteer motivation has offered an area in which both TS and the industry have followed completely different, and potentially complementary, approaches. Jiménez-Crespo (2014) identified this area as one in which industrial prescriptive approaches and TS research could be contrasted and complemented. TS scholars have delved into crowdsourcing from an empirical perspective, researching the motivation of volunteers to participate, and this will be explored in the chapter related to sociological approaches to the study of crowdsourcing (see Section 8.5 and 8.6). Meanwhile, the industry has compiled best practices that emerge from focus groups through experiences of those in charge of developing and managing initiatives. The two sides of the same coin can be contrasted: on the one side are the views from business agents who need active crowd involvement, and on the other the actual self-image and opinions of participants.

The significance of volunteer motivation in the industry appears in all industry best practice publications. In the one publication that emerged after the TAUS 2011 meeting, *Wanted: Best Practices in Collaborative Translation*, it is indicated that "[m]otivation issues are most critical in crowdsourcing scenarios, and this is possibly the main reason why it has yet to become widespread" (Desilets and Van de Meer 2011: 32). Similarly, DePalma and Kelly indicate that it is necessary to discover volunteer motivations, and organizations need to "keep nurturing them with rewards and incentives" (ibid: 401). Motivation appears so predominantly in industry publications that crowdsourcing quality is sometimes even less of a concern than motivation:

> Quality Control issues tend to resolve themselves, provided that enough of the "right" people can be enticed to participate and that you provide them with light-weight tools and processes by which they can spot and fix errors.
>
> (Desilets and van de Meer 2011: 41)

Motivation appears in the publications by Common Sense Advisory (i.e. DePalma and Kelly 2009; Kelly and Ray 2011) and those resulting from the TAUS 2011 meeting (Desilets and van de Meer 2011; Collaborative Translation Patterns 2011).[5] All publications include lists of similar areas. For example, the paper by DePalma and Kelly (2011) includes recommendations for:

---

5.   http://collaborative-translation-patterns.wiki4us.com/tiki-index.php

1. Planning for crowdsourced translation
2. Building and supporting the community
3. Creating a robust, sustainable community via best practices
4. Building a platform for collaboration

Motivation appears in the second and third areas, supporting the community and creating a robust and sustainable community. The TAUS report includes a compendium of the most commonly used decision-making patterns, previously identified issues in the implementation of crowdsourcing during a meeting with industry experts in 2011 and recommendations for how to best tackle each of them. As Pym indicates, rather than best practices, these design patterns could rather be called "formalized solutions to common problems" (Pym 2015a: 146), since the document merely identifies existing solutions in the industry to common problems, rather than providing actual best practices for different crowdsourcing scenarios.

The areas of interest in the TAUS report include the following sections:

1. Planning and scoping
2. Community motivation
3. Translation quality
4. Contributor career Path
5. Community rightsizing
6. Tools and processes

As far as the community motivation is concerned, industry experts suggest an extensive list of existing practices to increase motivation among participants. These represent potential strategies identified previously in existing crowdsourcing initiatives rather than a ranking or study of the best practices to motivate translators. The practices proposed to motivate the community in the TAUS publications include a long list with items such as establishing a campaign progress gauge, recognizing contributors, implementing leader boards, offering an official certificate of participation, point systems, offering double points, handing out unique branded products, showing the contributor of the month, granting special access rights, implementing playful casual translation, initiating campaigns, publishing contributions rapidly or establishing playful competition among contributors. It is apparent that most of them are related to the fostering of non-monetary motivations (12 out of 13), while only one of them relates to handing out branded products.

In research in Translation Studies, two studies asked translators whether they would be motivated if gifts were handed out. In the case of Skype (Mesipuu 2012) results showed that community events, such as getting together in beta releases, were a more powerful motivator than handing out T-shirts or other merchandise.

Similarly, in the study for the non-profit Rosetta Foundation (O'Brien and Schäler 2010), merchandise, gifts or monetary compensation came in at the bottom of the list of potential motivators for further engagement, while intrinsic motivations such as feedback from qualified translators or clients or invitations to events were reported twice as often as free gifts or payments in the survey. Additionally, subjects indicated that the least attractive incentives to motivate them in the future were practices such as translator of the month profiles or monthly top-ten lists. Practically all best-practice reports include these types of incentives and to some extent this finding contradicts these recommendations in industry publications. For example, DePalma and Kelly identify the main incentive to motivating participants is to "keep nurturing them [volunteer translators] with rewards and incentives…Something as simple as a certificate can be a powerful form of recognition" (2011:403). They also indicate the value of "Highlight[ing] and showcase[ing] member contributions. Companies in the article find the "leaderboard" to be an effective tool".[6] However, the study by O'Brien and Schäler (2010) also found out that top lists could be somewhat detrimental to the engagement of "lurkers", those with little time to volunteer (Nielsen 2006).[7] The authors indicated that:

> Some volunteers [...] mention factors that would demotivate them. In particular, turning their activities into a competition by making them bid against each other or simply compete for positions on leadership boards was highlighted as something that would demotivate the volunteers   (n.p.)

It is therefore necessary to address the existing discrepancies between initial industry practices to motivate volunteers and the opinions of those participating in motivation-related surveys. The differences, however, might need to contrast with caution. For example, the practice of including a leaderboard might actually be beneficial since it seems directed towards recruiting and retaining the low percentage of highly active participants that volunteer beyond the weekly average of two to five hours identified in studies (McDonough-Dolmaya 2012; Camara 2015). Thus, when surveys get a carefully balanced response from the population under study, the participants, it is necessary to take into consideration that participation in terms of engagement and committed hours varies across the board. This uncertainty of working with volunteers at their will and with dependence on their motivation presents interesting challenges that both the industry and TS are attempting to uncover. This and other areas represent interesting cases for bringing

---

6.   DePalma and Kelly (2011) indicate also that it is necessary to remember that all volunteers do not have the same amount of time and it is necessary to recognize them all.

7.   According to Nielsen 90% of participants in crowdsourcing efforts are "lurkers" who never contribute, while 9% contribute a little and 1% of participants account for all of the activity.

together industry and TS research since both interested parties are working in interrelated areas of a global research cycle, applied and prescriptive vs. theoretical and descriptive, and both feed into each other. Desilets and van de Meer concluded in their paper that "most practices […] are not that different from best-practices which are being used for crowdsourcing in other domains" (2011: 41). They also ask whether translation specifically requires a set of best practices. However, research by McDonough-Dolmaya (2012) identified clear differences in the motivations and types of participants if translation crowdsourcing is compared with studies in Free and Open Software (Lakhani and Wolf 2005). This means that the potential to research and identify best practices through the global cycle of research, whether it starts in the applied or the theoretical-descriptive side, is still wide open.

CHAPTER 4

Crowdsourcing and Cognitive Translation Studies
Moving beyond the individual's mind

> These developments [in embedded, embodied and extended cognition]
> indicate a shift of perspective from the individual to a network level,
> suggesting a need to revise the individualistic concept of 'the translator'.
>
> (Risku 2014: 341)

4.1 Introduction

For over three decades, the study and modeling of the complex cognitive as-
pects of translation and interpreting have been the objectives of the branch of
TS known throughout the successive stages as Process Research, Translation
Process, Cognitive Translation Studies (Shreve and Angelone 2009) or Cognitive
Translatology (henceforth CT, Muñoz 2010a).[1] Researchers in this branch have
attempted to shed light on what happens in the "black box" (Shreve and Diamond
1997), the translator's cognitive system, during translation and interpreting tasks.
Investigating what happens in the mind of the translator during the process is a
central issue in Translation Studies during the four successive stages of the development of Cognitive Translation Studies (see Muñoz 2013, 2014a), since understanding how translations are produced can help identify the main factors
that play a role in translation processes and how they influence each other (Risku
2014). Research into cognitive aspects of translation has proven essential to building more solid theories and to helping develop models for translation training
(Jääskeläinen 2013). It has also been significant in the development of translation
tools and aides, as well as in translation quality assessment (Shreve and Angelone
2009). As one of the key pillars of Descriptive Translation Studies, process-based
approaches strive for a solid empirical foundation, importing theoretical models

---

1. These labels do not mean the same thing, but clarifications are outside the scope of this
book. Suffice it to say that they all refer to cognitive and psycholinguistic approaches. Cognitive
translatology refers to approaches based on embodied, embedded, enacted, extended and affective cognition, or 4EA cognition (cf. Muñoz 2015). Cognitive Translation Studies refers to
the interface between cognition and translation, with no particular theoretical framework
attached to it.

and research methodologies from neighboring fields such as cognitive psychology, expertise studies, psycholinguistics, cognitive science neurolinguistics or neuropsychology, and at the same time adapting and creating new ones.

The classic approach to process research, in the words of Englund Dimitrova, has been mainly focused on understanding the "nature of the cognitive process involved in translation, with a focus on the *individual translator*" [emphasis added] (2010: 406). The initial underlying theoretical foundation based on the information-processing paradigm, understanding the brain to work as a computer (cf. Muñoz 2013), has been mainly responsible for the prevalent emphasis on the analysis of individual translators and interpreters across populations, such as professionals, bilinguals, novices or language teachers. This emphasis is also due to the need to develop a solid empirical paradigm within the discipline, firmly grounded on testing in highly controlled experimental settings to limit the number of variables. Research on individuals' cognitive systems in highly controlled experimental settings could thus be considered as the mainstream research approach of many works within Cognitive Translation Studies. This does not mean that it has stopped or limited its research to experimental settings, quantitative research, or the confines of an individual translator's mind. As will be explored later, current trends introducing situated, embodied, extended and distributed cognition (also, 4EA cognition) have also embraced the extended nature of translation processes beyond the individual (i.e., Risku 2002; Risku and Windhager 2013; Ehrengsberger-Dow and Massey 2014). Cognition in translation has therefore also been researched in terms of "translation networks, actors and environments" (Risku 2014: 333), extending the focus from the individual mind to the environment, tools used and the social networks during the cycle of production.

From the point of view of the intersection of CT and contemporary collaborative practices, it should be acknowledged that earlier approaches in this subdiscipline, mostly within computationalist models focused on individual, decontextualized problem-solving, display an overreliance on the individualistic model in experimental settings. This issue has also been the objective of criticisms mostly within more recent embodied, distributed and extended 4EA Cognitive Translatology approaches. According to Risku (2014: 335), it is somewhat problematic that this subdiscipline has mainly focused "on the mental processes of individuals in isolation", while the situated and embodied cognition approaches of Clark (1997, 2008) and Hutchins (2010) claim that the situation and context in which cognition occurs is "part of the thought process" (Risku 2014: 335). Recent developments in how human cognition is understood suggest a move from the individual as the sole unit of cognition, towards the network, cultural and social levels. This shift implies "a need to revise the individualistic concept of 'the translator'" (ibid: 341) including, among others, the possibility of collaboration among translators as well as other agents. This expansion beyond the individual mind of the translator is also supported by Muñoz (2010b) who, in his threefold restructuring and realignment of cognitive research, highlights how reinstating the "human, social and cultural dimensions of cognition has had an enormous impact" (2014a: 67) on the discipline. In Muñoz's proposal, the first level focuses on the mental states and operations that play a role when translating and interpreting, such as problem solving, decision making or understanding. The second level relates to the variable set of subtasks and observable operations that entail combining and managing the states and operations in the first level, such as reading, writing, information-seeking, or revising. The third level focuses on "the roles, cognitive contributions and relations of all relevant agents who interact in the production of translation and interpreting" (Muñoz 2014a: 71). This third level also has, in agreement with Risku's proposal, implications for the methodologies used, since traditional research methods have been designed for the study of "isolated, minimal units in laboratory settings" (ibid: 70).

Despite the fact that certain theoretical models and approaches have already moved beyond the confines of the individual mind, including these extended aspects of translatorial cognition, crowdsourcing and modern collaborative practices by volunteers have yet to make their way into CT. The initial theoretical and methodological ground is already laid down to move beyond the individualistic character of earlier approaches. For the purposes of analyzing and understanding online collaborative phenomena, two of the main issues that have attracted the attention of scholars working within cognitive paradigms can be of great interest. The first one is research into the notions of "expertise" and "competence;" the second one is the introduction of situated, extended and distributed approaches.

The study of "expertise" and situated and extended cognition has been often undertaken mainly from the perspective of professional translation, the prevailing emphasis in situated and extended cognition research projects (i.e., Risku and Windhager 2013; Ehrengsberger-Down and Massey 2014). This does not mean that Cognitive Translation Studies has not produced invaluable research on the cognitive processes of non-professionals that so overwhelmingly make up the majority of participants, but quite the opposite. Since its early days, experimental studies have incorporated language learners, bilinguals and translation novices to study a wide array of issues. Nevertheless, the focus of research has not been the processes of volunteer or non-professional translators *per se*. Including these subject populations in research studies has mainly been motivated by the need to contrastively identify components of translation expertise or translation competence through experimental research. In cases in which bilinguals or non-professionals have been main subjects in studies, this has been done mainly in order to identify "pre-translational" competence (Presas 1995) or "aptitude" towards interpreting (i.e., Angelelli 2010; Blasco Mayor 2015); that is, to identify in bilinguals traits or aptitudes that indicate a predisposition to succeed as a professional through deliberate and dedicated training.

The emphasis in professional settings also implies that CT has yet to explore in depth the impact of distributing the cognitive task of translation among several non-professional translators working on the same text, rather than the existing emphasis on researching the stages in isolation, such as translation and self-revision, online revision, or revision by itself as separate stages done by different people but with the focus on individuals (i.e., Conde Ruano 2009). In achieving this goal, the insights from the group of theories that have extended the limits of cognition beyond the individual minds and extended it to tools, social context and the environment, and those supporting several research strands within TS under the umbrella label of Cognitive Translatology (see note 1), play a key role.

4.2 Distributed and extended cognition in the age of translation crowdsourcing

The main premise of situated, embodied, extended, embedded and distributed cognition approaches is that cognition is not carried out solely with the brain. Human cognition is not constrained and limited by the human mind but, on the contrary, cognitive processes depend on the bodily, physical, social, and cultural context in which they are carried out (Clark 2008; Clark and Chalmers 1998; Hutchins 2010). These approaches to cognition extended the focus from beyond the individual's mind and claim that all cognitive processes occur thanks to the interaction of the body, mind, artefacts, as well as the social and environmental contexts in which processing takes place. Despite subtle differences between these approaches, a feature

> they have in common is a commitment to the idea that issues of material embodiment and environmental embedding play explanatorily significant roles in our understanding of human cognitive success. (Smart 2014: 326)

"Situated cognition" claims that human cognitive processing is adapted to the environment and that perception and action develop together (Lave 1988; Clark 1997). "Embodied cognition" claims that the human body, as the physical mechanism of the cognitive system, mediates perception and action planning, as well as the interactions with the external world and plays an essential role in cognition (Clark 1997). "Extended cognition" departs from the premise that cognition extends to the environment, and it is understood as a "form of coupled system between human organisms and external entities" (Risku 2014: 333). For instance, taking down notes is a way to extend one's memory store into the environment. Similarly, "distributed cognition" occurs when cognitive processes are distributed beyond the confines of the brain, and on to artifacts or members of a social group. It results from the constant interaction between people and their social and physical environments, such as the pilots in charge of a plane cockpit (Hutchins 1995b), or a group of translators or trainees working together to produce a single translated text (Muñoz 2010a). It embraces the possibility of the distribution of cognitive tasks, since a process is not cognitive "simply because it happens in a brain, nor is a process non cognitive simply because it happens in the interactions among many brains" (Hollan, Hutchins and Kirsh 2000: 172). This outward expansion means a "propagation of representational states across media" (Hutchins 1995a:118). By "media," Hutchins referred to representations made inside individuals' minds, such as abstract concepts or frameworks, overt representations that are embodied in verbal exchanges, movements or gestures, as well as artifacts such as paper, pen, compasses, maps, calendars, charts, etc. Media would also refer, in the case of translation, to the web, search engines, and TM tools (Christensen 2011), as well as community forums or the collaborative tools described in Section 3.4. This is a highly adaptive process in which networks of actors and artefacts interact, and it refers to all cognition and not only to some parts of it. These approaches highlight the fact that, once the focus moves away from a view of cognition as the sole property of the brain, and on to the environment, social systems and context, the study of cognition must include objects, artefacts, and symbolic processes of other people.

For the purposes of the study of collaborative practices, what is interesting in the "distributed cognition" paradigm is precisely the distribution of cognitive tasks onto artefacts and to a social community that it makes possible. This approach was initially applied to the design and analysis of human-computer interaction in the 90's, and applied to many other areas such as education, e-learning, game design, electronic collaboration, organizational synergy, etc. (i.e., Salmons 2008; Shapiro 2014). According to Hollan, Hutchins and Kirsh (2000), the fact that computers were networked and tasks could be completed by putting together individual brains, as well as the fact that computers are artefacts in which humans can share and support their cognitive tasks, meant that "distributed" cognition was an ideal theoretical foundation to understand the interactions between people and computers.[2] This approach has also been extended to the distribution of cognitive tasks to through the World Wide Web, since it is:

2.   A parallel development in sociology is Actor-Network Theory (see 8.2.2).

> a platform for social interaction and engagement, and this opens up the possibility
> that the Web may lead to new forms of socially-situated and socially-distributed
> cognition.   (Smart 2014: 332)

According to Hollan, Hutchins and Kirsh (2000), distributed cognition has three
basic tenets:

1. The embodiment of the cognitive act
2. The fact that distributed cognition needs to be researched in its cultural context since agents live in complex cultural systems, and
3. The social aspect of cognition

Cognition can therefore be distributed across three dimensions, first of all socially,
between different agents. Similar to how different cognitive functions can be allocated to different parts of the brain, distributed cognition argues that cognitive
functions of groups can be allocated to different group members. Task-related
cognitive processes can therefore be distributed and shared across members of
a community or social group, such as those linked to the production of a single
translation. They can also be shared through the neural structures, body or the
environment, such as a microscope for a biologist, a telescope for an astrologist or
a corpus-search tool for a translator. Thirdly, cognitive processes can be distributed
throughout time, and the products of earlier events can transform the processing
of the later. This refers, for example, to the impact of culture in distributing cognition and how future generations can benefit from cognitive processes of earlier
ones. For example, the invention of translation memory meant that the cognitive
distribution of translation tasks has transformed how freelance and collaborative
translators work. This is precisely why the use of translation memory, for example, has been argued to be a case of collective distributed cognition (Christensen
2011: 140), not only throughout the task but also beyond in its temporal dimension,
in terms of the development of these systems. Any translation memory used in a
translation task represents an additional long-term memory from which stored
information can be retrieved during the process. When a group of translators
works collectively in a translation and shares a TM, they can be "said to share
cognitive resources via the artifact" (ibid). Similarly, even if a single translator
uses the translation memory that he or she previously created, the cognitive task
is distributed to some extent between the individual cognition and the artefact.
Crowdsourcing processes mediated through collaborative platforms of different
kinds therefore implement a distribution of cognitive tasks not only between different agents through collaboration and use of existing memories and term bases,
but also between agents and technological artefacts. Examples of how cognition is
distributed in popular crowdsourcing initiatives could be the use of terminology
matches in the interactive workspace of the Translate Facebook App.

These main tenets of distributed cognition highlight that the production of translations in crowdsourcing and collaboration represent prime cases of how cognitive processing can be distributed through technological artefacts throughout a community. For example, cases of distributed processes range from the interaction between translator and reviser that occurs in Kiva to the multi participatory iterative proposal and voting process found in social networking sites. Distributed cognition in CT does not only belong to the study of professional translation in terms of the complex network of relationships and actor interactions that occur in any given professional translation process from beginning to end (i.e., Risku and Windhager 2013). It can also be the complex network of interactions between agents, community managers, programmers, initiators, volunteer translators, revisers, etc. that can take part in a variable way in any given volunteer collaborative project online. In this sense, throughout this book it has been argued that collaboration is not "just a special case of several translation scenarios, such as localization" (Muñoz 2010b: 172), but a rising phenomenon of still unforeseen scale.

4.2.1 The introduction of embodied, situated and extended cognition approaches to translation

The above-mentioned approaches, among others, can be said to be introduced to CT by the works of Hanna Risku. Since the beginning of the 2000's, she argued for the analysis of translation processes from these perspectives (2002), as well as subsequent distributed and extended cognition approaches (e.g., Risku 2014). Risku and Windhager (2013) have proposed an "extended translation" that combines a cognitive and sociological perspective. This approach, they claim, is needed due, first of all, to the radical changes in the translation profession in the last decades, not only in the wide range of new tasks assigned to translators (i.e., web localization or audiovisual digital translation), but also in the impact of technologies to move from the individual to the network level. The network economy and the impact of a digital wired world (Folaron and Buzelin 2007; Folaron 2010) implies that translation processes are mediated by a network of different agents and instruments or artefacts "in an increasingly longer chain and increasingly larger and more complex networks" (Risku 2014: 340). In fact, beyond the individual setting in which a translator might produce a segment or paragraph, the results of the studies conducted have identified that, even in a freelance translator setting, networks tend to be much larger than originally anticipated (Risku 2014: 333), both on the client and in the translator's side.

The second reason behind why CT benefits from an "extended cognition" approach is the need to move beyond experimental settings to study authentic translation cognitive processes. If one of the main caveats of psycholinguistic approaches is that cognition does not happen only in the brain, a second one is that cognition does not only happen 'in the lab'. This requires a contextualized study of "translators in their authentic, personal, historically embedded environments and translation situations" (ibid: 335). This is also what Chesterman (2009), analyzing Toury (2012), calls the interdependence of the complementary "cognitive translation act" and the "social translation event", where the cognitive act is embedded in the event. In this case, Chesterman would be advocating or supporting the notion of decontextualized cognition, while recent 4EA cognition approaches do not support this distinction (Muñoz 2015)

Risku's proposal calls for a move from the "purely mental" to a sociocognitive approach, and this requires a parallel between the underlying situated and extended cognitive focus and popular sociological theories in TS such as Action-Network theory (see also 8.1.2). In Action-Network theory, social processes can only be understood through careful observation of the interactions between the "actants", a collective label that includes both human actors and non-human artefacts used by the former. "Artefacts" can be defined as the material and immaterial objects formed and used by humans in cognition (Clark 1997), such as reminders, calendars, organizing apps in a smartphone or translation management systems used by companies. It therefore argues for the observation of artefacts used during translation tasks, such as information and media infrastructures, architecture and the spatial and geographic context, the biological and ecological environment, as well as the social spaces and the areas of interaction (see, for example, Ehrengsberger-Dow and Massey 2014). In order to account for the technological environment in which translation occurs, the "extended translation" proposal also incorporates Activity Theory (Leontiev 1978), a framework that developed from psychology in order to study and develop systems of computer-supported cooperative work. Activity theory sees human action as situated, object-oriented and tool-mediated.

Research carried out by Risku and collaborators has focused on ethnographic observation of the real workspace of freelance translators (Risku 2013), as well as translation management in a language vendor (Risku, Rogl and Pein-Weber 2016). The data collected in these studies follows the adapted model of translatorial cognition and action (Risku, Windhager and Apfelthaler 2013) that introduces the following six key aspects: cognition, action, social network, artefacts, environment, and time. Cognition in this model takes into account the

> self-organizing processes of interconnected sensorimotor sub-networks of the cognitive system [...] and includes all operations that work on internal and external representations with the aim of creating translations, building, for instance, on memorized knowledge (of languages, translation, business, communication and cooperation methods) and including all manner of associations, knowledge and expectations.   (Risku 2014: 340)

The second element is the "action", and it refers to all translation activities that "involve task-oriented operations", as well as actions as "behavioral, observable action patterns" (ibid). The "social network" comprises the totality of actors together with their roles both in informal and formal networks, as well as all the "relational ties" that refer to coordination of responsibilities in the global task and workflow patterns. "Artefacts" comprise "the material and immaterial objects used as tools", including software services, hardware, texts, calendar or mental and physical lists. The next one, the "translation environments" comprise:

> the source, target, client, and translator activity systems, as perceived and operative from the point of view of the translators or other actors involved in the translation process. They form the ecological, physical, geographic, economic, political, demographic and social boundary conditions of action.
>
> (Risku 2014: 340)

Lastly, the "time" in Risku's model refers to the temporal changes and the succession of developments in all the previous items, and it also includes their relations and the overall situation. In this sense, this last component cannot be perceived as an independent aspect, but rather it is indicated that it "is discussed as the temporal-historical dimension of the other five aspects" (ibid)

The results of the studies identify the rich network of interactions that occur in the translation process from beginning to end. Figure 4.1 shows the complex network of interactions that occurs in an online amateur translation network with more than 250.000 registered members (Risku, Rogl and Pein-Weber 2016). The researchers indicate that given the complexity of the network this figure represents merely a "schematic representation of the relationships analyzed" (ibid: 10) in the paper.

Similarly, previous studies by Risku (2014) have analyzed the networks in the case of freelance translators. Figure 4.2 shows this representation that resemble the classic principle agent/dyad and not a multinode network. The researcher points out that, even when this seems like the smallest translatorial minimal unit (Abdallah 2010), a complex network of interactions was identified on the client side. The study also focused on the interaction with the translator's space, the observation of the immediate physical context in which the translation was carried out, such as the computer, desk, notepads, etc., as well as the recurring actions that occurred during the observation of real translation behavior. This aspect is related also to the ergonomics of translation and has been the focus of recent projects in the real workspace (Ehrengsberger-Dow and Massey 2014). According to the results of the study, Risku argues that the object of research, the translation process, is widened: it starts with the decision to translate a document, and ends when the transaction is closed and paid and the translation is available

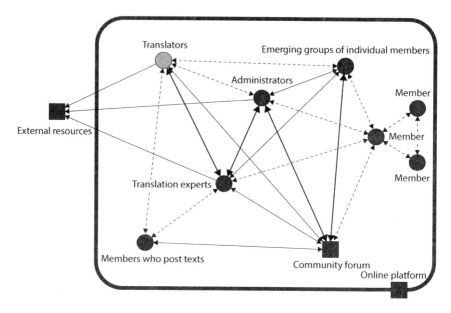

Figure 4.1 Schematic representation of an online amateur complete network (Risku, Rogl and Pein-Weber 2016: 10).

in the target settings. Additionally, taking the situated and extended cognition approach widens the cognitive object of research from some individual, isolated mental operations and systems to socio cognitive issues, including the social and artefact-mediated process that is an essential part of human cognition. The extension, nevertheless, focuses these studies on the macro context, meaning that these studies have focused on the networks and the macrocontext. It does not, however, focus from a process perspective on the micro level, that is, how the overall set of interactions between translators and artefacts or between translators and other agents shape actual decisions and problem solving activities in the translator. The observations carried out in the context of this research are one translated text or a set of texts translated by one translator and, therefore, refer to the broader type of translation collaboration in O'Brien's proposal (2011a) (see 1.3).

A study of crowdsourcing from this perspective could also take into account at the same time the social interactions as well as how cooperation occurs at the microlevel, that is, in each segment or identified problem. In this sense, this extended sociocognitive agenda could be widened to account for distributed problem-solving of actual translation problems and other aspects of "text induced text production" (Neubert and Shreve 1992: 25) in order to, as indicated by Neubert and Shreve (1992), not only focus on problem solving as the earlier cognitivists

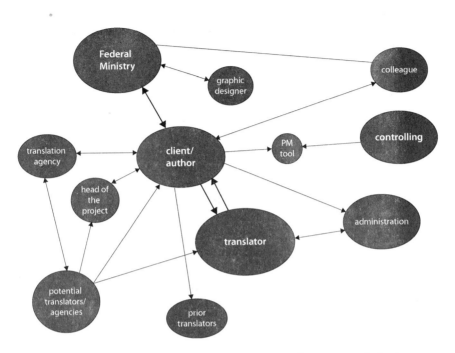

Figure 4.2 Network complexity in the study of a client/author process of a freelance translator (Risku 2014: 344).

mainly did. Following Hutchins (1995a) and Martín de Leon (2008), Risku and Windhager (2013) claim they have studied "cognition in the wild", translation as it happens in real situations in professional settings. Their agenda to study "translation in the wild" resonates in crowdsourcing approaches. This is not only due to the dichotomy of controlled experimental vs. real professional practices. It also resonates in the relative unpredictable, free and uncontrolled way in which translation processes are carried out, or planned to be carried out, in volunteer initiatives. Crowdsourcing processes should be studies in the "wild", immersed in the translation community, both because of the possibility of studying them outside controlled experimental conditions and in real context, and also due to the freedom to proceed outside the professional norms and constraints that translation as a business or economic activity entail. Does the different approach and freedom experienced by participants imply significant changes in their cognitive styles? In their performance? These aspects could also be seen in how the professional world of translation and the research community perceives this set of phenomena.

Translation in traditional and earlier cognitivist paradigms was understood as being focused on decision-making and problem solving procedures (i.e., Wilss

1994). The centrality of problem-solving from a micro-crowdsourcing approach is also often included in definitions across disciplines and fields (Estellés-Arola et al. 2015). In more current views, it is understood to incorporate "a subset of complex behaviours aiming to solve communicative needs, whose common thread is the use of at least two (spoken, written or signaled) languages" (Muñoz 2014b: 3). Crowdsourcing is at the same time often conceptualized as a means to achieve problem-solving; however, it is not the product of an independent mental module nor the result of applying (a combination of) mental algorithms, but rather the result of emerging processes of collective intelligence (Brabham 2013). The opening up of the individual cognitive problem resolution in translation beyond the mind of a single translation to the collective distribution of cognitive tasks in crowdsourcing was pointed out early on by Pym (2011b: 6), who discusses the benefits of this approach. He points out that the cognitive problem solving activities carried out "in the cognitive space of the individual translator", have been socialized and interspersed by discussions between users and the "machinery of democratic decisions". In other words, this entails a change from the high productivity approach embraced by the industry when adopting translation technologies to a "high sociability" approach. In the latter, speed and efficiency are not the main goal, but rather human involvement. Facebook exemplifies this opening up of translation problems to the collective. For example, at the same time that translations can be offered for one segment, participants also have the opportunity to mark any segment for problems inherent to the translation into the target language, such as marking a segment for variation for gender or number when variables are present. Thus, not only translations are offered but certain problems are marked or flagged by members, providing feedback at the same time to Facebook about how to tackle internationalization.

Plassard (2007) too has pointed out the impact of social distribution of problems through the Internet and shows that translation distribution lists have changed individual approaches to translation problem solving. Since the emergence of collaborative forums, problems in translation can now be solved collaboratively through the web by an unlimited number of participants. Forums such as Proz.com, in which individuals or translators can pose translation problems and ask for solutions from members of the forum, represent a clear example of this approach. Many crowdsourcing initiatives include discussion forums in order to serve as a discussion platform on the translations and engage the community. Nevertheless, it would be of interest to identify whether participating non-professionals do in fact identify problems differently from professionals and whether the volunteer status of participants also draws the attention to specific distinct issues or problems that are raised for discussion within the community. Since one of the hypotheses is also that non-professionals tend to identify fewer problems than professionals in individualistic experimental studies (Krings 1988; Jääskeläinen 1989), it would be of interest to know whether community participation and the distribution of the cognitive task of problem identification does result in fact in unprofessional communities identifying a similar number and spectrum of problems and potential solutions as single professional translators. Does the distribution of tasks result in fact in the identification of certain problem types that only professionals identify according to TS literature, such as issues related to linguistic levels beyond the lexical and syntactic ones, such as macrostructural, pragmatic, discursive or register issues?

4.3 But what is an expert anyhow? Insights from Cognitive Translatology

Debates on crowdsourcing and online collaborative practices often display a dichotomy either between the professional vs. non-professional approaches or between their business vs. free and altruistic nature. Narratives are often framed around the threats to the profession of translation from untrained participants who cannot possibly produce decent translational quality in their efforts, since only "professionals" with certain skills can be trusted to lead to successful translation results. The nature of "professionalism" appears at the center of these narratives that have attempted to defend the status of translators for decades in the public sphere. This notion is often meant to represent anyone who makes a living out of translation, whatever his or her background and education. In research literature, "professionalism" appears as a somewhat controversial topic; it has been associated with the capacity to produce acceptable target texts, and also with "translator professionalism", the ability of an individual to be accepted and attain professional status in any given community (Kiraly 2000).[3]

CT has, from its early days, attempted to uncover the differences in cognitive processing of translation between bilinguals, trainees (often called novices) and professionals, with a focus on uncovering the cognitive traits that distinguish each subgroup. Experimental studies initially focused on bilinguals that interpreted, and soon the interest also moved to translation novices and professionals. The goal of early studies was to uncover precisely what separated "natural translation" (Harris and Sherwood 1978), the innate capacity of all bilinguals to translate, from that of "professional translation". The drive behind this research

---

3. Scholars such as Tirkkonen-Condit (1996) use the term "professionalism" to refer loosely to the notions of "expertise" and "competence" in other studies.

agenda was motivated not only by the need to incorporate the existing interest of psycholinguistics in the study of translation and interpreting, but also because researchers (who were mostly university-level trainers) were interested in discovering the range of skills that trainees needed to acquire in university programs. The wide range of skills or competencies possessed by professional translators and not by bilinguals thus became one of the foci of research, framed in terms of "translation competence" and its acquisition (i.e., PACTE 2003, 2005; Göpferich 2009).[4] In the earlier studies, issues such as problem-solving and decision-making were the main focus, and depending on the design of the study, comparisons were made between bilinguals, novices, advanced students and professionals (see 4.3.1). Debates on the nature of "professionalism" or "professional performance" quickly emerged, since the strict experimental nature of these studies required limiting the number of variables and carefully defining what a "professional" was. In some early cases, professionals were advanced students (i.e., Krings 1995; Kiraly 1995); in others, and following principles from cognitive studies, only subjects with a minimum of 10 years of experience were considered (Göpferich 2009). The wide range of variation between so-called "professionals" in terms of background and translation performance soon lead to the introduction of another key research construct from cognitive psychology, that of "expertise". This notion subsumes the potential range of "cognitive, motivational and personal traits, habits and dispositions that will yield sustained outstanding performance" (Muñoz 2014a: 55). In these studies, the definition of "expertise" from Ericson and Charness (1994: 731) was often used: expertise means "consistently superior performance on a specific set of representative tasks for the domain." Following this approach, "translation expertise" was subsequently defined as:

> The capabilities which underlie the performance of human expert translators, including extensive domain knowledge but crucially also heuristic rules that simplify and improve approaches of problem solving, metaknowledge and metacognition, and compiled forms of behavior which afford great economy in skilled performance.
> (Muñoz 2009: 25)

One of the main caveats that separate "expertise" from natural translation is that the former can only develop through extensive, structured "deliberate practice" (Shreve 2006a). This deliberate practice results from "regular engagement in specific activities directed at performance enhancement in a particular domain" (ibid: 29), provided this practice has appropriate difficulty and informative feedback. "Deliberate practice" with a specific structure would be the main component

---

4.   Muñoz (2014) has pointed out that scholars often use the notions of "competence" and "expertise" indistinctively, but that they actually depart from and entail very different views.

of translation training programs if expertise were to be developed.[5] As Muñoz (2014b) points out, following Ericsson, Krample and Tesch-Römer (1993), this deliberate practice is the result of (1) general mechanisms for learning and adjusting behavior to task demands, (2) the individual commitment to improve his/her performance and (3) well designed training.

The focus on expertise allowed the discipline to differentiate between two related, but dissimilar populations. First of all, "translation professionals" would be those making a living out of translation, while "translation experts" would be those with consistent superior performance. Separating "translation professionals" from "translation experts" was necessary in the CT since early on it was identified that not all professionals could be considered "experts" (Jääskeläinen 2010). In fact, in some studies translation students performed better at translation tasks than professionals, or they did not perform as well as expected (Jääskeläinen 1999; Göpferich 2009). Explanations for this phenomenon started to emerge. Scholars started to borrow a range of research constructs from cognitive psychology and cognitive science in order to explain these contradictory findings. Rather than entertaining a notion of competence across-the-board, the cognitive notion of expertise could be domain specific; Jääskeläinen (2010) introduced Hatano and Inagaki's (1986) constructs of "routine" and "adaptive experts" in order to account for this phenomenon. This means that translation professionals could sometimes not achieve peak performance in non-routine tasks, such as having a professional translate a piece of news if his/her main job is to translate patents. Translation expertise was therefore considered to some extent to be domain specific. Another separation of expertise levels was introduced by Jääskeläinen using Bereiter and Scardamalia's (1993: 11) distinction between "experts" and "experienced non-experts". The latter would refer to those practitioners of a task whose task performance is not consistently of high quality. In this light, she coins the notion of "experienced professional" to refer to those practitioners who do not consistently excel at translation tasks.

Translation is a highly specialized task in different domains (Gouadec 2007), and this implies an additional difficulty in outlining what translation expertise entails. Scholars have pointed out the impact of domain knowledge and text types in experimental studies into "expertise" (2009: 25). Personal traits and different life experiences make it difficult to study expertise using specific domains and genres, and therefore, expertise should be studied in a non-domain specific way in order to make generalizations possible (ibid). Jääskeläinen (2012: 217) introduced the notions of "absolute experts" and "relative experts" from Chi (2006: 21–23). "Relative

---

5.   Recent studies in interpreting have tackled the issue of how simultaneous interpreters have achieved "expertise" status without "deliberate practice" (Tiselius 2013).

expertise" refers to a stage that novices can achieve with dedicated training. It implies that most people can become professionals with adequate training, as is the case with translation and interpreting nowadays. "Absolute expertise" would be the domain of a very few subjects in a similar way that only very few can become a top world tennis player. "Relative expertise" would therefore be closer to the notion of a professional in the discipline, whereas very few professionals can be considered as "absolute experts" in any given task. This adds an interesting dimension to the professional vs. non-professional debate on collaborative practices online, since often it might be difficult to identify professionals with domain knowledge in new or rare domains, such as role-play videogames. It is no wonder that initially, collaborative and fan translations were preferred by users under the argument that only fans would be experts in these "domains" and "genres". According to O'Hagan (2009), this intimate knowledge of the genres would compensate for the relative lack of general translation experience.

It should also be mentioned that "expertise", rather than "professionalism" is a dynamic construct and it is not something that is possessed or not indefinitely, since it is "in constant change through the lifespan of a translator" (Muñoz 2009). In this sense, certification exams, entry exams or university degrees might lead to an initial professional status in a permanent and static fashion, but expertise requires a constant dedication and practicing at the "growing edge" (Bereiter and Scardamalia's 1993). This means that expertise develops and is maintained when working at the edge of the competence level, rather than repeating automatic well-known tasks over and over throughout the life of a professional. The metaphor of expertise in tennis playing can also be illuminating in this case, since expert performance is not something that always improves in an upward movement. Expertise then is the result of efficient adaptation to specific working conditions, and these conditions can always change (ibid). As an example, nowadays expertise in professional settings could not be understood without the efficiency and speed that translation technology tools can provide. Any "expert" in the tasks would only be considered as such by the professional community if they successfully integrate the technology tools effectively within their translation processes.

Some models of translation expertise, such as Muñoz's (2014a) situated translation expertise, do not distinguish between professional and non-professional processes and behaviors. On the contrary, Muñoz proposes a model of expertise that aims to apply to all translational phenomena, including the types of volunteer translation. He argues that differences between these two types of translations are due to the "social understandings and norms of translation tasks and behaviors in different communities" (2014a: 35), so that the possibility of possessing "expertise" in non-professional settings is acknowledged. It is also indicated that "mental processing might be dissimilar in different translation tasks", and this could explain the findings by Jiménez-Crespo (2015b) when subjects were instructed to both translate the segments from a UI from a social networking site by direct translation or by selecting from a range of already existing translations. Translations that were produced by selecting among range of conventionalized forms previously found to fulfill the similar communicative purpose were significantly different and more explicit than those translations that were produced directly, that is, through a direct translation of a source text segment into a target text. Volunteer and crowdsourcing approaches have also been signaled as a new development that highlights the pertinence of research on "translation expertise", since "this research agenda has become even more important in recent years with the increase in crowd-sourcing and volunteer translation" (O'Brien 2015:8). Research, such as the above mentioned paper by Jimenez-Crespo focused on the differences between translation and selection or voting of candidates in social networking sites initiatives, is needed; professional translation is also moving to some extent towards the "paid crowdsourcing" paradigm. Consequently, processing models found solely in crowdsourcing approaches are now making their way into professional settings and raise new questions that deserve careful consideration.

4.3.1 Expertise in translation and non-professionals: Findings

Crowdsourcing, a paradigm that depends on the "wisdom of the crowd" (Surowiecki 2004) has attempted, for example, to produce "professional quality from non-professionals" (Zaidan and Calliston-Burch 2011). It has also attempted to produce "high quality translations through MT and crowdsourcing using only monolinguals (Hu et al. 2011). Models and workflows have attempted to subdivide the "professional" task into subcomponents and assign it to different collectives, effectively distributing the complex cognitive task typical of seasoned experts. Nevertheless, these models tend to be developed without using the body of knowledge of TS as a whole, and more importantly, without relying on the body of knowledge of Cognitive Translation Studies. How are these models supposed to produce outputs similar to professionals if they do not depart from clear definitions and models of the complex set of tasks and processes in which a professional excels? From a process-based perspective, empirical studies from the 80's–90's have identified the differences between experts, professionals, novices and bilinguals in terms of how they process translations. These finding could be helpful when delving into how workflows and models of crowdsourcing and collaborative translation could be improved or developed. The decomposition of the tasks for micro task crowdsourcing could be better developed from a micro and macro processing perspective in order to identify blind spots and synergies that could improve the process. It could also help develop differentiated crowdsourcing models for participants with different skill levels, from bilinguals to professional translators or bilingual domain experts.

The following summary of results can help shed light on precisely how the notion of professionals can be defined based on how they carry out translation tasks differently from non-professionals. This summary draws from previous reviews found in Göpferich and Jääskeläinen (2009), Pym and Windle (2011), Jääskeläinen (2012) and Muñoz (2014a) among others. For the sake of this review, the term "bilinguals" includes all types of initial translation students, often called "novices" and "early and late" bilinguals, while "professional" includes a wide range of participants labeled as such in experimental studies, from advanced MA students to translators with 10 years or more of practice. Also, the translation process is subdivided according to Jakobsen (2003) in three different stages: (1) planning, (2) drafting and (3) postdrafting. This does not mean that the translation process proceeds in a linear fashion, but it is rather a recursive and reiterative process in which some of these stages are dominant throughout different moments in the process. As a summary, professionals have been found to possess these specific processing characteristics. In general, professionals

1. Proceeded in a more strategic and efficient manner than the novices (Göpferich 2009)
2. Have a heightened awareness of translation problems and find more problems in translations than novices (Krings 1988). They also can find more solutions to problems (Jääskeläinen 1999)
3. Process larger translation units (Krings 1988; Jääskeläinen 1999)
4. Take into consideration to a higher degree the co-text and context (Krings 1988)
5. Show an increasing ability to process more complex translation problems rather than just lexical equivalence searches (Jääskeläinen 1999)
6. Spend longer time reviewing their work at the post-drafting phase (Lachat 2003) but making fewer changes when reviewing.
7. Automatize some complex tasks but also shift between automatized routine tasks and conscious ones. They possess a more automatic processing of translation problems, but the additional processing capacity is used to process more complex aspects of translation (Jääskeläinen and Tirkkonen-Condit 1991). This is related to what is called the "translation does not get easier" phenomenon (Gerloff 1988; Siken and Hakkarainen 2002)
8. Use more top-down processing (macro-strategies), moving constantly between the micro and the macro level and referring more to the translation purpose. This is essential in segment-based processing models such as crowdsourcing, where relating each segment to the macrocontext is essential (Jiménez-Crespo 2013a).

9. Use more periphrasis and less literal calquing strategies
10. Rely more on encyclopedic and world knowledge
11. Display more realism, confidence and critical attitudes in decision-making
12. Read the text differently than monolingual readers based on the task that they are going to perform later (Castro 2007)
13. Use translation resources differently (Gómez 2006). For example, bilinguals use more bilingual dictionaries for comprehension problems while more advanced translators use more monolingual ones (Jääskeläinen 1989). Professionals also use a wider range of resources and are more discerning about their use for specific problem types (Massey and Ehrengsberger-Dow 2011)
14. Express more principles and personal theories, an essential aspect in order to justify certain decision and strategies to team, group or other participants in the overall process such as clients, managers or translators. Professionals show a more dynamic approach to the understanding of translation beyond the simple linguistic equivalence approach (PACTE 2008, 2014)
15. Possess or develop the ability to produce the same quality regardless of the length of the deadlines (Jensen 1999; De Rooze 2003). A component of translation that novices need to develop is the ability to adapt their cognitive resources and mechanisms to maintain the quality of their output under time pressure. De Rooze (2003) found that the quality of translation in students decreased by 15% when the time available for the translation of a 250-word text was reduced from 15 to 10 minutes. Surprisingly, some students produced better quality translations under stricter time deadlines. This study also found that experts did not show any differential effects on quality under both experimental conditions. In comparing the effect of time pressure in translation and interpreting, translators may take 10 to 11 times longer to produce translations with similar quality to those produced by simultaneous interpreters (Hönig 1998; Gorm-Hansen and Dragstead 2007)
16. Base their decisions less on issues of fidelity, or on picking up variants blindly from dictionaries such as novices do
17. Spend more time in orientation and final revision, with superior speed potential (Jakobsen 2005). It is of interest that the most demanding difficulty for professionals is not the drafting of the target text but the continuous monitoring and editing of the TT output
18. Have stronger monitoring skills during the task
19. Possess differences in their metacognition (Göpferich 2008: 1), the ability to reflect on one's own mental processes
20. Better adapt their approach in response to the challenges presented by a particular text (Ehrengsberger-Dow and Massey 2013)

21. Use the mouse more ergonomically and they switch less from keyboard to mouse in their tasks than novices while producing more target text; that is, they have a more "purposeful automatized keyboarding and employments of computer peripherals" (Ehrengsberger-Dow and Massey 2014: 13) and this leaves more free cognitive resources to produce target text
22. Develop a concept self-concept to teamwork (Risku 1998)
23. Show unique traits in their mental representation of the languages they work with (Lacruz 2014)

These differences in cognitive processing found in empirical studies between professionals and non-professionals cannot be only considered to be positive or advantageous to the efficiency of the process. In some cases, some traits have been considered detrimental to translation tasks, such as "routinization". This effect is detrimental effect because it constrains decision making, reflective problem solving and the identification of creative solutions (Christensen 2011). This routinization effect has also been shown when professionals use TM tools. For example, Dragstead (2008) found that some expertise traits in translation, such as processing larger units or the ability to switch between the macro and the micro levels in processing the translation task, such as incorporating in the decisions the translation brief, the end-user, etc., could be detrimental when using TM. To some extent, without a sound adaptation of cognitive strategies to handle TM tools from a macroperspective, the segment-based processing might to some extent complicate experts' tasks if compared with bilinguals. This could be related to some extent to specific cases in general crowdsourcing in which solutions to problems are sought among non-experts in the field in question. For example, in Innocentive, a type of "knowledge discovery and management" according to Brabham's typology (2013), a prize is awarded to the member of the crowd that finds the best solution to a scientific problem. Often, specialists from a different area provide more creative solutions since scientists in the same field are constrained by their models and routinizations, unable to think to some extent "outside the box".

The significance of these findings for crowdsourcing research lies in that, since some traits of professional performance are identified, decomposing the tasks in micro-task crowdsourcing and distributing them to a crowd can be analyzed in terms of which aspects can and cannot be collectively carried out by bilinguals, which components might be left to experts, or which tasks might not be able to be produced by a single bilingual but achievable through crowd participation. Aspects that cannot be replicated through the distribution of text-processing and drafting among the bilingual crowd can be taken up by experts or by workflow and management mechanisms. As an example, Translate Facebook benefits from two basic traits of translation problem-solving, namely the generation of candidates and the selection among possibilities. The crowd through the translate-and-vote approach can collectively suggest and select the best translation candidate in each case, but this sentence base process suffers from the relative inability of participants to switch between the macro and the micro levels, relating the segment to the overall macrostructure of the website. In this case, workflow design works both at the pre translation and at the post translation stages to overcome the gap. The pre-translation stage involves preparing a style guide, a glossary, introducing a term-match functionality in the application, designing a translation problem feedback loop, etc. In the post stage, when a rendition is selected after the generative and selective stages, language coordinators guarantee the macrostructural coherence and cohesion, as well as the overall style. Another example can be found in that professionals have a heightened awareness of problems and they identify a wider range of solutions to any specific problem. In the translation stage, the combination of translation proposals and the voting stages precisely fills the gap since the identification of the problems, the generation of solution proposals and the selection is ultimately done in a distributed model, expanding beyond the limitations of a single non-professional cognitive system. In another case, the fact that non-professionals, for example, display less confidence and critical attitudes towards decision-making becomes then to some extent irrelevant, since it is ultimately the crowd who collectively makes selection decisions.

4.4   Other significant issues in CT: Cognition, technology and emotions

From a wider perspective, expertise and extended and distributed cognition are by no means the only issues of interest to analyze and conceptualize online collaborative practices. Probably the most significant area of research could be what Hurtado Albir et al. (2015) considered as the fourth stage in the development of CT, the interface of cognition and technology. Translation cannot be understood nowadays without the increasing interaction between humans and machines in the translation industry, a revolution that is changing the cognitive and ergonomic environment of translation tasks (O'Brien 2012b). This stage draws from research on distinct areas such as computational linguistics, studies on human-computer interaction and speech recognition. In this area, studies that analyze the intersection of human cognition with translation technologies such as translation memory systems are of interest (i.e., Dragstead 2006; O'Brien 2006, 2008; Colominas 2008; Mellinger 2014), since crowdsourcing and non-solicited collaborative translation cannot be understood without the technology platforms that mediate them. Empirical studies have identified that the use of TM can impact translators' mental processes (Christensen 2011). Similarly, the increasing intersection of crowdsourcing and MT crowd post-editing make relevant to some extent those studies that focus on cognitive effort during post-editing MT output (O'Brien 2007, 2011b; Mitchell, Roturier and O'Brien 2013; Mitchel 2015; Elming, Winther and Carl 2014) or how cognitive processes are impacted by post-editing tasks. Crowdsourcing for the improvement of MT systems, such as Google Translate or Bing, attests to the significance of these trends. Nevertheless, they also raise questions related to how professional and volunteer post-editing might differ not only due to the lack of training or skills, but also to how cognitive effort might impact the motivation of volunteers to translate, since the task can be abandoned whenever the participants deem it appropriate.

The role of emotions and motivation in the translation process are interesting too. Since motivation is one of the key elements of crowdsourcing translation (Olohan 2014), the impact of motivation and emotions in the process could lead to a better understanding of how better quality could be achieved. For example, CT studies have found that personal involvement in the translation might lead to higher translation quality, while a detached attitude might have an adverse effect on quality (Laukanen 1997; Rojo López 2014; Rojo López and Ramos 2015). In principle, the non-business nature of collaborative practices would demand a motivated attitude towards the project, and stronger commitments to any such initiative might improve the process and, subsequently, the product.

The type of feedback that volunteers receive is also a key issue discussed in industry literature. CT studies have identified the role of emotions in the translation process. In the study with novices by Rojo López and Ramos (2014), participants that were given negative feedback on an assignment performed worse in a subsequent translation than those that received highly positive feedback, and this finding was also replicated when the subjects of the experiment were professionals (2015). This issue brings to the surface not only the potential effect on motivation to engage in further translation, but the impact on the translation process and the quality of the output.

4.5   Reflections on new methodologies: Internet-mediated methods and collaborative translation protocols

As far as research methods are concerned, the development of Internet-mediated methods to research technology-mediated cognitive processes could be significant in this area (Dombek 2013; Mellinger 2015). Traditional laboratory experimentation requires the presence of participants in the same physical spot, constraining the potential recruitment of participants for studies. According to Mellinger

(2015:59), "[i]nternet-mediated research is a potential solution to this issue, it expands the size of participant pools and eliminates the need for participant travel". Since the foundations of online collaborative practices lie precisely on the global interconnectivity provided by the web in which participants can potentially be anywhere in the world, advances in Internet-based methods can only but benefit any research carried out in this area (i.e., Dombek 2013).

An extension of Think Aloud techniques (TAPs) — the methodology of concurrently verbalizing the subject's thoughts in groups or alone during translation tasks — namely "collaborative translation protocols", is worth mentioning (Pavlović 2007, 2013). Think aloud or concurrent verbalization represents a method of data elicitation that was borrowed from cognitive psychology (Ericsson and Simon 1984/1993) and that initially was applied by scholars such as Krings (1986), Lörcher (1991). Many criticisms were brought against this method since only conscious, and not automatized, processes are verbalized, and it represents an artificial situation and it can slow down the task (Krings 1995). Joint protocols were introduced in the discipline in experiments to translate in pairs (House 1988; Kussmaul 1995; Séguinot 1996) or in groups (Hönig 1990). Collaborative translation protocols are important, not because of the methodological innovation, but rather thanks to the discussions around it, regarding how collaboratively carrying out a translation and discussing it in pair or groups brings to the surface in a more natural way data that might help infer conjured cognitive processes. "Joint translation protocols" or "dialog protocols" appeared as a reaction to the deficiencies identified in TAPs that marked the early stages of development of translation process studies (Jääskeläinen 2012). In her study on directionality of translation, Pavlović reintroduced what she referred to as "collaborative translation protocols" to study collaborative translations, defined as tasks in which a pair or group of people translate the same source text together, basing their decisions on mutual consensus (2013: 552). This method can elicit process data that is different from regular TAPS, and considers that they cannot be called TAPs as such. The reasoning behind this claim is that they include social interactions as well as thinking aloud while subjects verbalize their thoughts spontaneously. As such, they are less artificial and can elicit richer data, even when she claims that neither TAPs nor collaborative protocols represent the real stream of thoughts. The dialogic nature of the interaction means that "the verbalization of thoughts [are] more natural than thinking aloud one's own [thoughts]" (Jääskeläinen 2011: 126). Disadvantages of these type of protocols are that they might elicit thoughts that otherwise would not have been verbalized in regular TAPs working individually, and they include a large amount of rationalizations, that is, justifications of decisions. They also depend on the interpersonal relationships between the subjects in question (Kussmaul 1995:11). Even when the data obtained does not allow the observation of "real" mental processes, it can provide important data to back inferences and hypotheses on conjured mental processes. They can serve as point of departure for testable these hypotheses. Rather than contrast the validity of both methods, Pavlović argues that it is best to see them are more or less suitable to study certain aspects of the process, and therefore, the research methodology depends on the goals of the project (Pavlović 2009). This method is also of benefit since it highlights and brings to the surface how subjects envision their process and their potential (a-)theoreical models of translation that shape how they carry out the translation tasks themselves. Additionally, from a product-based perspective, a study from Pavlović (2013) found that collaborating towards producing a translation often results in higher quality than producing it individually.

Beyond the application as a research methodology, scholars have also pointed out the benefits of using these protocols in translation education (Göpferich and Jääskeläinen 2010). Thus, despite the fact that collaborative protocols were introduced in the discipline as a methodological innovation (Séguinot 1996), this change of focus from research method to training tool implies that joint discussions while collaborating in the production of a translation by groups or pairs can be of interest for the analysis of crowdsourcing because they foster metalinguistic and metacognitive awareness. Certain collaborative processes by volunteers seem to underlie the principles of collaborative translation protocols, even if discussions are done asynchronously through discussion boards, voting of proposals, commenting of translations or commented translation revisions. The extension of individual cognition to a shared cognitive space is acknowledged by Pavlović (2013: 552), who claims that "the understanding of the source text meaning and the creation of the target text occur after individual cognitive processing and the interaction among the members of the group". Even when this process might be mainly asynchronous in web mediated spaces, some collaborative practices such as the volunteer translation of modern Buddhist texts is, according to Neather (2015), to some extent representative of a joint synchronous dialogic collaborative effort. This discussion resonates in recent research in distributed and extended cognition crowdsourcing mediated through ubiquitous mobile and computing devices (i.e. Whitaker, Chorley and Stuart 2015).

CHAPTER 5

Crowdsourcing
Challenges to translation quality

> Quality is definitely not under pressure. Translation is.
>
> (Muzii 2013: 12)

5.1   Introduction

Quality represents one of the most controversial issues in Translation Studies. While scholars often contend that a theoretical foundation is a prerequisite for assessment (House 1997, 2014), industry approaches have been moving towards a dynamic perspective in which all participants in the translation event, such as clients, managers, translators, user communities and targeted readers can jointly decide what can be a good enough level of a translation or its "fitness for purpose" (Drugan 2013; Göröj 2014a, 2014b). This evolution has been parallel to the expansion of raw and post-edited MT, crowdsourcing and collaborative translation, irrevocably shifting the paradigm from the search of absolute quality to a dynamic and realistic conceptualization that includes monetary, time and resource constraints (Wright 2006; Jiménez-Crespo 2013a).

   The exploration of quality in crowdsourcing and online collaborative translations is not an easy task. While top-down efforts in TS and the industry are guided by quality standards, QA models and norms, the collaborative scenarios are extremely open, creative and dynamic with a wide array of different approaches. According to Howe, crowdsourcing is an "umbrella term for a highly varied group of approaches that share one obvious attribute in common: they all the depend on some contribution from the crowd. But the nature of those contributions can differ tremendously" (Howe 2008: 280). The same can be said of translation quality; the nature of quality and the processes to evaluate it can be differently conceptualized across the board. In order to tackle this challenge, the focus of the chapter is both descriptive and analytical: it attempts to shed light on how crowdsourcing and volunteer approaches can help reconceptualize the notion of translation quality from a broad perspective. Thus, it describes current practices in crowdsourcing to ensure quality in these novel environments, as well as analyzes the impact of these novel practices on how society, the industry, translation professionals and scholars conceptualize this notion. It explores the synergies and attempts to bridge the gap between TS and the industry (i.e., Drugan 2013; Göröj 2014a). It also places current quality approaches in collaborative environments within the wider framework of translation theory and its applied translation criticism sub-branch (Jiménez-Crespo 2011), exploring the extent to which crowdsourcing approaches to quality can challenge or help expand theorizations and applied research in TS. The chapter ends with a review of the scarce number of empirical studies on quality of crowdsourced translations (Pérez and Carreira 2011; Jiménez-Crespo 2013b, 2016; Deriemaeker 2014).

5.2　Translation quality: A multifractal notion in constant evolution

The challenging nature of translation quality evaluation is widely recognized in TS, since "translation quality assessment has always been and still is a challenge for translation studies" (House 2013: 546). At the same time, industry experts claim that their view "on quality is highly fragmented, in part because different kinds of translation projects require very different evaluation methods" (Lommel et al. 2014: 455). Quality is thus continually the object of research because, no matter how fuzzy the notion of quality might be, the lack of consensus in either camp does not mean that quality evaluation is not implemented around the world. Right now, thousands of reviewers are editing human translations, volunteers are voting on their preferred rendition of a translated segment on Facebook or Twitter, professionals might be rating the translation for a segment in the crowdsourcing app Unbabel or grading an admission test for a crowdsourcing non-profit initiative, while others are post-editing the output of a free MT system.

All these real-world scenarios are guided by implicit notions of quality that frame practices and discourses. Invariably, quality evaluation tasks are "built up upon internalized frameworks of quality that guide subjects' decisions, even when they might lack operative theoretical foundations" (Jiménez-Crespo 2013a: 103). These internalized frameworks of what an ideal or adequate translation should look like diverge between different communities of practice, geographic locations, users' expectations or evaluation contexts. These models have been described as "anecdotal" or "experiential", based on the accumulated knowledge base (or lack thereof) of subjects, communities or organizations involved. Often, discourses revolve around notions such as "faithfulness to the source text", "equivalence", "lack of errors", "does not feel right", etc. They can be considered the prevailing ones among translation practitioners, non-professionals, philosophers or some industry experts (Angelelli and Jacobson 2009; Colina 2009). These real world models also vary according to how dynamic the notion of quality is understood to be, as well as the constraints that operate during the translation process (and review or evaluation). These economic, time or situational constraints not only limit efforts and resources assigned to evaluation, they also make top quality not always possible or, even desirable. Accepting these constraints has been crucial in the shift from perceiving quality as a relatively unachievable abstraction to a practical construct operationalized through a continuum of levels defined by situational criteria (i.e. O'Brien 2012a; Lommel et al. 2014). This shift has also been gaining traction in TS literature, with recent professional-oriented approaches, such as Gouadec (2007, 2010), O'Brien (2012a) Jiménez-Crespo (2013a: 127–131) or Drugan (2013), accepting and operationalizing different levels of quality.

Crowdsourcing and volunteer translations quickly made their way to the forefront of discussions on quality. Following the initial disruption caused by MT, these new translation production models started to challenge even further whether top quality is ideal for all situations, bringing to the equation other factors such as access to content or speed over quality. It quickly became clear, despite a constant stream of complaints by professionals, that the highly aspirational notion of "top quality" is an unachievable and imaginary myth. The main contention from scholarly and professional associations was the inability to produce "sufficient" quality if professionals were not involved (Kelly 2009), often pointing at the prevalent number of errors in non-professional translations (i.e., Bogucki 2009; Khalaf, Rashid, Jumingan and Othman 2014). Meanwhile, a segment of the industry quickly saw a potential to expand and develop a different business model that could capitalize on the wisdom of the crowd, leaving behind preconceived ideas about translation quality. New business models emerged, stretching the quality range offered to span from FOMT, volunteer crowdsourcing, volunteer post-editing of MT, paid crowdsourcing performed either by professionals and bilinguals, professional post-editing of MT all the way to high quality human translation. Quality then started to be conceptualized in a continuum, "with the enduring and critical at one extreme, and the ephemeral and inconsequential at the other" (García 2015: 340). Content prioritization became a reality in the industry (O'Brien 2012a): does the translation of an internal email or a tweet from a famous person always needs to be of high quality? The emergence of new highly dynamic approaches to quality evaluation witness to this evolution, with several proposed translation quality models, such as the TAUS Dynamic Framework (O'Brien 2012a; Göröj 2014a), and theoretical proposals such as Jiménez-Crespo (2013a:127–131). These proposals implicitly acknowledge the wide range of quality scenarios, including the potential to encompass non-professional translation and MT output. Dynamicity, adaptability and content prioritization thus have become the norm rather than the exception.

As a result, the 20th century has been marked by a move away from a static notion of quality, venturing beyond top-down models in which error typologies, quality control and quality management procedures are established a priori and applied across the board. In the other side of the spectrum, "bottom-up" approaches have been praised, "because they extend access. [...] Users drive supply, so there is less waste: material is only translated when needed" (Drugan 2013: 160). A new paradigm in TS emerges when quality appears disassociated from economic pressures and market imperatives, making it even become secondary to other considerations. Translations can often be driven by user demand, and in turn, these users can establish the "expectancy norms" (Toury 1995) (see Chapter 7) or the type of quality that might suit them depending on several factors, such as (1) their needs, (2) the speed at which the translation is needed (3) the relative permanence of the translation or (4) in long tail languages, even if a professional community of translators exists. Bottom-up approaches also bring to the surface that, in real life, the notion of quality is user and context-dependent. That is, the user and the relation between them and the situation of reception, among other factors, are ultimately what can help establish what an "appropriate" or "adequate" translation might be, or whether the translation is good enough for the purposes intended. In this context, dynamic models of quality become the norm.

5.3 Dynamicity in models of translation quality: Towards adaptable models of quality

While TS devoted in the past most of its efforts to establishing evaluation criteria perceiving quality as an absolute notion, industry and professional approaches identified that it was best to distinguish between different levels of quality depending on a range of factors or constraints. This means that current quality evaluation proposals embrace the dynamicity and highly constrained nature of evaluation. This dynamicity is present in the highly customizable evaluation metrics that have been recently proposed, such as the TAUS Dynamic Quality Framework (DQF) (O'Brien 2012a; Göröj 2014a), the Multidimensional Quality Metrics (MQM) framework developed by the EU-funded QTLaunchPad project (Lommel et al. 2014), two models that have recently harmonized their error metrics through another EU funded initiative, the QT21 project on human annotation of MT errors (Lommel et al. 2015). They embrace the diverse nature of quality and the potential different procedures for its evaluation. These metrics are also created with a broader perspective in mind, attempting to provide a platform to evaluate all types of translations in the industry, including MT output and non-professional ones. The reasons to include these two evaluation contexts are due to the fact that they are not an essential part of the mainstream language industry. Consequently, it is often necessary to compare and contrast these processes with the ones using professional translators. As García (2015: 31) indicates:

the translation industry has both room and need for a spectrum spanning professionals, semi-professionals, casual aficionados and even untrained volunteers. Quality is not always critical, and there is nothing inherently wrong with enterprises, institutions and NGOs using these approaches.

This does not mean at all that the industry is attempting to justify the provision of low quality levels. For example, the DQF model does not depart from the premise that models should be a justification for low quality, "but that a dynamic QE model would take into account the varying tolerance thresholds for quality that already exist in the professional sphere" (O'Brien 2012a: 68). It is also due to the fact that in certain situations, the industry has accepted that "it is best to provide some translations with available resources than none, even if quality is lower" (Drugan 2013: 180). This means that quality is de-facto already understood in the industry as a gradable scale depending on a range of factors, and it underlies the premise that the massive amount of content that needs to or could be translated is driven by user demand. In this respect Göröj (2014b: 389) from an industry perspective rightly indicated that:

> The only way to offer large amounts of information and goods in multiple languages fast while staying within reasonable budgets is by making a compromise and provide content with different levels of quality using new translation channels and translation technology.

This also means that different quality levels might not require an existing one-size-fits-all approach or depend on inadequate error-based quality approaches to evaluation (see Jiménez-Crespo 2013a: 116–120), but rather they "require new ways of evaluating the quality of translated content" (Göröj 2014b: 389). For example, in the overview of professional practices by O'Brien for TAUS (2012a), it was found that content was prioritized prior to the actual evaluation based on parameters such as utility, time and sentiment. Utility is related to the relative importance of the functionality of the translated content. Time obviously refers to how quickly the translation is needed and sentiment is related to the significance of the text for brand image etc. Other proposals such as MQM, incorporate several issues such as accuracy, fluency, design, locale convention, terminology, style, and verity, with an open customizable list of subtypes that includes 114 issue types (Lommel et al. 2014), with a core list of 19 basic ones. The models also open up the possibility of customizing the assessment through error-based or holistic evaluation procedures. Flexibility, thus, becomes the norm.

These dynamic and customizable evaluation frameworks can be seen as the industry response to the challenges posed by variable quality issues. However, the potential for endless customization in these new proposals also opens the door to issues of time and resource constraints. This was an issue with previous proposals with endless error types (Gouadec 1981, 1989) or complex contrastive procedures (i.e., House 1997, 2014; Williams 2003). In that regard, these new models can be understood as an effort to explain and facilitate customization, rather than complete new evaluation proposals. No matter how customizable a framework might be, customization models will probably tend to be replicated, and one or several customization types might eventually become the norm.

5.3.1   Quality tiers in MT: Towards a model for crowdsourcing and collaborative models

The introduction of the different levels of quality in TS and industry discourses can be traced back to the resurgence of MT in the 90's. The widespread adoption of MT started to cast a shadow when statistical architectures started to produce "acceptable" quality in certain areas and for certain purposes, such as customized engines in technical domains (Hutchins 2014). MT was thus a sort of Trojan horse that started to undermine the "top quality" mantra that pervaded academia for years.[1] Users and industry agents started to accept and use for certain purposes translation that could be mired with errors and inadequacies, but still, they fulfilled a precise purpose or need in a specific timeframe. No longer was quality, or better said, the absence of high quality, an impediment to translations circulating and fulfilling specific communicative purposes. The negative discourse surrounding MT raw output or "gist translation" in the discipline started to extend to non-professional translations. This type of translation was defined in professional circles as a rough translation "to get some essential information about what is in the text and for a user to define whether to translate it in full or not to serve some specific purposes" (Chan 2014: 42). Free Online Machine Translation systems (FOMT) has a relatively long history since it was first offered by CompuServe in collaboration with Systrans in 1994, and it has evolved and expanded with Google Translate translating over 100 billion words per day in its 90 language combinations (Google 2015).[2]

The emergence of post-editing to improve raw MT output led to the proposal of different quality tiers depending on the extent of human involvement (Allen 2003; Quah 2006; García 2009). The basic premise here is that evaluation is not an infinite, unlimited process, but rather it follows the "necessary and sufficient rule" (Wright 2006), assuming that a limited number of errors is unavoidable due to the

---

1. During these years, fan communities were also producing amateur translations that in a pre-Internet era did not have a wide impact on public and industry perceptions as FOMT did.

2. http://googletranslate.blogspot.in/2015/06/google-translate-keeps-getting-better.html

economic context in which this process is performed. Thus, MT approaches were also instrumental in operationalizing quality in terms of equilibrium between a wide range of constraints and the potential needs of users. For example, the Translation Automation Society (TAUS) (2010: 3–4) guidelines for post-editing MT introduce two quality levels: "good enough" and "publishable quality". The first one is defined as a translation that is comprehensible and accurate so that it conveys the meaning of the source text, but is not necessarily grammatically or stylistically perfect. Another approach based on how much post-editing is needed is found in Allen's (2003) study where different quality tiers of machine translation output emerge: "no post-editing", "minor post-editing intended for gisting purposes", and "full post-editing". The impact of MT post-editing approaches soon reached professional translation. Gouadec, for example, embraced a flexible paradigm and defended establishing degrees for different domains or situations upon which quality evaluation and quality judgments can be built. He proposed different quality tiers depending on how much a translation is "fit for delivery or broadcast" (Gouadec 2010: 273). The different customizable degrees of quality in his proposal were: "rough cut", "fit for delivery (but still requiring minor improvements or still not fit for broadcast medium)" and "fit for broadcast (accurate, efficient and ergonomic)" (ibid). In the light of the impact of post-editing MT in the industry, he also included also "fit for revision" grade to "describe translation that can be revised within a reasonable time at a reasonable cost" (ibid).

Other scholars such as Quah (2006: 154) resorted to MT approaches, identifying the need for quality levels depending on users' needs. She also established a cline based on whether machine translation or human translation would be needed (no post-editing is mentioned). The author placed highly creative and critical translation modalities as requiring full quality, and therefore, human-based translation, while translation for gisting purposes such as web articles is identified as a low priority process that can be achieved through machine translation. This cline was subsequently adopted by Jiménez-Crespo (2013: 110) who also added crowdsourcing to the potential levels of quality that could emerge in relation to the type of content.

Figure 5.1 adapts the traditional cline of MT quality and its relation to types of content or text, extending it to crowdsourcing and collaborative approaches. It is mainly based on industrial crowdsourcing initiatives and not in unsolicited self-organized environments. This does not mean that quality does not have different grades in fan or non-profit environments, but the distinctions are blurred in those cases. For example, crowdsourcing has been used in emergency situations that involve life or death scenarios, one of the top quality tiers in industry standards such as the SJAE J2450. In these humanitarian crises cases involving a high volume of texts, evaluation has been left to crowdsourcing since professional

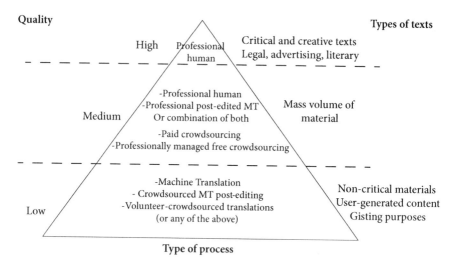

Figure 5.1 Translation quality cline in terms of human to MT including crowdsourcing. Adapted from Jiménez-Crespo (2013:2011) and Quah (2006:154).

environments could not possibly accommodate the volume and speed at which these translations are needed (Meier and Munro 2010).

The proposed categorization includes a high, medium and low grades of quality and associates them with different types of content that might in principle require distinctive processes. Crowdsourcing is placed in both the medium and the low quality spectrum of the triangle, and the different approaches are incorporated, from general crowdsourcing and MT post-editing by volunteers all the way to paid crowdsourcing in the middle of the spectrum. The medium grade also includes "professionally managed crowdsourcing", such as social networking sites, since they do produce highly usable translations in their processes (Jiménez-Crespo 2013b). The incorporation of "paid crowdsourcing" in the cline reflects current industry practices and business models (García 2015), and it also suggests that some contexts require professional translation. For example, paid crowdsourcing portals such as Gengo exclude highly critical, legal or marketing materials from their services. This business model also includes a wide range of potential quality with companies offering services from translation produced in collaboration, such as Translation Cloud, all the way to professionals and specialized experts working in crowdsourcing-inspired hive environments such as the specialized services by OneHourTranslation or Speaklike. The wide range of quality tiers and price ranges offered by paid crowdsourcing portals thus requires a closer analysis.

5.3.2 Paid crowdsourcing and the customization of translation quality

The different quality tiers offered by paid crowdsourcing portals depend on several parameters, such as the type of content, the type of crowd (professional or non-professional / generalist or specialist), or the type of process, such as translation by the crowd plus professional editing, translation by a crowd of specialists plus editing, open or closed community involvement, etc. Quality tiers that are often described in relation to "best suited" content types, rather than referring to any internal or external quality of the translation itself. This appears as a common practice in recent quality evaluation proposals (O'Brien 2012a).

Online companies such as Gengo.com and Speaklike both offer three tiers of paid crowdsourcing translation services that are not explicitly attached to quality levels, but rather to the type of content that they can handle. For example, Gengo offers "standard", "business" and "ultra" services, while Speaklike offers "basic", "marketing" and "specialized" levels. In the case of Gengo, the "standard" level is recommended for everyday content, "business" for professional content and "ultra" for business levels, such as static content, marketing etc. Gengo also implicitly includes two other levels that are not provided by the company, MT and "specialist". MT is displayed as having a 0 in terms of quality while the company does not provide "specialist translation", defined as texts related to legal, medical or safety critical content. They also do not provide creative texts or those related to image branding. Speaklike does offer specialized translations as part of the third quality tier, and they are related to medical, legal or transcription services. This service is provided by a different "specialized crowd" that is established by creating "specialized enterprise groups" with pre-selected specialized translators with domain-specific experience or qualifications. Thus, the levels of quality are interrelated with different levels of specialization by the participating translators, even when in principle Gengo has a team of "over 15000 pre-tested translators" and Speaklike has a "qualified translation team". Getlocalization also offers paid crowdsourcing but it offers different customized solutions to crowdsource the translation including the option of building or designing the crowd targeted, including employees of the firm requesting the translation, or building a crowd only of professional translators.

Other paid crowdsourcing vendors such as OneHourTranslation offer not only different tiers such as "general", "expert" and "exclusive", but also the possibility of including "or not" revision in the price. The types of translation recommended are also attached to the content requested and this company, in terms of quality, also offers different rates for translation than for translation plus proofreading. That is, not only does the customer need to select the type of quality requested, it also has to pay a higher rate if proofreading is also required. For example, "expert" translation is offered in late 2015 for 0.139 per word while translation plus proof-reading would be 0.239 cents per word. Again, the company claims that "only professional translators with rich translation experience" are pre-screened to work for them, and they also offer separate expertise groups in order to produce "expert translations".

Arguably, the dynamicity in these business models relies on the fact that users and clients ultimately decide what a "fit for purpose" translation is. In this change of paradigm, both business agents and users understand that that translation is a time, resource and money constrained process (Wright 2006; Jiménez-Crespo 2013a) and therefore, fit for purpose models could be considered as a "conscious attempt at using translation and revision resources intelligently" (Drugan 2013:42). In these business contexts, however, this conscious attempt shifts crucial decision-making on quality to relatively uninformed translation clients and /or users based on the price and the value that they place on the translated text or the service provided. This even occurs when clients might not possess any knowledge of the difference between a standard and an ultra translation or a basic and a specialist one. Quality is conceptualized as a scalable commodity that can be requested in different degrees depending on the characteristics of the crowd of participants, with a similar approach to how any other products or services are purchased in the market, such as a car or a house. This process has been argued to lead towards a downward pressure on prices, rather than improving the overall conditions in the industry (García 2015). But what conditions is García referring to: the actual translators, the innovators in the industry, the end users?

New paid crowdsourcing approaches also fail to define what translation quality means but in this case, rather than resorting to norms or standards, companies associate different quality levels, as previously described, to types of content or content prioritization. In this shift, translation quality is not defined per se, but rather replaced by a scale of potential value or worth of different types of content, from the trivial to the highly important, defining in this way the quality of translation through a preliminary analysis of the value of the source text rather than the actual quality. Again, if the industry resorted to process-based rather than product-based criteria through their norms and standards, paid crowdsourcing models have also resorted to extratextual parameters such as the estimated or sentimental value of the content. The process-oriented rather than product-oriented nature of previous normative standards in the industry has been heavily criticized in TS (Wright 2006: 256). The main argument against them is that they normally indicate how language vendors establish procedures for achieving quality, rather than providing normative statements about what constitutes translation quality (Martínez Mélis and Hurtado Albir 2001: 274). The same, then, can be said of paid crowdsourcing models: clients, users and the industry are often discussing properties of the process rather than the actual properties of the translated texts.

The very fact that translation quality can be secondary to other considerations can be witnessed in industry publications, where speed, cost or even the motivation of volunteers to participate can be a higher priority than top quality. For example, Muzii indicates that "[q]uality is no under pressure. Translation is" (2013: 12). The main premise of his article is that there is no increased pressure to bring the highest possible quality, in our fast pace networked world, there is just pressure to get the translations done as quickly as possible. Similarly, Desilets and Van de Meer indicate that:

> Quality Control issues tend to resolve themselves, provided that enough of the "right" people can be enticed to participate and that you provide them with light-weight tools and processes by which they can spot and fix errors.
>
> (Desilets and van de Meer 2011: 41)

In this case, the issue would be that even when quality might not be that significant in some scenarios, it is not defined what the "right" people or what the minimum amount of people might be. It shows a blind faith in a process-oriented or management-oriented approach in which setting up the process will lead to adequate quality, even when the notion of what quality is might not be defined.

5.4 Guaranteeing quality in crowdsourcing

Crowdsourcing quality evaluation has challenged the creative force of workflow industry experts and MT researchers to achieve the highest possible level of quality in a changing landscape. This new highly dynamic field has become an ideal breeding ground for innovations that might ultimately impact theorizations and professional practices. Mossop (2005) indicated that new technological phenomena might require novel theorizations, and these novel approaches can help point to areas that might ultimately redefine how TS conceptualizes quality.[3] Many approaches and models represent a radical departure from previous models in the industry and TS, influenced by a combination of "fit for purpose" models, MT

---

3. This does not mean that TS as a discipline cannot apply existing metrics, evaluation models and approaches to the analysis of quality for research purposes. In fact, quality comparisons based on error detection between professional and collaborative processes have been an initial approach to the study of these phenomena (Bogucki 2009; Hanes 2011; Pérez and Carreira 2011; Deriemaeker 2014).

approaches, usability and user-based models. Traditional professional cycles, such as those described in the EN 15038 standard, require a minimum of a two-step process with an a priori accredited translator and a reviser, as well as standardized metrics. Meanwhile, non-professional collaborative workflows have developed different mechanisms to achieve a sufficient or good enough level of "fitness for purpose". The following list emerged through a comprehensive analysis of existing models, industry and scholarly publications, with the goal of identifying and describing new practices and approaches of interest for TS. The list of practices to guarantee quality can be summarized as follows, in a continuum from those most similar to professional approaches to the least:[4]

1. Translation-Edit-Publish (TEP) approaches.
2. Pre-selection with exam.
3. Selection of the participants in the crowd.
4. Continuing evaluation of participant performance.
5. Creation of cloud workflow solutions with built-in QA measures.
6. Establishing common resources such as glossaries, guidelines, norms, or discussion forums.
7. Combination of automatic quality checking with professional human translator.
8. Presence of language experts or community managers.
9. Quality loops after the release of the text.
10. Iterative/Redundancy voting.
11. "Many eyes" principle.

Translation-Edit-Publish (TEP) models attempt to replicate the traditional professional model in which translations are followed by a revision and delivery. These initiatives assign one or several translators that have been selected or qualified in the eyes of the initiatives to a translation, and then a reviser reviews it in its entirety. Hierarchies are often part of these initiatives, and often quality is secured through the assignments of professional or good performers to the revision or management. For example, it has been reported that in the TED Open Translation

---

4. Some descriptive lists of best practices in crowdsourcing quality exist, such as the one that emerged from the TAUS workgroup (Desilets and van de Meer 2011; Collaborative Translation Patterns 2011). In this list some practices are included, such as the entry exam, peer review, automatic reputation management, random spot-checking, in-house revision, users as translators, voting, transparent quality level, publish then revise, refining redundancy, open alternatives, hidden alternatives. While some of them match practices described in this list, such as entry exams, in-house revision, publish then revise, others have been previously described in the workflow section in Chapter 3, such as open and hidden alternatives.

Initiative, professional translators tend to become revisers directly (Camara 2015). This is often also the case in some non-profits, such as Kiva. One benefit of this practices is that it allows revisers to provide feedback back to the translators in order to improve future performance, and this, stated in O'Brien and Schäler (2010), is one of the most motivating factors for volunteers.

Pre-selection with exams is the most common practice in the industry, instituted by language providers to accept translators to in-house or freelance positions. In crowdsourcing scenarios, this practice is often found in non-profit and paid crowdsourcing initiatives, such as Kiva, Watching America or the paid crowdsourcing initiatives described in Section 5.3.2. Exams are often graded by language managers or higher status participants. In some cases, the exam is only required for proofreading or editing roles, such as the cases of the translation into Chinese of the popular science website Gouker and its MOOC courses (Cao 2015).

The selection of the participants in the crowd for each project is one of the key elements according to industry publications (i.e., DePalma and Kelly 2011; Desilets and Van de Meer 2011). Open and closed models represent different approaches to this issue, but even in open models sometimes filters are set in place. Communities can be open only to professional translators, such as the case of Translators Without Borders that requires four years of professional experience. In "paid crowdsourcing" models, companies offer different types of crowds, from bilinguals, general translators to specialists, or even allow the creation of a crowd of selected professionals to participate in the translation process, such as in the case of GetLocalization. Launchpad Rosetta for open software localization for example allows users to set projects with different types of contributions or permission policy, such as "open", "structured", "restricted" or "closed". In open projects anyone can collaborate. In the structured model, a member or group of selected members can review and accept translation suggestions from the community. The restricted model is similar to the structured one, but languages without a management team are closed, while the closed model only participants assigned by the team can both translate and review/accept suggestions. In open initiatives, such as Translate Facebook, limitations are set in place, such as the fact that members have to be active for at least one month before participating. Changes to working languages are only allowed once a month. If a different language is selected to translate, the application flags the user and indicates that the language of translation is different from the language they are using. Basically it attempts to make sure that users are acquainted with the website and how it works before they participate. Other initiatives, nevertheless, do not have any time restrictions and in Twitter, users can participate immediately upon registering.

Whether the admission to the community is done in an open or closed process, *participants' performance can be continually evaluated* during their participation either manually or automatically. In manual cases, this can be accomplished by in-house or volunteer community managers, or also by peers, such as the Unbabel or Stepes smartphone apps. For example, the volunteer initiative to translate the Economist by ECOS into Chinese entails successfully translating seven articles in order to be fully accepted as a translator (Ray and Kelly 2011). In other cases, such as the bartering platform Cucumis, if translation performance in the review stage is consistently rated as superior, translators move to an "expert" category. When this happens, their volunteer translations cost more "translation points" in exchange. A similar approach has also been implemented in the Linqapp platform. Automatic evaluation cases are found, for example, in the crowdsourcing management platform Crowdflower. This platform can randomly insert multiple-choice questions during the crowdsourcing tasks in order to assess the potential reliability of participants. Similarly, MT approaches have also explored the ratings of translator contributors in Amazon Turks in order to select and / or reject participants based on their worker ratings or past performance (Yan et al. 2015). This selection of "super-users" or establishing user ratings also appears as a recommendation for general community evaluation by TAUS (2014).

Cloud workflow solutions are created with built in QA measures. Platforms to manage the translations by the crowd such as Transifex, Ackuna, Trommons or MNH-TT incorporate workflow solutions that resemble professional approaches to quality, with built in TMs and termbases, the assignment of managers, editors, reviewers or translators, feedback loops, etc.

Most crowdsourcing platforms include basic workflow management solutions that *establish common resources such as glossaries, guidelines, norms, or discussion forums.* Many can resemble professional practices (Orrego-Carmona 2012). This represents a common practice in crowdsourcing, i.e. Facebook, Twitter, Symantec, etc., and collaborative approaches such as fansub communities or non-profit initiatives.

Initiatives *combine automatic quality checking with professional human translators,* such as the case of Asia Online in their workflow to translate Wikipedia into Thai. One of the main steps to guarantee quality is that three different participants post-edit the same MT translated segment. If any of the two participants' post-edited outputs match, the segment is automatically selected and flagged for insertion in the target text. If the three renditions are different, then a "professional" contributor selects the best rendition. The quality approach does not end there, since the other two segments are fed into the MT engine for learning purposes with the hope of producing higher quality MT output in the future.

Involving language experts or community managers to oversee the crowdsourcing process from a macrostructural and professional perspective is a common practice in most social networking sites (DePalma and Kelly 2011). Their role involves the oversight of the process and the overall quality of the translation. In large initiatives, "language managers" appear online in all the fully-supported languages, while others are self-managed by the community. In general, the involvement of as many experts as possible is often recommended, with proposed workflows indicating that the process should involve "as many skilled translators as possible" (ibid: 380). Many initiatives and platforms implicitly include the role of managers or language experts with different roles, such as Microsoft Collaborative Translation Framework (Aikawa, Yamamoto and Isahara 2012) and most of the non and for profit platforms described in Section 3.4. In some instances, it is recommended that the expert become a company employee or, if that is not possible, a "top contributor" as indicated in the TAUS Community evaluation guidelines (TAUS 2014).

Many initiatives set up *quality loops after the release of the text*. These participatory mechanisms often take two forms, either the direct participation in open initiatives such as Wikipedia or Amara that anyone can edit, or in the form of discussion boards to report translation issues. Examples of this last practice are found in the Microsoft Language Portal, the discussion boards in all FLOSS localization communities or the Facebook forums for each locale version. In some platforms, such as Microsoft Collaborative Translation Framework, it is possible to authorize users to edit directly MT translated webpages.

Crowdsourcing approaches with *iterative/redundancy voting* mechanisms represent the extreme case in which the expectations and preferences of the end user crowds take center stage. Quality is achieved through the production of translation proposals that are subsequently voted. The translation renditions can be either proposed by the crowd, by experts or higher status participants or by MT engines. This mechanism involves segmentation of the source text and it is not successful with larger stretches such as paragraphs or entire texts (Jiménez-Crespo 2011).

The *"many eyes" principle or "Linus' law"* was first formulated by Raymond (2001) in reference to Open Software and it defined it as situations in which "[g]iven a large enough beta-tester and co-developer base, almost every problem will be characterized quickly and the fix will be obvious to someone" (2001:30), or as the author indicated less formally, "given enough eyeballs, all bugs are shallow" (ibid). This departs from a completely open paradigm in which anyone in the community can translate and edit the translation. Broad crowd participation in a process with many people going over the same materials will identify and correct any existing flaw. This can only work in systems that are totally open and in which they can or not incorporate a step called the "freezing" of the translation similar to the one in Open Software.

All existing approaches vary to a great extent, but all of them share the need to develop alternative mechanisms to secure quality under different external and internal constraints. According to the classification of internal and external constrains to translation quality in Jiménez-Crespo (2013: 108), evaluation processes can be restricted externally in terms of skills and competences of the participants, the QA process used, the translation procedure (post-editing, MT engine used, non-professional translation, etc.), cognitive constrains or norms as to what is considered quality. In the practices mentioned in this section, external constraints not only constrain the evaluation process, they also mold and shape the design of the mechanisms created to secure quality. It has also been observed that the wide range of quality evaluation settings extend in a continuum from approaches that attempt to replicate professional TEP workflows and norms, such as some post-anime TV fansub communities (Orrego-Carmona 2015), all the way to the Wikipedia reliance on the principle of "many eyes" or "Linus' Law" (Raymond 2001) where translation quality is left up to the whims and motivations of an active large crowd. After this review the next issue of interest would be what challenges these approaches entail for TS as a discipline.

5.5   Crowdsourcing, quality and challenges to TS

Even today, echoing the words of Larose (1998: 163), quality evaluation in the discipline "entails problems that are of cosmic proportions". Larose's words resonated in a time when TS was moving beyond linguistic and equivalence inspired models based on error detection. Didactic and literary applications still were the main concerns in scholarly contexts, and they required a maximalist approach to the notion of translation quality. The irruption of digital technologies added additional communicative situations, modalities and types of translation that have expanded what translation quality should (or could) be. It would seem that, in principle, problems might be getting bigger and more complex. And still, it also seems like quality might be less of a problem since industry circles willingly accept and encourage different tiers of quality, while users gladly accept low quality in cases where access, speed or trivial nature of the content might be more important. The notion of "translation quality" might have been substituted by a construct that could be best referred to as "acceptability" or "adequacy", all within a complex interaction of user attitudes, business decisions (or lack thereof), content types, translation types and the relative importance of the translated text. The dynamic and fluid status of new practices can be such that different translation quality tiers can even appear in the same text. For example, any non-English user of Facebook can potentially find a web interface that has been crowdsourced through a multiple translation voting system, parts of the translation carried out by professionals, a posting that might have been translated by a bilingual user, all alongside a comment from a friend in another language that has been automatically translated with Microsoft Bing MT through the "See translation" feature. That is, professional, crowdsourced, natural and MT translation can appear on the same screen at the same time.

The following sections review some challenges that crowdsourcing and collaborative approaches pose to TS theorizations and research, as well as the vantage point that TS provides to analyze these phenomena. The challenges and issues reviewed are whether translation theory is a prerequisite or not for evaluation, the flexible nature of the unit of evaluation, the challenges posed by processes in which quality can potentially worsen, the different types of assessment and their relation to crowdsourcing, as well as the radically different approaches present in MT research.

5.5.1 Translation theory: A prerequisite for quality evaluation?

From the early discussions on linguistic equivalence approaches (i.e., Nida and Taber 1969) to the functionalist (Nord 1991, 1997) or discourse-based approaches (Reiss 1971; House 1997, 2014), proposals have been firmly grounded in the underlying theoretical backgrounds of scholars. Publications often argue that translation theory, models and solidly defined constructs are a prerequisite for evaluation (Colina 2008; House 1997). The view from TS is to some extent summarized by Julianne House (1997: 7) who indicated:

> Evaluating the quality of a translation presupposes a theory of translation. Thus different views of translation lead to different concepts of translational quality, and hence different ways of assessing it.

For House, theory is not only a requirement for definitions of quality and assessment purposes; it also extends to how the process is established since "different theoretical stances lead to [...] different ways of ensuring (prospectively) quality in the production of a translation" (House 2013: 534). This dependence on translation theory for evaluation is often found in TS literature, frequently associated to the provision of reliability and objectivity in the process (House 2001, 1997; Williams 2003; Colina 2009; Angelelli 2009). Not only is theory a prerequisite, it is also argued that proposed models need to be empirically tested, that is, both industry and TS models need to be "validated by means of empirical research" (Martínez Mélis and Hurtado Albir 2001: 274).

In general, crowdsourcing and collaborative quality evaluation practices have been established without relying on the body of knowledge of TS, in an industry – academia gap previously mentioned (Dunne, 2006; Jiménez-Crespo 2013a, 2010b).

It can thus be argued from this perspective that theory-free quality evaluation provides neither a model for quality nor objective, valid and reliable evaluation results. This issue raises a number of questions that should be addressed in the discipline: are objectivity or reliability necessary beyond certification exams and the certification of the language service industry? Even in admission exams that occur in crowdsourcing initiatives, such an admission exam for Kiva, is objectivity even necessary or perceived to be essential when volunteers are contributing pro-bono? Outside professional circles when money, time or resource constraints disappear, are objectivity and validity necessary? What is the role of theory in these cases? It is a fact that, as argued in Jiménez-Crespo (2011: 132), crowdsourcing approaches contradict the frequent mantra in TS: only translation evaluation built around explicit TS theoretical models can provide reliable and objective results, or for that matter, useful ones.

Some reasons given by scholars to defend a theory-dependent approach are the need to control the subjectivity inherent in all evaluation processes (Hönig 1998: 14) or the differences in quality constructs between professionals and other agents in the process. As far as subjectivity, this has been a recurring issue from the first attempts to study translation evaluation. Nida (1964: 154–157), for example, believed that no translator or evaluator could avoid some degree of subjectivity and personal involvement in the interpretation of the ST. Subjectivity, likened to individuals, was considered to be present in all translation evaluation processes (Hönig 1998: 14), and relying on theoretical foundations often has been argued to be needed to separate this innate subjective component. In addition to theoretical foundations, for over two decades scholars have expressed the need to empirically test any proposed models (Martínez Mélis and Hurtado Abir 2001; Angelelli 2009; Colina 2009). The main issue in these approaches from a collaborative perspective is that scholarly discourses almost invariably assume an individualistic approach to quality evaluation, and the main challenge tends to be how to overcome the fact that a single evaluator might not provide an objective measure of quality (Rothe-Neves 2002). This can be true if the focus of analysis is, as it has been for decades, professional translation in individual settings. Nevertheless, other quality evaluation settings exist, and the industry has already been working towards incorporating them in their research efforts (i.e., Lommel et al. 2014; Göröj 2014a). This is yet to happen in TS. Collaborative approaches open up the window to revision by the crowd, and even when in MT this is a common research topic, the implication of using the crowd to achieve translation quality has yet been barely examined in TS. In contrast to professional approaches that require collaboration between one or more qualified translator (s) and reviser(s), as stated in the European EN 15038 standard, crowdsourcing models apply a range of distinct mechanisms to secure quality beyond the TEP model as described in Section 5.4. Individual biases can be controlled in approaches that rely on the "collective intelligence", either through voting or the "many eyes" principle. This last principle, for example, arguably keeps translations in Wikipedia of acceptable quality: an outstanding potential case study of theory-free implementation of quality evaluation.

Another issue of interest is how users and participants in crowdsourcing initiatives conceptualize translation quality and the differences with professional and /or scholarly approaches. Crowdsourcing takes to the extreme the fact that an acceptable degree of quality seems to be in the eye of the users and/or users-translators. This was the approach taken by de Wille (2014) who conducted a study on the perceptions of quality by the volunteer crowd. The research project explored the opinions of volunteer evaluating and editing translation for the Trommons platform by the Rosetta Foundation. The results of the survey found that feedback comments showed a certain level of agreement on how quality was conceptualized and perceived. In general, linguistic dependent issues such as grammar, spelling, terminology and style were mentioned more often than others related to design, verity, register, omissions and additions, etc. This, according to the researcher, shows a similar pattern to the analysis of industry practices conducted by O'Brien (2012a).

Theoretical models arguably attempt to apply to all evaluation contexts, and this universalist aspiration brings up whether different models should be proposed depending on the evaluation settings. Since early on, scholars pointed out that TS evaluation models are developed with certain translation types in mind framed from a universal perspective, such as literary, didactic or religious translations. Therefore, many of their underlying principles might not necessarily apply to other types of translations (i.e., Larose 1998: 164; Martínez Mélis and Hurtado Albir 2001: 284). Meanwhile, recent industry approaches widely accept that flexibility and customization to specific settings is required (O'Brien 2012a; Göröj 2014a; Lommel et al. 2014), since different kinds of translations "require very different evaluation methods" (Lommel et al. 2014: 455). The translation of an inconsequential tweet in which speed primes cannot be equated to the legal terms in a website. TS has been moving towards flexible evaluation models including and combining user-based methods, usability measures, reception studies, and other extralinguistic parameters. These approaches are moves in the right direction, and the proposal of flexible and dynamic parameters that can easily move and adapt according to the situation from a more intralinguistic to more extralinguistic quality approach could be the solution to the relative lack of impact of TS in industry developments related to new technology dependent translation phenomena.

To finish with, it should be born in mind that the relative shortcomings on TS in this area often means that models and approaches that emerged in other areas, mostly MT, or in industrial approaches, are often applied to the evaluation of crowdsourcing output. The question then arises of whether further theoretical efforts in TS can incorporate and / or promote the introduction of TS theories in industry practices, or to what extent TS theory can impact related theories and public perceptions.

5.5.2   The minimal unit to evaluate quality: Between internal and external quality

TS considers the entire text not only as the minimum unit of translation, but also as the minimal unit of evaluation. For example, functionalist views on translation depart from the foundation of "the text as a whole whose function(s) and effect(s) must be regarded as the crucial criteria for translation criticism" (Nord 1991: 166). The function pragmatic model of translation quality assessment of House (2013, 2014) also departs from a "specific text" and it results in a "pragmatically and semantically equivalent one [...] a translation text has a function equivalent to that of its original" (House 2013: 542). Other scholars with proposals that incorporate pragmatic or discursive approaches also invariably considered the text as the unit of quality analysis (Larose 1998; Williams 2003).

As seen in Chapter 3, texts in crowdsourcing initiatives are often disaggregated, segmented, and presented to volunteers in units of diverse nature, from terminology equivalents to full sentences, paragraphs or entire texts depending on the workflow. While some collaborative approaches do evaluate translation in complete and full texts, crowdsourcing workflow approaches have mainly adopted TM and MT segmentation approaches, and consequently, sometimes tend to use the sentence or segment as the unit of evaluation. In social networking platforms participants translate and assess one by one each sentence, and in MT post-editing models volunteers post-edit isolated sentences from a global text. Depending on the initiative, there might or might not be a macrostructural stage in which the global cohesion and coherence of the text is assessed as a whole. In a sense, these segment-based approaches to quality can often be reduced to the linguistic level, which Gouadec (2010) considers internal quality. According Gouadec, quality can be understood in terms of both internal and external quality. Internal quality refers to the intrinsic qualities that the translated text itself possesses, while external qualities have to do with how well it fulfills the intended purpose for which it was initiated, how it satisfied the implied client needs, etc. It is highly productive to separate both components, the internal and the external in quality analyses. Crowdsourcing approaches span both sides of the spectrum. In those that prime user involvement such as Facebook, the external quality in terms of user expectations and the reception of the text comes first, while MT post-editing approaches that focus on the translation task to the micro level mostly reduce it to an internal quality level. The extreme case of external quality can be found in cases such as user evaluation in Symantec. The website of this company contains MT translations of pages, and a crowdsourced user-based quality loop is inserted that asks users whether the webpage solved their issues or reasons why they read the page. The aggregation of contributions by the user community represents a case of evaluation of translations based on usability and external quality. A paradox emerges here: even when often the unit of evaluation can be anything from a segment to the entire text in crowdsourcing, while users might be judging internal quality in a proposed segment, the promoters of the initiative might have in mind as a goal external quality issues such as usability or the reception of the translation by users. A blending of internal and external quality paradigms emerges, with some agents focusing on external quality parameters while others based their decisions on a mix between external and internal quality.

Many iterative models are based on internal and external quality models such as Facebook. This initiative focuses on segments and community opinions at the segmental micro level. Inherent linguistic features of the translated segments together with communicative issues related to how users perceive the usefulness, naturalness or adequacy of the translation play a role in the evaluation process. In other new dynamic models, entire texts as the unit of evaluation, such as usability, adequacy or verity, require the consideration of the entire text as a unit of communication. For example, verity is incorporated in the MQM model and it refers to:

> issues with the text that relate to the broader world [...] and cannot be evaluated simply be reading the translation or comparing it to the source, but instead requires the evaluator to consider the text in its intended environment.
>
> (Lommel et al. 2014: 459)

Examples of this issue type would be the adaptation of a contract to be fully valid under the legislation of a different country or the incorporation of a different phone number. Obviously, without considering the entire text as a unit or a project, these types of issues cannot be solved merely with a micro-task crowdsourcing approach. Crowdsourcing approaches, thus, despite the emphasis on segmentation and micro-task approaches, do potentially involve a combination of evaluation models that require both considering the segmental and the textual level in a combination of internal and external quality evaluation.

5.5.3 Is translation quality always improving through the process?

Quality in TS is conceptualized in a metaphorical improvement journey that goes from low quality and moves towards achieving the desired higher level (if not the maximum possible). This is reflected in the traditional TEP model in the profession: no matter how good the translation is, revision and proofreading guarantee this incremental action towards higher quality. Participation by the community, with a wide range of skills and competences, implies that quality can both improve and worsen throughout time in open initiatives, a problem that is absent in TS theorizations and publications. In order to analyse this phenomenon, it is of interest to revise approaches that conceptualized quality as an incremental process of improvement only, such professional management, in cognitive approaches or in the study of revision.

In a professional cycle approach, this metaphorical improvement journey starts from the pre-translational quality management issues (Gouadec 2007), such as establishing quality assurance mechanisms, sharing glossaries and term bases, translation memories, securing "qualified" translators for the job, adapting or pre-processing source texts, etc. It is also established through the Quality Assurance and Quality control procedures. Quality assurance (QA) is intended to guarantee that whichever quality requirements have been pre-defined are met, and quality control (QC) is set up through the entire translation cycle, from source text development all the way to the delivery of the product and post mortem, such as keeping the translation memories for future projects or updating the terminology databases. Quality Control can expand beyond the delivery of the product and they can be circular in cases such as large social networking sites that are constantly updating and adding material translated by the crowd.

From the process-oriented point of view of the Cognitive TS, this motion towards higher quality is also perceived, for example, through the so-called "literal hypothesis" (Chesterman 2010) or the existence of the "monitor model" Tirkkonen-Condit (2005). These models that depart from the psycholinguistic process research approach and an individualistic perspective (see Chapter 4), claim that during the process of translation, translators move from the most literal and close rendition to the source text to a freer and supposedly better one. Chesterman defined the "literal hypothesis" as a general tendency by which during the translation process, "translators tend to proceed from more literal versions to less literal ones." (2010:5). Similarly, the "monitor model" proposed by Tirkkonen-Condit proposes that the translation process develops literally and semi automatically, only stopping when problems are identified. In this moment, translators move away from the literal rendition of the source text to a better and "freer" one of supposedly higher quality. Cognitive approaches have also extensively focused on the notion of "self-revision" (Englund Dimitrova 2005) that occurs during the translation process, a continuous process of improvement of the emerging product.

The extensive literature on revision and editing also defends this metaphorical continuous improvement of the translation during the overall production cycle. The objective of translation quality revision is to decide if a translation is of satisfactory quality, and also to make any changes that are needed according to the revision instructions (Mossop 2007, 2012). According to the European Union, the objectives of revision encompass improving the quality of the translation, as an instrument of quality control and as training mechanisms for translation and revisers (EU 2010: 6). Suojanen et al. (2015: 130) for example stresses the linear nature of the process when they indicate that:

> the central role of revision in translation quality models underlies the linear nature of the exercise [...] translation is seen as a cascade that runs from one phase to the next.

Once the target text is set for distribution, the quality control process can guarantee that once published or distributed, any errors in the text can be corrected. Some companies have extended crowdsourcing approaches beyond the distribution of the translated product, such as Microsoft. In their Language portal,[5] any user can provide feedback on erroneous translations in their products.

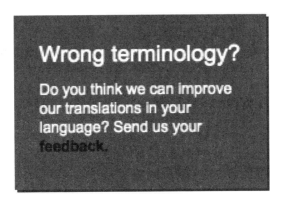

Figure 5.2 Microsoft Language Portal request for translation improvement by the crowd.

The issue here is that quality can get worse in crowdsourcing and collaborative approaches, where the potential exists to attract bad performers or even the so-called malicious "trolls" (Drugan 2011; Shachaf and Hara, 2010). Quality is thus seen as an ongoing process rather than a static one (Drugan 2013: 179). However, the ongoing process and incremental participation do not always necessarily lead to better outcomes, even if this is most often the case. This issue has never been addressed in TS literature, except in some experimental settings in which it has been reported that reviewers can insert errors in the target text (Conde Ruano 2012). In order to tackle issues related to quality worsening over time, crowdsourcing initiatives have set up mechanisms in order to handle the disruptions caused by bad

---

5. http://www.microsoft.com/Language/en-US/Default.aspx

performers or conscious wrongdoers. For example, Wikipedia, Amara or Dotsub have implemented what is known as translation "rollback", that is, "reverting to a previously existing version of the data [...] to support damage control" (Morera-Mesa 2014: 174). The main differences with other translation scenarios in which quality can potentially worsen, such as revision, is that in some crowdsourcing models this possibility is multiplied infinitely. Different types of mechanisms exist to control quality issues produced by trolls or bad performance. For example, MT crowdsourcing approaches have explored the possibility to control profiles in order to increase quality by means of eliminating automatically bad profiles or participants with poor performance (Yan et al. 2015). The dynamicity in the process of translation production implies that the path of quality throughout translation processes can go in either direction and translation theory should in principle also account for this possibility.

5.5.4 Crowdsourcing and different assessment types

Theoretical approaches also encompass a wide range of quality and evaluation scenarios that might not be equally relevant for the industry or the analysis of crowdsourcing efforts. Most research therefore focuses on two distinctive but related evaluation perspectives: the professional (i.e., Nobs 2006; Drugan 2013) and the didactic (i.e., Nord 1991; 1997; Waddington 2001). Not only do the different perspectives impinge on the objectives of the research, evaluation is also found in several settings depending on the outcomes, such as summative, diagnostic and formative evaluation (Martínez Mélis and Hurtado Albir 2001).

Summative evaluation is carried out in order to determine the end result or pass a final judgment. This type of evaluation would be carried out in certification examinations or professional contexts with publishable/non-publishable decisions. This type of evaluation can be performed in the entire document or in samples. It also appears broadly in crowdsourcing and collaborative translations since all "close" initiatives require some sort of translation test that has to be passed, either through pre-testing or testing through performance in a series of assignments. The nature of the tests and the quality performance thresholds represents an issue of interest that has not been researched to date. It is also a prevalent testing scenario in "paid crowdsourcing" approaches where translators are pre-screened and monitor throughout the early stages.

Formative evaluation appears in translation training and usually requires providing constructive feedback from the trainer to the evaluee (Kussmaul 1995; Washbourne 2014). The feedback is normally directed at the improvement of future performance, but in the process evaluators need to identify the etiology or cause of the error or inadequacy. In this sense, this type of evaluation entails looking at performance both back into the past and forward into the future. This type of evaluation has found its niche in volunteer and non-professional communities in cases in which revisers or managers provide feedback to volunteer translators to improve future performance, such as the cases of TED talks and the non-profit Kiva for example.

The last type, diagnostic evaluation, is directed towards placement, the identification of a relative level of quality achievement, and is mostly used during college admissions or hiring processes. It can also be said to be present in collaborative approaches since in some instances evaluation can lead to placements into different hierarchical roles, such as regular translator, senior translator or reviewer. The nature of these types of evaluations are also different in nature from professional approaches, since not only might quality thresholds be lower or different, but also the evaluation process takes place in a volunteer and not market-driven scenario, and in this situation, both evaluator and evaluee might be more comfortable and free to share feedback, accept mistakes, etc. (Drugan 2013).

5.5.5 Translation quality in MT

The issue of translation quality in crowdsourcing represents one of the most prolific areas of research in MT. The number of publications and paper presented in conferences is extensive if compared with the relative lack of attention the issue of quality in crowdsourcing has attracted in TS. A complete review of the findings from this discipline is outside the scope of this chapter but, nevertheless, an analysis of publications yields interesting reflections on how the nature of translation quality can expand beyond what is known in TS.

Two issues that are of interest are claims of the possibility of producing "professional quality" through crowdsourcing and whether non-professionals are equally valid to conduct the three evaluation scenarios in MT: sentences, systems and translation scores. The first and the one that has attracted the most attention was initially raised by Zaidan and Calliston-Burch (2011) paper on getting "professional quality from non-professionals" through crowdsourcing. The main focus is not on obtaining quality from regular translators, but rather using crowdsourcing as a tool to obtain translations to feed and improve MT engines (Zaidan and Callison-Burch 2011; Zbib et al. 2013; Yan et al. 2014). These processes uses "feedback translations" (Volk and Harder 2007; O'Hagan 2013), human post-edited MT output that is later on used to feed the MT engines. In this research line, studies have focused on the production of translation not for end users, but merely as a tool to produce parallel feedback texts that can help develop MT engines.

This entails a new model not explored in translation research, as it combines paid crowdsourced translation to volunteers using Amazon Mechanical Turk with the production of a translation that does not have humans or human communication as an objective, but rather computer engines. The quality notion in this area refers not to the quality of the translations themselves, but rather the quality of the output of the MT engine trained with these translated texts. This line of research has proven that crowdsourcing can produce, for the purposes of MT training, similar results to those from professional translations at one fifth of the cost (Zaidan and Calliston-Burch 2011).

Whether crowdsourcing quality evaluation of translation is feasible if compared to actual professionals has been the object of research by Goto, Lin and Ishida (2014). In a study of crowdsourcing MT quality, both professionals and volunteers assessed MT output in terms of a system comparison, sentence and translation scores. The results showed that when compared with professional scores, crowdsourcing is as valid as professional translation for the evaluation of quality in comparing MT systems, but not necessarily in sentence or translation scores and sentence score evaluation. Other similar studies have also resorted to the crowd to compare MT system performance. For example, in one of the stages of the study by Bowker and Buitrago (2016) into the usefulness of MT in the translation of library websites, users evaluated the performance of a statistical, a hybrid and a rule-based system in the translation of a library website. The results of the study showed that the statistical MT system, Google Translate, produced the most acceptable results for the users. The number of studies on MT quality are numerous and they would require a more extensive treatment. Nevertheless, this small review has highlighted two of significant issues that are a recurrent topic in the literature of interest to TS scholars, whether crowdsourcing can produce professional-like quality in MT, and whether crowdsourcing can be equally useful to perform the different evaluation scenarios in MT contexts.

5.6   A critical review of the iterative translate/vote crowdsourcing approaches in the light of Translation Studies

This section focuses on a review from a TS perspective of supposedly novel and innovative approaches that, as reviewed in Jiménez-Crespo (2011), had been proposed by TS scholars for decades. This section deals exclusively with the iterative model of Facebook, Twitter and others in which translation proposals are followed by voting by participants, a model that has been proven to produce similar texts to those naturally produced in the target language (Jiménez-Crespo 2013b). Iterative models in crowdsourcing embody and implement principles that have been present in TS literature, such as the recognition of the role of the expectations of the end user and the reader in the evaluation of quality introduced by Nida and Taber in the 60's (1964), and a novel, exciting gateway into the subconscious set of norms, conventions and expectations of users in fast evolving digital genres. These user expectations also play a key role in pragmatic and functionalist evaluation proposals (Reiss 1977; Reiss and Vermeer 1984; Nord 1997; Nobs 2006; Colina 2008, 2009). Iterative models also represent a combination of a mostly quantitative rather than qualitative process, an approach advocated by House (2001), and also by Bowker (2001) in her proposal for a corpus-assisted approach to translation evaluation. The lack of wide implementation of some of these proposals prior to its introduction by social networking sites is due to the impossibility of carrying out these complex processes in business environments without the technological innovations, a volunteer crowd and the participation capabilities afforded by the WWW and related technologies. The following section reviews the reader response approach and whether these models might represent an actual implementation of Nida and Taber's proposal.

5.6.1 The Facebook model and reader-response approaches

The works of Nida (1964) and Nida and Taber (1969) are recognized as the first approach to translation quality that included reader responses as a basic component. This can be described as a response-oriented or behavioral approach to translation evaluation and is based on Nida's notion of "dynamic equivalence"; that is, that the manner in which the receptors of the translated texts respond to the translation must be equivalent to the manner in which the receptors of the source text respond to the source text (Nida 1964). In general, the overall criteria suggested by Nida and Taber (1969: 173) in order to evaluate translations are (1) the correctness with which the receivers understand the message, (2) the ease of comprehension and (3) the involvement a person experiences as a result of the adequacy of the form of the translation. In order to achieve this goal, the authors suggest so-called "practical tests" to measure this apparently similar response: (1) the cloze technique, related to the degree of predictability of the translation, which is achieved by providing a translated text with certain blank spaces and asking that these be filled in with the word that would best fit. (2) The elicitation of the receiver's reaction to several translation alternatives. (3) Reading the translation aloud to another person and asking them to explain the contents of the text to other people who were not present during the original reading of the text. And finally, (4) reading aloud the translation to several individuals before an audience. The second "practical test", even when the author's proposal does not implicitly include the source texts, would be the closest to current Facebook practices.

These reader-response approaches to translation quality have been extensively criticized, mainly for the lack of an explicit theoretical model of quality that might guide readers in their criticism, for not using the source text in the evaluation process (House 1997), or for not controlling the inherent speculative and subjective component. However, the authors already indicated that the subjective bias could be overcome by sampling techniques, such as the ones used in Facebook. It has also been criticized because it is normally assumed that translation evaluation is carried out only by experts such as professional translators, researchers, as well as translation or language teachers (Rothe-Neves 2002), but not by non-professionals. Another point that has been criticized is that the method is based on the assumption that greater ease of comprehension might equal a better translation, or that reader response might not be equally important in all types of translation, such as in legal texts (Colina 2008).

It is interesting to note that in the review of Nida's approach by Colina (2008), all of the objections against this model are, in fact, beneficial for the crowdsourced Facebook model in the specific contexts of web localization. First of all, web localization is a clear case of instrumental (Nord 1997) or covert (House 2001) translations, and therefore, the ease with which readers can interact with the translated material is of utmost importance (Jiménez-Crespo 2009). In fact, localized websites are not called on to represent any previous source text, but rather a functional text in the target language (Pym 2004). Secondly, Colina (2008: 201) argues that "[t]he evaluation of the quality of a translation on the basis of reader response is time consuming and difficult to apply" (Colina 2008: 101). This might be the case in most QA settings, but the novel approach taken by Facebook might precisely prove that quality and translation evaluation is context-dependent and, in some cases, the inherent difficulty in crowdsourcing quality evaluation might be overcome by an active community of users. Additionally, Colina argues that "careful selection of readers is also necessary to make sure that they belong to the intended audience of translation" (ibid). Again, fans' knowledge of these newly emerging digital genres can definitely match the exact profile of the target user. Finally, it has also been suggested that the intended users of a translation might be different from the original ones, both culturally and temporally, and that the purpose of the translation might be different, so therefore measuring an "equivalent response" might be impossible. Again, the readers or users recruited to participate in the evaluation are basically those users to whom the translation is addressed. Despite the fact that the model is not necessarily grounded in Translation Theory, research using Facebook or Twitter data could provide data that is valuable in empirically revisiting reader response approaches not from a linguistic equivalence paradigm (Nida 1964), but rather from a functionalist approach such as in the empirical work of Nobs (2006). Additionally, Hönig (1998: 32) mentioned while discussing the subjective bias in evaluation that: "the speculative element will remain – at least as long as there are no hard and fast empirical data which serve to prove what a "typical" reader's responses are like". Given that evaluators are typical readers of these sites, empirical research with data from the site could help move the quality evaluation in translation within the discipline further along. It therefore seems, at least in principle, that all the potential shortcomings of reader-response approaches in most evaluation settings are in fact beneficial to a crowdsourced model.

This review has shown that, even when QA crowdsourcing seems like a completely novel process, at the dawn of Translation Studies some proposals already pointed to a few of the novel aspects of these models that could not be implemented prior to the unexpected explosion of Internet users around the world. In the evolution of quality evaluation research in the discipline, the next revolutionary development was the application of functionalism to quality assessment. The next section reviews how the shift towards the target context and the repudiation of any type of equivalence between source and target texts in the evaluation process (Nord 1997) can find a parallel in these approaches.

5.6.2 The iterative quality models and functionalist approaches

The development of functionalist theoretical approaches to translation in the 70s and 80s was instrumental in moving the focus of the evaluation process away from the highlighting of some sort of equivalence with the source text (Reiss 1971) and towards the purpose or "skopos" of each translation assignment (Reiss and Vermeer 1984; Nord 1997). This entailed a shift in the definition of a quality translation, from one that was somewhat "equivalent" to a source text to one that had the ability to fulfill the communicative purpose for which it was intended. This also introduced to mainstream Translation Studies the notion of "adequacy" in the evaluation process. In this switch, the receivers, together with their socio-cultural context, play an essential role. Their frameworks of expectations also become essential during the translation and evaluation processes. Within this context, functionalists highlighted the importance that conventions play both in the production and reception of translations, since they can potentially differ between the same genres in different cultures (Nord 1997: 54). During translation, and more importantly, during quality evaluation processes, it is key to guarantee that target texts contain whichever conventions users expect in whichever genre is translated, as non-compliance with different genre conventions might have a detrimental effect on the reception of the text (Jiménez-Crespo 2009). Within the functionalist paradigm, conventions are defined as:

> Implicit or tacit non-binding regulation of behavior, based on common knowledge and the expectations of what others expect you to expect from them (etc.) to do in a certain situation. (Nord 1991:96)

These regulations of behavior are normally associated with different levels, such as "genre conventions" (Reiss and Vermeer 1984), "style conventions", "conventions of non-verbal conduct" or "translation conventions" (Nord 1997). Genre conventions play an important role in the identification and translation of most localized genres (Nord 1997:53). First of all, they function as signs that facilitate the recognition of a given genre. Secondly, they activate the expectations of the reader. And finally, they are signs that coordinate the text comprehension process (Reiss and Vermeer 1984:189). Therefore, given that translation entails both a textual comprehension and a textual production process, conventions also play a crucial role in it (Göpferich 1995:168; Nord 1997).

However, it has been shown that localized websites tend not to comply with the conventions found in similar genres in target cultures (Jiménez-Crespo 2009, 2010). Normally, these websites show direct transfer of many source text conventions. As an example, Jiménez-Crespo (2009) showed that US websites localized into Spanish show source-culture conventions such as the more prominent use of direct imperative forms of the verbs in navigation menus, while Spanish websites prefer infinitives or other non-personal forms. As previously mentioned, fans' knowledge of certain genres can lead to texts with higher levels of quality than those produced by professional translators (O'Hagan 2009) and in part, this can be due to the fact that intensive users might possess what is known as "active competence" (Gläser 1990:72) in the knowledge of genre conventions. Normally, users and translators can possess active or passive knowledge of digital genre conventions (Jiménez-Crespo 2009). Active competence can be defined as the ability of speakers of a language to recognize and produce the conventional features of textual genres, such as writing a resume or an email. Nevertheless, most speakers might not be able to produce certain textual genres, such as a patent, a purchase contract or a privacy policy on a website, even though they might recognize prototypical instances of the genres and be able to identify the possible range of variation. This is referred to as passive competence (Gamero 2001:53). In the ever-changing nature of digital genres, it is possible that translators and quality evaluators might not possess an active competence on any given textual genre, a problem that is referred to as "genre deficit" or "text type deficit" (Hatim and Mason 1997:133). This text type deficit might lead to the production of digital genres that to some extent lack the conventions expected by users. Thus, enlisting large numbers of users in the quality evaluation process is not only adequate, but also essential in order to identify by consensus what the specific conventions expected by the discourse community of users might be in each locale.

It should be mentioned at this point that for a convention to exist, alternative variants need to exist that fulfill the same communicative purpose (Göpferich 1995). In the case where no alternative exists, conventions cannot exist, but rather, we would be talking about norms. The Facebook evaluation model therefore allows us to identify within the range of possible variants that fulfill any communicative purpose which alternatives are more frequent than others. This can naturally lead to websites that better match the framework of expectations of the community of users, and therefore this can be associated with higher levels of quality in the eyes of the end users. All these issues should be framed within the context of rapidly evolving "imported" genres into most cultures, and therefore, enlisting the community of users in order to gauge the evolution or establishment of the features expected in these genres represents a positive addition to the process.

5.6.3 Corpus-assisted approaches

The last evaluation proposal that has some parallels with these iterative processes is the corpus-assisted approach to quality evaluation (Bowker 2001). For over two decades, the use of corpora during translation and evaluation has been widely promoted, mostly from within TS for both didactic (i.e. Zanettin 1998, 2001; Bowker 2001; Beeby Rodríguez-Inés and Sánchez-Gijón 2009) and professional practices (i.e. Bowker and Barlow 2009). Lynne Bowker pioneered the use of corpora during translation evaluation because this process "entails making judgments about appropriate language use, [and] it should not rely on intuition, anecdotal evidence or small samples" (2001: 346). In translation, Bowker (1998: 631) also indicated that "corpus-assisted translations are of a higher quality with respect to subject field understanding, correct term choice, and idiomatic expressions." Additionally, the researcher indicates that the quantitative approach provided by evaluation corpora can be better than using conventional resources such as dictionaries because these "are not always highly conducive to providing the conceptual and linguistic knowledge necessary to objectively evaluate a translation" (2001: 346).

An electronic corpus can be defined as a large principled collection of machine-readable texts that has been compiled according to a specific set of criteria in order to be representative of the targeted textual population. Among different corpus types (Laviosa 2002: 34–38), a carefully constructed evaluation corpus constitutes a source of conceptual and linguistic information that can objectively support evaluation decisions and judgments. Very few studies have focused on the use of corpora in localization (Jiménez-Crespo 2010; Shreve 2006b), and the only existing proposal for an evaluation corpus in Translation Studies is that of Bowker (2001). This evaluation corpus is intended for a didactic setting and it was presented as assistance to evaluators while making evaluation judgments. It is comprised of four different components: a comparable corpus, a quality corpus, a quantity corpus and an inappropriate corpus. First of all, the comparable corpus includes both a translated and non-translated collection of texts. This corpus allows us to observe patterns in non-translated texts in the same genre and text type in order to produce more natural sounding translations; the second component is a quality corpus, a small handpicked corpus consisting of texts that have been selected primarily for their conceptual content. The next component is a quantity corpus, an extensive collection of carefully selected texts in the same domain, genre, text type, etc. Finally, Bowker proposes a section called inappropriate corpus, a corpus that contains "inappropriate" parallel texts, that is, texts that are very similar to the original text but that include different web genres or subgenres. The combination of the large amount of data in these corpora would "make it possible to spot patterns more easily, to make generalizations, and to provide concrete evidence to support decisions" (ibid: 353). It should be mentioned that the combination of corpora suggested by Bowker does not represent a corpus-based approach, but rather a corpus-assisted approach, as these corpora merely provide the necessary information to support evaluators' judgments. This use of corpora during evaluation has been criticized mostly due to the fact that the proposal for evaluation does not include a fully-fledged evaluation method, but rather, a way to support the evaluator's intuition (Colina 2009). The use of corpora is also reduced to the microcontext; that is, it is mostly geared towards finding the most common lexical or syntactic combinations or collocations and colligations. A collocation can be defined as is a co-occurrence of two or more words within a given span (distance from each other), while colligations are co-occurrences between specific words and grammatical classes, or interrelations of grammatical categories (Tognini Bonelli 1996:74). Collocations are therefore related to lexical or semantic relations, while colligations are co-occurrences of words and grammatical classes. Both of these features are related to the appreciation of naturalness in texts, as they point to the more frequent combinations in users' minds.

The basic premise behind the use of large computerized textual corpora in translation is that it can help produce more natural sounding translations (Zanettin 2001), as well as minimize to some extent the amount of "shining through" (Teich 2003) of the source text, or in other words, that lexical, syntactic or pragmatic features of the source texts might end up represented in the translation. In a sense, corpora provide a tool for translators to identify attested "units of meaning", that is, conventional ways of expressing specific meanings and performing specific functions in the relevant text-type variety within the target language (Tognini-Bonelli 1996: 131). This is due to the premise that a large body of texts that belong to the same text type and genre that have been naturally produced by speakers of any specific discourse community represents, to some extent, the subconscious set of expected features in any specific genre. This is shared knowledge of how specific genres and text types are accumulated by the repeated exposure of members of any discourse community to any genre. From a cognitive perspective, the experience of being exposed to any common textual genre is guided by "schemata" (Rumelhart 1980) or "frames" (Fillmore 1976). A frame can be defined as a network of concepts related in such a way that one concept evokes an entire system. This notion underlies the idea of the "structure of expectations", or in other words, that each member of a discourse community organizes knowledge on the basis of their own experiences, and then uses this knowledge to predict interpretations regarding new information or experiences.

The novel nature of social networking sites means that in most languages, in a so-called "imported genre", international users might still lack the set of expected features when they interact with a localized social networking site in their own languages. They might possess a subconscious framework of what the most natural sounding site would be, and then compare it to what they would like to see in these sites. The same can be said of translators and evaluators trying to produce the best possible localized site. Therefore, even when one or a group of evaluators might eliminate any language or cultural errors in the localization, and the sites might appear lexically and syntactically correct, the combination of lexical or syntactic items might not appear totally natural to end users. To a certain extent, this is due to the fact that the localized text does not show the collocations and colligations that users are primed to expect in specific communicative situations (Hoey 2005). In order to adjust translated texts to the expected primed features in the user's mind, one of the current approaches in TS is to resort to comparable corpora (Bowker 2001; Shreve 2006b; Bowker and Barlow 2009; Jiménez-Crespo 2009, 2010). Nevertheless, the compilation of a corpus of similar texts naturally produced in the target language is nearly impossible for emerging and imported genres. The Facebook approach to evaluation bridges this gap as it extracts from a large group of active users a snapshot of what would be more "natural" or "adequate", a notion related to their lexical and syntactic primings (Hoey 2005). The goal of the Facebook model, despite a totally different approach, is therefore to identify what a community of users is primed to expect in this social networking genre. Thus, if discourse communities around the world would produce from scratch social networking sites that could be compiled in a corpus, the results of analyzing them would be similar to what they are already expressing by voting on proposed translations in Facebook.

To sum up briefly, I have argued in this section that the Facebook evaluation model, in which a large number of users votes positively or negatively on proposed translations, can help guarantee that the resulting website complies with the expected features in a digital genre that any discourse community might have. This is quite similar to the goals of corpus-assisted approaches: to explore the most common linguistic and pragmatic features in any genre, features that are extracted through the analysis of textual corpora of texts naturally produced by the target discourse community.

5.7 Empirical studies on crowdsourcing translation quality in TS

Quality has been the focus of a number of studies in MT research and in fansub contexts (see Chapter 7), but few quantitative studies on the quality of translated products have so far been published within TS (Pérez and Carreira 2011; Jiménez-Crespo 2013b, 2016), together with one MA dissertation (Deriemaeker 2014). The first two studies focus on the quality of the translations on Facebook from different perspectives, while the later focuses on touristic translations using Duolingo. The MA dissertation of Deriemaeker (2014) replicates the contrastive approach between professional and non-professional translations that has become so widespread in fansubbing (see 7.4.1). It, however, compares professional published translations of Spanish tourist brochures with those resulting from an experimental task using the Duolingo interface. Thirty-six participants completed surveys and participated in the translations. The results show that overall, the number of errors between professional and non-professional translations tends to be similar, but neverthe-less, upon a closer look, the types of errors are more serious in the crowdsourced versions while errors in professional translations carry lower weights according to the quality evaluation model used. The study does suggest that the quality of non-professional translations is adequate for information purposes and are "very much understandable to readers" (ibid: 48).

Pérez and Carreira (2011) analyzed the FB Spain user interface using an er-ror measuring scale that identified patterns of inadequacies in this translated so-cial networking site. In tune with previous web localization studies, it identified calques, lexical selection, coherence, spelling and formatting as the main issues. Jiménez-Crespo used a corpus based approach to research crowdsourcing in TS (Jiménez-Crespo 2013b, 2016). The research questions for these studies related to previous corpus studies on the "language of translation" (Baker 1995), attempting to identify whether crowdsourcing can produce "natural" sounding translations, as well as whether the Facebook model in which volunteers propose translations that are subsequently voted on is more effective to reach that goal. In the first study, Jiménez-Crespo used comparable corpus-based methods in TS in order to research whether the Spanish version of Facebook included the most frequent lex-ical items in the potential range of variation in non-translated or original Spanish social networking sites. The comparable corpus included a translational section with 142 lexical items in interactive segments in the crowdsourced Spain version of Facebook. The non-translational comparable section included all the interactive and navigation segments in the 25 most popular Spanish social networking sites. The results showed that the localized version of Facebook included the most frequent lexical units and syntactic patterns for each communicative purpose investigated. This study therefore confirms that the method used by this company is effective in order to achieve texts similar to non-translated ones.

In the following experimental study (Jiménez-Crespo 2016), seventy-five fourth year translation students at the School of Translation and Interpreting, Granada Spain, were divided into three experimental groups. The first one had to directly translate a Facebook navigation menu from English (subjects were unaware that the segments belonged to the Facebook UI), the second one had to select the translation from the potential range of terminological variations found in the previous corpus study (i.e. "upload photo" can be expressed also as "change profile pic", "change your photo", etc.), and the third group consisted of a control group in which subjects were instructed to write from scratch directly in Spanish the navigation options for a social networking site. The testing instruments were directly created from the results of the corpus study (2013b), following a bottom up approach to experimental design. The results were triangulated with the existing comparable corpus. The results showed that the voting method used by Facebook, that is, participants offer translation proposals for each segment and others subsequently vote for the one they prefer, produces different results depending on the translation method (select translation, do a translation of a segment). On average, selecting a translation resulted in longer and more explicit renderings while translations were on average shorter and closer to the conventional items found in the corpus. This finding points to potential differences in translated products depending on the translation method used, opening the door to further research into the products of translation crowdsourcing.

CHAPTER 6

Texts and crowdsourcing

Perspectives from textual, discursive and linguistic approaches

> [T]o translate the overall message of the text, translators often
> need to work outside the artificial boundaries of sentences,
> so the sentence-by-sentence approach imposed by TMs may not be
> conducive to effective translation of the text's message as a whole.
>
> (Bowker 2006: 180)

6.1 Introduction

Recent developments in crowdsourcing and volunteer translation pose exciting new challenges to existing theorizations in TS that conceptualize texts as stable and complete units that are subject to translation activities. This chapter critically analyses textual and linguistic approaches in TS in the light of different models of textual processing, production, distribution and reception in an era of crowdsourcing and collaborative translation. The main issue that is analyzed is the relation between micro-task crowdsourcing and the necessary segmentation and disaggregation of source texts. This issue, the atomization of the source text through segmentation, distribution and reintegration continues to challenge some tenets of TS, such as the unit of translation, the necessity or not of complete cohesive texts as the units of analysis and processing, the role of cohesion and coherence or the emergence of new translation products. It explores how over the years the adoption of TM systems and the emergence of novel digital modalities, such as localization, with new textual forms, started to challenge the mantra that complete cohesive texts are necessary for both translation production and for translation research purposes. It explores approaches to textual segmentation and it provides two categorizations of texts in crowdsourcing depending on process or product-based parameters.

6.2   Defining texts in an era of dynamic texts produced in collaboration

Contemporary theories understand translation as a communicative, cognitive and textual process (Hurtado Albir 2001), as well as a social (Wolf 2010), cultural (Bassnet and Lefevere 1990) and technological one (Jiménez-Crespo 2013a; O'Brien 2012b). As a textual process, one of the underlying premises in translation theories, models and paradigms is the existence of stable unitary texts that are transferred, moved, transformed, processed, transcreated, modified, adapted or manipulated according to the approach taken. Stable and finite source and target texts are often contrasted for research purposes in linguistic, discursive or rhetoric approaches. They represent the minimal unit of translation and analysis from a pragmatic and communicative perspective (i.e., Hatim and Mason 1990; Hurtado Albir 2001; Bowker 2006), as well as the minimal unit in quality evaluation perspectives (i.e., Williams 2003; Colina 2009; House 2014).

As a whole, the notion of "text" has been at the core of TS since its inception (Neubert and Shreve 1992; Neubert 1997). It represents a fundamental point of departure for both scholarly discussions and it is so fundamental in the development of the discipline, that text linguistic approaches even departed from the premise that texts are "the central defining issue in translation" and also "[t]exts and their situations define the translation process" (Neubert and Shreve 1992: 5). Under this text linguistic approach, source and target texts during translation tasks are "communicative occurrences" that need to fulfill the seven standards of textuality according to Beaudegrande and Dressler (1981): cohesion, coherence, intentionality, acceptability, informativity, situationality and intertextuality. The existence of source texts and target texts that meet these seven standards represent the point of departure for product explorations in the discipline.

Textual approaches never gained much traction in TS, but nevertheless, the notion of "text" continues to be central to theories, research methodologies, translation training, etc. Discussions on the nature of what a "text" is abound in most directions and subdisciplines. For example, the study of scientific texts brought up how texts contain graphic and textual content, while AVT research expanded the notion of text to include multimodal, aural, visual or sound aspects of the audiovisual text (Diaz Cintas 2003; Remael 2010). Texts were also redefined in the hypertextual era in web localization (Jiménez-Crespo 2013a) or an era of internationalization of software (Pym 2004) to include interactivity, accessibility or cultural considerations. Cognitive TS has also focused on how texts are processed and how they are splitted into "units of translation" (Alves and Gonçalves 2003; Alves and Vale 2009). No matter how many issues surround the act of translation, the existence of source and target texts, together with the relationship between them, to paraphrase Toury's postulates (1995), represents the fundamental core of any translational phenomenon.

The underlying notion that stable texts were a premise in translation theory started to be undermined with the advent of translation technologies. Translation memory technologies and MT required the segmentation of cohesive ST into textual units, primarily at the sentence level. The reasons for textual segmentation were not due to cognitive processing or theoretical principles, but rather to programming imperatives (Shreve 2006b), thus imposing technology over discourse, linguistic or cognitive considerations. These discrete textual segments, if processed in isolation by crowdsourcing participants, can represent instances of language that are "non-communicative" according to text linguistics and, consequently, "non-communicative texts are treated as non-texts" (Beaudegrande and Dressler 1981:3). During the initial inquiries into the impact of TM technologies, the jury was out: could "non-texts" be the units of translation? (Bowker 2006; Shreve 2006b). Nowadays, this question seems to have fallen into oblivion. Nevertheless, it seems more pertinent than ever. It seems like the imperative that translation operates on fully formed texts is already out of the window in crowdsourcing approaches.

One of the basic premises of crowdsourcing is that a global task is decomposed into micro tasks that are subsequently taken up by the crowd (Brabham 2013), leading to a faster and more efficient task completion. The actualization of this premise in translation means that the material for the task, that source text itself, can be atomized and distributed to a multiplicity of agents that process discrete small tasks, the translation segments themselves as described in Chapter 3. Linguistic-inspired TS theories insist that processing at the macrotextual level is essential to the production of a coherent and cohesive target text (Baker 2011) with sufficient quality (Larose 1999; Williams 2004) and that fulfills the intended communicative purpose (Nord 1997). However, this micro task processing approach has completely tipped the balance towards a microtextual approach, completely ignoring global macrotextual considerations or, in cases, shifting them (or not) to be taken care of by alternative procedures as seen in Chapter 3. It is not only the macrotextual level that is forgotten; decades of research have added a multiplicity of layers to the analysis of translation production, such as pragmatic, communicative, rhetoric, or sociocultural layers. These all also seem to be completely absent in these novel approaches, apparently turning the tide and taking translation back to the early days of linguistic and equivalence based approaches at the sentence level (i.e., Vinay and Darbelnet 1958; Catford 1965; Vázquez Áyora 1977). Crowdsourcing and collaborative practices thus directly challenge the overpowering notion of the existence of a discrete textual unit, however it might be defined, that exists prior to the act of translation and that is subsequently processed as a unit, distributed and presented to end users.

6.3   The atomization of texts in TS: From TM to localization

This atomization and segmentation of texts in order to be processed in technological settings is nothing new to the discipline. It was in the late 80's with the technological revolution that the segmentation of texts into discrete units started to challenge existing theoretical models based on a static and stable text (i.e., Bowker 2006; Pym 2004). The segmentation paradigm only grew from there and today, it is the norm in professional approaches through TM tools, MT, localization models that separate translatable segments from programming code (Pym 2004; Jiménez-Crespo 2009, 2013; O'Hagan and Mangiron 2013) and obviously, crowdsourcing. Research on TM and localization offers invaluable insights into the challenges of textual segmentation in TS.

6.3.1   Textual segmentation and TM

Translation memories brought the first revolution in the way texts where processed during translation tasks. These software solutions used segmentation to align the source texts and target texts in order to facilitate future reuse (Macklovitch and Russell 2002; Bowker 2002; Sin-Wai 2014). TM systems process translations incrementally in segments, usually sentences separated by full periods, presented to translators one by one. When a usable TM exists prior to the translation itself, the leveraging of this asset can lead to what scholars refer to as "batch mode" (Bowker 2002) or "pre-translation" mode; that is, a process in which the TM system populates the target texts with existing full matches from previous translations. If selected, the system offers the option of presenting the translator only those segments that do not have an existing match. Translators can then work only on those segments without matches available in the database, shifting from the linear processing of the pre-technological era to a segmental and non-linear approach. Collaboration is also an essential element of TM tools, since they can also be used collaboratively in synchronic or diachronic models through networked TM servers.

The adoption of TM systems was related to significant gains in speed and efficiency of the translation process in the industry, leading to faster turnaround and higher productivity for professionals. According to Reinke, the gains were significant: "users in industry and international organizations usually claim a 25 to 60 per cent rise in productivity" (2013: 2). The same discourse on efficiency and productivity has been used in crowdsourcing, where speed and efficiency are often presented by the industry and scholars as one of the main benefits (DePalma and Kelly 2011).

The overall change of paradigm from a linear to a segmental non-linear approach introduced implications that publications quickly pointed out. Scholars early on started to theorize on the gradual disappearance of the notion of single unitary stable texts and the potential consequences for the practice of translation (i.e., Bedard 2000; Shreve 2006b; Bowker 2006). Overwhelmingly, the discourse on the consequences of segmentation and TM tended to be negative. For example, professional translators would lose control of the overall translation understood as an individual and linear process, always framed within the fight between the industrialization and globalization forces that demand higher productivity and speed (García 2009; Cronin 2013). It was feared that translators themselves, as one more agent in the streamlined industrial translation process, could become simple "sentence translators" (Bedard 2000). Who would have thought then that, nowadays, crowdsourcing could precisely inspire micro task approaches in professional contexts that take this model even further?

It was argued that the reducing of tasks from the text level as a whole to processing translations in a constrained segmental process was a substandard approach that hindered the production of quality in translation. The issues were both in the comprehension and reformulation stages:

> to translate the overall message of the text, translators often need to work outside the artificial boundaries of sentences, so the sentence-by-sentence approach imposed by TMs may not be conducive to effective translation of the text's message as a whole. (Bowker 2006: 180)

Translators, thus, as agents fighting against the impositions of technologies, were perceived to be in charge of preserving the text message as a whole as embodied in a complete text, the minimal unit of translation from a communicative and pragmatic perspective. Who would have thought that today, crowdsourcing has precisely continued expanding this much-feared "sentence translating" process through micro-task crowdsourcing in professional and non-professional settings?

A number of empirical studies ensued, attempting to discover the changes in how translators themselves processed translations within the cognitive paradigm (i.e., Dragstead 2006; Macklovitch and Russell 2002), a trend that has continued until today (Mellinger 2014; Cardoso-Teixeira 2014). The results of these studies suggest that segmental processing is inadequate since translation entails negotiation in the process between the macro and micro structural levels (Shreve 2006b), while translation in TM environments can reduce the task to the sentence level (Dragstead 2006). Not having the entire texts during the translation was supposed to be highly problematic for processing since this means that "the very notion of a document [is] lost" (Macklovitch and Russell 2002: 137). The loss was so significant that some authors even claimed the "death of the source text" through the intensive use of TM and GMS systems. In these cases, the "text is not called on to represent any previous texts, it is instead part of one and the same process of constant material distribution" (Pym 2004: 6). In this context, translator themselves, who were used to processing a text from beginning to end, would change the way translations were produced. It was feared that they would formulate texts in a way so as to maximize their future reuse with TM, for example avoiding anaphoric or cataphoric references. Heyn referred to this effect as "peephole translations" (Heyn 1998: 135), the result of an excessive focus on microstructures without a clear global macrostructural guiding model. Nevertheless, nowadays it is clear that this lack of context and co-text can affect differently professionals and non-professionals: a basic processing difference between professionals and novices or bilinguals in TS literature is the ability to negotiate and process any microstructure in a text within the overall framework of the macrostructure and overall translation specifications (Jääskeläinen 1989) (see 4.3.1). Thus, Jiménez-Crespo (2013: 54) argues that from a cognitive perspective, professionals, through prior accumulated experience with similar texts or by constructing a mental model of what the texts might be, consciously or unconsciously can possess a model of the global text that compensates for this potential lack of communicative context or co-text.

The conclusions of studies on TM segmentation also point out the drawbacks for the translation products, the translations themselves. The products of segmented translation processes appear as a hodgepodge of sentences produced by multiple translators without a consistent tone and style due to the combination of multiple authoring and the insertion of pre-translated segments. This is what scholars referred to with a myriad of terms such as "sentence salads" (Bedard 2000), "train wrecks" (Bowker 2006), or "collage texts" (Mossop 2006). Translated texts could be "inherently less cohesive or coherent, less readable and of lesser overall quality" (Bowker 2006: 180). Sentence-by-sentence processing would also result in target texts with exactly the same textual structure of source texts, resulting in what Larose (1998) refers to as "cloned texts". This was perceived as a serious issue in translation quality in cases when the language pair exhibits differences in the discursive structuring of texts (Jiménez-Crespo 2011). Translated texts, additionally, would not necessarily show increasing levels of coherence and quality as advertised by all industry publications if TM were used, since translated texts can show lower coherence and cohesion levels than naturally produced texts (Jiménez-Crespo 2009).

In a sense, all these effects and issues also appear in crowdsourcing. Sentence-based processing results in "cloned texts" with similar macrostructures to the ST, even when similar conventionalized genres in different cultures can possess totally different structures (Jiménez-Crespo 2011). Texts can be less cohesive and coherent, an issue that is often addressed in the industry with language managers or assigning reviewing to higher-status participants. Many initiatives include context with each segment assigned, and the most popular initiatives are those with embedded communities; that is, the users of a website, a software product or a videogame are the same ones translating. The segments are presented within the overall framework of the global cohesive text, the entire website, software product, etc., and therefore the macrostructural framework of reference is clear for participants.

This issues might nevertheless be more prevalent nowadays in crowdsourcing that in professional translation. Recent empirical studies seem to point at an adaptation of professionals to working with TM tools. For example, Bundgaard, Christensen and Schjoldager (2016) in an empirical study on the use of MT-TM tools observed that professionals do observe the coherence relationships in the work text and work outside the constraints of TM segmentation. In the discussion of their study it is indicated that

> the translator broke with the sequential, segment-by-segment method that is encouraged by the CAT tool, indicating that s/he was (still) focused on the text as a cohesive entity.   (Burndgaard, Christensen and Schjoldager 2016: 155)

Translation expertise might thus, in the context of translation as human computer interaction (O'Brien 2012b), entail an adaptation to the constraints of working with TM tools, while non-professionals working in segmental environments might rely on the fixed and strict segmentation approach offered by crowdsourcing platforms.

6.3.2 Textual segmentation and localization

The 90's also saw the emergence of new modalities, such as software, web and videogame localization that continued to challenge the notion of what a text in translation was. These modalities also inspired discussions on the negative effects of segmentation and the processing of isolated textual segments. Several issues emerged in addition to all that was previously described in relation to TM use, such as the multimodality of text, the processes set in place to handle the dynamic nature of digital texts or the role and significance of the translation of "text" in the overall process. In the first case, digital texts are multimodal entities that contain two superimposed structures: the presentation structure of what users see on screen, together with the deep or programming structure. The presentation structure is multimodal and interactive in nature, while the deep structure contains a representation of this presentation structure tangled with programming code. The translators work either directly on the surface structure using visual

WYSIWYG localization tools or translated lists of textual segments extracted from software products or videogames on Excel or txt lists (Esselink 2000; Pym 2004), or nowadays in-cloud solutions that separate textual segments from code. These last processes entail a complete decontextualization of the segments to be translated, often forcing translators to carry out the task without the global framework offered by the entire software or videogame package (Pym 2010). To date, this is a recurring practice despite the continuous development of technologies (Bernal-Merino 2015). This separation of coding structure and multimodal elements from the actual textual strings to translate still continues in crowdsourcing approaches, since it is the preferred model for crowdsourcing in all types of localization.

Another issue of interest was how to handle massive texts and their dynamic and unstable nature. Collaboration was necessary and it expanded exponentially since the emergence of dynamic processes in software and web localization. Software products and videogames are so large, with constant updates throughout time, that collaboration is the norm. The same would happen with localized websites, in instances of open dynamic texts in which new hypertextual nodes, content or web pages can be added continuously and a pipeline is necessary to efficiently localize hypertexts and updates into their chosen locales. New technologies were developed to produce, translate, integrate and distribute web content seamlessly. TM tools evolved into more complex Content or Global Management Systems (CMS and GMS) with the objective of handling an ever-increasing number of language versions of multilingual documentation dynamic websites. These systems combined the previous textual segmentation capabilities and functionalities of translation memories and dynamically managed the translation of updates or changes into multiple languages. GMS facilitate translation processes by means of identification and feeding to translators precisely the textual segments or "chunks" that have been modified or added to any large project. Crowdsourcing platforms represent the natural evolution and adaptation of these systems to novel practices, with platforms such as Glotpress integrated into the web content creation system Wordpress, in order to seamlessly localize new user-generated content by the crowd.

The last issue of interest with the emergence of localization was the role of "textual" aspects in the overall process. Discourse and narratives often delved into whether translation of the "text" is just one, often unimportant, of the many steps within a larger production chain. Back then, this debate was framed within the insistence by the localization industry that translation simply dealt only with "texts", while localization, and its programming, management, internationalization or globalization dealt with issues of higher importance (Jiménez-Crespo 2013: 14–17). In industry publications, translation was seen as "the core skill of converting text from one language to another, whether on hard copy or electronically" (Sprung

2000: 10). In other cases, localization related to "significant, non-textual components of products or services in addition to strict translation" (LISA 2007: 11). After
decades of scholarly reflection in TS in order to dispel the notion that translation
was merely a linguistic replacement process, new technological developments and
workflows have again reduced the work of translators to a micro-linguistic level.
Meanwhile, management, programming, and integration are seen as something
"more sophisticated than [textual] translation" (Pym 2004: 25). How important
might the actual translation of segment by a volunteer be when twenty other members might also propose a different translation for this same source segment? Is
the translation of textual segments as important as management, localization engineering or quality assurance? A parallelism can be seen here. Crowdsourcing
also emphasizes workflows, management and practices to motivate and manage
a non-professional crowd. The participants can be any bilinguals in many cases,
or even monolinguals (Hu et al. 2011), while highly skilled managers and developers appear in highly recognized positions. Crowdsourcing paradigms might
have taken to the extreme those practices that started with software localization
related to having translators deal within "linguistic content" or the "text", while
other agents handle a wide range of extralinguistic and extratextual tasks such as
management, engineering, etc.

6.4 Texts in a crowdsourcing era: Insights from linguistics and TS

Even when crowdsourcing represents a case in which texts are atomized, processed
and reconstructed in innovative way never seen before, target texts do emerge
from this process and final users have available fully operational texts. Users in
Russian interact with the crowdsourced Russian version of Twitter or audiences
in Chile can enjoy their preferred subtitled TED talks online. Insights from the
different strands of linguistics and TS can assist in identifying features that helped
conceptualize for research purposes the notion of text in modern collaborative
practices. Following the theoretical review by Jiménez-Crespo (2013: 48–49) for
texts in web localization, this list summarizes the key features of what represents
a text from different perspectives:

1. First of all, texts are "units". This can be considered the most repeated mantra
    from all perspectives. As an example, from a systemic – functionalist ap-
    proach, this notion is understood as an essential property of a text, a "unified
    whole" (Halliday and Hassan 1976: 1). From a text-linguistic approach, they
    represent a single "communicative occurrence" (Beaudegrande and Dressler
    1981), or the fundamental unit of language from a communicative perspective.

In TS, and departing from these systemic-functionalist, text linguistic or discourse approaches, a text is a "coherent and cohesive unit" (Hatim and Mason 1990) or a "coherent whole" (Göpferich 1995). In localization, they are simply "whatever unit is distributed as a unit" (Pym 2004:170), or "a digital interactive entity that is coherently developed as a unit and presented to users as such" (Jiménez-Crespo 2013:51). Crowdsourcing represents a new paradigm, but the approach, as far as TS is concerned, is very similar to the localization of dynamic digital texts. Even if during translation tasks participants might not have access to the entire source text, it "does exist, even when at specific moments [...] translators might not have access to the global text" (Jiménez-Crespo 2013:54). The disappearance of the source text as a complete textual unit "has to be understood in the context of [cognitive approaches to] translation [...] and not necessarily a product-based one" (ibid).

2. The unitary character of any text is represented in its inherent nature, referred to as "textuality" (Beaudegrande and Dressler 1981:3). This nature combines semantic and linguistic aspects (close to structuralist and generativist linguistic theories), as well as pragmatic ones (adopting the perspective that highlights the important role of extralinguistic aspects). Textuality, as the global essence of any text is related to the notion of "texture" (Hatim and Mason 1997), defined as the property of any text by virtue of which it has a conceptual and linguistic consistency, that is, it has a continuity both in its sense (coherent) and in its surface elements (cohesive), and also possesses a clearly articulated thematic progression (Hurtado 2001:415). Coherence is often highlighted as one of the most important properties of translated texts, and in translation it is often associated with a dynamic approach in which coherence is defined as a mental action (not just a static property of texts) that is assigned by language users in their interactions with texts and discourse (Van Dijk 1988:62). Coherence is seen as a necessary tool to make the text "hang together conceptually" (Hatim and Mason 1990:239) and it is "the result of the interaction between the knowledge presented in the texts and the reader's own knowledge and experience of the world" (Baker 2011:219). In this regard, coherence cannot be understood as a universal feature of text, but rather as dependent on the receiver's intervention through a process of inference during textual processing. This overall "texture" or global cohesive nature of the text is one aspect that crowdsourcing workflow models take into account (or not) in their development, such as hybrid collaborative models that hire "experts" to oversee the entire global process. In other systems with voting mechanisms, it is expected that the crowd as a whole through its "collective intelligence" might produce similar, more or less cohesive results throughout the process in terms of linguistic traits. The achievement of this overall global coherence

can also be achieved through mechanisms, such as glossary matches as in the case of Facebook, or the intervention of participants of higher status that oversee the overall process.

3. A text is "situated"; that is, it is only considered as such through the "actualization" that a specific receiver does in a specific reception situation (Reiss and Vermeer 1984: 90). This implies that there could be as many instances of any texts as potential receivers (Nord 1997). This dependence on the context of reception in the "actualization" of a text makes reading a unique act that depends on this reception situation. According to Beaudegrande and Dressler, reading is "a process subject to the particular contextual constraints of the occasion, just as much as the production of the texts is" (Beaudegrande 1978: 30). From Neubert's (1997) text-linguistic approach, the fact that any translation depends on the unique reading and comprehension process of a translator has been referred to as "translational relativity". This notion is of interest in crowdsourcing research for two reasons. First of all, this unique actualization process can differ considerably between end users' reading processes and those of translators. Depending on the workflow selected for the collaborative and crowdsourcing practices, participants can work with lists of segments or discrete units that are often not the final communicative structure of the text. Consequently, the distinct comprehension process during translation can lack certain communicative cues that often reflect the configuration and features of localized TTs (Jiménez-Crespo 2009b; 2013). The crowdsourced texts with multiple participants can also be the result of a multitude of processes of "translational relativity" (Neubert 1997), with a range of interpretations of the source segment by participants. However, iterative and participatory models represent a mechanism to level the individual "translation relativity" and achieve a collective interpretation and rendition of the source text. In these cases, the "situatedness" of a text and the implications for individualistic translation processes disappear.

4. Texts are defined not only by linguistic or verbal aspects, but also by non-verbal ones such as graphics, typographic, visual (Nord 1991; Göpferich 1995), and multimedia elements (Remael 2010), as well as interactive ones in the case of digital texts (Jiménez-Crespo 2013a). This global entity represents a unitary whole whose value is greater than the sheer sum of their verbal and non-verbal elements (Snell-Hornby 1996: 55). Nord, for example, defined a text as "the totality of communicative signals used in a communicative interaction" (1991: 14). A text, therefore, is not merely expressed by linguistic means, but rather, it is a communicative action that can be "realized by a combination of verbal and non-verbal means" (Nord 1991: 15). Similarly, Göpferich defined texts in technical translation as "a coherent whole made up by linguistic

or graphic-linguistic elements" (Göpferich 1995a: 57).[1] Crowdsourcing approaches range from those that reduce the task to the linguistic level with isolated sentences, to those that include the multimodal nature of translated texts in YGWYS environments. This last approach appears in a variety of initiatives, such as the cases of crowd post-editing of websites using Microsoft Collaborative Translation Framework (Aikawa, Yamamoto and Isahara 2012), Wikipedia, Duolingo or the open reviewing of subtitles in Amara.

5. All texts possess a specific textual configuration or structure that is determined by its communicative purpose. Texts as such cannot exist without this communicative purpose (Göpferich 1995: 40). Many types of texts possess highly conventionalized textual structures (García Izquierdo 2005), and this is similar in many digital genres, web texts (Jiménez-Crespo 2009, 2010, 2011, 2013a), software products and videogames (O'Hagan and Mangiron 2013). The crowdsourcing processing paradigm also invariable reproduces source text super and macrostructures due to the technological processing, not taking into account the possibility of genre-dependent structural differences between cultures (Jiménez-Crespo 2011).

6. Texts can be classified as "simple" and "complex texts" (Reiss and Vermeer 1984). "Complex texts" can incorporate other instances of texts in their open structure. This distinction between simple and complex texts is highly productive for the purposes of social networking sites, the prime target of crowdsourcing practices online, as most websites can incorporate instances of simple texts in their structures. For example, users can find a video blog, a recipe or a poem within a social networking site, or a privacy contract inside a social networking site. In crowdsourcing, it is common to disaggregate global texts such as software products or websites and offer online some parts of the texts, such as user interfaces or embedded games to the crowd, while other more serious texts, such as legal texts, are translated by professionals. Reiss and Vermeer also proposed the notion of "complementary texts", those that depend on the existence of prior texts, such as a book review or a search engine. Search engines, such as Google, have also been subject to translation by the crowd (Google in Your Language Campaign).

---

1. The definition used by Göpferich is: "a coherent whole made up by linguistic or graphic-linguistic elements that presents a textual and-or functional orientation. It was created with a specific purpose, the communicative purpose, it fulfills an identifiable communicative function […] and represent a unit with a thematic and functional unit" (Göpferich 1995: 57).

6.5 "Entire texts" as the unit of translation: The crowdsourcing perspective

For over two decades, the notion that entire texts are the minimal unit of translation recurrently appears in the discipline in discussions on text linguistic approaches, research on the "unit of translation" or the impact of TM use. Complete texts are seen as necessary for successful translation processes in opposition to current segment-based technological paradigms in which the overall text is often unavailable (Mossop 2006). According to Bowker in discussing TM use:

> To understand the message contained in the source text (ST), translators must read the entire text through at least once before beginning to translate.
>
> (Bowker 2006: 176)

The necessity of processing the entire text as a whole is related to issues of cohesion or coherence. In this regard and from a Discourse Analysis perspective, Hatim and Mason argued that complete texts are necessary since "it is of vital importance for translators to identify text boundaries" (1990: 178). Textual boundaries in finite texts are essential in this approach to correctly processing the ST since they assist in the identification of coherence and cohesion relationships in the comprehension processes. Subsequently, they also help produce appropriate cohesive TTs.

The perspective provided by Discourse Analysis can be highly beneficial at this point to understand the significance the unitary nature of texts, especially the distinction between super, macro and micro superstructures of texts. These three structures represent the three levels of text representations according to the psychological model of text processing of Van Dijk and Kintsch (1983). Micro and macrostructures refer to the meaning or propositional content of the text, the lexico-grammatical content or semantic meaning made up of propositions or sentences. The macrostructure represents the global meaning structure or the gist of the entire text and it is formed through the text base provided by the microstructures or propositions. Superstructures represent the global structure container or global structure in which the macrostructure or textual content is presented. For example, the superstructure of a news report would be the headline, lead, context, and event. In the case of an online contact form, the superstructure would include the presentation of the contact form and invitation to use it, fields to fill out with contact details, and submission of the contact information (Jiménez-Crespo 2010a). In micro task crowdsourcing approaches, tasks are often reduced to syntactic and lexical issues at a microstructural level. Macrostructural level issues, related to a greater degree to pragmatic, discursive and communicative issues, are therefore limited. Often, the global macrostructural coherence and as well as superstructural considerations are delegated (or not) either to experts or "premium" members of the community. In other cases such as Wikipedia, micro, macro and superstructural considerations, from lexical choices to the different sections and subsections included in the article, are left up to the "wisdom of the crowd". This issue brings about whether non-professionals or bilinguals that typically participate in these processes might possess the ability to be guided by any sort of "macrostructure" in order to process any specific segment. The ability to negotiate and process any microstructure in a text within the overall framework of the macrostructure and overall translation specifications represents a basic processing difference between professionals and novices or bilinguals in TS literature. Nevertheless, it has been argued that in specific cases such as fansubs or videogame localization (O'Hagan 2009), fans might possess a better understanding of the genre — that is, the macrostructure of the text and a number of extratextual parameters guiding the translation — than professionals. In a sense, a collective of users as a whole might possess knowledge about linguistic, pragmatic or discursive features of these fast evolving digital genres that professional translators might lack.

In collaborative and crowdsourcing models, it could also be argued that the responsibility put on the translators' shoulders by successive translation theories, models and paradigms to operate in these three structural levels has been compartmentalized and shifted (or often ignored) by agents managing and developing the processes from single translators and their reviewers to a collectivity or one or more agents that oversee specific aspects of the process. One example can be the language specialists hired by Facebook to oversee the entire website, considered here as a complete text (Jiménez-Crespo 2013a), Asia Online leaves the decision to human experts to select the best translation in cases in which the three versions of a segment that are post-edited by volunteers are different, and in paid crowdsourcing companies, such as Clickworker, expert translators always oversee the entire process. According to this website:

> We set the project up online, divide it into individual microtasks and make it available to translators [...] Every translation undergoes a final check by a qualified corrector with regard to spelling, grammar and adherence to the task specifications.

This means that rather than ignoring the significance of issues beyond the microstuctural level, crowdsourcing models decompose tasks that were the domain of professional translators or the components of translation expertise to specific agents in the process. These tasks related to macrostructural considerations can be related to maintaining global lexical or syntactic coherence (Baker 2011), or keeping a target user-based orientation. The atomization of the task, a basic step in crowdsourcing management, therefore extends not only to the separation of segments, but to specific skills, steps, or tasks identified as part of the production of a quality translation that are understood to be possessed by translation professionals. These skills are recognized and assigned as an additional task in the overall process to different agents (or not) depending on the workflow.

If crowdsourcing initiatives are classified in the light of how texts are segmented, a broad spectrum of interaction types emerge according to how participants interact with the ST. Figure 6.1 introduces this wide diverse range of approaches to process STs. It is based on a workflow process-based analysis of crowdsourcing initiatives and it includes only those in which the control is within an organization and not the community. Both side of the cline include whether participants access isolated segments or full texts during the process.

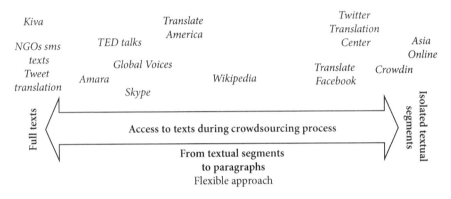

Figure 6.1 Access to the text during collaborative translation processes.

In some cases, participants engage in regular processes translating self-contained texts from beginning to end, such as the case of Kiva microloan applications, the translation of tweets (Arend 2012; Šubert and Bojar 2014), SMS messages (Munro 2010) or even the possibility of subtitling an entire video (Baker 2015). On the other side of the spectrum appear translations of highly dynamic texts, such as Wikipedia, that can be translated directly through the Wikipedia site, or through selected workflows such as the Asia Online Wikipedia initiative (see 3.4.4). While the first examples would entail the interaction with complete texts, the latter simply entails processing decontextualized textual chunks similar to what happened with localization (Jiménez-Crespo 2011). For example, social networking genres are ever expanding textual forms that change throughout time, requiring a constant flow of crowdsourcing. Even when the Spanish version of Facebook was supposedly localized in one week in 2007, today the crowdsourcing platform continues to display segments for translation into Spanish-Spain. It would be of great interest to delve into linguistic or corpus-based analyses of the different textual population that emerge from these different processes. The discipline would also benefit from the study from a cognitive perspective of the potential differences in processing in the different process settings in Figure 6.1.

6.6   The "unit of translation" and crowdsourcing

Decomposing any text into discrete textual segments units for crowdsourcing brings about another important notion in TS: the "unit of translation". This notion has throughout the years been a core concept in Translation Studies (Kenny 2009, 2011a), and different proposals have argued that the minimal operative unit can be anything from a lexical unit to the text or the entire culture (i.e. Bassnet and Lefevere 1990). As previously mentioned, crowdsourcing adopts the technology approach that separates translation units according to programming or workflow imperatives rather than cognitive or communicative ones. Nevertheless, a review of existing approaches in TS can be beneficial in a comprehensive overview and analysis of crowdsourcing. For these purposes, several trends are of interest. The first one emerges from natural language processing and language automation, and the other two, contrastive linguistics and cognitive approaches, are part of TS.

Crowdsourcing approaches to textual segmentation are mainly grounded on research carried out within natural language processing approaches or those related to language automation. From this perspective, Bowker defined this notion in the context of TM as "a source text segment stored in a memory along with its corresponding translation" (Bowker 2002: 155). This notion is often referred to as a "translation memory entry" and it also incorporates the necessary metadata to make the bilingual pair indexed and retrievable. In TM parallel corpus-based research, the textual segmentation is normally carried out at the level of punctuation or sentence level, with modern systems incorporating the possibility of alignment and retrieval at the word or clause level, known as "subsentential matches". This approach does not claim any psychological validity of the translation unit extracted (Kenny 2009: 84), since the main objective is to produce useful data for translation-related applications, and therefore, units are extracted and validated based on technological criteria. Segmentation is often achieved in technological platforms using the SRX standard (Segmentation Rules eXchange) developed by OSCAR group in the now extinct LISA organization. It was designed as a vendor-neutral standard for segmentation in translation memory exchanges created by different types of computer-assisted tools. Crowdsourcing platforms often incorporate TM functionalities for collaborative translations, except for those iterative models in which volunteers both translate and vote for the best proposals.

The two perspectives that are of interest in TS for the purposes of analyzing the notion of units of translation in crowdsourcing are comparative stylistics and cognitive approaches. In cognitive approaches (see Chapter 4), translation units are research constructs. In earlier psycholinguistic approaches that perceive the "mind as a computer", and this "computer" processes discrete tasks that can relate to translation problems, solutions and strategies. Translation units are often defined as the textual segment upon which a translator focuses his/her attention at any given moment and therefore it is a dynamic notion that varies according to each translator and the task at hand. One of the most influential definitions of this notion was offered by Alves and Gonçalves (2003:10–11):

> segments of the source text, independent of specific size or form, to which, at a given moment, the translator's focus of attention is directed. It is a segment in constant transformation that changes according to the translator's cognitive and processing needs.

This definition stressed the dynamic and flexible nature of translation units, since the cognitive environment of the subject is constantly adapting depending on a number of factors. The benefits of this approach have been to identify differences between professionals and novices or bilinguals. Research into translation units has identified that the former usually work with larger units than the latter (Lörcher 1991; Krings 1995), with novices or bilinguals normally working at the syntagma or word level. However, it should be noted that even when experts process larger units, they still work mostly at the sentence level (Krings 1995).

Alves in a later project proposed the existence of two operative constructs, micro and macro TUs. The former were defined as "the flow of continuous TT production which may incorporate the continuous reading of ST and TT segments separated by pauses during the translation process as registered by key-logging and/ or eye tracking software" (Alves and Vale 2009: 257). Macro TUs were defined as "a collection of micro TUs that comprise all the interim text productions that follow the translator's focus on the same ST segment from the first tentative rendering to the final output that appears in the TT" (ibid). This distinction draws the attention to the fact that, during the translation process, translators consider a number of "interim solutions", working within the boundaries of a flexible TU. In this stage of the processing, translators proceed to what is known as the "online revision" of the unit under consideration, until the final target text unit is written or edited. Even when these empirical and cognitive approaches to the notion of the translation unit are of less interest to the analysis of what happens with the text during crowdsourcing, it can draw the attention to those iterative processes in which a vast number of volunteers propose interim solutions and others vote for them. The final target text might display just one final target segment, but the crowd will produce a large number of interim solutions that can impact subsequent participants' cognitive processes during their participation (Jiménez-Crespo 2016).

The third and last perspective of interest is that of comparative linguistic approaches in TS. Vinay and Darbelnet (1958/1995:21) defined it as "the smallest segment of the utterance whose signs are linked in such a way that they should not be translated individually". This definition focuses on providing the foundation for their renowned translation strategies, attempting to identify correspondences at the lexical and clause level. The dependence on contrastive linguistics implies that the unit of translation serves merely as a construct in order to facilitate the contrastive analysis, and the focus was often at the subsentence level. Nevertheless, this approach had a great influence on subsequent theorizations, and scholars, such as Newmark have proposed having the sentence as "the natural unit of translation" (Newmark 1998: 165). Departing from Hallidayan systemic functional linguistics, the author considered the text as a macro translation unit that can represent the minimal unit of translation in some instances, since "all lengths of language can, at different moments and also simultaneously, be used as units of translation in the course of the translation activity" (1998: 66). With a broader perspective and from a target-oriented position, Toury (1995: 122) defines the translation unit as "the linguistic-textual unit in the original text within which the translator tended to work". Translation units were therefore defined from his descriptive perspective after the observation of translation behaviors and norms, and not fixed a priori. Despite placing the locus of the definition of translation within the variable of a translator's cognition (without mentioning it), Toury defines it as a linguistic textual unit, bringing an interesting combination of linguistic approaches with the specificities of a translator's performance and variability.

Later linguistic-centered approaches within communication or textual approaches shifted towards the entire text as the main unit of translation (Neubert and Shreve 1992; Hatim and Mason 1990; Neubert 1997). In these approaches, the text is the biggest possible translation unit; go "beyond the level of the text, [and] it is difficult to perceive any regularly occurring patterns which would enable us to identify a unit of discourse" (Hatim and Mason 1990: 178). Nevertheless, culturalist approaches took a step further and argued that higher possible units of translation are entirely culture. In the words Bassnett and Lefevere "neither the word, nor the text, but the culture becomes the operational 'unit' of translation" (1990: 8). After years of discussions, the popularity of crowdsourcing seems to swing the pendulum back to the clause or the sentence.

The reasons to go back to the sentence level stress the gap between translation theory and the industry. In crowdsourcing, platforms and workflows are developed by programmers and engineers following natural language or language automation approaches. The obvious unit of processing and segmentation, and hence the unit of translation, is therefore the sentence. It is up to developers and managers without any knowledge of the body of knowledge of TS, to decide on how to arrange workflows. This goes in line with the words of crowdsourcing theorist Brabham, who indicates that the parties that "conceive new crowdsourcing arrangements in theory can create [...] those arrangements" (Brabham 2013: 54). That is, developers often design and implement their ideas about ideal crowdsourcing workflows from language automation perspectives, and the cognitive or linguistic implications of selecting sentences as the unit of translation are ignored. Nevertheless, this does not mean that pragmatic and communicative perspectives that defend the idea that entire texts are the minimal unit of translation are completely absent in micro task crowdsourcing practices. As mentioned above, the unitary and functional nature of the text is recognized in many crowdsourcing workflows, mostly when the global coherence at the terminological, syntactic or style level is taken into account in the process. The incorporation of glossaries in many crowdsourcing efforts, for example, addresses the need for global terminological coherence or style guides that might include basic syntactic guidelines regarding tone and style. Revision stages and the authorization to freeze a version by qualified contributors when the crowd carries out translations brings about the conceptualization of the text as the minimal unit of translation in these environments.

6.7 Redefining crowdsourced "texts" as a translation product

Translation is seen both as a process and as a product (Munday 2008), and in this regard the notion of "text" can be seen in a different light from process and a product-based perspective. From a "product based" perspective, the discipline has showed an interest in defining what a "translated text" is from two distinct perspectives. First of all, debates have centered on whether a translated text is such in contrast to adaptations, transcreations or versions. On the other hand, corpus-linguistics approaches have defined the notion of what a "translated text" is in order to incorporate them to translational corpora (Baker 1995; Laviosa 2002). Parallel and comparable corpora studies, those with aligned ST and TT pairs or those that contain translations and similar non-translated texts, respectively, have attempted to study the specifics of language resulting from translation processes. Translation in the corpus-based TS (CBTS) paradigm is understood as "a communicative event which is shaped by its own goals, pressures and context of production" (Baker 1996: 175). The product of this process, the "translated text", presents specific recurring linguistic features due to specific constraints that operate during the translation process:

> Translated language reflects the constraints which operate in the context of pro-
> duction and reception: these constraints are social, cultural, ideological, and of
> course, of cognitive nature.   (Baker 1999:285)

Empirical research has focused on the specific features found in translated texts, the so-called "universals of translation" (Baker 1993), "general features of translation" (Chesterman 2004), or "general tendency of translation" (Olohan 2004). A limited number of studies extended the initial research into the general features of translation to study the impact of technologies, such as the impact of TM tools on translation products (Jiménez-Crespo 2009) or the necessity of testing these general tendencies in new technology-dependent textual populations, such as web localization (Jiménez-Crespo 2011). CBTS research prototypically understood "translated texts" as the result of professional processes (Laviosa 2002). In some cases, such as learner corpora, the objective of the study was texts resulting from trainees engaged in translation competence acquisition processes (i.e., Lopez and Tercedor 2009; Espuña 2014).

Collaborative and crowdsourcing models have already expanded the notion of "translated text" both in the discipline and in industry discourses. Crowdsourced texts represent a distinct textual population of interest in CBTS, even when to date only one corpus study has explored the distinct nature of "crowdsourced texts" in comparison with regular translation processes (Jiménez-Crespo 2014). On its part, industry discourses already reflect this expansion in the notion of "translated text". For example, paid crowdsourcing companies offer different translation "products", from crowdsourced texts produced by "translation professionals", to texts produced by "motivated fans", to crowdsourced texts produced by competent bilinguals, or in some cases, even language learners.

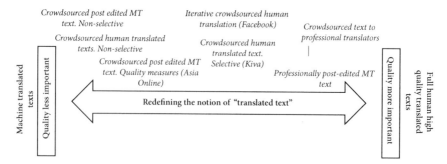

Figure 6.2 Expanding the notion of "translated text".

Figure 6.2 offers a graphic representation of the cline on the expansion of the notion of translated text. It shows the polarity of practices in which the significance of the levels of quality defines a more segmental or textual approach and these practices are also associated to the higher or lower dependence on MT. In each extreme are located the two most commonly confronted cases, "full human high quality translated texts" and "machine translated texts". Somewhere in the middle would be the "non-professionally translated text". The cline of potential textual forms that emerge range from post-edited MT without any type of quality or workflow models to professionally post-edited text by the professional crowd. The incorporation of MT in the workflow therefore does not automatically associate with lower quality, since in some cases professionals can collaboratively post-edit MT output in certain paid – crowdsourcing initiatives.

CHAPTER 7

Fansubs and AVT norms

> Subtitling conventions are not set in stone and only time will
> tell whether these fansub conventions are just a mere fleeting fashion
> or whether they will [...] become the seed of a new type
> of subtitling for the digital era.
>
> (Díaz Cintas and Muñoz Sánchez 2006: 51)

7.1 Introduction

Audiovisual Translation (AT) represents an area in which professional norms and practices have been challenged the most by the freedom and empowerment of users, primarily the "fan-produced, translated, subtitled version" of audiovisual products known as fansubbing (Díaz Cintas and Muñoz Sánchez 2006: 37). This set of practices emerged from an initial discontent of fans with existing professional and industry approaches, embodying how fans conceptualize the creation and reception of subtitled products in opposition to mainstream professional practices. As one of the most productive area in TS research on collaborative and volunteer translation, studies have shown that fans working without the influence of professional conventions, as well as market and regulatory forces, are often emboldened to defy established norms and standards, taking into their hands the creation of subtitles that satisfy their own needs (ibid). The interest in the analysis of this phenomenon lies beyond the benefits of descriptive analyses or empirical research in TS. It also lays in the fact that volunteer subtitling has actually had an impact on the evolution of professional norms and practices (Massidda 2015; Katan 2015), a reverse process in which non-professionals can potentially impact and gradually change the professional world. The goal of this chapter is therefore to analyze how research into fansubbing has provided a new perspective on the emergence, consolidation and evolution of translation norms. It examines how professional norms have been challenged by the freedom and creative drive of fansubbers, subsequently providing new insights into the notion of norms in the discipline and the consequences and dynamics of "norm flouting" and norm evolution.

7.2   From professional norms to "abusive subtitling" … and back

Already in the early days of fansubbing research, Asian and Media Studies scholar Nornes (1999, 2007) introduced the notion of "abusive subtitling", a notion taken up by audiovisual TS scholars and referred to by Pérez-González (2012) as "transformative subtitling". Abusive subtitling was defined as a type of subtitling that primed experimentation, freedom and instincts rather than "the inertia of convention" (Nornes 1999: 18). According to Nornes, this practice emerged from the propensity to play with formatting, graphics, location of subtitles or explicitation of cultural items in glosses that could potentially fill a screen. It also arose as a reaction to professional practices that he described as "corrupt", since they "[smooth] over its textual violence and [domesticate] all otherness while [they pretend] to bring the audience to an experience of the foreign" (ibid). Mainstream subtitling practices were conceptualized as a mechanism that corrupts the source text, eliminating important aspects in order to conform "the foreign to the framework of the target language and cultural norms" (Nornes 2007: 178). The abusive subtitler, in a reaction against traditional norm-guided practices, "pretends to locate his or her subtitles in the place of the other […] abusive subtitles always directs the spectator back to the original foreign text" (ibid: 32). This notion brought to the surface the potential interventionist force of fansubbing communities to ignore or remodel professional subtitling norms as they please (Pérez-González 2012). They brought back the pendulum from an excessive domesticating approach in professional settings to a more literal target-oriented one, displaying more foreignized subtitles that bring the audience closer to the source text and culture.

The reasons that drove fans to challenge and reshape audiovisual norms lay in several factors. The professional subtitling norms and conventions for wide consumption in receiving communities were perceived as "outmoded, inadequate and above all excessively 'target-oriented'" (Massidda 2015: 11). This target-oriented, naturalizing and domesticating approach was often brought up as a source of discontent. Professional subtitling was blamed for eliminating and adapting culture-specific items of source texts, a common practice that allegedly upset fans with intimate knowledge of the source culture of the audiovisual product (Innoccenti and Maestri 2010). This target-orientedness was criticized for distorting important issues related to:

> signification, idioms, register and style, and also for impoverishing the sense of otherness inherent in the foreign dialogue in the name of fluency, readability and the questionable notion of transparency.   (Massidda 2015: 11)

As a consequence, fans perceived that professionally subtitled products displayed an excessive adaptation of culture, humor or style, eliminating the flavor and feel of the original sociocultural context. In other cases, it is not the translation but the power of regulatory agencies and audiovisual boards which impacted existing norms, such normalization or standardization of foul language or cursing (Ameri and Ghazizadeh 2015). The emergence of participatory cultures helped raise the voice of fans who started to criticize the professional subtitling of their favorite TV series and films, expressing "disagreement with commercial subtitling practices and [imposing] linguistic and cultural mediation strategies of their own" (Pérez-González 2007: 4). In this context, fans and volunteers took into their hands the development of new practices that suited their expectations, empowered by the freedom provided by working outside professional and market pressures. They started to cater to fans as a distinct active audience from the mainstream, a viewership segment with a deeper knowledge of the source language and culture.

After over two decades of a creative surge in fansubbing in Japanese anime, the so-called "post-fansub" era emerged around other audiovisual genres, such as TV series and films around the world. US TV series are fansubbed around the world, while in other cases other trends have emerged, such as, among others, Korean TV dramas in Thailand or the Philippines (i.e. Rossum 2015). In the second decade of the 20th century, some established fansub communities started to move away from the experimental nature of early anime practices and shifted to replicate professional approaches in their organizations and workflows (Barra and Guarnaccia 2008: 2; Orrego-Carmona 2013: 14; Massidda 2015: 41; Rong 2015: 20). The pendulum started to swing back in some genres and attempting to produce products as close as possible to professional ones became an aspirational value in these communities. A new type of fansubber emerged: individuals that pursue certain activities as an amateur but attempt to closely follow professional practices. Orrego-Carmona (2013) refers to these individuals as "pro-am's" borrowing the notion of Leadbeater and Miller (2004). This attempt to replicate professional practices entails that amateur processes tend to "resemble a job more than a hobby" (Massidda 2015: 41). Witness to this is the fact that almost all nightly TV series in the USA are subtitled within 8 hours in Chinese by highly structured fansub communities (Wu 2010). Only through carefully crafted structures and workflows, the power of the crowd and near professional organization and work ethics, can this be achieved.

These fansubs communities have not only started to replicate professional workflows and structures, they have also started to comply to the highest possible degree with professional subtitling norms. Orrego-Carmona (2012), for example, identified that out of 26 main professional norms, the subtitling group ArgenTeam in Argentina includes 19 of them. This represents a point of departure from the total freedom of initial anime fansubbers to a desire to comply as much as possible with professional practices in certain groups. Some new norms and standards started to emerge, with some communities abiding by strict codes and standards of practice. The new, more diversified fansub era had started, and it will only get bigger from there.

7.3   Translation and subtitling norms in fansubbing research

The study of norms in fansubbing has been primarily framed within the system approach to the study of translation norms of Toury (1995) and Chesterman (1997). It has also been built upon the corpus of AVT studies focused on audiovisual norms from both descriptive (i.e. Días Cintas 2003; Díaz Cintas and Remael 2007) and empirical perspectives (i.e. Karamitroglou 2000; Pedersen 2011). From a broad TS perspective, norms have been defined as general values or ideas that are shared by specific communities or groups as to what is right or wrong, adequate or in-adequate, and their transfer into performance instructions that can be applied to specific situations (Hermans 2013b). They have also been defined as "regularities of translation behavior within a specific sociocultural context" (Schäffner 2010: 237). Norms specify what is tolerated, prescribed and permitted (Toury 1998). They also indicate what kind of consequences can exist for deviant behaviors, such as the po-tential to discard the translation, assume the non-professional status of the trans-lator with its implications, refuse to accept the translation product, etc. According to Chesterman, translators that do not comply with norms "threaten normality, produce difference and are quickly ostracized or punished" (Chesterman 1997: 54). Since they hold a social dimension, they are relatively stable and they hold a relative durability despite differences between individual translators' styles and critical responses to them (Hermans 2013b).

AVT studies normally depart from the classification of norms by Toury (1995) and/or Chesterman (1997). The seminal work of Toury (1995) proposed three sets of norms that guide the translation process: initial, preliminary and operational norms. "Initial norms" deal with the choice a translator has to make in order to operate within the norms of the source text or the target text. They guide the trans-lator towards a more domesticated or foreignized approach, bringing the reader more towards the source text and culture or the target one. "Preliminary norms" relate to what type of text should be translated in terms of genres, authors, periods, etc. Meanwhile, "operational norms" affect the actual process of translation. They are subdivided between "matricial norms", norms that account for the macrostruc-ture of the text and to what extent the structure of the source text should be ob-served, as well as "textual norms" related to the stylistic and textual decisions at the microtextual level. Toury identified the potential for creative uses and deviations from the norms when placing them in a continuum of "socio-cultural constraints" between the personal "idiosyncrasies" of single translators and "absolute rules". In the case of fansubbing, the "idiosyncrasies" could also be approached in terms of "collective idiosyncrasies", since many studies have also identified recurrent differences between the procedures and released products from different communities within and between countries (see 7.4).

Studies into non-professional subtitling norms have often also incorporated Chesterman's proposal (1997: 175–187). While Toury was more concerned with translators' decision making, the work of the former introduced the interaction between translators, receivers and other translators in the study of norms. This introduction of the end-users represents one of the main reasons why Chesterman's proposal provides a good framework for the study of fansubbing. He distinguished between two types of norms: "expectancy norms" and "professional norms". Professional norms account for what a community or group expects a translation to be like, and therefore, delimit what a community might accept as a proper or legitimate translation. They "regulate the translation process itself" (1997: 68) and they shape translation products. Professional norms were subdivided between "accountability", "communication" and "relation" norms. "Accountability norms" relate to ethical issues and govern the relation between the translator and the other parties in the translation process, such as clients, authors, the readership, etc. "Communication norms" relate to the necessity of behaving in a way "to optimize communication" (1997: 69) during the translation process. The most important of the professional norms, the "relation norm", focuses on the relation between the ST and the TT, where "the translator should act in such a way that an appropriate relation of relevant similarity is established and maintained between the source text and the target text" (ibid: 69). What constitutes "relevant similarity" and what type is appropriate and how this can be achieved depends on many factors, including translation traditions, the client's brief, the type of text to translate or the expectations of the audience. The relation norm can help disentangle translations from adaptations or transcreations. For example, this relation norm can be used in the study of fansubs to separate legitimate fansubs from other derivative subtitling or dubbing practices by amateurs such as "fake translation" (Izwaini 2014), "fundubbing" (Nord et al. 2015) or "parodic dubbing" (Nornes 2007: 195), the subtitling or dubbing of a video with a fabricated target text for fun often using local references, accents or slang. The last norms embody the role of the audience and they are referred to as "expectancy norms". They are "established by reader's [and client's] expectations on a translation" (Chesterman 1997: 68) and concern "what a translation (of this type) should be like" (Chesterman 1997: 64). "Expectancy norms" are of a higher order than professional norms, since the former give shape to the expectations that professionals attempt to conform with to create an acceptable TT.

In terms of research into fansubbing, Chesterman's proposal rightly highlights this role of the reader and the possible expectations. Some researchers, such as Pedersen (2011) have highlighted that expectancy norms "focus on the reader, and the reader is in focus in subtitling, due to the transient nature of the medium and because of its constraints" (2011: 36–37). Thus, norms are understood as linked between individual or collective translation behaviors with collective expectations (Hermans 2013b: 80). Chesterman's proposal has thus been relevant in the study of fansubbing cultures, since the "prosumers" or the fans themselves are the ones adapting and experimenting with the way they would like to receive these subtitles. In the age of "prosumers" (Toffler 1980), expectancy norms can be shaped by the same agents that produce translations working outside the constraints imposed by "professional norms". The translation process is carried out by the same individual or collective that both produces the translation and that shapes and establishes norms, a phenomenon that deserves further study. Expectancy norms are also related to notions of "correctness" of a translation, shaped by the ideas in any specific community about what kinds of translations will be recognized as proper, correct or acceptable (Hermans 2013b).

Chesterman's emphasis on the reader and the target orientedness of the norms closely relates his proposal to that of functionalist Christiane Nord (1991). She suggested two types of norms, "constitutive" and "regulatory" ones. The latter account for the professional norms and regulatory norms would guide the process itself. Nord also delved into the differences between norms and conventions in TS. The notion of convention has been defined from a philosophical perspective as regularities in human behavior in situations of cooperation (Lewis 1969). From functionalist approaches in TS, this notion has been defined as:

> Implicit or tacit non-binding regulation of behavior, based on common knowledge and the expectations of what others expect you to expect from them (etc.) to do in a certain situation. (Nord 1991: 96)

From this definition it should be stressed that conventions are non-binding, an aspect that distances this notion from norms. Breaking a convention does not imply any potential penalty or consequence beyond the possible impact on the ease of communication; that is, flouting a convention can be seen as a creative or strange strategy and does not lead to any penalty.

7.4 Fansubbing or how collaboration can challenge translation norms

A significant aspect that fansubbing brings to the surface is the potential of norms to be challenged, to adapt, or to evolve throughout time. Norms in general are not conceived as static and fossilized, but quite the opposite. They can change "because they need to be constantly readjusted so as to meet changing appropriateness conditions" (Hermans 1999:84). These changes are due to the fact that the nature of norms involves "conflicts, challenges and changes over time" (Hermans 2013b:80), and these collective practices prove to be a case in point. In the case of fansubbing, the potential conflict appears between professional subtitling norms and the expectations and preferences of certain audiences empowered by technological advances. These active collectives can define the "appropriateness" or "correctness" of a translation outside market pressures, from the style used to the placement of subtitles. In this process, fansubs bring to the surface that professional and non-professional versions are often directed at different audiences (Wilcock 2013). While professional ones are addressed to the mainstream audience, fansubs are directed at audiences with a more comprehensive knowledge of the source culture that the "average viewer". This "average viewer" requires a specific set of established norms to facilitate the enjoyment of the audiovisual product, while fans crave a richer approach to culture and language transfer. An interesting process emerges in the "user-generated translation" paradigm: the merging of the audience from whom "expectancy norms" emerge and the translators that operates under them. Thus, the "expectancy norms" reshape and help establish "operational norms" that subsequently guide the translation process in fan communities. If, as Hermans indicated (2013b), the study of norms can help gain insights into concepts of translation held by particular communities at certain periods, the existing studies of how fansubs deal with professional norms and the study of the actual impact of non-professional norms in reshaping actual professional practices (Massidda 2015; Katan 2015), can contribute to expanding the notion of translation and AVT translation in the way (Gambier 2014).

Another significant issue is fact that norms require validation and enforcement by a "norm authority" (Chesterman 1997:66). This authority handles cases of norm deviation, since in the professional context: "[n]orm flouters threaten normality, produce difference and are quickly ostracized or punished" (Chesterman 1997:54). This authority becomes a more flexible and fluid notion across different fansubbing initiatives and settings. Since the early days of anime fansubbing, communities with different degrees of authority levels and hierarchy have emerged, from highly structured workflows, hierarchies and established norms or conventions (Bold 2011; Orrego-Carmona 2012) to completely free and experimental cases that differ across initiatives and national boundaries. For example, volunteer subtitling communities, such as TED, have highly structured guidelines that resemble professional ones. Participants are categorized according to their status, from general translators to reviewers/managers. In some cases, subtitling guidelines for non-anime communities can include the majority of professional standards, such as the case of the volunteer community ArgenTeam[1] (Orrego-Carmona 2012). Similarly, the great majority of Chinese fansubs possess a highly rigid structure that enforces certain norms. Thus, the emergence of different norms in non-professional subtitling communities does not necessarily entail the absence of norm authority. This authority is implicitly present in non-professional participation guides and codes of ethics where non-compliance to common self-established norms often leads to dismissal from the amateur community (Drugan 2011).

7.4.1 Challenges to professional audiovisual norms from fansubbing

Fansubbing in part emerges as a form of expression of disagreement with professional subtitling practices and therefore, as previously described, communities consciously attempt to develop their own linguistic and cultural mediation strategies (Pérez-González 2007:7). In general, collaborative audiovisual translation has been the main ground for a systematic, conscious and willful violation of professional translation norms, something that has not happened necessarily in other realms in which volunteers participate. This process treads the fine line between the flexibility inherent in norms and the conscious violation when some constraints are not accepted by fans. This flexibility is present in theorizations of norms in TS. For Hermans (2013b), not all norms have the same force, and not all norms imply necessarily that experimentation might be curtailed:

> [n]orms may be strong or weak, more or less durable, and narrow or broad in scope. They can and will be breached, but they are able to cope with a relatively large amount of discrepant behavior. (2013b: 3)

This discrepant behavior in fansubbing started to jump into commercial versions of programs in the beginning of the 20th century (Díaz Cintas 2005). The adoption of glosses and information on the screen is nowadays common in some audiovisual TV genres, such as MTV programs or the recent incorporation of intralingual titles with information in series such as Sherlock. Current research (McClarty 2012; Fox 2015; Katan 2015) as well as TV stations, such as the BBC, are also exploring subtitle placement in different locations on the screen. Research is also

---

1. According to Orrego-Carmona (2012) the ArgenTeam subtitling group guidelines in 2011 include 19 of the 26 standards of subtitling in professional codes.

currently exploring the reception of norm-breaking creative subtitling (Caffrey 2009; Orrego-Carmona 2015), since norm deviation can potentially cause different effects in terms of comprehension, cognitive load, etc.

Another area in which fansubbing has been argued to impact professional practices is the shortening of the time gap between the original release and the release of the subtitled version. This effect has been perceived in many cases of the official release of many highly popular US TV series and the time they are released in other audiovisual markets. Massidda (2015) presents the last episode of Lost in 2010 as a case in point. The original version of the episode was aired in several countries at the same time. Within hours the subtitling communities ItaSA and Subsfactory released their fansubbed versions, while the professional subtitled version was released 24 hours later. According to Massidda, "never before had Italians experienced such a speed in dealing with audiovisual translation" (2015: 39). Similarly, Orrego-Carmona (2014a) introduces the case of the fourth season of *Games of Thrones* that was released with subtitles in Spain 18 hours after it was broadcasted in the USA. He also concludes the non-professional subtitling has "influenced changes in media flows" (ibid: 67). These changes in the temporal dimension of translation production and distribution can also be seen in other initiatives such as the PBS TV station crowdsourcing of US presidential speeches to reach as many locales as possible.

As a whole, fansubbing also challenges the established mantra that the AVT process is defined as "a loss with very little intervention by the translator" (Gambier 2013: 54). Subtitlers normally attempt to make their work as transparent and unobtrusive as possible (Pedersen 2011: 22). The visibility of fansubbers is often enhanced through the inclusion of the name of the collective or individual responsible for the translation, both for fansubbing communities (Orrego-Carmona 2012) or crowdsourcing ones like TED (Olohan 2014). The interventionist role of the fansubber can emerge as a transformative figure (Pérez-González 2007; 2014), challenging the invisibility of the translator through conscious interventions such as glosses with cultural or linguistic explanations.

This distinct nature of non-professional subtitling has attracted the attention of an increasing number of researchers, mainly focused on a popular trend of empirical studies that contrast audiovisual norms between the two polarities of practice, fansub and professional, in different countries (i.e., Pérez-González 2007; Feitosa 2009; Verbruggen 2010; García-Manchón 2013; Miloševski 2013; Wilcock 2013; Wang 2014; Ameri and Ghazizadeh 2015; Massidda 2015; Okyayuz 2016), including parallel corpus studies of non-professional translations that include STs and TTs (Bogucki 2009; Sajna 2013; Khalaf, Rashid, Jumingan and Othman 2015). Researchers have tackled the study of non-compliance with professional norms, an issue that has been pointed out as a necessity in the field. For example, Schäffner

(2010) precisely pointed out that the study of norms in TS has often ignored the issue of non-compliance with dominant norms. She identifies deviations, exceptions and creative uses in translator strategies as potential indications of the role of the translator as an active agent (Baker 2006; Pérez-González 2007), modeling the translation to match their activist or interventionist role. In this sense, early anime fansubs have helped pave the way for creative and experimental subtitling practices in other domains, such as activist subtitling (Baker 2015, 2016). Fansubbing represents an ideal locus for the study of the conflict between professional norms and practices of fansubbers that currently either attempt to operate within the scope of professional norms or those communities that consciously decide, in a merging of expectancy and operational norms in the same collective, to experiment with these norms. They also represent a great locus to study the effect of compliance or deviancy from norms on the reception of the audiovisual texts (i.e., Caffrey 2009; Orrego-Carmona 2015). The following section reviews the different challenges that fansubs have posed to professional norms and practices through a summary of published results in relevant literature.

7.5   Challenges to subtitling norms: A summary

This section offers an overview of the most common deviations from professional norms identified in fansubbing in a series of published descriptive and empirical studies (Ferrer-Simó 2005; Díaz Cintas and Muñoz Sánchez 2006; Pérez-González 2006, 2007; Gambier 2013; Wilcock 2013; Massidda 2015). It is important to bear in mind that not all types of fansubbing incorporate all of these practices. In broad terms, scholars differentiate between the experimentation of early anime fansubbing and more recent practices attempting to replicate professional standards based on North American films or TV series (Pérez-González 2014). Therefore, different communities of practice across geographic areas might not equally share all characteristics. The main features discussed are:

1. The literal source-oriented approach
2. More creative and individual renditions of source texts
3. Subtitle positioning, layout and font
4. Number of lines per subtitle
5. The addition of glosses and notes
6. The addition of discussion bands to add comments
7. The role of omission and addition
8. Different approaches to taboos and improper language
9. Different quality standards

First of all, fansubs are characterized by a more literal source-oriented approach. This is one of the most common features identified in fansubbing (Díaz Cintas and Muñoz Sánchez 2006; Orrego-Carmona 2015; Massidda 2015). Fansubbers tend to highlight the foreignness of the source text and they dismiss the more domesticating approach, both linguistic and cultural, that professional subtitling embraces. Fansubs are often "closer to the original, wordier, more word-for-word, making the reading time shorter" (Gambier 2013: 54). This also entails that fansubs preserve linguistic idiosyncrasies of the original in the target text. As a result, fansub viewers normally accept to a higher degree foreignized translations with literal language often heavily marked by interference form the source text. In a comparative study of French fansubs with professional ones, Wilcock (2013) identified clear differences in the strategies used in both cases. Fansubbers preferred a more complete rendering of the source text dialogue and a more source-oriented approach, which retains elements of spoken language found in the film dialogue. This meant the inclusion of discourse markers and marks of orality that are normally the linguistic first elements to be eliminated in order to condense the oral text into subtitles (Díaz Cintas 2003). A study by Tang (2014) focused on a contrastive study of cultural representations in the movie Kung Fu Panda in dubbing and subtitling by professional and non professionals. Results showed that both versions showed a marked preference for interventionist strategies such as adaptation, rephrasing and replacement. The study concludes both practices highlight the active role of the translation in the shaping of cultural representation. More recent studies have identified an impact from the tendency in structured communities to replicate professional norms and standards. For example, in the study by Matielo and Spindola (2011) comparing professional and non professional subtitles of the US series *Heroes*, the study was inconclusive as to whether both versions would diverge in terms of foreignizing and domesticating cultural items. It was found that both versions showed a similar tendency to foreignize some items. Differences were nevertheless present in some categories of analysis, such as the translation of anthroponyms and forms of entertainment.

The freedom of volunteers can lead to more creative and individual renditions of the source text (Gambier 2014). This contrasts with the ideal of a more literal and source-oriented approach seen in many fansub communities. One extreme case in this area is the above-mentioned case of "fundubbing" or "funsubtitling" (Nord et al. 2015; Chaume 2013). These cases are characterized by the "the witty and humorous nature of this type of home-grown dubbing" (Chaume, 2013: 111). A cline can be observed, therefore, in this area between the more literal approach on the one side, all the way to the extreme case of "fundubbing" or "fake subtitling". Some studies have explored the role of creativity in the subtitling of humor (Verbruggen 2010; Wu 2013; Okyayuz 2016). In a MA thesis study of Dutch professional and non-professional subtitles (Verbruggen 2010), it was reported that professional subtitling of movies such as Faulty Towers, Shrek or Monty Python contained more humorous puns translated as pun (55%) than those in non-professional versions (32%). Thus, creative solutions and the constraints in subtitles can also lead to difficulties in identifying creative solutions in some cases. For example, it is common for Chinese communities to include puns and jokes with references to the target Chinese culture, replacing US cultural references with Chinese ones (Wu 2013), while this is not the case in many other geographic areas. Creative spelling that appears in subtitles has also been the object of research (Secara 2011), since spelling mimicking text messaging has emerged as a novel tool for creativity in audiovisual texts. The results of a pilot study by Secara confirmed that creative "spellings do not hinder the viewing process as a whole" and they facilitate the viewing since it allows "viewers to spend more time fixating outside the subtitled area" (ibid: 168). Creativity also extends not only to spelling, but also to how subtitles are displayed.

The experimentation and creativity in fansubs is mainly reflected in the positioning, layout and font of subtitles. Díaz Cintas and Muñoz Sánchez (2006) indicate that subtitles have been generally very standardized in terms of positioning, while fansubs playfully approach how to display them in certain cases. Fansubs challenge the fixed positions of subtitle lines on the bottom, or the top when text or the attention is directed at the bottom of the screen (Díaz Cintas and Muñoz Sánchez 2006 Cintas 2003). Subtitles can appear anywhere on the screen; they emerge in the form of speech or thought bubbles. They can appear and fly from the sides or from different angles (Fox 2015). Font can be used in order to indicate the foreignness of the speech or differences in the speech delivery, "blending in with the aesthetics of visual semiotics" (Pérez-González 2014: 54). Subtitles can also change in color in order to indicate, for example, alternation of talk. Fansubs also sacrifice the maximum or optimal visibility to aesthetic considerations.

Professional norms indicate a maximum of two subtitle lines per segment (Díaz Cintas 2003). Due to the literal approach and the tendency to explicitate cultural items, fansubs can incorporate up to three full lines of subtitles. They often flout the limit of characters per line (Gambier 2013; Massidda 2015). This general tendency is not always the case. For example, Feitosa (2009) studied a corpus of excerpts of professional and non-professional subtitles in ten movies commercialized in Brazil in 2000. The results found no differences in the duration of subtitles or the amount of subtitle lines.

The desire to include more cultural and linguistic information leads to the potential incorporation of glosses and notes. These glosses can appear as pop ups inside the subtitles. Explanatory notes are usually placed at the top of the screen (Díaz Cintas and Muñoz Sánchez 2006) and normally appear and disappear with the subtitles that they accompany. They can also appear in different locations of the screen if any visual item needs to be explicitated. This practice challenges the invisibility of the translator, purposefully breaking the "suspension of disbelief" that subtitles are supposed to help create in order to enjoy the audiovisual product. The overload of potential information can add difficulty to the task of reading subtitles. In the eye tracking study by Caffrey (2009), it was shown that a significant correlation between the appearance of these glosses and cognitive effort in the reception exists. It was also shown that more subtitles lines were ignored if compared to subtitles without glosses. Less time was also spent on the bottom of the screen when glosses were displayed. This reception study clearly correlates the desire of fansubbers to add to the viewing experience with the enjoyment of the audiovisual text on the other. It also signals, as previously mentioned, the different audience expectations and the emergence of different subtitles for different audiences (Wilcock 2013).

In addition to glosses, some volunteer subtitling sites have incorporated discussion bands where fans and audiences can potentially add comments. For example, in the case as the case of the Korean drama fansub website Viki (Dwyer 2013) a comment band can appear on the top of the screen were viewers and fansubbers can add information. This represents a case of user intervention in the filmic text that is not accomplished by means of manipulating the subtitles themselves. Rather, these comment bands represent a mechanism for emotional community building. In fact, the comments themselves in Viki are usually unrelated to the subtitles themselves, such as gossip or viewer reactions (ibid). These mechanisms open up the participatory process to the audience at large of these subtitles, resulting in "a more open if chaotic model of participation" (ibid: 220).

Omission and condensation represents one of the cornerstones of professional subtitling practices due to the limitations of the number of characters displayed on screen at a time and in specific time constraints to facilitate comfortable reading (Díaz Cintas 2003). The reduction can normally entail up to 40%–44% of reduction in the subtitled version (ibid). In order to achieve this reduction, redundant language, markers or orality tend to be eliminated. Since fansubbers defend a return to a literal source-oriented approach, they show a tendency to convey everything in the original dialogue, even when the result might be too much text on screen. According to Massidda (2015: 59):

> [s]ubbers aim to convey "everything" belonging to the original dialogues, deeming it of paramount importance to detach themselves from the mainstream practices of "domestication" and the excessive conciseness of professional subtitling.

These practices have been examined in a number of contrastive studies between professionals and non-professionals. One of the major contributions to the body of knowledge of fansubbing is the potential to pay attention to that which professionals discard (Massidda 2015: 59). These omissions are often framed in what Nornes (2007) referred to as "corrupt translation", and these textual and graphic violations could be an interesting area of research in TS. The previously mentioned study of Feitosa (2009) focuses on a contrastive corpus study on explicitation in professional and non-professional subtitles in Brazil, and even when explicitation was found in both textual populations, non-professional subtitles tended to be longer and more explicit. This indicates the recurring tendency in non-professional subtitles to render all the materials without omissions and including a higher degree of explicitation.[2] The dissertation by Bruti (2015) focused on contrastive analysis of the translation of compliments in the subtitles of the TV series *Lost*, one of the discursive features which are guidelines often recommend reducing or eliminating in case of constraints. The results showed that contrary to the expectations of the researcher, compliments were almost always translated, and with no differences in the strategy adopted by professionals or amateurs. In another study, discursive markers and register were studied in the translation of Korean honorifics in subtitles (Rossum 2015), a specific issue in Korean culture. Generally, fansubs of several Korean dramas, such as *Coffee Prince* and *Reply*, included a more foreignized approach which included more foreignizations and the different honorifics as compared to the professional versions. Nevertheless, differences were identified between the translations of two different series, pointing to significant variation between subtitling collectives in terms of their approach to subtitling cultural items.

Subtitles tend to show a standardized and normalized language (Díaz Cintas 2003). One of the main targets of this tendency is taboos and improper language. Studies, for example, have identified that non-professional subtitling can be more direct in the case of cursing and swearing. It is common to identify that official dubbed and subtitled versions tend to be neutralized and tend to avoid sexual and foul language (Massidda 2015). Two different studies of professional and non-professional subtitles and/or dubbed versions in Iran (Ameri and Ghazizadeh 2015) and Spain (García-Manchón 2013) showed that fansub versions tend to have a much more direct translation of the original swearing language with stronger discursive force. This tendency conforms to the more literal and direct approach to subtitling in fansub communities.

One of the early goals of contrastive studies was quality standards. Generally, and not surprisingly, several studies have analyzed the lower quality of

---

2. The presence of explicitation as a general feature of translation in professional subtitles was identified in the study of Perego (2008).

non-professional subtitles in comparison with professional ones or from a professional perspective (i.e. Bogucki 2009; Khalaf, Rashid, Jumingan and Othman 2015). As was seen in Chapter 5, working without the boundaries of professional translation also means that quality norms and standards in professional settings might not apply, priming speed and accessibility to compliance with industry quality standards. Nevertheless, with the evolution of subtitling communities, some studies have found that in certain cases professional versions can have more inadequate renderings than the non-professional ones (Massidda 2015).

This review has not only highlighted the diverging nature of fansubbing, but it has also shown the diverse nature of fansubbing practices across genres, initiatives and geographical areas. This makes an overall description of fansubbing difficult. This challenging task has been attempted by Massidda (2015), who proposed a "hybrid proposal" for fansubbing norms. The researcher indicates that post-anime fansubbing norms tend to include "minor modifications" to the professional ones. In general, the overall goal of fansubbing processes is to allow viewers to enjoy the audiovisual product in a literal and source-oriented approach, paying attention to the distinct audience to which the text is addressed. It includes the above-mentioned characteristics of the general literal approach and the more direct approach to cursing and taboo language. The layout proposal includes two lines in white with 45 characters, while omission is limited only by the spatio-temporal constraints. It is of interest that the foreignizing approach can be achieved through "loanwords (cultural-bound expressions explicitated by notes, for example)" and neologisms "(derived from youth culture slang) in order for obscure foreign concepts to enter the target culture" (Massidda 2015: 63). Finally, it offers the same guidelines for punctuation and segmentation as professional codes. This set of norms seems to fit within post-anime film and TV subtitling, but nevertheless the different contexts and audiovisual genres in which fansubbing occurs requires a more open and flexible approach. Rather than a normative approach that goes contrary to the free and open nature of fansubs, the proposal by Massidda (2015) would be best described as a descriptive apparatus to conceptualize existing TV fansubbing in Western contexts.

This chapter has mainly focused on norms, one of the most significant and exciting challenges that fansubbing poses. Other issues of relevance to TS that have been explored in the literature, such as interventionist or ideological issues (i.e. Pérez-González 2007, 2014), do deserve further study that has not been possible in this project which is focused on how online collaborative translations can help expand the limits of translation. There are still a lot of areas to explore and fansubbing will continue to provide ample areas of inquiry, witness to the high interest fansubbing attracts among young and seasoned scholars alike. Fansubbing flows are only going to increase in the future, parallel to the ever-increasing penetration of the Internet around the world. The creative force of fans will continue to evolve and run across geographical areas and initiatives, both parallel and contrary to professional practices.

CHAPTER 8

Crowdsourcing
Insights from the sociology of translation

> When we speak of an ethics of translation, do we mean
> to include amateurs as well as "professionals"?
> One way of answering this question would be to
> distinguish between someone "who is a translator"
> and someone "who does translations (sometimes).
>
> (Chesterman 2001: 146)

8.1   Introduction

Sociological approaches have gained increasing popularity in TS since the late 90's, shifting the focus of attention from more linguistic-related issues towards the central role of translators and the sociocultural and socioeconomic contexts in which they translate. From this perspective, translators and interpreters are seen as agents that interact with social structures and hierarchies, and whose decisions and predispositions are marked by their socializations and education (Inghilleri 2009; Wolf 2010; Angelelli 2012). The expansion of the highly varied sociological approaches in the discipline (Buzelin 2013), including the theoretical foundation provided by Bourdieu or Latour and the popularization of imported methodologies from the social sciences, created the groundwork for the initial empirical inquiries into collaborative practices. This context provided the fertile ground for the most fruitful point of departure for TS research projects into crowdsourcing and online collaborative translation to date, with research objectives such as motivation to translate, ethics, socio-professional or socio-economic implications of free and volunteer activities (i.e., McDonough-Dolmaya 2012, 2015; Olohan 2014). This chapter analyzes the highly productive combination of the imported theories and methodologies in the "sociological turn" (Wolf and Fukari 2007; Wolf 2010) and how they combined with the "technological turn" (O'Hagan 2013) to serve as a point of departure of these studies. It also reviews how, in this context, other turns of interest from a crowdsourcing perspective overlap, such as the "activist" (Wolf 2012) or the "economic" turns (Gambier 2014). The chapter then moves on to fundamental issues in this field, such as research on the role of ethics in volunteer initiatives or the role of imported methodologies. It ends with a summary of empirical studies from a sociological perspective into the two main questions that have been addressed by a growing number of researchers (O'Brien and Schäler 2010; McDonough-Dolmaya 2012; Dombek 2013; Chu 2013; Deriemaeker 2014; Luczaj and Cwiek-Rogalska 2014; Camara 2015); that is, why do volunteers translate (motivation) and who participates in these initiatives (volunteer profiles)? At a time when MT research into collaboration has been mostly concerned with issues such as translation quality or workflows, the impact of sociological approaches in the discipline is thus clear when TS has been so far mostly intrigued by sociological aspects related to motivation or participant profiles.

8.2   The "sociological turn" in TS

The sociocultural model in Translation Studies "[…] comprises the cluster of questions dealing […] with the networks of agents and agencies and the interplay of their power relations" (Wolf 2010: 29). It has provided conceptual tools on how concepts and theories from "sociology and neighboring disciplines can offer new productive ways of understanding translation" (O'Brien and Saldanha 2013: 150). It focuses on what Chesterman calls "translator studies", a branch of TS whose objectives are "the social role and status of translators and the translators' profession, translating as a social practice" and "people and their observable actions" (2007: 173–174). The interest in the social aspect of translation was initially introduced through literary translation approaches (Simeoni 1998; Gouanvic 1999; Hermans 1999), and it was subsequently expanded to other contexts in which translators and interpreters themselves conduct their professional, non-professional or unprofessional activities. Diverse in nature, it cannot be considered a unified approach. Buzelin (2013) identifies a wide spectrum within sociological approaches that, nevertheless, is united by the belief in the key role social aspects play in shaping translational activities: "it takes for granted that translation is inherently a social activity that both reflects and shapes social interactions" (2013: 187). Initially focused mainly in professional activities, it is of interest that sociological studies also focus on the "hierarchies and values underlying the way professional translators organize themselves and perceive themselves" (ibid). Volunteer practices, once free from market imperatives, bring to the fore questions related to how new emerging practices can offer new insights into hierarchies and organizations, or how volunteers perceive not only themselves, but also how they perceive professionals in the area. These novel practices can have an impact both on professionals and on the public at large. They hold the potential, if still to be proven, to disrupt the socio-economic status of existing translators (Pym, Orrego-Carmona and Torres Simón 2016) and how professionals see themselves, their status, and their place in society. They also can have an impact on public perceptions of both translation and the socioeconomic and cultural role of translators in society.

One of the greatest contributions from sociological approaches, in addition to providing a powerful theoretical apparatus, or providing "sets of analytical concepts and explanatory procedures to theorize the social nature of translation practices" (Inghilleri 2009: 279), is the invaluable introduction of a "number of [empirical] methodological approaches for investigating translation and interpreting as a social activity" (ibid). Methodologies imported from sociology and related disciplines, such as surveys and questionnaires or ethnographic field work research, have gained popularity in research in collaborative practices, since identifying and describing the agents, their motivations, profiles, socializations, potential hierarchies or structuring, their ethics, ideologies, how they interface with professional practices, etc., have proven to be some of the most intriguing questions for the discipline.

The main theoretical frameworks in sociological approaches are Bourdieu's theory of fields (Simeoni 1998; Gouanvic 1999; Inghilleri 2005, 2009), Latour's Action Network theory (Buzelin 2005; Abdallah 2010, 2014) and Luhmann's theory of social systems (Hermans 1999, 2007; Tyulenev 2009, 2014, 2015). Despite the fact that they have provided a theoretical foundation for TS research, the theories that helped shape the sociological research agenda are surprisingly often missing in existing research into online collaborative practices. Nevertheless, several main issues emerging from these approaches are of interest for the conceptualization and research into online collaborative practices and crowdsourcing: the incorporation of the Bordieuan notion of "habitus" in researching professionalism in translation (Abdallah 2014), the study of professional collaborative translation networks using Latour's Action Network theory (Abdallah and Koskinen 2007; Abdallah 2010, 2014) and the impact of the notions of agency in activist and engaged approaches to translation (Wolf 2012).

8.2.1 Bourdieu's theory of fields and the translator's "habitus"

Bourdieu's theory of fields was introduced in TS in a shift of the focus of attention to the pivotal role of translators and interpreters (Inghilleri 2005). In general, his theory can be seen as an attempt to "unveil the mechanisms underlying relation of domination in various social contexts" (Buzelin 2013: 187). The main constructs in the theory are the notions of "field", "symbolic capital" and "habitus". The "field" refers to a sphere of interaction where the different agents share the field with specific rules and agendas. It is seen by Bourdieu as a "locus of struggle". As far as "capital", a notion that he also refers to as "power" (Bourdieu 1986: 242),[1] his proposal differentiates between four types: economic, social, cultural and symbolic. All these types relate to the position in the field of agents who possess a share of capital of any of those types. Capital can be inherited, cultivated, exchanged or accumulated. The most significant type is the "symbolic capital", related to the recognition, prestige or honor that is associated with acquisition or accumulation of one of more of the other three types. The "field" is governed by a process by which agents attempt to acquire more symbolic capital, and in this notion is embedded that of "habitus", the most widely-used concept in TS to research the role played by different agents of translation, and how they think, interrelate and communicate (Simeoni 1998; Gouanvic 1999; Inghilleri 2005, 2009; Wolf 2010; Vorderobermeier 2014). It is defined by Bourdieu as "a system of durable, transposable dispositions" of "internalised structures, common schemes of perception, conception and action" (Bourdieu 1990: 53–60). The habitus mediates between the personal experiences of translation and the social sphere in which their activity takes place, and it is acquired through a process of "inculcation in a set of social practices" (Inghilleri 2005: 70). Thus, an examination of the habitus of the translators allows one "to analyse critically their role as social and cultural agents actively participating in the production and reproduction of textual and discursive practices" (Inghilleri 2005: 126). The habitus is therefore seen as the complex structured network of dispositions that translators acquire through their education and their social interactions that in turn help establish norms and conventions of behavior (Simeoni 1998: 21–22).

The notion of habitus includes not only include the professional side of individuals, but also encompasses the entire sphere of any socialized individual. As such, a fluid distinction is drawn between the "general habitus" and the "professional habitus". These two notions have been referred to in literary translation as "primary habitus" and "specific habitus" (Gouanvic 2005) or "social" and "specialized" habitus (Buzelin 2013: 186). The specific or specialized habitus is therefore related to the study of professional translation contexts. Since in principle Bordieuan theories depart from the positions of dominance and struggle, research in TS has been mainly focused on the habitus of professional translators and their struggles for recognition and visibility. Crowdsourcing research therefore needs to tread the fine line between the general and professional habitus, since participation in volunteer initiatives straddles the line between them.

Some fundamental points of departure in Bourdieu's approach question whether the notion of habitus from a Bordieuan perspective is relevant to the study

---

1. According to Bourdieu, the "symbolic capital" represents the power granted to those who have obtained sufficient recognition to be in a position to impose recognition (1989: 23).

of non-professional or volunteer translators. First of all, it departs from a sociology for nations with groups in conflict and it focuses on conflicts and domination. According to Pym (2011a), this means that it has little to say about cooperation or interculturally essential notions in collaborative environments. Additionally, it is a notion that can overlap with other wide concepts such as professionalism, socialization or disposition (ibid). After all, initially the notion of habitus was introduced to denounce the fact that literary translators were subservient within the overall system (Simeoni 1998). The self-determination of volunteers in the web to participate according to their own motives and outside the pressures of markets or social structures therefore questions the pertinence of using this term and its associated sociological theoretical underpinnings. In fact, few studies have used the notion of habitus to study non-professionals in general, such as literary translators (Meylaerts 2008). Another frequent criticism of the inclusion of this notion in TS is the fact that the notion of habitus is also reduced to an individualistic perspective, in which the locus of agency is the individual (Buzelin 2005:215; Abdallah and Koskinen 2007; Meylaerts 2008). This complicates or makes impossible using the notion of habitus in collaborative environments. The reliance on this individualistic perspective, among others, such as the significance of the theoretical points of departure and the pertinence of different theories, is one of the points of departure of Abdallah's (2014) research into collaborative translation networks and how Bourdieu's notion of habitus and the objective of the next section, Latour's notion of agency, can potentially interface. The use of Latour's Actor-Network theory to study collaboration in translation therefore requires a closer analysis.

8.2.2 Latour's Actor-Network theory and collaborative translations

The individual focus on translators and their habitus in TS literature contrasts with the ethnographic approach of Latour and his Actor-Network theory. The aim of ANT is therefore to "unveil the strategies actors use to enroll others and fulfill their objectives" (Buzelin 2013: 189). It focuses on the relational ties between actants, which can be human and non-human artifacts, to come together and act as a cohesive whole. This theory has been used in the discipline to study collaboration between agents in the process (Risku and Windhager 2013) and collaborative networks (Abdallah and Koskinen 2007; Abdallah 2010, 2014). This focus on the collective, rather than the individual, is the reason why Latour's theory is more relevant to the study of crowdsourcing and volunteer translation, since it allows the analysis of collaborative social and socio-technological processes.

Contrary to the conflict and domination inherent in Bordieuan approaches, ANT departs from the premise that the world is flat and tries to understand how categories and inequalities emerge. Elements according to this theory do not have meaning by themselves but only in relation to the others in the network, including artifacts such as technologies, texts, computers, etc. According to Muñoz Martín (2014: 12–13) and Risku and Windhager (2013), ANT is extremely well suited to account for interactions and task constellations and to fully describe collaborative translation settings within technological contexts as distributed cognition. Studies using ANT therefore "highlight the multiplicity of interactions involved in the making of a translation [...] and the hybridity of the resulting product" (Buzelin 2013: 189). This approach therefore allows for the incorporation of both translation technologies and collaborative processes mediated through them with the focus of the networks that emerge within social structures (Buzelin 2005; Alonso and Calvo 2015). From Latour's theory departs the notion of agency, which Buzelin (2011:7) argues, is "the ability to exert power in an intentional way". Kinnunen and Koskinen (2010:6) defined agency as the "willingness and ability to act" building on Kaptelinin and Nardi's (2006:33) account on agency where they defined it as "the ability and need to act". Agency also represents a necessary construct in the study of volunteer activist communities since the motivations for participation are based on this "ability and need to act" in situations of perceived injustice or inequalities (see 8.2.2). The notion of agency thus opens a door to much needed studies on the role of agency in volunteer collaborative settings.

8.3 Overlapping turns: When the sociological and the technological turns collide

The "technological turn" started to be acknowledged towards the end of the 20th century when the consolidation of translation technologies and their impact slowly made their way into TS. It represents a process by which:

> translation theories begin to incorporate the increasingly evident impact of technology, in turn providing a relevant theoretical framework to language and translation technology researchers. (O'Hagan 2013: 513)

In this sense, it is still too early to judge whether translation theories are providing a relevant theoretical framework to translation technology researchers (Jiménez-Crespo and Singh 2016). The potential emergence of this turn was anticipated by Snell-Hornby who coined the term "globalization turn", a process due to:

> outside influence of globalization, along with the breath-taking developments in information technology and hence worldwide communication, which have revolutionized many aspects of modern life and brought radical changes for language industries. (2010: 368)

The emergence of the "sociological turn" in TS during the 90's coincided with the "technological turn" (Cronin 2010; O'Hagan 2013; Malmkjaer 2013). This parallel process has, over the last decade, provided an ideal breeding ground for a research agenda marked by the combination of two distinct and consolidated research trends or directions. The combination is to some extent coincidental; the inevitable impact of technologies in translation practices occurred at the same time as the discipline was starting to embrace the "sociological turn" that pulled the pendulum in the discipline completely away from the previous popularity of linguistic or discourse approaches (House 2013). According to Pym (2010), turns in translation studies are cumulative and they overlap, but, even when the consolidation of the sociological turn is widely acknowledged, it is still unclear if the "technological" turn can be considered as such in Snell-Hornby's terms. This researcher describes translation turns as "a paradigmatic change, a marked 'bend in the road' involving a distinct change in direction" (Snell-Hornby 2010: 366). Translation turns represent a dynamic process that "can only be assessed as such in retrospect" (ibid). Has technology therefore made a "paradigmatic change" in TS with a "distinct change of direction"? The volume of research in the discipline on technology-dependent phenomena seems to suggest that this turn is clearly consolidated. A prime example of this interface of the technological and sociological turn could be found in the doctoral dissertation of Dombek (2013), who researched from a sociological perspective the motivations and profiles of participants in the Facebook Translate community in Polish, and at the same time focused on the interactions of participants with the technological platform deployed by Facebook using Activity Theory (Leontiev 1978/1987; Kaptelinin and Nardi 2012).

8.3.1 Crowdsourcing and the "economic turn"

Volunteer translation has also been linked to what is starting to be known as the "economic turn" (Gambier 2014), a necessary link between translation and the economic factors behind it which was anticipated by Pym, Shlesinger and Jettmarova (2006). This turn or developing research direction owes its emergence to the fact that "economic and financial dimensions can no longer be ignored. There are [economic] factors that orient, and even determine, specific choices and decisions" (Gambier 2014: 8). Economic aspects are significant for the analysis of motivation to translate. Pym indicates from a Bordieuan perspective that

> The discussion of commerce is still very relevant, but we now have to recognize that the kind of value for which effort is exchanged is not just economic: translators also work, legitimately, for value of a social, symbolic and cultural kind
>
> (Pym 2012: 4)

The search for social, symbolic or cultural capital, using Bourdieu's terms, that individuals engage in translation might seek also matches the findings of empirical studies into motivations to volunteer in which intrinsic or non-monetary motivations are seen as the main factor (see. 8.5). Research into economic considerations is very much needed in TS to analyze the potential market disruption brought by collaborative approaches. The interest of economic perspectives lies in the fact that research into translation has often been theorized as a professional economic process in which agents act mainly according to economic motives. In volunteer settings, different conceptualizations of translation and the forces that shape it might emerge when business aspects are taken out of the picture. Volunteer initiatives precisely fill an existing gap between translation as an economic activity based on ROI principles and translation as a "natural" skill performed across centuries and geography to facilitate cross-cultural communication based on different interests, such as cultural, linguistic, moral, ethical, ideological, political, etc. The motivations to participate might vary, but in crowdsourcing, companies tap into this ability in bilinguals and language learners to engage and "empower" them in social media platforms. Economic forces are also responsible, not only for the emergence of solicited crowdsourcing, but also for the continuous evolution of initiatives and the introduction of micro-task crowdsourcing workflows in professional environments. Instances of this evolution are companies offering different tiers of translation quality based on the qualifications (or lack thereof) of the community of participants, with different price points depending on the skills of the crowd. Not only are "skilled" translators perceived in these initiatives as different from bilinguals, but "skilled" translators are also divided between general or specialized translators for distinct translation types, offering different economic conditions for both the participants and the clients (see 5.2.2). In this context, crowdsourcing emerges as "a business model [...] [that] makes it possible to blend efficiency with highly skilled professionals by recruiting specially selected communities of paid translators" (Muzii 2013: 12). Crowdsourcing is de-facto stretching and widening the business models in the industry, filling the gap from free and volunteer translation all the way to high quality, and high cost, professional translation. Nevertheless, it should by no means be perceived as the first phenomenon exploited by the language industry to push prices downwards: globalization for years has meant that the language industry has moved most production to low cost locations. Crowdsourcing only represents a new step in the exploitation of new technologies to lower costs or create new business niches.

Again, the question to ask is if an "economic turn" exists. If turns can only be defined or perceived after they are completed (Snell-Hornby 2010: 368), then the call for a research agenda into the economic aspects of translation could also not be considered a turn as such. Therefore, simply the call to engage in linking economic aspects in the study of translation is insufficient for a turn to exist. However, the initial interest in the discipline of a research trend marked by economic issues, such as the 2017 special issue on the economic turn in the TS journal *Perspectives: Studies on Translatology*, makes true that turns can overlap or that one turn can motivate another. This can be perceived in the fact that the influence of economic and market forces was part of the research agenda of the "sociological turn" (Inghilleri 2009; Pym 2012). Thus, the interdisciplinary nature of TS means that importing theories and principles from Economics and Business studies could potentially bring about new insights into the role of these forces in shaping translation practices, decisions, socio-professional considerations, etc. One example of this interdisciplinary process could be the incorporation of the notion of "asymmetric signaling" from the economist Spence (1973) in the study of how volunteer practices can potentially disrupt the professional market of translation (Pym, Orrego-Carmona and Torres-Simón 2016). Another example can be study of the connections between different price points and the offering of diverse quality tiers in paid crowdsourcing initiatives examined in Section 5.2.2.

8.3.2 The "activist turn" and collaborative practices

Another potential "turn" of interest is Wolf's notion of "activist turn" even when, again, its existence is questionable in Snell-Hornby's terms (2008). The relation between activism across linguistic borders and crowdsourcing is very close since activist activities depend greatly on the labor of volunteer translators to accomplish their goals, such as the case of Amnesty International (Tesseur 2014a, 2014b), Translators Without Borders (O'Brien 2016), Migrant Watch International, the Haiti Relief Effort or Green Peace. The combination of political positions and translational practices has led scholars to propose terms such as "engagement in Translation Studies" (Tymoczko 2000: 23) or the "activist turn" (Wolf 2012). Activist volunteer translation has been referred to as a new context in which previously inexistent "codes of reference have been created for translatorial activity" that subsequently can pose "questions for Western concepts of translation and their social implications" (ibid 2012: 129). The same activist approach is also perceived in engaged approaches of actual researchers analyzing these political phenomena, and it is guided by the "shared belief that the task of the researcher is not only to describe and explain but also to attempt to improve the situation or to offer solutions to a perceived problem" (Koskinen 2004: 153). Thus, the activist turn both involves the object of study and the perspective the researcher him/ herself brings to the picture. Chesterman has called for a more in-depth study of the motivation of these engaged practices, which he refers to as the "teloi" of participants in activist initiatives. He rightly considers that this study can make "worthwhile contributions to a better understanding of their attitudes and personal goals and ethics and how they are realized in what and how they translate" (Chesterman 2009:17). This focus on the "teloi", or motivations, of volunteers has not been fully explored in interpreting settings but it has, as will be shown later, been the main objective of crowdsourcing research in TS.

Studies in TS have mainly viewed this activist approach in the context of organizations such as Amnesty International (Tesseur 2014a, 2014b). Nevertheless, it has been most prominently the objective of interpreting research through the analysis of narratives produced by volunteer communities and individuals (Baker 2006), such as Babels or Peace Brigades International. This research trend can be said to have been initiated by Baker in her study of interpreting "communities set up outside the mainstream institutions of society", and focuses on the "narrative framework within which the work of communities of translators and interpreters who may be involved in political or social agendas may be explained and critiqued" (2006: 462). In this context, Boeri (2008, 2010, 2012) has studied the case of Babels, a pro-bono community of conference interpreters that contribute and arrange conference interpreting in the World Social Forum. It focuses on the "narratives that circulate among members of the conference interpreting community, especially those relating to issues of volunteering, activism and professionalism" (p. 29). It departs from an analysis of the positioning of professional conference interpreters and the fact, similar to what happens in professional translation in relation to the emergence of crowdsourcing practices, of the lack of binary positions but rather the network-like constellation of positionings that are available to and taken up by members of the conference interpreting community. On its part, Hokkanen (2012) focuses on volunteer simultaneous interpreting in Pentecostal churches in Finland. The study identified the type of volunteer interpreting performed as a twofold service, both to the members of the community and to God.

8.4   Ethics of translation in a participatory digital world

Ethics and ethical behaviors are a key area of study in sociological approaches, both from general professional translation (i.e. Pym 2001, 2012; Chesterman 2001; McDonough-Dolmaya 2011a; Van Wyke 2013), from a didactic perspective (Baker and Maier 2011) or even from the point of view of online collaborative activities (McDonough-Dolmaya 2011a; Drugan 2011; Pym 2012; Flanagan 2016: 158–160). Translation ethics can be said to encompass a range of settings, such as professional activity, the process or performance of translation, translator training or translation as a field of study (McDonough-Dolmaya 2011b). In professional-oriented settings, ethical behaviors are supposed to be guided by the innumerable existing deontological codes put forth by professional associations, such as the North American ATA, the Australian NAATI, the International Association of Conference Interpreters (AIIC) or the International Association of Medical Interpreters (IMIA), to name a few. Compliance with these codes is often related to one of the key components of the general notion of "professionalization" and for that purpose, many certification exams around the world include sections on ethics. Despite the relative consolidation of the profession in the 20th century, an agreement on what represents ethical behavior in translation is still far from clear. To date, the multitude of professional codes in different parts of the world "[seems] to agree on very few ethical or professional practices" (McDonough-Dolmaya 2011b: 30). Codes tend to agree on basic issues such as the confidentiality of the material translated and on the necessary preparations to be part of the profession, similar to what happens in other fields, such as accounting. Other issues in which most codes agree that professionals are supposed to be able to behave ethically include towards the process of translation and texts involved, towards the parties involved in the translation, towards the larger community of translators and towards training the future generations.

The emergence of all types of collaborative practices has opened up the discussion into the wider question of whether the study of translator ethics should involve practices in which non-professionals participate or those outside market circles, such as activist or non-profit initiatives. Chesterman, for example, before the emergence of online collaborative practices, questions if research into ethics refers to professionals or amateurs:

> [w]hen we speak of an ethics of translation, do we mean to include amateurs as well as "professionals"? One way of answering this question would be to distinguish between someone "who is a translator" and someone "who does translations (sometimes)". (2001: 146)

Chesterman sees the role of professional codes of ethics as promoters of the professionalization of the translation industry, helping boost the status of the profession at large: "an internationally accepted Hieronymus Oath would help to distinguish between professionals and amateurs, and promote professionalization" (ibid: 154). The emergence and consolidation of collaborative practices nowadays requires a more nuanced approach rather than separating amateurs from professionals, as will be seen later. The answer might also lie in whether ethical issues would encompass just translators or the wider network of agents involved in the processes.

Chesterman also argues that one of the main issues with the professionalization of translation, if compared with other fields, is precisely that some would argue that translation is not a true profession in the first place. The argument for this claim is that translation professionals do not seem to have a monopoly on a value goal that is not shared by other groups (ibid: 145). He argues that cross-cultural communication is not the exclusive domain of translators, and therefore, the boundaries are quite blurry. Other scholars, such as Tyulenev (2015), have also indicated that the multiplicity of objects in translation, including online collaborative practices, is "the factor that undermines its claims to be a fully formed professional field" (n.p.). Obviously, all types of free collaborative process online have only helped expand this issue with the subsequent effect on the profession. Chesterman (2001) in his proposal distinguishes four types of ethics involving the relation between the source text and the author (the ethics of representation), the negotiation and loyalty towards the client (ethics of service), the role of communicating efficiently (ethics of communication) and the specific expectations of the target audience (norm-based ethics). He also adds a fifth element, the "ethics of commitment", which relates to the inclusion of deontological aspects such as the codes of ethics for professionals.

Another researcher who delves into the ethical issues of having professionals and non-professionals sharing a similar activity is Pym (2012). He explores the issue of ethics in the age of digital voluntarism in which not all individuals engaging in translation do so through a professional model (2012: 81–86). He wonders whether any study into ethics should recognize that the translator is not always a professional: "translator ethics has now more to consider than the professional translator" (2012: 84), and consequently "this opens up new terrain for ethical inquiry" (ibid: 4). He does not trace a radical distinction between what would be expected in ethical behavior in both professionals and non-professionals, or what he calls the "paraprofessional". He insists that issues such as responsibility or trust in the final products should not be forgotten: "[o]n the contrary most things we have been talking about remain strangely operative in the field of collaborative translation" (2012: 85). From the point of view of advancing the profession, in tune with what Chesterman indicated, Pym argues that the basic ethical difference between professional translators and other people that translate is the issue of trust: "what translators exchange, first and foremostly, is their trustworthiness" (2012: 70). Meanwhile, volunteer and non-professional translators basically do not request the trust of those members of the society or participants in the wider translational context (ibid). In these contexts, the higher responsibility often falls on the shoulders of managers and workflow engineers that attempt to produce the highest possible quality within the limits of the initiatives, or sometimes on "professionals" or higher status participants that oversee the process, revise or post-edit the final work. That is, ethical issues in some translational contexts expand far beyond the actual agents that carry out the translation task. Another issue that regulates ethics in professional environments according to Pym is responsibility: responsibility to the matter, the client or the profession. In this regard, the proposal is similar to Chesterman's proposal, only the latter also includes the essential responsibility towards the end users or the audience. The study by Flanagan (2016) on the attitude of professionals towards crowdsourcing also raises the question of the issues related to this shift of responsibility in this paradigm. One of the issues noted by professionals is that responsibility no longer falls squarely on the shoulders of the translators, but rather on the organization.

One of the main issues that needs to be addressed is whether ethical behavior in TS is solely reduced to the focus on the individual, the single translator. Normally, the collective layer of translational activities is forgotten beyond the individual responsibility of the translator towards the global professional community. Crowdsourcing and collaborative translations open up the field to issues related to ethical behavior of other parties involved in the overall translational interactions. For example, when a social networking site attempts to engage users in segmental micro task crowdsourcing that results in a translation preferred by the majority, do the ethical implications rest on the shoulders of the non-professional or volunteer translator who votes on a preferred segment, or the collective of participants who in combination select their collective translation of choice? It seems like it might also fall on the shoulders of the company requesting the translations or even the initiator who requests a cheaper translation process. The focus on the individual is often related to the main philosophical points of departure, and the ethical behavior of the individuals is collectively employed as a mechanism to build "trust" in society and to gain "respect" and "status" in society. Once this need to build trust is devoid of economic exchanges or service provision issues, can the study of translation ethics also incorporate initiators, commissioners, clients, end users that prefer or use post-edited FOMT or amateur subtitles? This could be part of the distinction that the author makes between the "ethics of translation" and "translator ethics" (Pym 2012).

The above-mentioned extension of ethical responsibility beyond the individuals engaged in translational activities has already been discussed by Kenny (2011b) in reference to the mainstream adoption of MT in society. In her study of on the ethics of MT she brings certain arguments related to the question posed above. She claims that "ethical decisions are reasoned decisions that take others into account" (n.p.), such as developers of MT, post editors, free crowdsourced post editors, commissioners and consumers of MT, etc. When developers of statistical MT systems that depend on carefully built and aligned corpora of professional translations use them to produce translations through complex statistical algorithms; are they behaving ethically when they are "using" the product of innumerable professionals? Kenny does not necessarily provide an answer to this question, but there is an implied shift from translators behaving ethically towards other parties and the issue of whether others behave ethically towards translators. Suddenly, the equation seems to be reversed. It is professional translators and researchers who claim that "others" should behave ethically towards their profession. Similarly, the question to ask is whether those companies behind MT free systems, such as Google or Bing, behave ethically, not only by using or "harvesting" professional and amateur translations, but also by requesting free training for their engines by anonymous post editors of their output. Kenny is mostly concerned with the fact that engines are trained with the labor of professional translators that are unrecognized, and she finishes with an ambiguous call for further research: "these issues is still unclear, but what is clear is that we will need some kind of an ethical basis to help us rise to the challenge" (n.p.). The issues in this regard can be exponentially multiplied in current crowd post-editing MT approaches that not only make use of MT systems, but also use the crowd in the process. New business models that include crowd post-editing of MT output thus extend this discussion on the ethical responsibilities of a wide range of agents engaged in MT and crowdsourcing processes.

The ethics of collaborative and crowdsourcing environments would require further research into the many participants beyond the professional or non-professional translators. If the motivation of a bilingual student to participate in one crowdsourcing initiative is to practice their foreign language and they get satisfaction from their activity, the question emerges of the main locus of ethical considerations, in the participant or in the company or organization behind it. If so, are ethical implications radically different if the initiative is non-profit or done without any financial gain? Pym (2015a) and McDonough-Dolmaya (2011a) question whether the issue of ethics relates exclusively to whether any party is making any financial gains. Activist and non-profit collaboration in principle cannot be opposed to other contexts in which a company can obtain any economic benefit. But again, in some cases such as Facebook and other social networking sites, there are not any savings associated with moving to a crowdsourcing paradigm; managing the process might even cost more than using professionals (Desilets and van de Meer 2011). Nevertheless, if the trail of implications is followed, when a company offers paid-crowdsourcing translations at a third of the cost (see 3.2.2), do the ethical implications revolve around the company, the client that selected this less expensive option that they deemed appropriate for their purposes, the volunteer or paraprofessional translators that participate by the millions in these initiatives, or the developers of the MT systems that many of these initiatives use? It would be logical to think that the ethical responsibilities in these environments shift from the central role of the translator to a wider network of participants and, consequently, the role of codes of ethics and standards of conduct, such as the ones that a paid-crowdsourcing company might publish, might provide clues towards the better understanding of ethical issues in collaborative environments or industry standards.[2]

Collaborative environments not only expand the reach of the ethics of translation, but they also bring about new potential dilemmas. For example, as noted by Pym (2012: 86), nowadays translators can be requested to oversee or post-edit the output of MT and crowdsourcing translations. The final product can therefore be the result of the potential exploitation, in Kenny's terms (2011b), of both translators that produced the translations that fed the MT engine and of the volunteers that collaborated pro-bono. In this case, is the translator that post-edits a combination of crowdsourcing and MT output behaving ethically? It rightly seems so. Is the company that developed the MT systems or that developed and managed the crowdsourcing initiative behaving ethically? The answer of service providers tends to be similar: they are doing what is "legal", and their responsibility and allegiance is towards the legal systems and the wider society, and not necessarily towards translators as a loosely defined professional community. This model is gaining traction in the industry, and novel "community manager" positions appear in the industry. Further research is needed on what could be the implications of this shift. The field is thus wide open for additional research studies that can further expand on all these research questions.

8.4.1 TS research into the ethics of crowdsourcing

A handful of studies have delved into the ethics of translation in these contexts, either from a theoretical point of view (McDonough-Dolmaya 2011a; Pym 2012) or from a more empirical approach using documentary research methods (Drugan 2011). Other disciplines have also delved into the ethics of crowdsourcing using ethnographic or interventionist methods, such as Lee's (2010) analysis of copyright interpretation by fan communities in several countries. Similar studies from a TS perspectives including not only fansubs, but other crowdsourcing scenarios, are also dearly needed in this area.

The publication by Drugan (2011) analyzed professional codes and compared them with "codes" or guidelines for participation in a number of different volunteer online initiatives using documentary methods, from free and open software localization to social networking sites. The point of departure was a similar

---

2. The European Language Industry Association (ELIA), for example, indicates in their website that one of their objectives is "to promote ethics in the translation industry".

premise to Pym's (2012) claim that professional codes are to some extent repressive and normative in nature, as opposed to the more open and inclusive ethos of the "volunteer translator" ethics. In this line, Drugan attempts to identify areas in which volunteer guidelines for participation could help reframe professional codes. Several areas of interest are identified, among which are the "shared values and an explicit community vision" (2011: 117) in non-professional communities, a component that can be contrasted with the more individual approach in professional codes based on the rights of the translator. She also argues that professional codes could benefit from the sense of "shared ethos and continuing fostering of new leaders" (2011: 121) that promotes mentoring programs and support structures. The third area of interest is the open and transparent nature of online discussions geared towards establishing the ruling codes. Finally, she contends that all these issues (the openness, shared ethos and values, and sense of community engrained in many initiatives) represent an "inspiring and positive ethical model" (p. 122) that could benefit the often-isolated work of many freelancers. In any case, professionals have available highly popular and active online communities in forums in which freelancers participate, such as Proz.com or TranslatorCafe, in which discussions on ethics are, for example, open and transparent. One of the most significant findings in the study is that, contrary to what the open and free natures of these initiatives would suggest, non-professional explicitate quite clearly the penalties for non-compliance with the ethical provisions. For example, trolling a translation initiative or not complying with some of the norms in the volunteer community might result in immediate dismissal. Surprisingly, professional codes of ethics do not include a mention of what direct consequences might be associated with non-compliance, unlike other board-governed professions, such as medicine or law. The more prominent presence of penalties for non-compliance also involves an "emphasis on community policing" (2011: 118), but always framed in a positive light so as not to harm motivation.

The positive perspective in which community policing and compliance are framed in non-professional initiatives involves addressing more directly issues related to community mediation and the steps taken to contribute to the discussions on translation solutions. Collaborative initiatives often include tips and recommendation on how to participate and engage in translation discussions in productive ways, a component of professional translation competence that might not always be followed by translators in case of conflict. An interesting example of how discussions on translation solutions are displayed is the Osho Talks Translation Project, an initiative to subtitle talks related to meditation and mindfulness. In the community building section on the mediation principles for reviewing and discussion of translation solutions, it is indicated that

Meditative Collaboration [...] If there are any problems in the review process, please work them out in a meditative manner! If necessary – for stress release – do Osho Dynamic Meditation! [...] Reviewers are expected to contact the translator and confer over major changes made. Be clear and kind. We're all working on the OSHO TALKS Translation Project as contributors so find a way to be supportive as opposed to critical".[3]   (Osho Talks 2015)

The confrontational nature of the review process is anticipated and participants are reminded, if so needed, to even meditate and watch the meditation videos on the website to foster a collaborative, peaceful and constructive environment. In many cases, the mediation process not only refers to the code of ethics of the translation organization, but ethical codes related to the more general codes of ethics. For example, Translators without Borders includes not only the guidelines for participation, but also mentions of the Code of Conduct for The International Red Cross and Red Crescent Movement and NGOs in Disaster Relief.

McDonough-Dolmaya's (2011a) publication also analyses issues related to ethics in volunteer initiatives departing from a previous study on the shortcomings of professional codes (2011b). The main ethical issues she identifies are remuneration, visibility and the role of minor languages. First of all, remuneration and pricing are two of the most contentious issues in this area, and she contends that companies that profit from the labor of love of volunteers represent an ethical problem, extending the implications beyond the actual activity of translators themselves. The main issue here is the ethical behavior changes or lack thereof in cases in which participants carry out tasks for non-profit causes. In this last case, McDonough-Dolmaya refuses to separate from an ethical perspective for-profit and non-profit initiatives. Her main contention is that participation might help reduce the compensation for professional translation. Others, from the voice of professional translators, claim that crowdsourcing means pushing production costs to consumers while companies retain profits and rights to content (Dodd 2011). In any case, the lowering of the rates in general that has been experienced lately (DePalma et al. 2013) cannot be attributed solely to the disruptions on the market by MT and crowdsourcing alone. Other factors, such as globalization and outsourcing, might play a larger role in this area. In addressing ethical issues, some positive aspects should also be considered. In for-profit initiatives, volunteers pick up content that might not have been translated from a ROI point of view, thus not engaging in actual competition with professionals and extending access to content. In addition, the management of crowdsourcing and other related positions has also created new job profiles similar to what has happened in other crowdsourcing

---

3. http://www.oshotalks.com/CMS.aspx?pid=5

areas (Brabham 2013). The issue is less clear in cases in which non-professionals attempt to make a living out of initiatives. Brabham, for example, wonders whether modern societies will see "individuals who consider themselves full time members of crowds and who make a full time living through participation in one of multiple crowdsourcing platforms?" (2013: 114). The scholar answers himself by indicating that this is already happening, and wonders if these participants will or do have their own sense of professional ethics and habitus. This issue represents an interesting case that deserves further study in TS: the emergence of this hybrid "paraprofessional" does pose interesting challenges to the discipline, filling a gap between free FOMT, volunteers and professionals, and also, in terms of ethics, a middle position between volunteers and professionals.

The next issue of interest that McDonough addresses is translator's visibility. The paradox here is that while scholars have denounced for years the invisibility of translators (Venuti 1995), collaborative practices mainly in non-profit and MT settings have made translation more visible to the wider society. Nevertheless, McDonough-Dolmaya argues that if visibility emerges under the guise that everyone can translate, enhanced visibility does not imply that the working conditions of professionals might improve. Meanwhile, other scholars point out the beneficial aspects of increased visibility in general. While MT over the years has promoted the invisibility of the translation process, these models made visible both the process and demands of users globally (Cronin 2013). In principle, the "desire to translate" of the crowd should be welcomed by the translation community at large (Gambier 2012, 2014). Translation, after all, is seen in a positive light as an activity in which the wider public wants to engage in their free time and at their free will. In principle, it can be argued that the wide popularization of translation as an activity that is desirable and exciting to do should be welcomed by the scholarly community, since it also brings about low quality results that might enhance the perceived need for professional services in achieving quality. For example, in fansubbing, Massidda claims that "a majority of fans [...] are more than glad to access their favourite TV shows as soon as possible even if the final and fairly mediocre output is more of a nuisance than a pleasure", and even if these fans "seem unaware of these widespread mistakes" (Massidda 2015: 41). The wide visibility of these non-professional translations, in tune with the perceived low quality by the society at large of FOMT services, also brings about the discussion on the need for improvements in translation, highlighting along the way the role of professional translation. Some industry models based on MT bring up the visibility of human translation through this approach. For example, the free MT system Translate. com or the CAT tool Matecat based on a TM MT model, always include a link to "human" or "professional" translation. Rather than denouncing the low quality of MT, these business models attempt to attract those customers that would, probably, first attempt anyhow a gist MT translation, perceiving their need for human translation through being exposed to low quality output.

The third and last issue brought up by McDonough-Dolmaya is the ethical implications in cases in which collaborative translations are used to provide access to information to minority languages that would otherwise be impossible through market forces. It is argued that even when the opening of translation to minor languages might break down the limitations to access, the responsibility shifts from the company who shows the "willingness" to provide content in that language to the community of participants. In this regard, ethical implications of translation extend beyond the participants and include not only companies, but also language activists with a drive to enhance the presence and daily use of some minority languages in their communities. The fact that users often request companies to open up the translation to the crowd does not mean that it will be completed, but nevertheless, it acknowledges that they accept their limitations to produce translations under market forces and opens up a potential third way.

8.4.2 Copyright infringement and fansubbing

One of the most relevant ethical dilemmas brought up by the digital society, the emergence of the "sharing culture" and the rise of the "co-creational" user, relates to the legality of many practices common to a sharing culture paradigm, such as copyright infringement by fan communities that engage in translations of audiovisual products, comic books, journalistic texts or literary works. The ethical implications of these activities do not stop at the translation and distribution of copyright materials; they also extend to many supporting activities, such file sharing and file distributing, downloading or hacking. To date, this difficult balance between ethical and legal issues has been mostly addressed in the study of fansubbing (Díaz Cintas and Muñoz Sánchez 2006; Lee 2011; Hemmungs Wirtén 2012; Massidda 2015), but not in other areas such as literary works, scanlations or romhacking. The debate on the ethical or illegal nature of many collaborative activities is often framed in the wider debate of the "sharing cultures" (Castells 2003) fostered by the open web, and frequently under the light of issues such as piracy.

In their defense, many of the fansub communities invoke the access to information and critical content as their main drive. Generally, collaborative fan translations depend on the exploitation of intellectual works that are not accessible to the target sociocultural communities. In these cases, the fine balance between legality and ethical behavior is bridged by communities indicating that the fansubbing activity or the distribution will stop as soon as the material is available in whichever region they operate in. However, in more specific cases in which the activity is carried out due to the fans' expectations or desires not being satisfied when commercially subtitled or dubbed (Barraand and Guarnaccia 2008; Massidda 2015), the fine line gets murkier. To solve this issue, it is often necessary to draw distinctions between ethical and illegal considerations. For example, O'Hagan (2014) claims that crowdsourcing represents a legal, unethical activity while fansubbing is an illegal, ethical activity. As seen previously in this chapter, generalizing crowdsourcing as an unethical activity would be inadequate in certain settings, since, in line with McDonough-Dolmaya's (2011) and Pym's (2015a) arguments, the potential economic benefit of initiating companies cannot per se be seen as grounds to identify these activities as unethical. In a similar line, Massidda (2015: 18) sees the altruistic and free nature of fan translation as an ethical activity "because it is intended as an unselfish activity, a form of social disobedience, and a reaction to professional translations that do not meet fans' needs". The question then is whether social disobedience as such can be enough for breaking copyright laws. Recent legal developments, such as closing of fansubbing and general file-sharing sites, seem to suggest the opposite. Fansubbing has recently encountered an increasing pressure from institutions in line with the closing of P2P networks around the world and a tighter enforcement (or pretense of) copyright laws globally. For example, copyright infringement has led legal actions against communities, as seen in the closing by the Chinese government of the Schooter.cn and Yyets fansubbing sites in 2014. These institutional efforts by the Chinese government that forced these has been studied by Zhao and Gu (2015), who argue that the closing of popular fansubbing sites is due to the consolidation of the legal online video industry in China and the need to control these illegal activities. A similar effort was launched by the Japanese Government, the MAG project (Manga-Anime Guardians)[4] in order to protect this import cultural sector in Japan. As often happens with these fluid and dynamic communities, adapting to new circumstances happens rapidly. For example, one result of the increasing threat from institutional and commercial bodies is forcing subtitling communities to exclusively offer the subtitles without the video recording itself (Rong 2015). This is what is called "soft subs" as opposed to "hard sub" practices (Massidda 2015). Soft subs are basic .srt subtitling files that can be read by any media player in conjunction with the digital audio file itself, as opposed to the distribution of the video files with the subtitles hard coded in the file. This mechanism shifts the brunt of the legal responsibility to the end user that might need to download illegally the actual video file, sparing the fansub communities from one of their potential legal issues.

---

4. http://manga-anime-here.com/guardians

Copyright infringement does not automatically mean that companies cast a negative light on collaborative practices. In many cases, companies do not pursue legal actions against fansubbing since these activities can "have a very positive impact in the promotion of a given anime series in other countries" (Díaz Cintas and Muñoz Sánchez 2006: 44). This is similar in some journalistic context, such as the translation by ECOS of the Economist in China. In this case, it was reported that the journal gave permission to continue with the activities since they promoted the journal and the values associated with them internationally (Ray and Kelly 2011). As a defense, the social benefit of fansubbing is often brought up in the two potential illegal activities that fansubbers might engage in, namely piracy and copyright infringement. Rembert-Lang (2010) argues that the social benefits should outweigh the potential negative impact in terms of copyright infringement of fansubbing. She argues that "copyright law takes great care in protecting the needs of the author, but does not take into account the needs of the consumer" (2010: 33). Others, citing the social benefit and the benefit to the visibility of the translated products, argue that the "fair use" provisions could be extended to the activities of fansubbers (Díaz Cintas and Muñoz Sánchez 2006). Either way, it is important to remember that the WWW is a global network and savvy users can access content anywhere in the world, and therefore legal actions at the local level might not be sufficient.

Participants' attitudes and beliefs towards copyright and ethical issues help shape the debate and their actions. Lee (2011) researched the attitudes of fans towards copyright infringement and identified that the interpretation of the law depended on the geographical area, with different attitudes and interpretations across countries. In general, and maybe due to lax attitudes in young generations towards file sharing and downloading, copyright infringement does not represent a barrier for participation. An interesting case can be found in the study by Luczaj and Cwiek-Rogalska (2014). When fansubbers in Poland and the Czech Republic where asked about whether they were committing a crime through copyright infringement, the results were quite low at 19.2% and 12.1% respectively. Nevertheless, when asked about whether the subtitles they produced should be protected by copyright, the percentages almost tripled, with 59% and 64% of participants agreeing to this possibility. Thus, attitudes towards copyright infringement tend to vary not only according to countries or regional areas, but also on whether the participants are the users or creators of intellectual work. It is also of interest that, regardless of copyright protections, translation communities might have a strong sense of proprietorship towards the work produced. In the study of Chinese fansubs communities by Rong (2015), individuals did not show a sense of ownership over the subtitles they produced, but this was highly marked at the community level due to perceived competition. Subtitling communities often complained about other fansub communities "stealing" their work, an interesting contradiction that highlights the fact that their products are seen more as work rather than a hobby.

To finish with, the case of open software and any intellectual work developed under the Commons License deserves a special mention. The General Public License or GPL was initially developed by the FSF during the 80's in an attempt to protect free software that was developed collaboratively. This license extends to its subsequent collaborative localization of open software such as the browser Mozilla or the operative system Linux. The works of innumerable volunteer localizers have also been produced under open licenses that are less restrictive in what has been called the "copyleft" paradigm (Fondevilla and Lopez 2015). While the UNESCO translator's Charter (1963/1994) indicates it is a right of the translator to own the copyright to the translation and have his name mentioned on the translation, a radical distinction appears in collaborative environments between those initiatives by the legal owners of the copyright and those that might infringe it. While open source and commercial software, as well as some audiovisual initiatives such as TED might include the name of the participants, other illegal activities might hide behind community names or aliases.

8.5   Methodologies from the social sciences in research into collaborative practices

Sociological approaches have inspired empirical participant-oriented and context-oriented research in TS (O'Brien and Saldanha 2013), focusing on the interaction between agents, texts and the contexts of production and reception. Research into crowdsourcing thus reinforces the premise that TS represents an interdiscipline (Snell-Hornby 2010), with a wide range of theoretical models being imported and distilled. This foundation has provided the groundwork for the main questions that have been the object of enquiry: (1) what are the motivations of volunteers, (2) what are their profiles, and (3) how are these volunteers organized (Orrego-Carmona 2012)? As previously mentioned, these questions have been mainly researched using imported methodologies from the different strands of sociology, the most common of which have been:

1. Online survey methods
2. Ethnographic or "netnographic" approaches in which the informant immerses him-herself in the online community (Kozinets 2010)
3. Mixed methods (Creswell and Plano 2012), such as combining online surveys with "netnographic" approaches (Dombek 2013)
4. Documentary research methods

Before summarizing the main findings of these empirical studies in terms of volunteer motivations and profiles, the impact of the sociological research paradigm in the methodologies used needs to be explored.

8.5.1   Questionnaire and survey methodologies in the study of crowdsourcing

Questionnaires or online survey methods can be considered as the main current approach to questions related to the motivations of participants and their profiles, mainly through Internet mediated data collection using surveys.[5] Crowdsourcing studies have taken advantage of the evolution of survey research to the possibilities afforded by the Internet, giving rise to online research methods (ORMs), also known as Internet Research or web based methods (Fielding and Blank 2008). These types of methods have been used to study the cases of the main crowdsourcing initiatives such as Wikipedia (McDonough-Dolmaya 2012), Facebook (Dombek 2013), TED Open Translation initiative (Camara 2015), Duolingo (Deriemaeker 2014), Proz.com (Risku and Dickinson 2009), non-profits such as the Rosetta Foundation (O'Brien and Schäler 2010), subtitling communities in China (Chu 2013) and the Czech Republic and Poland (Luckaj and Cwiez-Rogalska 2014) or even to compare the attitudes of professionals towards MT and crowdsourcing (Anastasiou and Gupta 2011).

Motivation has primarily been the most widely studied issue in these publications. Most studies differentiate between intrinsic and extrinsic motivations (Frey 1997).[6] Intrinsic ones are those related not to financial compensation or reward but rather to personal enjoyment or to a feeling of obligation to a specific community, such as self-improvement or enjoyment of the task. Examples of this motivation type in the studies are "to gain intellectual stimulation" (O'Brien and Schäler 2010: n.p) or "make information available to other language speakers" (McDonough-Dolmaya 2012: 182). Extrinsic motivations are related to direct or indirect rewards, such as personal benefit (i.e. gaining more clients or reputation, getting presents or the potential to attract customers).

---

5.   Survey research was imported early on into TS in a wide variety of subfields, such as translation training, translation policy, social approaches to translation, audiovisual translation, translation quality, etc.

6.   Olohan reports on the discussion on the appropriateness of this binary intrinsic-extrinsic construct, since "volunteers are often motivated by a combination of factors, and can be seen as behaving simultaneously altruistically and egoistically" (2014: 19)

8.5.2   Netnographic approaches and mixed methods

Online surveys were also used in the study researching volunteer motivation in Facebook (Dombek 2013) in combination with "netnographic approaches".[7] This methodology represents an adaptation of ethnographical methods to research online communities on the web, a medium in which subjects or participants themselves cannot be directly observed. It was developed by Kozinets (2010) who defined it as a:

> written account resulting from fieldwork studying the cultures and communities that emerge from on-line, computer mediated, or Internet-based communications, where both the field work and the textual account are methodologically informed by the traditions and techniques of cultural anthropology.
>
> (1998: 366)

This methodology collects data of online communications in order to analyze behaviors and interactions. It involves the direct observation of subjects in online communities, similar to ethnographic fieldwork with the direct involvement and interaction of the researcher in the community. The field sites for this type of research are the online communities where participants communicate and build communities (Kozinets 2010). In netnography, researchers gather and analyze several types of data, such as archival data, or data that the researcher co-elicits through direct interaction with the community and the researcher's field data.[8]

Dombek's (2013) doctoral dissertation thus combined netnographic approaches with online surveys, online interviews, as well as observational studies. These observational studies were used to research the impact of the translation platform in participants' motivation and efficiency.[9] The study can therefore be described as a "mixed – method approach", because even when netnography can be considered a stand-alone methodology, it is better suited as a potential component of a mixed-method approach since virtual communities also manifest themselves in

---

7.   It is also known as "online ethnography" or "cyberethnography".

8.   Scholars indicate that blogs and forums are similar to archives of letters in newspapers that historians have been studied for years.

9.   This observational second stage is related to the interaction with the translation platform "Translate Facebook". The study used remote analysis of translation processes followed by TAPs in which the translation activity was recorded and displayed back to the subjects. For the latter method, the researcher adapted Activity Checklist approaches (Kaptelinin and Nardi 2006), a methodology used to handle the "interpretation of empirical evidence about complex phenomena of the technological mediation of everyday practices." (2006:97).

other realms of general society (Kozinets 2010).[10] The results of the study show that the motivations for this group of Polish FB translators were varied. For example, respondents reported that participating in FB: (1) promoted their feelings of competence, autonomy, and relatedness; (2) met their expectations of personal and social benefit; (3) produced a sense of reciprocity, self-efficacy, group commitment, and reputation gain, and (4) was perceived as fun and enjoyable. Additionally, the observational part of the study using Leontiev's (1974) Activity Theory showed that the technological platform designed by FB "often constrained attaining users' goals instead of facilitating them" (Dombek 2013: 262), which was often a source of frustration for the volunteers. The shortcomings identified by the subjects in the study were detrimental to the motivation of the volunteers in all four of the motivations identified above. Finally, it is worth mentioning that this netnographic study showed that the collaborative communicative platforms and discussion fora served as a means for the volunteers to arrive at solutions to the technological problems they faced.

8.6 Motivation to participate in online collaborative initiatives: A summary

This section summarizes the existing results from the different studies into motivation in Table 8.1. O'Brien and Schäler (2010) studied the motivation of volunteers in the non-profit The Rosetta Foundation, the results showed that the main drive behind volunteer motivation was the support for the causes to which the organization was committed, such as providing equal access to localization for minor languages. Participants also reported that the possibility of improving translation skills was a main drive behind their motivation. The main suggestion by participants was the possibility of getting professional feedback for their translations, both from peer translators and from the organizations. This is the only empirical study in which volunteers were asked about any motives that would make them more engaged in the future. This represents one of the main concerns of organizations and companies that organized crowdsourcing activities, since maintaining and expanding volunteer activity is key to their success (Ray and Kelly 2011).

---

10. A wide range of theoretical frameworks were used, such as (1) self-determination theory (SDT), (2) functional approach to volunteer motivation, (3) motivation to collaborate online and (4) gamification.

Table 8.1 Summary of initiatives and participants in studies into motivation

Researcher(s)	Initiative	N. of subjects in survey
O'Brien and Schäler (2010)	Rosetta Foundation	139
Mesipuu (2012)	Facebook & Skype	10 each (20 total)
McDonough-Dolmaya (2012)	Wikipedia	75
Dombek (2013)	Facebook / Poland	19 + 20
Camara (2015)	TED	177
Luckaj and Cwiez-Rogalska (2014)	Fansub communities Poland & Czech Republic	68 in Czech Republic 40 in Poland
Deriemaeker (2014)	Duolingo	36

McDonough-Dolmaya (2012) researched the motivation of Wikipedia volunteer translators using an online survey. The study departed from an adaptation of a previous motivation survey used in the field of Free and Open-Source Software (FOSS) (Lakhani and Wolf 2005) to identify specific motivations of translators. Translation participants were divided into non-professional and professional categories. Overall, intrinsic motivations were consistently the most significant ones, such as making the content available in other languages and supporting the initiative but, nevertheless, the findings identified a combination of different types of motivations to volunteer. Differences were also found between the professional and non-professional groups. For example, extrinsic motivations, such as gaining experience and feedback from others, were highlighted mostly among the professional participants. McDonough-Dolmaya also found empirical proof of what others have previously indicated (Ray and Kelly 2011): that volunteers do not see all initiatives equally and some of them are considered to have higher status than others. For example, professionals or participants with advanced translation skills carefully select the initiatives they chose to participate in. It is of interest that the results were also compared with studies in FOSS to identify differences between both fields (Lakhani and Wolf 2005). This comparison showed, for example, striking differences in the percentage of participants with university training in their field of voluntarism: while over 60% of volunteers had been trained on software development, this was true for less than 10% in Wikipedia, or 16.4% in TED talks (Camara 2015). These results echo the reflections on professionalism by several scholars and the relatively low barriers to entry into the field or practice (Chesterman 2001; Pym 2012; Tyulenev 2015).

Two studies have focused on the motivations of volunteers in TED Translation initiative: Olohan's (2014) and Camara (2015). Camara's study conducted a survey of volunteers, while Olohan employed documentary research methods and a qualitative approach using the published interviews in the TED website with participants. The data for this last study was obtained from blog entries in which the organization asked their main contributors "Why do you translate?". The documentary sources were only 11 blog entries, and it is clearly indicated that this cannot be considered representative of the over 8000 translators in TED, since, "the aim here is not to uncover all possible motivations [...], but rather to assess the usefulness of a qualitative analysis of data of this kind in studying motivation" (2014:23). In line with most studies, a combination of motivations seems to be behind volunteers' efforts, such as the support for the cause behind TED, "ideas worth spreading", or the opportunity to be part of a community. Meanwhile, Camara's study delved into both the motivations and the profiles of participants in the TED study with 177 respondents and a clearer picture of the motivations and participant profiles in this initiative. The main motivations identified relate to intrinsic motivations such as participants identifying themselves with the initiative or to help spread knowledge. Less important were issue related to learning, such as 53% of participants who indicated that they participated to gain translation experience and 52% to learn about the content of TED talks in general.

In order to compare and consolidate all results, it should be mentioned that the process is made somewhat difficult by the (1) different theoretical approaches taken, such as Volunteer Motivation Inventory used in the studies of Camara (2015) and Olohan (2014), (2) the different measuring scales, such as the Likert scale of O'Brien and Schäler (2010) or Luckaj and Cwiez-Rogalska (2014), to the multiple choice options in McDonough-Dolmaya (2012), or (3) the differences in the formulation of the potential motives in instruments developed. Nevertheless, the reliance on previous studies on volunteer motivation means that the underlying principles in survey questions are quite similar. For the purposes of presenting an overview of results, the data from all studies with quantitative studies were used and, for comparability issues, all motivations results were ranked and subsequently aggregated.[11]

The outcome of this analysis resulted in motivations being ranked in three different tiers. Tier one represents the most common results in all studies, and they all represent intrinsic motivations.

---

11. The qualitative results of the study by Olohan (2014) were not included since the motivations identified in the blogs by TED translators were not ranked, but in general lines the findings are similar to the others.

1. Making information in other languages accessible to others
2. Helping the organization with their mission or a belief in the organization's principles
3. Achieving intellectual stimulation and intellectual reasons. Probably related to what Shirky (2010) refers to as the "cognitive surplus"[12]

A second tier of motivations as reported by participants combines intrinsic and extrinsic ones:

4. The desire to practice the second language
5. Professional motivations related to the need to gain translation experience or increase one's reputation

Finally, a range of other motivations that appear consistently at the lower end of the results are:

6. The desire to support lesser-known languages
7. The satisfaction of completing something for the good of the community
8. The perception of this activity as something fun or as a hobby
9. The sense of belonging to a community or network

It should also be kept in mind that all studies, in tune with findings in motivations in other crowdsourcing and volunteering areas, conclude that a combination of motives, rather than one, is behind volunteer motivation. In any case, the only study that separated between professional and non-professional translators, that of McDonough-Dolmaya, identified that the main difference between both populations is the greater significance of extrinsic motivations in translation professionals, i.e. reputation, attracting clients, etc. To some extent, it is surprising that the community component of this participation, that is, being part of a network, tends to be at the bottom of the motivations reported by users.

It is also worth mentioning the results from the only study that questioned what would further motivate participants (O'Brien and Schäler 2010). It was shown that the most agreed upon option was feedback from professional translators and the organizations involved. This can be also due in part to the fact that most participants in this study self-reported being professional translators (86.4%). As far as the least motivating factor, having top translator lists was perceived as the least motivating factor according to participants, a widely implemented feature and one of the main recommendations in industry publications (Ray and Kelly 2011). Other

---

12. One study (Dombek 2013) asked whether participation was due to "boredom", and this could be considered to some extent related to the desire to expend the extra cognitive surplus that volunteers feel the need to expend.

issues related to motivation that emerge from these studies are the attachment to the content, genre or material translated. For example, in Luckaj and Cwiez-Rogalska (2014) it was reported that fansubbers mostly work with the audio-visual material they enjoy and only a small percentage (35% in Poland and 23.5% in the Czech Republic) would work on subtitles that others requested from them.

To finish this section, it should be mentioned that Olohan's qualitative study with an open probe approach, which examined the motivations of volunteers in blogs, to some extent agrees with the results of these studies.[13]

8.7   Volunteer profiles: A summary

Another question of interest that survey studies have attempted to uncover is the profile of the participating volunteers or fans. This has been explored in most of the studies and initiatives in the previous section (O'Brien and Schäler 2010; McDonough-Dolmaya 2012; Dombek 2013; Luckaj and Cwiez-Rogalska 2014; Camara 2015) and also in fansub communities in China (Chu 2013). These studies explore questions related to the educational and the professional profile, previous experience with translation, the age ranges and gender of the participants, potential time devoted to the initiative weekly and previous or concurrent crowdsourcing experiences, among others. Some, for example, explore other sociological issues, such as the religiosity or economic wellbeing of participants (Luckaj and Cwiez-Rogalska 2014). Some of the main conclusions that emerge from an overview of results are that significant differences exist between the average profiles of participants depending on the type of initiative and geographical area, but nevertheless, some common trends of interest emerge in how profiles of participants and initiatives interrelate. They relate to education, professional profiles, average age, other initiatives in which they participate and previous experiences in volunteer contexts.

Significant differences exist in the educational profiles between crowdsourcing initiatives. The surveys on Wikipedia and TED Translation initiative yield an approximately similar percentage of participants with a full degree (BA, MA) or a partial education in translation (certificate or some coursework), around 32% to 33% of participants. Only the study by McDonough-Dolmaya explicitly asked about a degree in translation and interpreting, and the percentage was 6.7%. The

---

13. The motivations identified are: (1) Sharing TED benefits, (2) effecting social change, (3) deriving "warm glow" (feel-good factor or the sense of satisfaction derived from altruistic behavior which differentiates pure from impure altruism), (4) participating in communities, (5) enhancing learning and (6) deriving enjoyment.

smaller study on the Polish translation community yielded a much different profile, the highest education achieved by the majority being middle school followed by high school. Similarly, in the case of fansubbing in the Czech Republic, only 31% of participants held a college degree. This difference can be significant from the point of view of the hierarchy of crowdsourcing initiatives in the minds of volunteers, with "certain initiatives having more symbolic value [...] than others" (McDonough-Dolmaya 2012: 183). Thus, findings could confirm that different initiatives do attract different volunteer translation profiles. McDonough-Dolmaya (2012) compares her results to those of previous studies into the crowdsourcing of open software and found that almost 60% of participants have college training (51%) or on the job IT training (9%), and reflects upon the difference in training profiles in both fields. It can be argued that, rather than lament the lower translation-specific training of volunteers, it could be related to the existence of unprofessional "natural translation" ability in all bilinguals (Harris and Sherwood 1978). This "natural" ability might not exist in most technological professions and skills. Also, these studies identify that in product-driven cases, such as software, the extrinsic motivations of participants are more prominent, since they use their professional expertise to develop a product that they themselves use later. Significant differences can be found if compared with fansub communities with lower or no barriers to entry. In Luckaj and Cwiez-Rogalska (2014), it was reported that 5% of Polish participants and 14% of Czech ones had a degree in languages, while the study by Chu (2013) yielded a 26.5% of participants with degrees in languages in China.

Regarding the current occupation of volunteers, results are again quite varied and participants arrive to these initiatives from all professional areas. The participants in the Rosetta Foundation non-profit project in 2010 were mainly professional translators (86.6% translators, 13.6%),[14] while in the study on Wikipedia 12% were translators, and 16.4% were translators in the TED initiative. In TED, professional translators also tend to occupy directly higher status positions, such as managers or revisers (Camara 2015). Student participation ranged from 37% in Wikipedia to 17.5% in TED, while academics were 4% and 8.5% respectively. This finding dispels that notion that volunteer translation is solely the domain of non-professionals, and further studies should be conducted to uncover the motivations and reasons for professionals to participate.

As far as the ages of participants, it can be seen again that different initiatives attract different age groups, even when only three studies implicitly requested this information. The Polish Facebook study reported 16 to 25 as the main age group,

---

14. Some initiatives such as Translators Without Borders are exclusively open to professionals.

with no participants over 40 years of age. The TED translation initiative attracts mainly 26 to 35 year-olds, followed by the 18 to 25 year-old range, and 27.6% of participants were from 36 to 61 and even 1.1% were over 61 years old (Camara 2015). Fansub communities seem to attract, on average, a slightly younger population, with an average of 26 years in Poland and the Czech Republic.

Another issue of interest is whether participants do or have participated in other translation crowdsourcing initiatives. In general, the percentage ranges from 40% (McDonough-Dolmaya 2012) to 50% (Dombek 2013). It can therefore be seen that translation voluntarism tends to be a recurrent practice and once participants become engaged, new or different initiatives might attract them. Volunteerism is also seen as a potential developer of translation skills. When asked whether subjects had formal training, 29.9% of subjects in Camara's study (2015) indicated that they had gained experience through previous volunteer participation.

Finally, the experience with the type of texts, modalities or the genres should be mentioned. As far as experience with textual genres, according to the small study by O'Hagan (2008), the advanced knowledge of the genres by fans prior to translation could compensate for the lack of knowledge or skills in translation. Consequently, fan translations could potentially produce translations of certain fan genres such as manga of quality similar to professional ones. Results from some of the studies mentioned in Chapter 5 might show that this could be, in principle, not the case. Another issue is whether participants have previous experience with the translation modality in the initiative. In the study by Camara (2015), 73% of participants reported no previous experience with subtitles before joining, and only 4% had previously been engaged in a pair or professional subtitling project. This might be possible due to intuitive platforms such as Amara that simplify the process, but nevertheless, despite the learning support offered by TED Translation Initiative, many collaborative initiatives might attract volunteers with no or relatively little knowledge of the genres, text types or modalities involved. To conclude this section then, it could be argued that the opposite of the claim by O'Hagan (2008) might be true across translation initiatives: many non-professional volunteers learn and engage with textual genres and modalities that they did not know before their participation.

CHAPTER 9

Crowdsourcing and translation training

> Collaborative work environments make the learning process easier,
> maintaining students' [...] positive attitude towards teamwork and improve
> students' self-confidence with regards to computers and translation tasks.
>
> (Olvera-Lobo et al. 2009: 179)

9.1   Introduction

Volunteer translation in non-professional contexts has often been used as a pedagogical tool to transition from classroom-based learning to real-world experiences. The emergence of web communities has made widely available translation possibilities in which trainees can engage in hands-on learning, expanding the contexts in which trainees can practice, and learn in casual, relaxed and self-directed ways. The question of whether volunteer communities can be integrated into training contexts has been dealt with by several researchers (i.e. O'Hagan 2008; Edfeldt, Fjordevik and Inose 2012; Orrego-Carmona 2014b; Michalak 2015), but this issue requires further efforts that can highlight the positive contribution they can provide to competence acquisition processes. Industry initiatives have been taking advantage of the availability of language learners since the early 2000's, many of which might be involved in translation training, for crowdsourcing efforts in paid and unpaid models, such as in the cases of Gengo and Duolingo respectively. The significance of translation trainees for many initiatives can be perceived in the development of platforms specifically designed to integrate crowdsourcing into both translation and language learning, such as the MNH-TT platform (Babych et al. 2012) or the academic extension of the crowd post-editing platform ACCEPT (Gulati et al. 2015).

This chapter explores how collaborative online platforms represent an ideal environment for socio-constructivist approaches to translation training (Kiraly 2000). From a cognitive perspective, it analyses the central role of feedback as a core component of the necessary "deliberate practice" in order to develop higher professional competence. Departing from an existing typology of pedagogical translation feedback in online courses (Neunzig and Tanqueiro 2005), the chapters offers a categorization of initiatives in terms of their positive contribution to the development of translation competence. The proposal is based on the type of feedback provided by different translation initiatives. The chapter ends with a reflection on how and if engagement in different types of crowdsourcing efforts can help achieve the development of professional translation competence according to recent models such as PACTE, TRANSCOMP, or translation expertise models from a cognitive perspective (Muñoz 2014b).

9.2 Crowdsourcing and collaborative translation in training: The path from volunteer to professional

The ultimate goal of translation education in institutions of higher learning is providing an entry to a professional community of practice. In a wider sense, this is accomplished through a two-pronged approach. On the one hand, it is necessary to prepare students to process and produce translations at entry-level standards, whatever they might be. On the other, students need to develop their professional habitus and self-concept, helping achieve a sense of belonging to a community of practice through their socializations. This is easier said than done. The transition from institutionalized structured learning to actual professional practice tends to be a complex process, and the results often entail a knowledge and performance gap between the exit point for university programs and the professional market (i.e., Lafeber 2012; Optimale program 2013). As one of the potential ways to bridge this gap, volunteer translation in non-professional or professional contexts has been used as a pedagogical tool to transition from classroom-based learning in institutions of higher learning to real-world experience. Traditionally, these efforts have taken shape of unpaid internships, with or without on-the-job supervision, an outstanding learning platform for situated learning models. According to Mareschal (2005), internships serve to fill the gap between the academic setting and the professional world, since they are an excellent way to reinforce the ties with the industry and to keep abreast of the latest developments and trends:

> un excellent moyen de renforcer ses liens avec le milieu professionnel, de se tenir au courant de l'évolution de la profession et du marché, et partant, de mettre à jour ses programmes et d'améliorer le produit qu'elle diplôme.
>
> (Mareschal 2005: 259)

These internships bring up the often-mentioned need of a closer connection between the language industries and university education. A need for closer connection between what happens in the classroom and the real professional practice has been a common position in TS since the 70's (González Davies 2004; Jääskeläinen 2011; Pym and Windle 2011; García 2015). This connection needs to link not only the latest developments in the language industries with training, but also with how the findings of research are applied to translation education:

> The links between research and the reality of the translation market may need critical scrutiny in terms of how we define our concepts, how we design and implement research, how we use research findings to bring about changes as well as how we educate future translators.
>
> (Jääskeläinen, Kujamäki and Jukka 2011: 145)

This is more so in a time when the language industry is inexorably moving towards different models, such as MT post-editing and paid crowdsourcing (García 2010, 2015), that require a deep analysis of their impact on translation education, demanding further pedagogical inquiry. This change of paradigm in the industry thus demands a close analysis in terms of how training institutions respond and embrace new industry trends. As an example, in new contexts such as post-editing MT, achieving maximum quality might not be a priority (Doherty and Moorkens 2013; Doherty and Kenny 2014); translators might be requested to produce light editing of MT output, quickly post-edit texts that have been crowdsourced, or just produce a "quick" low cost translation. In these cases, scholars have started to argue that translation training needs to acknowledge and include these different industry practices that prime speed or time constraints over quality, since traditional training focused on high performance might even be counterproductive (Pym 2013; García 2015).

A benefit of the potential incorporation of collaborative participation training is that they provide two basic notions in modern pedagogical approaches: collaboration and the immersion in real or simulated working environments. Both are a de-facto practice in most translation education programs due to several influential approaches, such as functionalism (Nord 1991), project and task-based models (i.e., Hurtado Albir 1999; González-Davies 2004), as well as socio-constructivist approaches (Kiraly 2000, 2012) together with their extension to online learning (i.e. Olvera-Lobo et al. 2009). They all introduced different variations of the collaborative nature of translation in the classroom mirroring the professional world. They emerged as an alternative to the classic "chalk and talk" approach in which an instructor comments on each translation segment of a text previously translated by students (Nord 1991), the central model in outdated transmissionist approaches to translation learning (Kelly 2005). Collaboration also made its way into training thanks to the impact of new translation technologies on translation training (i.e., Bowker 2014), as well as by the emergence of new modalities that require collaboration between different agents in the professional world, such as game localization (O'Hagan and Mangiron 2013), web localization (Jiménez-Crespo and Tercedor

2012; Jiménez-Crespo 2013a: 159–187) or MT post-editing (Doherty and Kenny 2014). The collaborative nature of some of these new modalities is such that web localization has been, for example, defined by its collaborative and team approach and in opposition to other types of "regular" individual translation processes. This type of collaboration is thus present in localization training. The introduction of real-world scenarios in the translation classroom also made its way there through different avenues, such as the consideration of clients and the expectations of the audience or the social and collaborative nature of learning. This trend soon made its way into theoretical and applied research with an interdisciplinary proposal in TS literature with different points of departure, such as theories of learning, second language acquisition and cognition (i.e. Nord 1991; Kiraly 2000, 2012, 2015; Olvera-Lobo et al. 2009; Risku and Peschl 2010).

The significance of crowdsourcing and online collaborative translation communities lies on the fact that they can be ideal platforms for practicing and building both general translation competence and specific translation subcompetences. Aside from that, they have become a source of new professional profiles that trainees can aspire to, such as "community language expert" or "community managers" (DePalma and Kelly 2011) or professional micro-task crowdsourcing models such as Unbabel, Stepes or Translate.com. Therefore, if translation education needs to look into current practices in the industry to prepare students for the real world, it should be acknowledged that many of these types of crowdsourcing, such as professional paid crowdsourcing in which professional translators collaborate in a "hive" model (see 3.4 and 5.2.2), are now part of the language industry. Consequently, students should be aware and knowledgeable about both paid and unpaid variations of this phenomenon as a fourth stage of revolution of translation technologies in the profession following the revolutions brought by translation memory, localization models and MT post-editing.

9.3   Are online collaborative practices "accidental training" environments?

The emergence of collaborative communities on the web has made available translation possibilities in which trainees can engage in hands-on learning unthinkable a couple of decades ago. Volunteer translation can happen anywhere, anytime; even mobile apps for volunteer translation in phones and iPads offer the possibility of practicing translation while waiting for a bus. This ubiquitous presence of translation crowdsourcing and collaborative process has found its reflection in translation training literature, with an increasing number of scholars questioning whether these communities can be integrated into learning settings. O'Hagan (2008) initiated the debate on whether fan translation represented an "accidental training environment", that seemed to offer "authentic and situated learning environments for amateur translators who are well motivated" (2008: 178). She indicated that the study of fan communities, one of the many possible collaborative settings, "could inform an alternative paradigm to translation training" (2008: 178). In assessing the impact of crowdsourcing in audiovisual translation, Gambier also defends that "fan translation forms a potentially highly effective learning environment" (2012: 55). Similarly, Edfeldt, Fjordevik and Inose (2012) indicate that there is "great interest when studying the interaction between formal and informal learning that puts the student in focus" (2012: 105). The collaborative nature of these approaches and the similarities with popular socio-constructivist approaches that prime social interaction and real world scenarios has been pointed out by scholars such as Orrego-Carmona (2014b) and O'Hagan (2008), and this combination is seen as "a suitable translator-training environment" (Orrego-Carmona 2014b:131). Meanwhile, Declercq (2014: 47) rightly indicates that crowdsourcing "as a concept and activity should be embraced by the translation education community as an additional asset in translation training". The benefits of potentially including volunteer translation as a learning tools has thus been rightly pointed out by these scholars, but to date, research has yet to explore how to operationalize and integrate this learning into the translation competence acquisition continuum.

Conceptualizing the participation in volunteer communities as an "additional" or "complementary asset" as Declercq (ibid) indicates rightly captures the benefit and the main proposal that serves as the connecting path throughout this chapter. If the acquisition of translation competence in institutions of higher learning is considered as the acquisition of "expert knowledge" (Shreve 2006a) that develops through "deliberate practice", then any guided and structured intensive "deliberate practice" setting, with different levels of difficulty and appropriate feedback to develop expertise (Ericsson 2000), should be mostly welcomed by the training and professional community. This is also true when considering that, similar to many basic cognitive activities such as tennis or playing an instrument, translation is also considered up to 80% procedural-operative knowledge (knowing how to do things), while declarative knowledge (knowledge about something and the ability to reflect upon the performance) is often consider to be around 20% (PACTE 2005). In this case, any additional guided practice in tune with how expertise or the integration of translation subcompetences develops (PACTE 2000; Kiraly 2012), can only be beneficial to the development of expertise in the field.

The question that needs to be answered then is (1) how to operationalize or establish how to incorporate or merge this "deliberate" or "free and undeliberate" practice into the translation competence acquisition continuum in university programs, (2) how to solve issues related to differences between the professional goals and the goals of the practice outside market pressures, or (3) how certain social and ethical issues related to the development of the professional habitus can vary between professional and non-professional settings (Gambier 2014). It is therefore more necessary than ever to analyze the possibility of incorporating collaborative and crowdsourcing approaches not merely as "accidental learning environments", but as "complementary learning foci"; how collaborative communities potentially represent an ideal setting from a socio-constructivist approach (Kiraly 2000, 2015); how these practices relate to cognitive-based research into translation competence and its acquisition; and how collaborative online practices can be part of the overall education process.

In the spirit of the proposed goal of this chapter, the focus is not the development or the emergence of a potential "alternative paradigm" separate from institutionalized learning, but rather an exploration of how both settings can contribute and be blended in order to lead to the ultimate objective of preparing students for the professional job market. In doing so, it needs to be acknowledged that successful or intensive participation in non-professional crowdsourcing initiatives seldom ever leads to high-level professional careers (De-Palma and Kelly 2011). Nevertheless, it can also be argued that, on the other hand, many successful professionals have not been trained in university training programs and, therefore, the paths from non-professional to being able to make a living out of translation is not necessarily mediated through institutionalized translation training globally. O'Hagan (2008) rightly advances that one locus of research in these areas should be which skills translating fans have successfully acquired in terms of performing either individually or collectively at professional standards (whatever they might be). Researching the mechanisms by which these volunteers and fans can acquire close to professional competence then becomes an imperative.

The answer to whether collaborative translation initiatives and crowdsourcing represents an "accidental environment" or a "complementary environment" for translation training can be found in two key elements. First of all, collaboration represents the backbone of socio-constructivist approaches and the following section examines how many initiatives, despite the non-professional nature, represent an ideal environment for situated learning in a semi-professional setting. The second issue to consider is the differences between initiatives and the approaches taken to the provision of feedback after performance. In principle, it will be argued that any collaborative initiative with sufficient informative feedback loops can be, ideally, a beneficial setting for enhancing translation competence acquisition.

9.4 Socio-constructivist approaches and crowdsourcing

Collaboration and networking are also at the core of professional translation (Gouadec 2007). This fact has been acknowledged since the 1980's by functionalist scholars such as Holz-Mänttäri (1984) or Nord (1991). The ubiquitous presence and penetration of the Internet in modern lives nowadays means that professional translation is a de facto networked collaborative endeavor mediated through digital technologies, in which the social networks are normally wider than anticipated (Risku and Windhager 2013). Any type of crowdsourcing and collaborative projects mediated through the web inevitably leads to the highly influential socio-constructivist approaches proposed by Kiraly (2000). This is reflected in TS pedagogy literature, where it is often argued that online collaborative learning platforms represent a perfect setting for socio-constructivist approaches (Massey 2005; Robinson, Lopez and Tercedor 2008; Babych et al. 2012). Socio-constructivist approaches claim that collaborative translation projects based on real world scenarios should represent the foundation of translation learning. This model has helped move the 20th century translation education from transmissionist teacher-centered approaches, in which instructors had the ultimate say in students' translation proposals, to models in which translation learning is fundamentally an interactive, collaborative, "socio-personal process". The main aspects are "learner autonomy, cognitive apprenticeship, and authentic collaborative project work in the classroom" (Kiraly 2015: 20). Learners socially construct their own knowledge through interaction in a social learning environment. Students are thus at the center of the learning process and are expected to take control and self-direct their own learning. They discover knowledge by themselves and collaborate in real life professional translation assignments. It highlights the interpersonal component in knowledge construction, in which collaboration and interaction is a key feature. Immersion and interaction in a "translation community" becomes an essential part of the learning process (Kiraly 2000: 13). Instructors are seen here as counselors or facilitators helping students to find information and build their own learning structures, known as "scaffolding" (ibid: 49). The author has recently questioned whether, rather than a move forward, socio-constructivism took translation education backwards, taking:

> translation education from largely desituated instruction and practice to increasingly collaborative work on authentic translation projects [...] back to the learning on the job that once formed the core of "training".   (Kiraly 2015: 13)

The acquisition of translation competence has recently been tackled by the Kiraly, departing from a criticism of subcomponential translation competence models (see 9.5). He presented a model for the emergence of translation competence from a fractal perspective that attempts to depict the "tremendous complex interplay of translational subcompetences and their non-parallel emergence over time" (ibid: 27). It is based on the premise that each person's life experience is unique and different, and therefore the acquisition of subcompetences for each individual is framed in the context of an emergent vortex of integration of competencies. The interesting aspect in this issue is that the emergence of translation competence interfaces "with the community of other individual vortices with which the translator interacts while translating and while learning to translate" (ibid: 29). The emergence of translation competence can therefore be only understood in the context of an ever-changing social, cultural and physical context. Social interaction, again, plays a key role not only in socio-constructivist learning models but also in the development of translation competence.

Collaboration in networks with mentoring structures or feedback loops represents an environment in which students can potentially engage in real-world projects that can help enhanced their translation competence. For example, some initiatives such as Translators Without Borders offers fully fledged training courses and programs for potential volunteers,[1] while many fansub communities offer training and mentorship programs for novel fansubbers (i.e., Bold 2011; Orrego-Carmona 2014b). They can also approach certain textual genres and contexts that hardly ever made their way into institutionalized learning (O'Hagan 2008). Receiving reviews from translations, the provision of detailed feedback, discussion forums, defending proposed solutions in groups, collaboration in one single translation or collaboratively building translation resources, such as term bases, are all key essential ingredients of these approaches that can be found in many of these initiatives. If the role of the instructor is to serve as a guide for students in socio-constructivist approaches, the question is whether highly experienced peers or higher status participants in non-professional contexts can serve in the same role as the instructor in regular translation classrooms from a theoretical perspective.

9.4.1 The development of online collaborative training models

Several collaborative learning projects have applied socio-constructivist approaches to online translation training in models that highly resemble many collaborative and crowdsourcing initiatives (Olvera-Lobo et al. 2005, 2009; Ramirez Polo and Ferrer Mora 2010; Vargas Sierra and Ramirez Polo 2012). For example, the Aula.Int project at the University of Granada implemented a model, known as the Professional Approach to Translation Training (PATT), based on this theoretical foundation. The main goal of this project is to:

1. http://translatorswithoutborders.org/Training-Center-Students

> [I]ntroduce translation students to the professional market and help them get acquainted with working conditions in the real labor market by means of a simulated translation agency. (Olvera-Lobo et al. 2005: 138)

The project was created using an online platform named Basic Support for Cooperative Work, where the research team developed a network consisting of the various interconnected roles within a translational transaction: teacher as a client, project manager (also the reviser), documentalist, terminologist, reviser and typesetter. This type of platform clearly resembles more recent crowdsourcing and collaborative platforms such as Trommons by Rosetta Stone (De Wille, Exton and Schäler 2015), or Transifex, as well as others that have been specially adapted for learning, such as MNHTT (Babych et al. 2012) or ACCEPT (Gulati et al. 2015). Students in several courses are initially assigned to groups of five participants, and then periodically receive translation assignments with clear translation briefs. Students then "telework" collaboratively to complete the assignments under the supervision of the instructor. Throughout the semester, students rotate to different roles in order to become acquainted with all positions in the translation cycle. The goal of this project is also geared towards getting students used to "teleworking" as well as to actively participating in translation projects mirroring the reality of the professional world. These types of initiatives have been highly praised in the TS community, and therefore, the question arises, if students participate in similar volunteer activities outside academia in which specialized genres are part of the text to translate, i.e. specialized texts for Translator Without Borders, highly specialized articles from The Economist in Ecos, microloans in Kiva or Open Source software and smartphone apps, what are the differences between both settings? The feedback and the formative evaluation processes? The progressions of texts, tasks and difficulties carefully structured (Kelly 2005)? The savvy guidance of the instructor? If in certain cases collaborative platforms can, indeed, be quite similar to highly popular socio-constructivist approaches, the main argument here would be that the initial step towards an attempt to blend institutionalized training with non-professional approaches is the selection of initiatives with feedback loops.

9.5 The search for constructive feedback: On the identification of initiatives that can enhance student's learning

Within constructivist and situated learning approaches, constructive feedback represents one of the key pillars to the development of translation competence. The need for formative feedback is not necessary only in educational context; in professional translation, feedback through revision of translations and other performance-related criteria is a common feature in a cycle to improve future performance (Gouadec 2007). The reasons why feedback is essential throughout the professional lives of translations is that translation acquisition is a non-finite process (Neubert 2000): highly professional translators are continually adding new knowledge and merging it with existing knowledge. A large part of the knowledge that professionals add comes from feedback on the translations performed, and it is a necessity for the continuous development of translation expertise (Shreve 1997; 2006). Feedback is so critical that the lack of continuous meaningful feedback in translation has been related to the relative inability of professionals to perform tasks in experimental settings at the level that would be expected from their formation and years of experience (Göpferich 2015: 74).

Feedback is often sought after by participants in volunteer initiatives. This is supported by the results of the study on volunteer motivations in the non-profit Rosetta Foundation (O'Brien and Schäler 2010); when participants were asked what would be the most motivating factor to continue participating, feedback on their translations was the most common response. Collaborative and crowdsourcing initiatives offer a wide range of feedback loops. In some of them participants receive detailed feedback; in others, communities even incorporate didactic assessment in order to train newcomers, such as several fansub or non-profit communities. In other cases, feedback is completely inexistent and participants do not know what happens once they translate a segment, paragraph or text. This can be part of the so-called "hide alternative translation model" (Morera-Mesa 2014), in which, even if several participants translate the same segment, they are unaware of this fact and no feedback is received from the initiative, such as Asia Online Wikipedia initiative or crowdsourcing initiatives through Amazon Turks.

Feedback can appear in the two most common types of evaluations: formative and summative, while feedback in the latter comes in the form of whether or not the participant passed a pre-established threshold. In formative evaluations, feedback is provided with the intent of continuing to build the translation competence of the student. Formative evaluation can be defined as "any marking, correction or comment which gives students feedback on their learning precisely in order to help them learn more, or better." (Kelly 2005: 133). If seen from this perspective, it could be argued that initiatives that incorporate any type of feedback loop in their workflow and models could be of interest for institutionalized translation training.

9.5.1 Neunzig and Tanqueiro's (2005) classification of online translation feedback

The type of feedback that can be provided in training situations, from the red-pen error marking settings to elaborate holistic models, all the way to peer feedback (Wang and Han 2013; Massey and Brändli 2015), represent a complex issue and it is interrelated with the type of pedagogical model adopted. In their empirical study of translation feedback in online courses, Neunzig and Tanqueiro (2005) offered a useful classification of possible formative feedback in online settings. Since the objective was the study of online classes in which students interact online with the instructors, the foundations and results of the study can be of interest for the analysis of formative feedback in crowdsourcing and collaborative initiatives. The proposed comprehensive classification of translation feedback in online situations depends on variables such as whether the feedback is individual or not, whether it is anticipatory (such as providing a glossary or discussing the difficulties in the text), contiguous or delayed. Anticipatory feedback, despite the contradictory nature of the term used, is defined as feedback that is provided when "the translation has not yet been formulated in writing" (ibid: np). Individual feedback was separated between informative feedback or corrective feedback, and in this latter category it was further divided between simple and elaborate. The empirical study focused on these last categories, "simple" and "elaborate", and it also considered the moment in which the feedback was presented; before the translation was initiated, during the translation process or as a follow-up. The empirical portion of the study concludes that the translation process and the quality outcome partially correlate to (1) the type of feedback employed, (2) how it is administered and (3) when it is presented. It indicated that "elaborate feedback", that is, feedback "provided directly after commission of errors [comprising] prompts or indications of the most appropriate strategy to be applied to find an acceptable solution" (2005: np), in whichever required form of presentation, was more effective than other forms of online teacher intervention, such as providing a translation model (this can even prove counterproductive) or traditional feedback. Online elaborate feedback also produced the highest acceptance rate among students. In addition, the researchers indicated that it was most influential in terms of modification of translator behavior and resulted in the highest rate of acceptable translations, thus indicating a positive effect on translation quality.

Feedback in online learning contexts does not necessarily need to be provided by the instructor. In collaborative environments it can also come from fellow students (Kiraly 2000: 84; Massey and Brändli 2015). In an empirical study, Wang and Han (2013) discuss the use of online peer review of translation as a tool for translation training. Participants were randomly assigned a marker to whom they would send their translation and at the same time they would receive feedback. The results showed students appreciate online peer feedback as a valuable activity that facilitates improvement. Students reported that the entire process of marking, receiving feedback and perusing was the most beneficial as a whole, followed by simply receiving feedback. Interestingly, none of the students indicated that simply marking a translation was beneficial to them in any way, reinforcing the perception that receiving feedback is an essential part of the online translation experience.

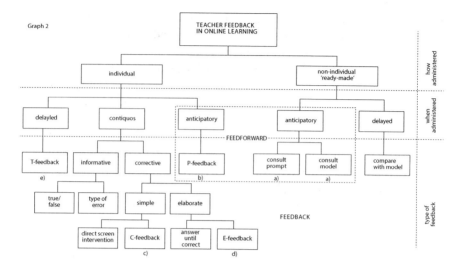

Figure 9.1 Classification of online translation feedback by Neunzig and Tanqueiro (2005: np).

Peer-feedback can also be problematic; in certain instances, peer-feedback can be too harsh or, in tune with findings that indicate that students tend to not identify translation problems (Krings 1986), it can be too superficial or lenient (Kim 2008). Massey and Brändli (2015) also studied peer feedback in a socio-constructivist real project-inspired situation, and it was found that peer feedback could result in quality levels in projects similar to professional ones (ibid: 187). In this project, students reported that less than one fifth of the feedback came from the instructor and client combined, but, nevertheless, they appreciated this feedback the most. That is, despite the value of peer feedback in collaborative settings, students still identify and highlight the different authority levels perceived by students in this approach. The type, form or content of feedback by instructors and clients still can be the most valuable in terms of development and efficiency of intervention.

9.5.2 A classification of collaborative initiatives on the basis of feedback

As previously described, crowdsourcing and collaboration online can be introduced in institutionalized learning as grounds for playful experimentation for future professionals. In this case, a classification of initiatives based on the type of feedback can help identify additional training initiatives that could help students in their path towards professional competence. Figure 9.2 proposes a categorization of initiatives partly inspired by Neunzig and Tanqueiro's (2005) classification.

It departs from an initial distinction between whether or not initiatives provide any type of feedback that can be beneficial to participants to develop their competence. The first category would be those initiatives that do not provide feedback, such as post-editing translations in Google Translate, Bing or other MT engines, participating in Amazon Turks, translating Wiki articles in which there is no direct oversight or providing feedback on published translations in language portals such as the Microsoft one. In principle, these initiatives should not be completely disregarded from translation training since they can provide a platform to practice translation, analyze proposals, provide materials for didactic units or task-based approaches (González Davies 2004), and serve as a minimal practicing environment for language related competences (García 2012). Nevertheless, in both a situated learning perspective and a cognitive expertise approach, the lack of direct feedback hinders the potential advanced development of competences or skills. They could still be used during regular didactic units with specific learning goals, carefully incorporating them in didactic units with specific purposes, such as MT post-editing modules (Doherty and Moorkens 2013). Cases in which feedback is provided are subsequently subdivided into individual and non-individual feedback models. Non-individual feedback is provided through learning guides, preparatory materials, problem guides, existing glossaries, norms and codes in crowdsourcing or collaborative initiatives. This can be referred to as "preventive or orientative feedback" in Neunzig and Tanqueiro's (2005) classification. "Individual feedback" is provided to each participant in different ways, and for the purposes of this proposal is divided between "delayed crowd feedback" and "corrective elaborate or simple feedback by peers". The delayed crowd feedback refers to cases in which the participant can eventually receive feedback from the community using the "wisdom of the crowd". It can appear either as simple feedback, such as iterative models in which eventually one's proposal can be accepted, or elaborate feedback that occurs in forums, either related to the initiative such as the forums in Facebook or TED or those independent ones such as the discussions in translator platforms such as Proz.com. In these forums, participants elaborate on their proposals, peers can vote, discussions among peers can occur and ultimately the requestor of the question, based on the responses and the votes from the crowd, can select the most appropriate answer from his or her point of view. Differences can be found, such as the cases of Facebook or Twitter in which the first only shows three proposals for voting, while Twitter directly shows an unlimited number of them. The value of this feedback model from the perspective of the development of translation competence can also be found in the generative and selective nature of these iterative models. According to Hönig (1995) and the subsequent adoption of this model by Pym (2003), professional translators possess a "macrocompetence"; the ability to select and produce different valid solutions confronted with a problem and, therefore, the ability to produce different target texts from a single source text.

> The ability to generate a series of more than one viable target text (TT1, TT2 … TTn) for a pertinent source text (ST) [This corresponds to what Hönig calls associative competence.]; The ability to select only one viable TT from this series quickly and with justified confidence. [This corresponds to Hönig's macro-strategy and the ability to employ it consistently.] (Pym 2003: 489)

In these iterative contexts with voting mechanisms, participants can translate and vote, opening up the potential limited exercise of both the generative and the selective features of this macrocompetence. In Twitter Translation Center for example, if a participant attempts to provide a translation for a segment that already exists, a message box indicates that it is not possible to propose that translation, but it is possible to vote for it. In this case, this minimal feedback can be considered to be valuable for earlier stages of the learning process.

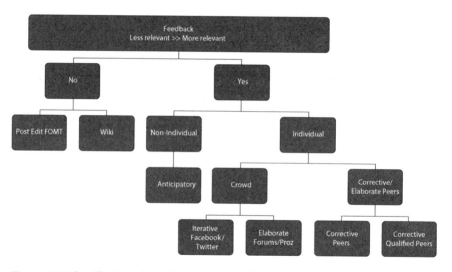

Figure 9.2 Classification of crowdsourcing and collaborative initiatives based on feedback received.

The following type of individual feedback would be the corrective and elaborate feedback present in platforms that attempt to replicate the Translation-Edit-Publish mechanisms. In this model, translations are subsequently edited by peers following the established model in the industry. This means that feedback of different form and detail can be provided to the participant. Under this model, two different types are proposed: feedback by peers that occupy a similar rank in the initiative, or feedback by qualified participants. The notion of "qualified participants" is understood here as those in initiatives that have ranked participants according to any type of criteria. The selection can be through performance, professional experience, frequent users, etc. For example, Camara identified that professional translators tend to occupy reviewing and managing positions in TED Talks (Camara 2015). TED Talks also includes a detailed evaluation process in which translators can receive elaborate feedback by qualified participants. Initiatives with revision processes abound in non-profits, subtitling communities, etc. This type of feedback has been shown to be beneficial to students. In the study of Orrego-Carmona (2014: 138), after participation in volunteer subtitling communities with mentoring programs, 83% of participants thought the communities could be a good source of feedback for their translations. Settings in which more meaningful feedback is obtained also respond to initiatives with close models in which admissions tests are often administered, and also often possess mentoring strategies to form volunteers.

9.6 Translation competence models in Cognitive Translatology, the development of translation competence and collaborative voluntarism

In Translation Studies, the notion of translation competence has been studied for over 15 years primarily from cognitive approaches. The last part of the chapters delves into an analysis of cognitive inspired competence models and the reasons why they can be beneficial to the process of conceptualization and integration of participation in crowdsourcing and online community translation in university programs. Cognitive models such as PACTE and TRANSCOMP will be described, followed by a detailed treatment of the notion of competence acquisition and participation in volunteer activities can be incorporated in the acquisition continuum. Last but not least, Section 9.7 will present the reasons why these componential cognitive inspired models represent an ideal foundation in order to conceptualize the integration of crowdsourcing and online community translation as opposed to other points of departure.

9.6.1 Translation competence in TS

It was early on, when the first translation training manuals appeared, that scholars started to describe the notion of translation competence from a didactic perspective as the main component of translation education (Deslisle 1980). It was then described as both the knowledge shared by professional translators that trainees did not possess and the learning objective of translation training. The basic underlying premise is that professional translators, as opposed to non-professional ones, possess a certain degree of this competence, which has been defined as the underlying knowledge system needed to translate (PACTE 2011a, 2005) or "the knowledge and skills the translator must possess in order to carry out a translation" (Bell 1991: 43). Among several other terms used in the discipline, this notion has also been referred to as "professionalism" (Kiraly 2000). It is normally understood to be expert knowledge that is not possessed by all bilinguals; it is mostly procedural-operative knowledge (knowing how to do things) as opposed to declarative knowledge (knowledge about something).

From the onset, one of the basic points of departure upon which translation competence was built was "natural translation" (Harris and Sherwood 1978), the innate ability of any bilingual to translate. This has also been referred to as native translation by Toury (1995: 248–254) or circumstantial interpreting and translation from the perspective of language acquisition (Angelelli 2010). Natural translation is often the objective of crowdsourcing initiatives that include different management and workflow solutions. The goal of educational programs is to move trainees from a departure point, ideally near college level fluency in two or more languages and/or a small degree of translation competence, together with natural transition skills, to a graduation moment in which students are closer to — though not yet fully developed — professional translation competence. This is precisely why this notion plays a key role in translation education, as translation competence represents precisely the core knowledge to be acquired throughout institutionalized translation programs.

A number of scholars have proposed more or less detailed theoretical models of translation competence since the 80's (Deslisle 1980; Bell 1991; Pym 2003; Hönig 1995; Kiraly 1995; Shreve 1997; Neubert 2000; González-Davies 2004; Kelly 2005). Nevertheless, only two research groups from a cognitive perspective have engaged in extensive empirical research efforts in order to validate the proposals: the PACTE group in the Autonomous University of Barcelona (http://grupsdere-cerca.uab.cat/pacte/en) and the TRANSCOMP group led by Göpferich (2009; Göpferich et al. 2011). Both models are componential and account for a number of interrelated subcompetences.

From the cognitive paradigm, definitions of translation competence focus more on the way professionals cognitively process translation tasks as opposed to bilinguals or trainees:

> What distinguishes the translator/interpreter from the non-translating bilingual are the nature and development of the relevant Long Term Memory (LTM) resources and the way that they are activated in the different communicative tasks.
> (Shreve and Diamond 1997)

That is, translation competence is conceptualized as the accumulation of resources and the creation of connections that activate the accumulated knowledge through systematic training in an efficient manner. In this sense, professional translators can be experts (Shreve 2006a; Muñoz Martín 2009) on this specific task. As previously mentioned, Shreve (2006a) specifically emphasizes the importance of systematic training or "deliberate practice", underscoring the importance of task selection for translation training.

9.6.2 The PACTE and TRANSCOMP translation competence models

The PACTE and TRANSCOMP are the only models that have been used in longitudinal empirical research into translation competence and its acquisition. Both models are mostly inspired in previous psycholinguistic models such as Hönig's (1995) and are componential in nature. Despite criticisms of componential models (i.e., Kiraly 2015), this chapter argues that incorporating crowdsourcing and online collaborative translation in translation education can greatly benefit from the implicit disaggregation of the overall holistic competence into subcompetences. This allows for the identification of subcomponents and tasks that can be learnt, practiced or reinforced by means of participating in volunteer initiatives.

The PACTE research project has its roots in the theoretical research carried out by Hurtado (1996, 1999), leading to the first version of their model in 1997. PACTE has been empirically testing their model for over a decade with translation students, translation professional and language teachers. The PACTE group is currently at the validation stage after a decade of research (2011a, 2011b, 2014, 2015; Hurtado Albir 2017), attempting to overcome one of the most common criticisms addressed towards existing theoretical models, namely the lack of empirical validation (Hurtado 2001; Kelly 2005; Pym 2012). This model identifies five interrelated subcompetences: (1) bilingual, (2) extralinguistic, (3) instrumental, (4) knowledge-about-translation and (5) strategic. Together, all these subcompetences represent "a system of competences that interact, are hierarchical, and subject to variation" (PACTE 2000: 100). Figure 9.3 illustrates this model.

The bilingual subcompetence includes "pragmatic, socio-linguistic, textual and lexical-grammatical knowledge in each language" (PACTE 2005: 610). It includes knowledge about the communicative situation, such as participants and sociocultural norms, illocutionary competence (knowledge about the functions of language) and advanced textual competence. As an example, this sub competence would include the recognition and production of specialized textual genres, such as a contract, a patent, a legal disclaimer on a videogame or information leaflet in both languages. Obviously, not all college-educated bilinguals possess the ability

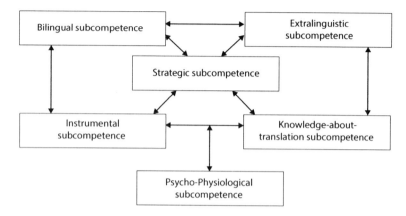

Figure 9.3 PACTE group translation competence model (PACTE 2005: 610, 2007: 331).

to draft legal or technical texts that are acceptable by specialists as appropriate and efficient in form and style. This requires the acquisition of advanced writing skills and the socialization in specialized groups. This subcompetence also includes the ability to control the interference between the language pair or interference control. It also includes the terminological competence in both languages. Some other scholars differentiate between language and textual competence (Neubert 2000; Kelly 2005). It could be argued that separating them explicitly might be productive in order to highlight the acquisition of advanced knowledge of writing styles, specialized genres, text types, different registers, etc. In fact, an approximation based on genre theory has been proposed as an effective tool in order to acquire the textual competence required for specialized translation. Additionally, as previously mentioned, participants in some communities, such as fans, can have advanced knowledge of the genres that can compensate for their lack of translation competence in some cases (O'Hagan 2009).

The PACTE group indicates that bilingual subcompetence is shared with other bilinguals and professionals, similar to what happens with many components of translation competence (Kiraly 1995: 108). For example, a volunteer bilingual manga editor might possess a similar degree of bilingual subcompetence in this setting as a professional translator. Therefore, this component in isolation could not be considered a differentiating component of the translation competence possessed by medical translators.

The extralinguistic subcompetence includes "encyclopedic, thematic and bicultural knowledge" (PACTE 2005:610). It includes both the entire accumulated knowledge about the world a subject might have, in addition to specific advanced domain knowledge related to translators' specialized field(s), such as knowledge about legal processes or how a patent might be registered. To a certain degree, this subcompetence is also shared with other bilingual professionals. The participation in any type of online community activity rightly expands the extralinguistic knowledge of participants in different domains and areas.

The knowledge-about-translation subcompetence is mostly declarative knowledge about what translation is and aspects of the profession. It includes:

> Knowledge about how translation functions: types of translation units, processes required, methods and procedures used (strategies and techniques), and types of problems; (2) knowledge related to professional translation practice: knowledge of the work market (different types of briefs, clients and audiences, etc.).
>
> (PACTE 2003: 92)

The instrumental subcompetence refers to two distinctive types of knowledge, (1) the translation technology tools and other technology applied to the entire cycle, and (2) research and documentation sources and strategies, including paper or online dictionaries of all kinds, encyclopedias, grammars, style books, corpora, translation memories, etc. The significance of this subcompetence has been increasing exponentially during the last two decades, as the translation profession cannot be understood nowadays as being independent of the technologies that support it (O'Brien 2012b; Bowker 2014).

At the center of the model is the main and most important component, strategic subcompetence. Its purpose is to solve problems and guarantee the efficiency of the process:

> It intervenes by planning the process in relation to the translation project, evaluating the process and partial results obtained, activating the different subcompetences and compensating for deficiencies, identifying translation problems and applying procedures to solve them. (PACTE 2005: 610)

This subcompetence entails mostly operative knowledge and interrelates and mobilizes all other subcompetences in order to solve any given translation problem that translators might encounter during their tasks. Recent studies by the PACTE have also "revealed the specific characteristics of the way in which Knowledge of Translation, Strategic, and Instrumental sub-competences operated within the group of translators." (Hurtado Albir, Amparo 2017: 282).

Finally, the PACTE model includes a separate physio-psychological component that is not considered a subcompetence as such, but rather, "an integral part of all expert knowledge" (PACTE 2003: 91). It includes:

> cognitive components such as memory, perception, attention and emotion; (2) attitudinal aspects such as intellectual curiosity, perseverance, rigor, critical spirit, knowledge of and confidence in one's own abilities, the ability to measure one's own abilities, motivation, etc.; (3) abilities such as creativity, logical reasoning, analysis and synthesis, etc. (PACTE 2003: 93)

The development of these components, despite not being part of translation competence per se, can be easily related to the goals of the translation education in institutions of higher learning (Pym 2011b), many of them, such as creativity, being key to a successful professional translator (Kiraly 1995). It also relates in part to the benefits of the development of cognitive skills that higher education in general provides.

The TRANSCOMP model is based on Hönig's (1995) and PACTE models with certain variations. It is used as the framework for reference for their longitudinal study on translation competence acquisition. This model includes six subcompetences: (1) communicative competence in at least two languages, (2) domain competence (3) tools and research competence (4) translation routine activation competence (5) psychomotor competence (6) strategic competence.

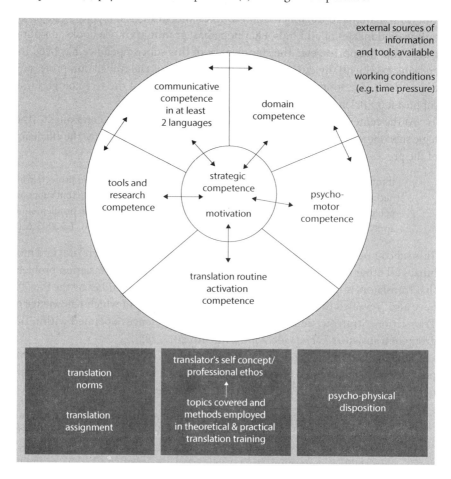

Figure 9.4 TRANSCOMP translation competence model (Göpferich 2009: 21).

The impact of PACTE research can be seen clearly in this model: four subcompetences out of six perfectly correspond to others in PACTE's: both models include the strategic subcompetence as a key element, the communicative competence in the TRANSCOMP model corresponds to the bilingual subcompetence, the tools and research competence with the instrumental subcompetence, the strategic subcompetence and the domain competence correspond approximately to PACTE's extra-linguistic subcompetence. This last one comprises not only "general and domain specific knowledge that [...] is necessary to understand the source text and formulate the target texts" (Göpferich 2009: 22), but also the ability to recognize what additional knowledge from external sources is needed at any specific moment. Given that this latter model indicates that general knowledge is also key in this component, it can be argued that extralinguistic competence might be a better term for this component than domain competence, as the latter leans more towards the specific knowledge in specialized translation settings.

Göpferich is renowned for her research in the cognitive paradigm within Translation Studies, and this partly explains the differences between her model and PACTE's. The last two subcompetences that differ between both models are thus related to the development of cognitive abilities. The model includes a translation routine activation competence that represents the knowledge and ability to recall and apply some transfer operations of shifts that frequently occur between specific language pairs. The last subcompetence is referred to as psychomotor competence, related to the abilities to read and write using technologies. This last subcompetence was included because the more developed this competence is, the less cognitive capacity is required to control this effort.

This model also includes three factors that determine the employment of these subcompetences. One of them is common between both models: the existence of a psychophysiological disposition such as intelligence, perseverance or self-confidence. Göpferich indicates that these components might accelerate the development of translation competence. The other factors are (1) the translation brief and the translation norms, as well as (2) the translator's self-concept of professional ethos in which:

> [T]he contents conveyed and the methods employed in theoretical and practical translation training courses have an impact and which form the component of [the] model where aspects of social responsibility and roles come in.
>
> (Göpferich 2009: 22)

These last two factors are included in the other model in the knowledge-about-translation subcompetence in PACTE, as subjects with advanced competence might be able to make strategic decisions depending on the instructions provided and the translation norms under which they might operate. At this point it should be indicated that the model to some extent combines general acquired skills and knowledge, with task-dependent issues such as translation briefs and norms. Even though all the theoretical models thus far have been created with a didactic objective in mind, the combination of task-dependent issues with other general ones highlights the situatedness of the cognitive paradigm from which this last research group approaches their project.

9.6.3   The acquisition of translation competence

Once these two models have been described, a less researched question is how does this translation competence develop? This process is addressed in translation research by the notion of "translation competence acquisition". This is of great significance for the integration or analysis of the impact of online collaborative practices in the overall development of translation competence. Despite the relatively large number of theoretical proposals of translation competence, fewer efforts have been devoted to how it is acquired. Generally, it can be defined as the progression in which professional translation competence is acquired by bilinguals (PACTE 2001; Toury 1995: 241–258; Shreve 1997; Göpferich 2009; Kiraly 2012). The point of departure would be the ill-defined and variable notion of "pre-translational competence" (Presas 1996), the body of knowledge that subjects possess prior to the acquisition of translation competence. This pre-translational competence includes natural translation skills (Harris and Sherwood 1978). Nowadays, pre-translational competence can also include the students' participation in online activities prior to admission in university programs, that is, prior to engagement in the willful acquisition of "professional translation competence".

The acquisition process is understood as a dynamic and cyclical process in which the development of the strategic competence or operative translation knowledge plays an essential role. The set of interrelated subcompetences can be somewhat acquired in isolation in earlier stages. This could respond to the task-based approach (González Davies 2004). Task-based approaches precisely support the potential use of crowdsourcing and collaborative translation as an addition towards the acquisition of translation competence. Many initiatives, even those with iterative and voting models, allow translators to practice subcomponents of translation competence in an approach that closely resembles the activities proposed in these task-based approaches. However, the advanced stage in competence acquisition is characterized by the development macrocompetence that prioritizes and interrelates individual subcompetences depending on the translation problem or communicative situation. This advanced stage does not necessarily mean that that students acquire or store new declarative knowledge but, rather, existing knowledge is restructured (PACTE 2000). The development of this macrocompetence thus implies that not all initiatives might be equally suitable for the acquisition of more advanced translation competence skills. The form of participation and the feedback in some initiatives might operate at a subcompetence level, such as electing translation candidates out of a pool of renderings. Nevertheless, some initiatives that include full texts with feedback loops might promote a global approach that might assist in the development of earlier stages in the advanced macrocompetence.

The heterogeneous and complex nature of this competence implies that the acquisition is a non-finite process (Neubert 2000): highly professional translators are continually adding new knowledge and merging it with existing knowledge. Participation in volunteer initiatives prior to enrolment in university programs can be considered part of this progressive and continuous process. Even in professional settings, some genres, text types or language combinations might not be potentially available to translate from a market and business perspective, and professionals could then even continue developing their skills through volunteer activities. This is precisely one of the main arguments to defend the inclusion of translation and interpreting within regular graduate and undergraduate university programs, as opposed to ad-hoc professional training courses: trainees and translators need to develop the capacity to be creative and adapt themselves to novel and existing situations, a basic skill that can be acquired in a variety of settings, such as any online collaborative translation endeavor. This issue also refers to the notion of "adaptive expertise" in which the ability to adapt the cognitive resources to novel situations is part of the baggage of a translation expert (Muñoz 2014b).[2]

Only three models of translation competence acquisition have been put forward: that of PACTE (2014: 93), Shreve (1997), and Kiraly (2012, 2015). In the PACTE one, subjects depart from a pre-translational competence and develop individual subcompetences but, most importantly, the integration of all of the subcompetences take place in order to prioritize them depending on the specifics of the task or the communicative situation. This integration process and the restructuring of existing competences (i.e. bilingual competence in any specific communicative situation or textual genre) can only occur when a competence is activated by specific learning strategies. For example, research participants of the PACTE project (Hurtado Albir 1999) and others have proposed learning strategies based on task-learning (González Davies 2004). As previously mentioned, in this

---

2. Adaptive expertise is defined as "the ability to develop new strategies to cope with novel situations" (Muñoz 2014b:9).

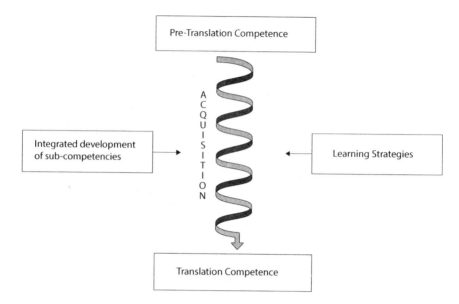

Figure 9.5 PACTE translation acquisition model (2014: 93).

didactic approach translation is acquired through a series of tasks that do not necessarily entail translation proper, but rather components of the translation competence or related tasks are gradually integrated.

It should be mentioned that the different components that make up individual subcompetences do not develop at the same time or in parallel fashion, but rather, they are acquired unequally and progressively as they interrelate and compensate. The process might also develop at different speeds. It should also be mentioned that depending on the translation types (legal, medical, journalistic, literary) and modalities (localization, audiovisual, etc.) some components of subcompetences might be more relevant than others. As an example, the advanced acquisition of technological competence is paramount to modalities such as the localization of websites, while legal translation courses need to focus heavily on the acquisition of advanced monolingual and contrastive knowledge of legal genres and their terminology and conventionalized phraseology, a component that belongs to bilingual subcompetence. Participants in online initiatives might be able to develop faster any type of subcompetences related to the specifics of the tasks performed, be it text type dependent, extratextual knowledge, instrumental competences, etc.

9.7 Componential translation competence models from the perspective of collaborative voluntarism

Despite criticisms (i.e. Kiraly 2015: 24–27), one of the positive aspects of using translation competence models, is that it allows one to itemize the prototypical components of each subcompetence, and it can provide a flexible tool to establish training curricula (Kelly 2005). It can also subsequently help identify components of subcompetences that can be added or reinforced through collaborative participation in volunteer settings. Prototypical components can be implicitly addressed in curricula and learning programs at universities (Hurtado 2015). The analysis from the perspective of volunteer practice can allow setting the learning process from a componential perspective that will not be assessed from a formal perspective (Kelly 2005), but rather through alternative mechanisms. Using the PACTE model as a foundation, the following lists explore components of subcompetences that can be practiced or improved through participation in online volunteer initiatives. The examples for each subcompetence are illustrative and are mainly intended to show this subcomponential approach in order to identify initiatives that might be beneficial to integrate or promote in translation education, as well as to identify initiatives that might serve as learning tools within specific modules (Orrego-Carmona 2014b). Due to the large range of initiatives and possibilities, the list can be arranged or expanded as necessary.

1. Specialized bilingual subcompetences. This subcompetence, together with the extralinguistic subcompetence below, are shared to some extent between general bilinguals, advanced bilinguals or general translators. Nevertheless, the bilingual subcompetence include specialized components that need to be specifically developed including different genres, text types and specializations, such as legal, technical, literary, journalistic, advertising, and audiovisual translations. This area has been widely explored in the literature, with a number of studies focusing on language learning and translation crowdsourcing initiatives (García 2012; Furuhata-Turner 2013; Liu 2014). As far as the bilingual subcompetence, students can increase their language competence in two or more languages, their contrastive knowledge of specific language pairs, general contrastive knowledge of main transfer strategies between the language pair, increase the specialized language writing skills in the target languages in initiatives with specialized textual genres, and increase textual production skills in different domains or producing texts that comply with initiative guidelines.

2. Extralinguistic subcompetence. The possibility of acquisition of general and domain specific knowledge depends widely on the initiative. Students can generally increase the knowledge of cultures involved, as well as potentially acquire knowledge related to specific domains.

3. Instrumental-technological subcompetences. Instrumental or tools and research competence is an essential element in all modern translation competence models, and constantly reshapes translation training around the world (Pym, Perekrestenko and Starink 2006; Pym 2012). This subcompetence is subdivided into technological and research-documentation. The technological subcompetences that participants can acquire are related to enhanced basic computing skills for participants that are "digital natives" (word processing, handling of files, different file types, internet communications, etc.), general understanding of technology tools applied to translation, knowledge of translation memory tools, terminology database integration and content management systems such as Trommons (De Wille, Exton and Schäler 2015), MH NTT (Babych et al. 2012), etc. In audiovisual initiatives, students can learn about basic subtitling and dubbing workflows, basic subtitling tools (Orrego-Carmona 2014b), while in Open Software communities, they can learn about basic localization workflows, basic open source tools, etc. In crowd post-editing platforms such as academic ACCEPT (Gulati et al. 2015), it is possible to learn about Basic knowledge of MT systems, as well as pre-editing and post-editing in general. In many initiatives, students that move up to higher status positions can increase their knowledge of quality management processes and tools. As far as the research-documentation skills, participants can increase their ability to identify appropriate Internet resources to solve specific problems through a wide range of dictionaries, terminology databases, such as IATE, or the ability to assess paper resources necessary to support translation decisions.

4. Knowledge about translation subcompetences. This is the knowledge that is often targeted in internships and volunteer work and it includes knowledge about basics of the translation cycle, stages, and involved agents, knowledge about the basics of project management, improvements in communication skills to negotiate and defend decisions or proposed solutions to problems, and putting into practice ethical issues regarding translation, globalization, and the role of translators in society. It can generally help establish and consolidate in real-life scenarios the metalanguage of translation and the specifics of different modalities such as software or web localization, audiovisual translation, etc.

5. Strategic subcompetence. Strategic subcompetence is the most important of all and it entails mostly operative knowledge. It, therefore, requires not only the ability to solve the most recurrent problems in all translation tasks, but

also the ability to cope with new and unpredictable ones by applying specific strategies and solutions based on situation, context, translation brief, initiator of translation, textual genre, community guidelines, etc. In this sense, translation is understood as a problem-solving activity (Lörcher 1991; Wilss 1994) and an expert skill (Shreve 2006a). All types of translational activity can, in the context of the integration of translation subcompetence during the institutionalized acquisition process, help develop the strategic subcompetence. For example, it can help to increase the toolset necessary to solve general transfer problems due to source text comprehension or target text reformulation. Also, it can help in identifying tasks and problems that might appear and how to propose different viable solutions based on the specific translation tasks and problem at hand, applying internal (mental) and external support (dictionaries, online resources, reference materials, etc.) to solve source text comprehension problems and target text reformulation, conceptualizing problems at the microtextual or segmental level within the wider framework of the macrotextual overall textual structure, switching between both levels in cognitive tasks, applying world, sociocultural and specialized knowledge, sociocultural and translation norms, acquired skills and common sense to specific problems, developing the ability to continue learning specific methods for resolving classes of problems and organizing the application of those methods in optimal ways, including problem representation or "chunking" at higher levels of abstraction or according to different principles than novices (Shreve 2006a). In initiatives with deadlines, it can help translators to solve problems effectively and efficiently within short deadlines. Since many initiatives are based on textual segmentation (see Chapter 6), students can apply advanced knowledge of certain genres and their communicative situations in order to solve instances of lack of context in the comprehension of disaggregated textual segments.

This proposed decomposition of subcompetences into small components that can be practiced and developed is intended solely for the purposes of illustrating the potential benefits of the componential models of translation competence and its acquisition. The overall goal should be a holistic approach in the successful integration of crowdsourcing and online collaborative translation in institutionalized translation education programs. The proposal is complementary, combining voluntarism and traditional education, rather than oppositional. The general integration of crowdsourcing into education in all walks of life is already a reality, with distributed learning models appearing in combination with MOOCs (i.e. Ahn, Butler, Alam and Webster 2013; Paulin and Haythornthwaite 2016). Rather than departing from a fractal perspective based on post-positive epistemology of Kiraly (2015), this chapter defends the subcomponential nature of PACTE or the Transcomp, since their models help identify small components of translation competence that can be integrated throughout the translation acquisition process in combination, or even as part of the "learning strategies" (PACTE 2000: 14) in the process. This does not mean that volunteer initiatives do not have a place in other non-componential models. Kiraly precisely indicates that his proposal is based on:

> [T]he undertaking of, as well as the reflection on, real [...] translation projects by the students [...] rather than the decontextualized instruction revolving around the translation of desituated textual material.   (2015: 11–12)

Crowdsourcing and online collaborative initiatives precisely revolve around the translation of authentic material. The potential benefit of these initiatives in Kiraly's proposal is also based on the fact that the role of the trainer disappears, placing students at the center of their learning processes. In that case, and in tune with his new post-positivist epistemological approach, any learning is "the result of a complex interplay of processes and only incidentally and occasionally the direct result of teaching" (ibid: 28). Thus, it seems logical to argue that participation in volunteer initiatives should be seemingly welcomed by proponents of this approach, even when it is still to be mentioned in their literature.

Needless to say, this conceptualization of initiatives in terms of the subcomponents of translation competence that can be integrated into modules, courses, or overall programs depends also on the feedback categorization proposed in Section 9.5.2. Again, and as previously indicated, if the acquisition of translation competence in institutions of higher learning is considered to be the acquisition of "expert knowledge" (Shreve 2006a) that develops through "deliberate practice", then any guided and structured intensive "deliberate practice" setting, with different levels of difficulty and appropriate feedback to develop expertise (Ericsson 2000), should be mostly welcomed by the training and professional community. Any type of participation in initiatives in which the "deliberate practice" includes any of the subcomponents of translation competence should be seen as beneficial in the path towards higher levels of competence, even the selective component of participating in iterative voting models such as Facebook. To finish with, it should be mentioned that the path towards professional translation competence is a long and effortful process. Crowdsourcing and online collaborative initiatives, carefully integrated or even left to the students' whims and preferences, represent a ground for playful experimentation or serious "deliberate practice". Since students are constantly attempting to achieve and strive for professional performance in university courses, volunteer and non-professional initiatives can rightly serve as the translation exercise treadmill for their cognitive systems engaged in the acquisition and integration of knowledge.

CHAPTER 10

Conclusions

> The twenty first century is witnessing the advent of new
> technological devices for people's entertainment and
> interaction and the future is likely to bring new forms
> of translation which will be able to cope with the constraints
> of small, portable screens. These futuristic modalities are,
> at present, almost unimaginable.
>
> (Chiaro 2004: 163)

10.1 Introduction

This book was initiated with the intention of providing an in-depth look at translation crowdsourcing and online community translation from the vantage point of Translation Studies. It has primarily focused on four interrelated objectives: (1) first of all, to describe these fast-evolving set of phenomena from an interdisciplinary approach, (2) to provide a critical review of existing literature and research trends in the field, (3) to identify areas of interest for TS with an eye on the future evolution of the discipline, and (4) to provide an analysis and self-critical look at TS and its many subdisciplines from the perspective that these novel practices can provide. In this sense, this exercise required a detailed look at the current and past state of the language industry and online translation communities, as well as TS, its subdisciplines and other disciplines with which they interact.

At this point, readers might be wondering why these technology-dependent and forward-looking practices have still not been examined with more of an emphasis on the future. The conclusions of this book should, in principle, attempt to delve into what the following years will hold, both in terms of industry developments and for the impact on TS. Nevertheless, a forward-looking analysis represents a complex and difficult enterprise. The most up-to-date perspectives and future outlooks can and will be found mostly in publications with an industry focus, such as those released by organizations such as TAUS, or from think tanks such as Common Sense Advisory, this lasts often inaccessible to scholars due to prohibitive cost. Papers in academic and industry conferences, as well as articles on industry journals, such as *Multilingual*, can also provide the most current developments in the area.

As it has been seen throughout this book, this set of phenomena could be considered as some of the most unpredictable ones in the translation context due to the free and unrestrained nature of volunteers and technological innovation. The reason why formulating such an analysis proves to be such a difficult enterprise can be illustrated by a technology-based revolution birthed at the time of writing: the global commotion on international media about the augmented reality mobile app *Pokemon Go* has not subsided yet in late summer 2016. This is an "augmented reality" (AR) game, or in other words, a game based on technologies by which "real-world objects are annotated with a virtual layer of information that is displayed on a smartphone's camera" (Hodson 2012: 19). It was developed by Niantic, a 2010 startup company that until 2015 was part of Google. Since its creation, it has developed similar games using the geolocation feature of smartphones to create a layer that interacts with the reality of the world. A previous game, *Ingress*, was released in 2012 by this company with exactly the same GPS technology integrated in Google Maps. Prior to this, other companies had also created similar "augmented reality games," such as *Shadow Cities* and *Endgame*. Nevertheless, the technology in itself did not create the massive growth experienced by these types of AR games. It was precisely the unpredictable combination of technologies with an existing cultural phenomenon since the 1990s, Pokemon, to create a modern-day sensation. This unforeseen combination of technology and cultural phenomenon quickly becomes the most played smartphone game in the world (El Pais 2016).[1]

The same, to some extent, happens in the context that surrounds crowdsourcing and online collaborative translations. The initial quote found in the introduction to this book from a NPR interview of Yuval Harari, the author of the 2015 best seller *A Brief History of Humankind,* was missing an important and key sentence that, at this point in the monograph, is now indispensable. The following includes this important missing part:

> We control the world basically because we are the only animals that can cooperate flexibly in very large numbers. *And if you examine any large-scale human cooperation, you will always find that it is based on some fiction like the nation, like money, like human rights. These are all things that do not exist objectively, but they exist only in the stories that we tell and that we spread around.* This is something very unique to us, perhaps the most unique feature of our species.[2]

This sentence indicates that humans can cooperate in large numbers based on fictions that we create ourselves, such as money or human rights. It is precisely

---

1.   http://economia.elpais.com/economia/2016/07/14/actualidad/1468523279_247313.html

2.   http://www.npr.org/2015/02/07/383276672/from-hunter-gatherers-to-space-explorers-a-70-000-year-story

"[t]he ability to create an imagined reality out of words[that] enable large numbers of strangers to cooperate effectively" (Harari 2015: 32) with specific goals. Other species can cooperate in very large numbers for food, shelter, survival, etc., but only humans can create fictions that make them cooperate and work together to accomplish abstract objectives. This is precisely why the next developments in both paid and volunteer crowdsourcing models, as well online collaborative translations, are to some extent quite unpredictable. The technologies required to collaborate flexibly in translation in large numbers, to include all types of crowds, from bilinguals to specialized translators, from amateur subtitlers to human rights activists, are already in place. They will likely improve and expand to other realms, such as chat-based crowdsourced mobile translations with Stepes. Nevertheless, if the evolution of CAT tools since their creation is used as a comparison, it can be argued that many instances of crowdsourcing technologies might continue to be used in their current form for years to come with small variations. However, what might change, evolve, and emerge are new motivations to "cooperate flexibly in large numbers [...] based on some fiction" (ibid), such as the cases reviewed in this monograph: to help spread the love for Manga, help Facebook expand to the user's language, help with human rights campaigns, help others learn a language, spend the "cognitive surplus," or earn some money with skills that the crowdsourcer might find of value.

The upcoming waves that will combine the desire to participate and cooperate with others in new initiatives with the intersection of existing and novel technologies will continue to raise questions of interest for TS scholars for many years to come. The last monograph the author of this book wrote on web localization ended with a quote found in *Don Quixote* by Cervantes, when idealist Don Quixote indicates to the more realist Sancho Panza "Thou hast seen nothing yet." This quote can certainly be applied to this case. Who, for example, would have predicted in 2009, when professionals rose in arms against crowdsourcing (Kelly 2009; American Translators Association 2009), that an increasing number of professional translators would willfully make a living or supplement their incomes participating in paid crowdsourcing models in the so-called "selected" or "specialized" communities set up by translation crowdsourcing companies? Even when non-profit scenarios were considered appropriate for volunteer professionals in position publications by translation associations (i.e., ATA 20029), who would have thought that many initiatives would incorporate different hierarchies in which professionals manage and review translations, providing their expertise beyond simply translating? Crowdsourcing technologies and workflows were set in place over the years (see Chapter 2), but it was not until the limitations of crowdsourcing started to be evident (DePalma and Kelly 2011), that micro task approaches expanded from free and low compensation to incorporate selected or specialized professional translator participation. This was done in order to include, on the one hand, high-risk or high-value types of content and, on the other hand, the content that would otherwise not motivate participants either due to its nature or due to the relative low pool of participants in certain language combinations. Nowadays, professional translation and translation crowdsourcing seamlessly coexist side by side as services offered by many language providers. Professionals have already accepted this phenomenon as a natural evolution of the translation industry. As Flanagan indicates in her study on the attitudes of professionals on crowdsourcing on blogs:

> [T]he discourse among professional translators in this study suggests that professional translators and translation crowdsourcing can coexist without being in competition. This might very well be within different translation markets (e.g., bulk vs. premium), and this decision is one the professional translators need to be involved in making.   (Flanagan 2016: 164)

10.2   Language industry perspectives and impact on the profession

In terms of industry developments, new initiatives will continue to emerge, and many others will consolidate and expand. It is likely that most social networks or companies with a loyal user-base will continue to use and expand their embedded communities for translation purposes following the trail of industry giants such as Facebook. Others will continue to grow, such as the case of the largest crowdsourcing portal in China, 365 Fanyi [365 translation] that was bought in 2015 by the Chinese e-commerce giant website Alibaba, the largest e-commerce platform in China. Towards the end of 2016, it will offer crowdsourcing translation services with a potential participant base of millions. The merging of all types of modes of production under one company is probably the present trend that will continue to increase. This trend to incorporate "professional" translation as an additional option to any free or low-fee service emerged with companies that offered MT or CAT tools services, such as Matecat. Free FOMT or cloud CAT services have been offered with a visible option on the interface to the user to demand professional services. This is meant to attract users that might initially attempt a free service but that then think it might not be worth the risk. Translation decision-making has already been studied under the perspective of risk avoidance (Pym 2015b), and possibly a research question of interest in the coming years will be the study of clients' decisions based on risk taking. What are the reasons that steer clients towards certain processes or quality tiers? Nowadays, most crowdsourcing companies offer, in addition to free or low-price options, the possibility of requesting a higher quality translation, be it referred to as "professional," "premium," or "ultra" (see

5.2.2). For instance, users can request a free translation from the community in the language and culture exchange app Flitto, and they also have the option to request a "Pro Translation" with its 1-on-1 feature. According to the app website, users can "Select a professional translator for [their] request. Communicate directly to the translator with 1:1 Message feature."[3] Pro translators are pre-vetted and they have reviews from others. Similarly, the smartphone localization crowdsourcing app "El Loco" offers developers the possibility of instantly including MT renditions of the textual components of the app during development to visually test the app, and it offers the opportunity to translate the app by the same developers, through a community built and approved by the developer, or through their professional services called "El Loco Translation Services."[4]

It is not only the clients who will continue to be puzzled and confronted with the multiple translation possibilities that MT and crowdsourcing are opening up for them. An increasing percentage of "professional" translators will continue to be confronted with a range of options that did not exist before, continuing to make the "profession" as a sociological construct more fluid and dynamic in different settings and geographic contexts (Kiraly 2000; Gouadec 2007; Jääskeläinen 2010; Jääskeläinen, Kujamäki, Jukka 2011). Some of these "professionals" will be faced with the selection of tasks that they would like to complete based on different price points. Unbabel, for example, always offers in its mobile crowdsourcing app the opportunity to engage in free or paid tasks. Others offer the possibility to participate in tasks directed as vetted higher status or "specialized" communities or lower paid ones. The merging and blending models also offer participants the option to participate in translation, editing or MT post-editing. The range of possibilities seems to be only expanding and pulling away from the Translation – Edit – Publish model. This does not mean that this development necessarily involves an impact on all professionals in the terms indicated by Cronin. This scholar indicated that crowdsourcing "has far reaching consequences for the profession of the translator in an age of globalization" (Cronin 2013: 99). Nevertheless, micro task crowdsourcing applied in professional context will still represent an increasing, still small percentage of the overall volume of professional translation worldwide. Also, it is not certain that the volume of translation for professionals have decreased due to crowdsourcing. The greater fluidity and dynamicity that these new market dynamics and business models will bring thus do not only affect clients' or users' choices, but also open up the field for the entire chain, including translators and language providers who have to decide which models to offer.

3.   https://www.flitto.com/

4.   https://www.elloco.com/

As it was indicated previously, the impact on the industry and the profession in terms of whether established professional practices would reduce their business volume or market share does match the initial fear and hype (DePalma and Kelly 2011; Valli 2015; Elia 2016). Also, the latest 2016 European Industry Survey indicates that only 11% of the 445 LSPs that participated in the survey are willing to try crowdsourcing, a decrease in interest from previous years that might be "linked to the effect of the unknown" (Elia 2016:7). As far as García's mid-2016 prediction that "translation for localisation will be pushed into simple MT post-editing, while other sectors will see a shift towards call-centre conditions and a return of the amateur" (2009: 211), it has not completely come true. There are more amateurs participating in translation tasks around the world, but this has not meant that the volume of business for high-quality, higher compensation professional translation has necessarily been reduced globally. The potential volume of translation requested by users vastly outweighs the possibilities that the professional market can cope with (Gambier 2014). Similarly, crowd participation in both paid and unpaid tasks differs widely between language combinations. The phenomena under study here, in combination with different MT approaches, have allowed for a greater ability to tackle different aspects, such as efficiency, speed, quality, or cost, of the translation needs that might have otherwise been unfulfilled had those two technologies, MT and free/paid crowdsourcing, not existed. As DePalma indicates from an industry perspective, "given the huge volumes of content that need to be in many more languages than they are today," these new models should be seen as engines to expand "access to information and income in the networked economy" (DePalma 2015:np). In fact, the areas of impact in the translation industry in a previous Common Sense Advisory publication cover issues unrelated to professional translation, such as expanding to bilingual tasks other than translation, MT training, and testing of software components (2013: 2). Similarly, online collaborative translations have put in the hands of end users the translation of content that was not provided or that was provided in a time and fashion that did not fulfill their needs. As Chapter 7 highlighted, fansubbers not only demanded access or quicker access to their favorite programs, but also rebelled against the domesticating, sanitizing, or censored nature of professional practices in many geographical locations. It is not simply that users did not receive the translations that they wanted, but also that they wanted them rendered a specific way the professional translation did not or could not provide and in the timeframe they wanted.

Publications in TS vary in their approach on how the profession might be impacted. As mentioned previously, some predict radical changes (i.e., García 2010; Cronin 2013). Others indicate how it might be "harming professional translation" (Massidda 2015: 16), while at the same time defending the labor and empowerment of the subtitling fans. What is clear is that crowdsourcing and online collaborative practices are here to stay, and there will continue to be a massive volume of translation that requires high quality provided by expert professionals, be it directly or through supervision, management, or revision of crowdsourced and MT post-editing output. It has been reported that, during recent years, prices for translation have decreased globally due to global outsourcing (Muzii 2009; García 2015). However, it is not clearly indicated whether the average price drop might be due to an increased volume of translation through these new production models that were probably not accounted for previously. Many crowdsourcing companies do not offer legal, medical, or marketing content translation through their free and paid crowdsourcing services. Has, therefore, the price of high-quality legal translation dropped also? New research framed within the "economic turn" is direly needed in this direction to help clarify whether prices are dropping across the board or more for some type of content than others. It has been argued in this book that one of the main contributions of crowdsourcing in the industry has been the further adoption of content prioritization models. Many studies are needed in this direction.

10.3 Impact on Translation Studies

In addition to the ongoing impact on the industry, the objective of the second part of this book has been the impact on TS in an attempt to analyze this phenomenon both from a generalist perspective and from a subdisciplinary approach. It has attempted to analyze and distill the implications for many theories, paradigms, methodologies, or sub-branches. The objective has also been to foster intradisciplinary connections between research conducted from different paradigms or departing points. Since 2008, crowdsourcing and online collaborative approaches have opened up a new and exciting avenue for research as this monograph and the multitude of papers, books, and conference presentations cited can witness. The approach taken in this book has been to place TS at the center, and though the project has been interdisciplinary in nature, it has been structured around and derived from current discussions, existing research trends, and issues of interest to TS as a whole and to the many subdisciplines within it. The analyses and discussions have thus been anchored in the perspective TS provides, rather than from the frequent introduction of imported current trends, theories, paradigms, or perspectives from other disciplines. In the interdisciplinary context of TS, it is invariably necessary to defend the benefits of interdisciplinarity since "it challenges the current conventional way of thinking by promoting and responding to new links between different types of knowledge and technologies"

(Munday 2008: 14). Nevertheless, it is necessary to highlight the tensions and discussions on whether bringing imported theories and paradigms from other disciplines is always beneficial to TS, and, relatedly, whether TS actually impacts other disciplines (Gambier and van Doorslaer 2016). In certain cases, incorporating related disciplines can also constitute a threat if greater financial means, status, or power lays in the partner discipline (Gile 2004: 29). Additionally, it is often pointed out that methods, models, and procedures are frequently borrowed from the associated disciplines without a full understanding of the partner discipline (Chesterman 2002). Furthermore, the effort to incorporate perspectives from other disciplines might not have an actual impact on subsequent research in the same area. This is precisely why this book places TS, its current issues, debates, and trends at the center.

The questions and issues that have been addressed are many, and it is expected that they offer a wide range of research questions for future scholars to address. It is expected that each chapter will offer innumerable threads that future novel and seasoned researchers can develop further. After years of conceptual and terminological confusion, the first part of the book has first mapped crowdsourcing and its different subtypes within the framework of TS. It has helped disentangle the related network of concepts, proposing to use the term crowdsourcing when a call to a community to participate over the web is made and the control is within the initiating organization. Meanwhile, "online collaborative translations" refers to volunteer initiatives in which the initiator is the community itself, even if there is some sort of hierarchy or structure within it to manage participation. The roots of translation collaboration since ancient times have been briefly analyzed to set the stage for the study of these phenomena from a TS perspective. Also, industry approaches and workflows have been studied in order to discover and identify patterns or practices that could help advance TS.

The main questions of interest for TS in the third part of the book have delved into cognitive, translation evaluation, text linguistic, AVT, sociological, and educational perspectives. The main trends analyzed show that existing research makes true the premise that consecutive turns and directions in TS are not cumulative, but rather they overlap (Pym 2010). The existing main research trends in TS have been seen to combine the "sociological turn" that started in the 1990s with the "technological turn" of the 20th century. The emergence of the "economic turn" is already pushing for new research directions. A range of studies have explored the motivations and profiles of participants, an issue of interest to translators and scholars attempting to question why participants take part in these initiatives without monetary compensation. Studies have confirmed a series of factors, such as the popularity of a cause that potentially limits crowdsourcing. Since volunteer translators do not often benefit themselves from the resulting product, only initiative or causes that might attract the attention of the crowd, and those in which a "fit for purpose" quality will suffice, will be successful in this area. New research trends also might foster the consolidation of the "economic turn" in TS: business and economic aspects advance to the front once free or low-compensation tasks come to the surface.

The issue of motivation of participants might be sufficiently researched so far, but many other research questions related to ideology, policies, ethics, quality of the products, impact on society, real impact in the profession, etc., are still wide open for research. Similarly, as evidenced by the many discussions in this book, the impact of crowdsourcing to widen and revise existing translation theory is vast. Crowdsourcing helps revisit many existing models and paradigms within the discipline, such as the individual character of translation as a social, cognitive, or textual activity. Research from cognitive approaches should further explore empirically how collaborative models change how translations are processed. Some work in this direction has already been started (i.e., Jiménez-Crespo 2016). Researchers could also continue to explore from the perspective of "situated cognition": how networks impact decision-making (Risku and Windhager 2013). Similarly to what has been done with CAT tools, cognitive studies should research to what extent crowdsourcing platforms mold or constrain translation processes. As far as CBTS, this subdiscipline could benefit from the ability to test the "general features of translated language" in crowdsourced texts. In this regard, this novel textual population that did not exist merely a decade ago represents an additional "textual population" or "translation subset," if Chesterman's (2004) terminology is used, to test any hypothesis that attempts to make any generalizations about the "language of translation."

To conclude, it could be argued that crowdsourcing represents an exciting, dynamic phenomenon that has the potential to foster and inspire exiting research projects within the discipline. It has increased the visibility of translation in society (Cronin 2013), blurring "distinctions which generally presuppose active translation agents and passive or unknowable translation recipients" (ibid: 100). Still, crowdsourcing can be considered to be in "its infancy" (Estellés and González 2012a: 198), with a future only limited by the shifting interests of online communities and the combination of existing technologies and technologies to come. In this sense, the potential research paths and trajectories into this dynamic set of phenomena are as unpredictable as crowdsourcing itself.

References

Abdallah, Kristiina. 2010. "Translators' Agency in Production Networks." In *Translators' Agency*, Tuija Kinnunen and Kaisa Koskinen (eds.), 11–46. Tampere: Tampere University Press

Abdallah, Kristiina. 2014. "Towards Empowerment of Students' Ethical Reflections on Translating in Production Networks." *The Interpreter and the Translator Trainer* 5(1): 129–154. doi:10.1080/13556509.2011.10798815

Abdallah, Kristiina and Kaisa Koskinen. 2007. "Managing Trust: Translating and the Network Economy." *META* 524: 673–687. doi:10.7202/017692ar

Ahn, June, Brian S. Butler, Alisha Alam and Sarah A. Webster. 2013 "Learner Participation and Engagement in Open Online Courses: Insights from the Peer 2 Peer University." *Journal of Online Learning and Teaching* 9(2). Accessed March 1, 2016. http://jolt.merlot.org/vol9no2/ahn_0613.htm.

Aikawa, Takako, Yamamoto, Kentaro and Hitoshi Isahara. 2012. "The Impact of Crowdsourcing Post-editing with the Collaborative Translation Framework." In *Proccedings of JapTAL 2012, Advances in Natural Language Processing 7614*, 1–10. Berlin: Springer. Accessed March 1, 2016. http://research.microsoft.com/pubs/172592/JapTal2012.pdf.

Alabau, Vicent *et al.* 2014. "Casmacat: A Computer-Assisted Translation Workbench." *Prague Bulletin of Mathematical Linguistics* 100: 101–112.

Alcina, Amparo. 2008. "Translation Technologies: Scopes, Tools and Resources." *Target* 20 (1): 79–102. doi:10.1075/target.20.1.05alc

Alegria, Iñaki *et al.* 2015. "Overview of TweetMT: A Shared Task on Machine Translation of Tweets at SEPLN 2015." In *Proceedings of the Tweet Translation Workshop co-located with 31th Conference of the Spanish Society for Natural Language Processing*, Alicante, Spain. Accessed March 1, 2016. http://gplsi.dlsi.ua.es/sepln15/sites/gplsi.dlsi.ua.es.sepln15/files/attachments/2-paper1-overview.pdf

Allen, Jeffrey. 2003. "Post-Editing." In *Computers and Translation: A Translators Guide*, Harold Somers (ed.), 297–317. Amsterdam-Philadelphia: John Benjamins. doi:10.1075/btl.35.19all

Alonso, Elisa and Elisa Calvo. 2015. "Developing a Blueprint for a Technology-mediated Approach to Translation Studies." *META* 60 (1): 135–157. doi:10.7202/1032403ar

Alves, Favio and Jose L. Gonçalves. 2003. "A Televance Theory Approach to the Investigation of Inferential Processes in Translation." In *Triangulating Translation: Perspectives In Process Oriented Research*, Favio Alves (ed.), 11–34. Amsterdam: John Benjamins. doi:10.1075/btl.45.04alv

Alves, Favio and Daniel Vale. 2009. "On Drafting and Revision in Translation: A Corpus Linguistics Oriented Analysis of Translation Process Data." *Translation: Computation, Corpora, Cognition* 1: 105–122.

Ambati, Vamsi, Stephan Vogel and Jaime Carbonell. 2012. "Collaborative Workflow for Crowdsourcing Translation." In *Proceeding CSCW '12 Proceedings Of The ACM 2012 Conference On Computer Supported Cooperative Work*, 1191–1194. Accessed March 1, 2016. https://www.cs.cmu.edu/~jgc/CollaborativeWorkflowforCrowdsourcingTranslationACMCoCSCW2012.pdf

Ameri, Saeed and Khalil Ghazizadeh. 2015. "A Norm-Based Analysis of Swearing Rendition in Professional Dubbing and Non-Professional Subtitling from English into Persian." *Iranian Journal of Research in English Language Teaching* 3: 78–96. Accessed March 1, 2016. http://journals.khuisf.ac.ir/ijrelt/browse.php?a_code=A-10-131-1&slc_lang=en&sid=1&sw=

American Translators Association. 2009. "Head of the Largest Translators' Organization Blasts LinkedIn CEO for 'Thoroughly Unprofessional Practices'." *Press Release*. Accessed July 24, 2016. http://atanet.org/pressroom/linkedIn_2009.pdf

Anastasiou, Dimitra and Rajat Gupta. 2011. "Comparison of Crowdsourcing Translation with Machine Translation." *Journal of Information Science* 37 (6): 637–659. doi:10.1177/0165551511418760

Anastasiou, Dimitra and Reinard Schäler. 2009. "Translating Vital Information: Localisation, Internationalisation, and Globalisation." *Synthèses* 3: 11–25.

Angelelli, Claudia. 2009. "Using a Rubric to Assess Translation Ability: Defining The Construct." In *Testing and Assessment in Translation and Interpreting Studies. ATA Scholarly Monographs Series*, Claudia Angelelli and Holly Jacobson (eds.), 13–47. Amsterdam: John Benjamins. doi:10.1075/ata.xiv.03ang

Angelelli, Claudia. 2010. "A Professional Ideology in the Making: Bilingual Youngsters Interpreting for Their Communities and the Notion of No Choice." *TIS: Translation and Interpreting Studies* 5: 94–108. doi:10.1075/tis.5.1.06ang

Angelelli, Claudia. 2012. "The Sociological Turn in Translation and Interpreting Studies. Introduction." *TIS:Translation and Interpreting Studies* 7 (2): 125–128 4. doi:10.1075/tis.7.2.01int

Angelelli, Claudia and Jacobson, Holly (eds.). 2009. *Testing and Assessment in Translation and Interpreting Studies. ATA Scholarly Monograph Series*. Amsterdam: John Benjamins. doi:10.1075/ata.xiv

Antonini, Rachele. 2011. "Natural Translator and Interpreter." In *Handbook of Translation Studies* Vol. 2, Yves Gambier and Luc. Van Doorslaer (eds.), 102–104. Amsterdam-Philadelphia: John Benjamins. doi:10.1075/hts.2.nat1

Appiah, Kwame A. 1993. "Thick Translation." *Callaloo On "Post-Colonial Discourse": A Special Issue* 16: 808–819. doi:10.2307/2932211

Arend, Thomas. 2012. "Social Localisation at Twitter: Translating the World in 140 Characters." Paper presented at the *17th Annual LRC Internationalisation and Localisation Conference*, University of Limerick. Accessed March 1st, 2016. https://www.youtube.com/watch?v=eGb5-MLcLr0

Arjona Reina, Laura, Gregorio Robles and Jesus M. González-Barahona. 2013. "A Preliminary Analysis of Localization in Free Software: How Translations are Performed." In *Open Source Software: Quality Verification*, Etiel Petrinja *et al.* (eds), 153–167. Springer Berlin Heidelberg. doi:10.1007/978-3-642-38928-3_11

Armstrong, Tom. 2016. "The Evolution of Mobile Translation." *Stepes Blogs*. Accessed July 29, 2016. https://blog.stepes.com/the-evolution-of-mobile-translation/

Austermühl, Frank. 2011. "Of Clouds and Crowds: Current Developments in Translation technology." *T21T*. Accessed March 1, 2016. http://www.t21n.com/homepage/articles/T21N-2011-09-Austermuehl.pdf

Austermühl, Frank. 2000. *Electronic Tools for Translators*. Manchester: St. Jerome.

Babych, Bogdan, Anthony Hartley, Kyo Kageura, Thomas Martin and Masao Utiyama. 2012. "MNH-TT: a Collaborative Platform for Translator Training." In *Proceedings of Translating and the Computer 34*. Accessed March 1st, 2016. http://www.mt-archive.info/Aslib-2012-Babych.pdf.

Baker, Mona. 1995. "Corpora in Translation Studies: an Overview and some Suggestions for Future Research." *Target* 7: 223–243. doi:10.1075/target.7.2.03bak

Baker, Mona. 1996. "Corpus-based Translation Studies: The Challenges that Lie Ahead." In *Terminology, LSP and Translation: Studies in Language Engineering in Honor of* Juan C. Sager, Harold Somers (ed.), 175–186. Amsterdam and Philadelphia: John Benjamins. doi:10.1075/btl.18.17bak

Baker, Mona. 1999. "The Role of Corpora in Investigating the Linguistic Behaviour of Professional Translators." *International Journal of Corpus Linguistics* 4 (2): 281–298. doi:10.1075/ijcl.4.2.05bak

Baker, Mona. 2006. "Translation and Activism: Emerging Patterns of Narrative Community." *The Massachusetts Review* 47 (3): 462–484.

Baker, Mona. 2011. *In Other Words. A Coursebook on Translation*, 2nd Ed. New York-London: Routledge.

Baker, Mona. 2015. *Translating Dissent: Voices from the Egyptian Revolution*. New York-London: Routledge.

Baker, Mona. 2016. "The Prefigurative Politics of Translation in Place-Based Movements of Protest: Subititling in the Egyptian Revolution." *The Translator* 22 (1): 1–21.

Baker, Mona and Carol Maier (eds). 2011. *The Interpreter and Translator Trainer: Ethics and the Curriculum* 5(1).

Banks, John. 2009. "Co-creative Expertise: Auran Games and Fury - A Case Study." *Media International Australia* 130: 77–89.

Barra, Luca and Fabio Guarnaccia. 2008. "Essere Fansubber. Alla Scoperta Delle Comunità che Sottotitolano le Serie TV." *Link* 6: 243–251. Accessed March 1, 2016. http://www.link.mediaset.it/bin/63.$plit/C_23_sguardilaterali_6_Group_Scheda_lista_scheda_item_0_fileUpload.pdf.

Baslez, Marie-Françoise. 2014a. *Chrétiens Persécuteurs. Destructions, Exclusions et Violences Religieuses au IVe Siècle*. Paris: Albin Michel.

Baslez, Marie-Françoise. 2014b."Traduire en collectif dans l'Antiquité: signification et enjeyx d'un mythe." Paper presented at *Conference La Traduction Collaborative de L'Antiqueté à Internet*, Paris, France, 5th, 6th, 7th June, 2014.

Bassnett, Susan. 1998. "Still Trapped in the Labyrinth: Further Reflections on Translation and Theatre." In *Constructing Cultures*, Bassnett, Susan and André Lefevere (eds), 90–108. Clevedon: Multilingual Matters.

Bassnett, Susanand and Andre Lefevere. 1990. *Translation, History and Culture*. London -New York: Pinter Publishers.

Beaudegrande, Robert. 1978. *Factors in a Theory of Poetic Translating*. Amsterdam: Rodopi.

Beaudegrande, Robert de and Dressler, Wolfgang. 1981. *Introduction to Text Linguistics*. London: Longman.

Beaven, Tita, Anna Comas-Quin, Mirjam Hauck, Beatriz de los Arcos and Timothy Lewis. 2013. "The Open Translation MOOC: Creating Online Communities to Transcend Linguistic Barriers." *Journal of Interactive Media in Education*. Accessed March 1st, 2016. http://www-jime.open.ac.uk/jime/article/viewArticle/2013-18/html doi:10.5334/2013-18

Bédard, Claude. 2000. "Translation Memory Seeks Sentence-Oriented Translator." *Traduire* 18: 641–649. http://www.terminotix.com/eng/info/mem_1.htm. Accessed January 5, 2014.

Beeby, Alison, Pilar Rodríguez Inés and Pilar Sánchez-Gijón (eds.). 2009. *Corpus Use and Translating: Corpus Use for Learning to Translate and Learning Corpus Use to Translate*. Amsterdam: John Benjamins doi:10.1075/btl.82

Bell, Roger. 1991. *Translation and Translating*. London: Longman.

Benkler, Yochai. 2006. *The Wealth of Networks: how Social Production Transforms Markets and Freedom*. Yale: Yale University Press.

Bentivogli, Luisa *et al.* 2011. "Getting Expert Quality from the Crowd for Machine Translation." In *Proceedings of the MT Summit 12*, 521–528. Accessed March 1, 2016. http://www.mt-archive.info/MTS-2011-Bentivogli.pdf

Bereiter, Carl and Marlene Scardamalia. 1993. *Surpassing Ourselves: An Inquiry into the Nature and Implications of Expertise*. Chicago, IL: Open Court.

Bernal-Merino, Miguel A. 2015. *Translation and Localization in Videogames*. New York-London: Routledge.

Berners-Lee, Tim. 2000. *Weaving the Web: The Past, Present and Future of the World Wide Web by its Inventor*. London: Texere.

Berners-Lee, Tim *et al.* 1992. "World Wide Web: the Information Universe." *Electronic publishing: Research and Applications* 1: 52–58. Accessed December 3, 2013. http://www.emeraldgroup-publishing.com/products/backfiles/pdf/backfiles_sample_5.pdf

Bestué, Belen. 2013. *Collaborative Translation and Multi-Version Texts in Early Modern Europe*. Burlington: Ashgate.

Bey, Youcef, Kageura Kageura and Christian Boitet. 2005. "A Framework for Data Management for the Online Volunteer Translators' Aid System QRLex." *In Proceedings of the 19th Pacific Asia Conference on Language, Information and Computation*. Taiwan, China, 51–60. Accessed March 1, 2016. http://www.aclweb.org/anthology/Y05-1005.

Bey, Youcef, Kageura Kageura and Christian Boitet. 2006a. "Data Management in QRLex, an Online Aid System for Volunteer Translators." *International Journal of Computational Linguistics and Chinese Language Processing* 11(4): 349–376.

Bey, Youcef, Kageura Kageura and Christian Boitet. 2006b. "The TRANSBey prototype: An Online Collaborative Wiki-based CAT Environment for Volunteer Translators." In *Proceedings of the Third International Workshop on Language Resources for Translation Work, Research & Training LR4Trans-III*, Elia Yuste (ed.), 49–54. Paris: ELRA.

Bhatia Vijay. K. 1997. "Genre-Mixing in Academic Introductions." *English for Specific Purposes* 16: 181–195. doi:10.1016/S0889-4906(96)00039-7

Blasco Mayor, Maria J. 2015. "L2 Proficiency as Predictor of Aptitude for Interpreting: An Empirical Study." *Translation and Interpreting Studies* 10: 108–132. doi:10.1075/tis.10.1.06bla

Boeri, Julie. 2008. "A Narrative Account of the Babels vs. Naumann Controversy. Competing Perspectives on Activism in Conference Interpreting." *The Translator* 14: 21–50. doi:10.1080/13556509.2008.10799248

Boeri, Julie. 2010. "Emerging Narratives of Conference Interpreters' Training: a Case Study of Ad Hoc Training in Babels and the Social Forum." *Puentes* 9: 61–70.

Boeri, Julie. 2012. "Translation/Interpreting Politics and Praxis: The Impact of Political Principles on Babels' Interpreting Practice." *The Translator* 18: 269–290. doi:10.1080/13556509.2012.10799511

Bogucki, Lucasz. 2009. "Amateur Subtitling on the Internet." In *Audio-visual Translation: Language Transfer on Screen*, Jorge Díaz Cintas and Gunilla Anderman (eds.), 49–57 Oxford: Palgrave Macmillan.

Bold, Bianca. 2011. "The Power Of Fan Communities: An Overview of Fansubbing in Brazil." *Cuadernos de Traduçao 11*. Accessed March 1st, 2016. http://www.maxwell.vrac.puc-rio.br/18881/18881.PDF.

Bourdieu, Pierre. 1986. "The Forms of Capital." In *The Handbook of Theory: Research for the Sociology of Education*, John Richardson (ed.). New York: Greenwood Press.

Bourdieu, Pierre. 1990. *The Logic of Practice*. Sanford: Stanford University Press.

Bowker, Lynne. 1998. "Using Specialized Monolingual Native-Language Corpora as a Translation Resource: A Pilot Study." *Meta* 43: 331–351.

Bowker, Lynne. 2001. "Towards a Methodology for a Corpus-Based Approach to Translation Evaluation." *META* 46: 345–364. doi:10.7202/002135ar

Bowker, Lynne. 2002. *Computer-Aided Translation Technology*. Ottawa: University of Ottawa Press.

Bowker, Lynne. 2006. "Translation Memory and Text." In *Lexicography, Terminology and Translation*, Lynne Bowker (ed.), 174–187. Ottawa: University of Ottawa Press.

Bowker, Lynne. 2014. "Computer-Aided Translation: Translator Training." In *The Routledge Encyclopaedia of Translation Technology*, Sin Wai Chan (ed.), 88–104. London-New York: Routledge.

Bowker, Lynne and Michael Barlow. 2008. "A Comparative Evaluation of Bilingual Concordancers and Translation Memory Systems." In *Topics in Language Resources for Translation and Localization*, Elia Yuste Trigo (ed.), 1–22. Amsterdam-Philadelphia: John Benjamins. doi:10.1075/btl.79.02bow

Bowker, Lynne and Gloria Corpas. 2015. "Translation Technology." In *Handbook of Computational Linguistics*, Ruslan Mitkov (ed.). Oxford: Oxford University Press.

Bowker, Lynne and Jairo Buitrago. 2016. "Investigating the Usefulness of Machine Translation to Newcomers in the Public Library." *TIS: Translation and Interpreting* 10(2): 165–186. doi:10.1075/tis.10.2.01bow

Brabham, Daren. 2008. "Crowdsourcing as a Model for Problem Solving: An Introduction and Cases." *Convergence: The International Journal of Research into New Media Technologies* 14: 75–90.

Brabham, Daren. 2013. *Crowdsourcing*. Cambridge: MIT Press.

Brough, Melissa and Sangita Shresthrova. 2012. "Fandom Meets Activism: Rethinking Civic and Political Participation." *Transformative Works and Cultures* 10. http://journal.transformative-works.org/index.php/twc/article/view/303/265

Bruti, Silvia. 2015. "Compliments in Fansubs and in Professional Subtitles: The Case of Lost." *Rivista internazionale di tecnica della traduzione (International Journal of Translation)* 16: 13–34.

Bundgaard, Kristine, Tina Paulsen Christensen and Anne Schjoldager. 2016. "Translator-Computer Interaction in Action: an Observational Process Study of Computer-Aided Translation." *Jostrans* 25: 106–130.

Burke, David. 2013. "Foreword: Vital Aspects of the KJV Genius." In *The King James Version at 400: Assessing its Genius as Bible Translation and its Literary Influence*, David Burke *et al.* (eds.), ix–xix. Atlanta: Society of Biblical Literature.

Buzelin, Hélène. 2005. "Unexpected Allies: How Latour's Network Theory Could Complement Bourdieusian Analyses in Translation Studies." *The Translator* 11 2: 193–218. doi:10.1080/13556509.2005.10799198

Buzelin, Héléne. 2006. "Independent Publisher in the Networks of Translation." *TTR* 19 1: 135–173. doi:10.7202/016663ar

Buzelin, Hélène. 2011. "Agents in Translation." In *The Routledge Handbook of Translation Studies*, Vol. 2., Yves Gambier and Luc van Doorslaer (eds.), 6–12. Amsterdam-Philadelphia: Johh Benjamins.

Buzelin, Hélène. 2013. "Sociology and Translation Studies." In *Routledge Handbook of Translation Studies*, Carmen Millán-Varela and Francesca Bartrina (eds.), 186–200. London: Routledge.

Caffrey, Colm. 2009. *Relevant abuse? Investigating the effects of an abusive subtitling procedure on the perception of TV anime using eye tracker and questionnaire.* PhD thesis, Dublin City University.

Camara, Lidia. 2015. "Motivation for Collaboration in TED Open Translation." *International Journal of Web-Based Communication* 11 (2): 210–229. doi:10.1504/IJWBC.2015.068542

Cao, Yixin. 2015. "Crowdsourcing Translation in Contemporary China: an Inspiring Perspective of Translation in the Web 2.0 Age." *META* 60 (60): 316. doi:10.7202/1032867ar

Cardoso-Teixeira, Carlos da Silva. 2014. *The Impact of Metadata on Translation Performance: How Translators Work with Translation Memories and Machine Translation.* PhD Thesis. Universitat Rovira i Virgili, Spain.

Carson-Berdsen, Julie, Harold Somers and Carl Vogel. 2009. "Integrated Language Technology as a Part of Next Generation Localization." *Localisation Focus* 81: 53–66.

Castells, Manuel. 1996. *The Rise of the Network Society.* Malden, MA: Blackwell.

Castells, Manuel. 2003. *The Internet Galaxy: Reflections on the Internet, Business, and Society.* Oxford University Press.

Castro, María. 2007. "Procesos de lectura y comprensión al traducir." In *Aproximaciones cognitivas al estudio de la traducción y la interpretación*, María M. Fernández and Ricardo Muñoz (eds.), 31–55. Granada: Comares.

Catford, John C. 1965. *A Linguistic Theory of Translation.* Oxford University Press: London.

Chan, Sin-Wai. 2005. *A Dictionary of Translation Technology.* Hong Kong: Chinese University Press.

Chan, Sin-Wai (ed.). 2014. *Routledge Encyclopedia of Translation Technology.* New York-London: Routledge.

Chaume, Federic. 2013. "Research Paths in Audiovisual Translation: The Case of Dubbing." In *Routledge Handbook of Translation Studies*, Carmen Millán-Varela and Francesca Bartrina (eds.), 288–302. London: Routledge.

Chesterman, Andrew. 1997. *Memes of Translation: the Spread of Ideas in Translation Theory.* Amsterdam-Philladelphia: John Benjamins. doi:10.1075/btl.22

Chesterman, Andrew. 2001. "Proposal for a Hieronymic Oath." *The Translator* 7 (2): 139–154. doi:10.1080/13556509.2001.10799097

Chesterman, Andrew. 2002. "On the Interdisciplinarity of Translation Studies." *Logos* 3: 1–9.

Chesterman, Andew. 2004. "Beyond the Particular." In *Translation Universals. Do they Exist?*, Anna Mauranen and Pekka Kujamäki (eds.), 33–49. Amsterdam-Philadelphia: Benjamins. doi:10.1075/btl.48.04che

Chesterman, Andrew. 2005. "Consilience and Translation Studies." *Revista Canaria de Estudios Ingleses* 51: 19–32.

Chesterman, Andrew. 2007. "Bridge concepts in Translation Sociology." *Constructing a Sociology of Translation*, Wolf, Michaela and Alexandra Fukari (eds.), 171–183. Amsterdam-Philadelphia: Benjamins. doi:10.1075/btl.74.12che

Chesterman, Andrew. 2009. "The Name and Nature of Translator Studies." *Hermes-Journal of Language and Communication Studies* 42: 13–22.

Chesterman, Andrew. 2010. "The Space between the Data and the Concepts." In *Electronic Proceedings of the KäTu Symposium on Translation and Interpreting Studies 4.* Accessed March 2, 2016. http://www.sktl.fi/@Bin/40686/Chesterman_MikaEL2010.pdf

Chesterman, Andrew *et al.* 2003. "Bananas – on Names and Definitions in Translation Studies." *Hermes* 31: 197–209.

Chi, Michelene T. H. 2006. "Two Approaches to the Study of Experts' Characteristics." In *Cambridge Handbook of Expertise and Expert Performance*, K. Anders Ericsson *et al.* (eds.), 21–30. New York: Cambridge University Press. doi:10.1017/CBO9780511816796.002

Christensen,Tina Paulsen. 2011. "Studies on the Mental Processes in Translation Memory Assisted Translation – the State of the Art." *Transkom* 42: 137–160. Accessed March 2, 2016. http://www.trans-kom.eu/bd04nr02/trans-kom_04_02_02_Christensen_Translation_Memory.20111205.pdf

Chu, Donna. 2013. "Fanatical Labor and Serious Leisure in the Internet Age: A Case of Fansubbing in China." In *Frontiers in New Media Research*, Francis L. F. Lee, Louis Leung, Jack Linchuan Qiu and Donna S. C. Chu (eds), 259–277. New York-London: Routledge.

Clark, Andy and David J. Chalmers. 1998. "The Extended Mind." *Analysis* 58(1): 7–19. Accessed March 2, 2016. http://consc.net/papers/extended.Html.

Clark, Andy. 1997. *Being There: Putting Brain, Body, and World Together Again*. Cambridge, MA: The MIT Press.

Clark, Andy. 2008. *Supersizing the Mind: Embodiment, Action, and Cognitive Extension*. Oxford: Oxford University Press. doi:10.1093/acprof:oso/9780195333213.001.0001

Colina, Sonia. 2008. "Translation Quality Evaluation: Empirical Evidence from a Functionalist Approach." *The Translator* 4 (1): 97–134. doi:10.1080/13556509.2008.10799251

Colina, Sonia. 2009. "Further Evidence for a Functionalist Approach to Translation Quality Evaluation." *Target* 21 (2): 235–264. doi:10.1075/target.21.2.02col

Collaborative Translation Patterns. 2011. Accessed March 2, 2016. http://collaborative-translation-patterns.wiki4us.com/tiki-index.php

Colominas, Carme. 2008. "Towards Chunk-Based Translation Memories." *Babel* 544: 343–354. doi:10.1075/babel.54.4.03col

Conde Ruano, Tomas. 2009. *Proceso y resultado de la evaluación de traducciones [Process and Result of Translation Evaluation]*. PhD Thesis, University of Granada, Spain.

Conde Ruano, Tomas. 2012. "The Good Guys and the Bad Guys: The Behavior of Lenient and Demanding Translation Evaluators." *META* 57: 763–786.

Consalvo, Mia. 2013. "Bringing a Japanese RPG to North America." In *The Participatory Cultures Handbook*, Delwiche Aaron and Jennifer J. Henderson (eds), 59–69. New York-London: Routledge.

Consalvo, Mia and Ess Charles. 2011. *The Handbook of Internet Studies*. Oxford: Wiley. doi:10.1002/9781444314861

Cordingley, Anthony and Céline Frigau Manning (eds.). 2016. *Collaborative Translation: From the Renaissance to the Digital Age*. London: Bloomsbury.

Costales, Alberto. 2012. "Collaborative Translation Revisited: Exploring the Rationale and the Motivation for Volunteer Translation." *Forum – International Journal of Translation* 10:115–142.

Costales, Alberto. 2013. "Crowdsourcing and Collaborative Translation: Mass Phenomena or Silent Threat to Translation Studies?" *Hermenus* 15: 85–110.

Creswell, John W. and Vicki L. Plano Clark. 2012. *Designing and conducting mixed methods research*. 2nd ed. Thousand Oaks: Sage Publications.

Cronin, Michael. 2010. "The Translation Crowd." *Tradumática*, 8. Accessed March 2, 2016. http://www.fti.uab.es/tradumatica/revista/num8/articles/04/04central.htm.

Cronin, Michael. 2013. *Translation in the Digital Age*. New York-London: Routledge.

de Almeida, Giselle. 2013. *Translating the Post-Editor: An Investigation of Post-Editing Changes and Correlations with Professional Experience across Two Romance Languages.* PhD Thesis. Dublin City University, Ireland.

de Rooze, Bert. 2003. *La traduccion, contra reloj [Translation against the clock].* PhD Thesis. University of Granada, Spain.

De Wille, Tabea, Chris Exton and Reinhard Schäler. 2015. "Multi-Language Communities, Technology and Perceived Quality." *International Reports on Socio-Informatics* 12: 25–33.

De Wille, Tabea. 2014. *Competence and Motivation in Volunteer Translators: the Example of Translation Trommons.* MA Thesis. University of Limerick, Ireland.

Declerq, Christophe. 2014. "Crowd, Cloud and Automation in the Translation Education Community." *Cultus* 7: 37–56.

Delisle, Jean. 1980. *L'Anayse du discours comme métode de traduction.* Ottawa: Université d'Ottawa.

Delwiche, Aaron and Jennifer J. Henderson. 2012. "Introduction: What is Participatory Culture?" In *The Participatory Cultures Handbook*, Delwiche Aaron and Jennifer J. Henderson (eds), 3–9. New York-London: Routledge.

Delwiche, Aaron. 2012. "The New Left and the Computer Undergroud: Recovering Political Antecedents of Participatory Culture." In *The Participatory Cultures Handbook*, Delwiche Aaron and Jennifer J. Henderson (eds), 10–21. New York-London: Routledge.

DePalma, Donald. 2011. "The Largest Translation Project…So Far." *Common Sense Advisory.* Accessed March 2, 2016. http://www.commonsenseadvisory.com/default.aspx?Contenttype=ArticleDetAD&tabID=63&Aid=1180&moduleId=390

DePalma, Donald. 2015. "CSOFT Swipes Left for Translation, Right for the Source to Mobilize Translation." *Common Sense Advisory.* Accessed July 24, 2016. http://www.commonsenseadvisory.com/Default.aspx?Contenttype=ArticleDetAD&tabID=63&Aid=36417&moduleId=390

DePalma, Donald and Kelly, Natalie. 2008. "Translation of, for, and by the People: How User-Translated Content Projects Work in Real Life." *Common Sense Advisory Reports.*

DePalma, Donald and Nataly Kelly. 2011. "Project Management for Crowdsourced Translation: How User-Translated Content Projects Work in Real Life." In *Translation and Localization Project Management: The Art of the Possible*, Keiran Dunne and Elena Dunne (eds.), 379–408. Amsterdam-Philadelphia: John Benjamins. doi:10.1075/ata.xvi.19dep

DePalma, Donald, Vijayalaxmi Hegde, Helene Pielmeier and Robert Stewart. 2013. *The Languages Services Market. The Languages Services Market.* Cambridge, MA: Common Sense Advisory.

Deriemaeker, Jen. 2014. *Power of the Crowd: Assessing Crowd Translation Quality of Tourist Literature.* MA Thesis. Universiteit Ghent, Belgium.

Desilets, Alain. 2007. "Translation Wikified: How will Massive Online Collaboration Impact the World of Translation?" In *Proceedings of Translation and the Computer 29.* Accessed December 3, 2014. http://www.mt-archive.info/Aslib-2007-Desilets.pdf

Desilets, Alain and Jaap van de Meer. 2011. "Co-Creating a Repository of Best-Practices for Collaborative Translation." *Linguistica Antverpiensia* 10: 11–27.

Diaz Cintas, Jorge and Aline Remael. 2007. *Audiovisual Translation: Subtitling.* Manchester: St. Jerome.

Díaz Cintas, Jorge and Pablo Muñoz Sánchez. 2006. "Fansubs: Audiovisual Translation in an Amateur Environment." *Journal of Specialised Translation* 6: 37–52.

Diaz Cintas, Jorge. 2003. *Teoria y Practica de la Subtitulación: inglés-español.* Barcelona: Ariel.

Díaz Cintas, Jorge. 2005 "Back to the Future in Subtitling." In *Proceedings of MuTra Conference 17.* Accessed March 2, 2016. http://www.euroconferences.info/proceedings/2005_Proceedings/2005_proceedings.html.

Diaz Fouçes, Oscar and García Gonzalez, Maria. 2009. *Traducir con software libre*. Granada: Comares.

DiNucci, Darcy 1999. "Fragmented Future." *Print* 53 (4): 32 and 221–222.

Dodd, Sean M. 2011. "Crowdsourcing: Social[ism] Media 2.0." *Journal of the Northern California Translators' Association*. Accessed March 2, 2016. http://translorial.com/2011/01/01/crowdsourcing-socialism-media-2-0/

Doherty, Stephen and Kenny Dorothy. 2014. "The Design and Evaluation of a Statistical Machine Translation Syllabus for Translation Students." *The Interpreter and Translator Trainer* 8 (2): 95 – 315. http://dx.doi.org/10.1080/1750399X.2014.937571

Doherty, Stephen and Joss Moorkens. 2013. "Investigating the Experience of Translation Technology Labs: Pedagogical Implications." *Journal of Specialised Translation* 19: 122 – 136. Accessed March 2, 2016. http://www.jostrans.org/issue19/art_doherty.php

Doherty, Stephen. 2015. "The Impact of Translation Technologies on the Process and Product of Translation." *International Journal of Communication Studies* 9: 1–23.

Dombek, Magdalena. 2013. *A Study into the Motivations of Internet Users Contributing to Translation Crowdsourcing: The Case of Polish Facebook User-Translators*. Unpublished Doctoral Thesis. Dublin City University.

Dragsted, Barbara. 2006. "Computer-Aided Translation as a Distributed Cognitive Task." *Pragmatics and Cognition* 14 (2): 443–464. doi:10.1075/pc.14.2.17dra

Dragsted, Barbara. 2008. "Computer-aided Translation as a Distributed Cognitive Task." In *Cognition Distributed: How Cognitive Technology Extends our Minds*, Itiel E. Dror and Stevan. Harnad (eds.), 237–256. Amsterdam-Philadelphia: John Benjamins doi:10.1075/bct.16.16dra

Drugan, Johanna. 2011. "Translation Ethics Wikified: How Do Professional Codes of Ethics and Practice Apply to Non-Professionally Produced Translation." *Linguistica Antverpiensia* 10: 97–111.

Drugan, Johanna. 2013. *Quality in Professional Translation*. London: Bloomsbury.

Du, Jinhua, Way, Andy, Qiu, Zhengwei, Wasla, Asanka and Reindhard Schaler. 2015. "Domain Adaptation for Social Localisation-based SMT: A Case Study Using Trommons Platform." In *Proceedings of the 4th Workshop on Post-Editing Technology and Practice*, O'Brien, Sharon and Simard, Michael (eds.), 57–75. http://amtaweb.org/wp-content/uploads/2015/10/MTSummitXV_WPTP4Proceedings.pdf

Dunne, Keiran and Elana Dunne (eds.). 2011. *Translation Management: the Art of the Possible*. Amsterdam: John Benjamins.

Dunne, Keiran. 2006. "A Copernican Revolution." In *Perspectives on Localization*, Keiran Dune (ed.), 1–11. Amsterdam-Philadelphia: John Benjamins. doi:10.1075/ata.xiii.01dun

Dunne, Keiran. 2011. "Managing the fourth dimension: time and schedule in translation and localization projects." In *Translation and Localization Management*, Keiran Dunne and Elena Dunne (eds.), 119–152. Amsterdam-Philadelphia: Jonh Benjamins.

Dutton, William (ed.). 2013. *The Oxford Handbook of Internet Studies*. Oxford: Oxford University Press. doi:10.1093/oxfordhb/9780199589074.001.0001

Dwyer, Tessa. 2013. "Fansub Dreaming on Viki." *The Translator* 18: 217–243. doi:10.1080/13556509.2012.10799509

Eagle, Nathan. 2009. "Txteagle: Mobile Crowdsourcing." *International Conference on Internationalization Design and Global Development* 5623: 447–456. Accessed March 2nd, 2016. http://realitycommons.media.mit.edu/pdfs/hcii_txteagle.pdf

Edfeldt, Chatarina, Fjordevik, Anneli and Hiroko Inose. 2012. "Fan Culture as an Informal Learning Environment." Paper presented at the *NGL 2012 Next Generation Learning Conference*. Accessed March 2, 2016. http://www.du.se/Global/dokument/NGL/conference%20summary.pdf

Ehrengsber-Dow, Maureen and Gary Massey. 2014. "Cognitive Ergonomic Issues in Professional Translation." In *The Development of Translation Competence: Theories and Methodologies from Psycholinguistics and Cognitive Science*, John W. Schwieter and Aline Ferreira (eds.), 58–86. Cambridge: Cambridge Scholars Publishing.

Elia. 2016. *Expectations and Concerns of the European Language Industry. EUATC European Union of Associations of Translation Companies*. Accessed October 10, 2016. http://ec.europa.eu/dgs/translation/programmes/languageindustry/platform/documents/2016_survey_en.pdf

Ellis, Roger and Liz Oakley-Brown. 2009. "British Tradition." In *Encyclopedia of Translation Studies*, Mona Baker and Gabriela Saldanha (eds.), 344–354. New York-London: Routledge.

Elming, Jakob, Laura Winther and Michael Carl. 2014. "Investigating User Behaviour in Post-editing and Translation using the CASMACAT Workbench." In *Post-Editing of Machine Translation: Processes and Application*, Sharon O'Brien, Laura Winther Balling, Michael Carl, Michel Simard and Lucia Specia (eds), 244–272. Cambridge: Cambridge Scholars Publishing.

Englund Dimitrova, Birgitta. 2005. "Combining Product and Process Analysis: Explicitation as a Case in Point." *Bulletin Suisse de linguistique appliqué* 81: 25–39.

Englund Dimitrova, Birgitta. 2010. "Translation Process." In *Handbook of Translation Studies*, Volume I, Yves Gambier and Luc van Doorslaereds (eds.), 406–411. Amsterdam/Philadelphia: Benjamins. doi:10.1075/hts.1.tra6

Ericsson, K. Anders. 2000. "Expertise in Interpreting: An Expert-Performance Perspective." *Interpreting* 5(2):187–220. doi:10.1075/intp.5.2.08eri.

Ericsson, K. Anders, Krampe, Ralf, and Tesch-Roemer, Clemens. 1993. "The Role of Deliberate Practice in the Acquisition of Expert Performance." *Psychological Review* 100: 363–406. doi:10.1037/0033-295X.100.3.363

Ericsson, K. Anders and Simon, Herbert A. 1984. *Protocol Analysis. Verbal Reports as Data*. Cambridge, MA/London: Massachusetts Institute of Technology.

Espasa, Eva. 2013. "Rethinking Performability through Metaphors." In *Theatre Translation in Performance 29*, Silvia, Bigliazzi, Peter Kofler and Paola Ambrosi (eds.). 38–49. New York-London: Routledge.

Espunya, Anna. 2014. "The UPF Learner Translation Corpus as a resource for translator training." *Language Resources and Evaluation* 48(1): 33–43 . doi:10.1007/s10579-013-9260-1

Esselink, Bert. 2000. *A Practical Guide to Localization*. Amsterdam-Philadelphia: John Benjamins.

Estellés, Enrique and Fernando González. 2012a. "Towards and Integrated Definition of Crowdsourcing." *Journal of Information Science* 38 (2): 189–200. doi:10.1177/0165551512437638

Estellés, Enrique and González, Fernando. 2012b. "Clasificación de iniciativas de crowdsourcing basada en tareas." *El profesional de la información* 21(3): 283–291. doi:10.3145/epi.2012.may.09

Estellés, Enrique *et al.* 2015. "Crowdsourcing: Definition and Typology." In *Advances in Crowdsourcing*, Simon Garrigos, Pechuan Gil and Miguel Estelles (eds.) 33–48. Springer International Publishing. doi:10.1007/978-3-319-18341-1_3

European Commission. 2011. "Crowdsourcing Translation. Studies on Multilingualism and Translation." *Brussels: Directorate General of Translation*. Accessed March 2, 2016. http://ec.europa.eu/dgs/translation/publications/studies/crowdsourcing_translation_en.pdf>

European Union. 2010. *Revision Manual.* Accessed March 2, 2016. http://ec.europa.eu/translation/spanish/guidelines/documents/revision_manual_en.pdf

Exton, Chris, Wasala Asanka, Jim Buckley and Reinhard Schäler. 2009. "Micro Crowdsourcing: a New Model for Software Localization." *The International Journal of Localization* 8: 81–89.

Federico, Marco *et al.* 2014. "The MateCat Tool." In *Proceedings of COLING 2014*, the 25th International Conference on Computational Linguistics: System Demonstrations, 129–132. Accessed March 2, 2016. http://www.aclweb.org/anthology/C14-2028.pdf.

Feitosa, Marcos. 2009. *Legendagem comercial e legendagem pirata: um estudo comparado.* PdD Thesis. Universidade Federal Minas Gerais, Brazil.

Ferrer Simó, María Rosario. 2005. "Fansubs y Scanlations: La Influencia del Aficionado en los Criterios Profesionales." *Puentes* 6: 27–43.

Fielding, Nigel, Raymond Lee and Grant Blank. (eds.). *The SAGE Handbook of Online Research Methods.* London: SAGE Publications Ltd.

Filip, David and Ó Conchuir, Eoin. 2011. "An Argument for Business Process Management in Localisation." *Localisation Focus: The International Journal of Localisation* 10: 4–17.

Fillmore, Charles J. 1976. "Frame semantics and the nature of language." Annals of the New York Academy of Sciences: Conference on the Origin and Development of Language and Speech 280: 20–32. doi:10.1111/j.1749-6632.1976.tb25467.x

FIT. 2015. "FIT Position Statement on Crowdsourcing of Translation, Interpreting and Terminology Services." Accessed March 2, 2016. http://www.fit-ift.org/?page_id=4355

Flanagan, Marian. 2016. "Cause for Concern? Attitudes towards Translation Crowdsourcing in Professional Translator's Blogs." *Jostrans: the Journal of Specialized Translation* 25: 149–173. Accessed July 23, 2016. http://www.jostrans.org/issue25/art_flanagan.pdf

Flew, Terry. 2008. *New Media: An Introduction*, 3rd Edition. Oxford: Oxford University Press.

Folaron, Debbie and Helene Buzelin. 2007. "Introduction Connecting Translation and Network Studies." *META* 52: 605–642. doi:10.7202/017689ar

Folaron, Debbie. 2010. "Networking and Volunteer Translators." In *Handbook of Translation Studies*, vol. 1, Yves Gambier and Luc van Doorslaer (eds.), 231–234. Amsterdam-Philadelphia: John Benjamins. doi:10.1075/hts.1.net1

Fondevila, Gascón, Joan Francesc and Raúl López García-Navas. 2015. "New Digital Production Models: The Consolidation of the Copyleft." In *Cultures of Copyright*, Dànielle Nicole Devoss, Martine Courant Rife (eds), 64–74. Berna: Peter Lang.

Fox, Wendy. 2015. "Modular Guidelines for Integrated Titles based on a Comparative Eye Tracking Study." Paper presented at *6th International Conference Media for All*, University of Western Sydney, Sydney, Australia, 16th-18th, July, 2015.

Fraser, Ryan. 2004. "Past Lives of Knives: On Borges, Translation, and Sticking Old Texts." *TTR: Traduction, Terminologie, Rédaction* 17 (1): 55 – 80. doi:10.7202/011973ar

Frey, Bruno. 1997. *Not just for the money. An Economic Theory of Personal Motivation.* Cheltenham and Brookfield: Edward Elgar Publishing.

Furuhata-Turner, Hamako. 2013. "Use of Comics Manga as a Learning Tool to Teach Translation of Japanese." *The Journal of Language Teaching and Learning* 2: 72–83.

Gambier, Yves. 2012. "Denial of translation and desire to translate." *Vertimo Studijos* 5: 9–29.

Gambier, Yves. 2013. "The Position of Audiovisual Translation Studies." In *Routledge Handbook of Translation Studies*, Carmen Millán-Varela and Francesca Bartrina (eds.), 45–59. London: Routledge. doi:10.1075/hts.4

Gambier, Yves. 2014. "Changing Landscape in Translation." *International Journal of Society, Culture and Language* 22. Accessed March 2, 2016. http://ijscl.net/pdf_4638_8301154b3b-fe303a6e1c541f62c4e18a.html.

Gambier, Yves and Jeremy Munday. 2014. "A Conversation Between Yves Gambier and Jeremy Munday about Transcreation and the Future of the Professions." *Cultus: the Intercultural Journal of Mediation and Communication* 7: 20–36. Accessed January 10, 2016. http://cultusjournal.com/files/Archives/conversation_gambier_munday_3_p.pdf

Gambier, Yves and Luc van Doorslaer (eds.). 2016. *Border Crossing: Translation Studies and Other Disciplines.* Amsterdam-Philadelphia: John Benjamins.

Gamero Pérez, Silvia. 2001. *La traducción de textos técnicos.* Barcelona: Ariel.

Gao, Huiji, Geoffrey Barbier and Rebecca Goolsby. 2011. "Harnessing the Crowdsourcing Power of Social Media for Disaster Relief." *IEEE Intelligent Systems* 26 (3): 10–14. Accessed July 24, 2016. http://www.dtic.mil/cgi-bin/GetTRDoc?AD=ADA581803

García Izquierdo, Isabel (ed.). 2005. *El género textual y la traducción. Reflexiones teóricas y aplicaciones pedagógicas.* Berna: Peter Lang.

García-Manchón, Paula. 2013. *A Corpus-Based Analysis of Swearword Translation in DVD Subtitles and Internet Fansubs.* MA Thesis. Universidad Complutense, Spain.

García, Ignacio. 2009. "Beyond Translation Memory, Computers and the professional translator." *Jostrans* 12: 199–2014. Accessed July 5, 2015. http://jostrans.org/issue12/art_garcia.pdf.

García, Ignacio. 2010. "Is Machine Translation Ready yet?" *Target* 22 (1): 7–21. doi:10.1075/target.22.1.02gar

García, Ignacio. 2012. "Learning a Language for Free While Translating the Web. Does Duolingo Work?" *International Journal of English Linguistics* 3:19–25. Accessed March 2, 2016. http://www.ccsenet.org/journal/index.php/ijel/article/viewFile/24236/15350.

García, Ignacio. 2015. "Cloud Marketplaces: Procurement of Translators in the Age of Social Media." *Jostrans* 23: 18–38. Accessed March 2, 2016. http://www.jostrans.org/issue23/art_garcia.pdf

Gargatagli, Marietta. 1999. "La historia de la escuela de traductores de Toledo." *Quaderns. Revista de Traducció* 4: 9–13.

Gaspari, Federico. 2014. "Online Translation." In *Routledge Encyclopedia of Translation Technology,* Sin-Wai Chan (ed.), 578–593. London: Routledge.

Geiger, R. Stuart and David Ribes. 2010. "The Work of Sustaining Order in Wikipedia: the Banning of a vandal." *In Proceedings of the 2010 ACM Conference on Computer Supported Cooperative Work, CSCW '10,* 117–126, New York: ACM. Accessed March 2, 2016. http://static1.1.sqspcdn.com/static/f/1070098/14615049/1318519402800/Geiger+Ribes+-+Sustaining+Order+in+Wikipedia.pdf?token=lkHP1PSRBTu49zopmq%2BnxYuExC4%3D

Gerloff, Pamela. 1988. *From French to English: A Look at the Translation Process in Students, Bilinguals, and Professional Translators.* Ann Arbor: University Microfilms International.

Gile, Daniel. 2004. "Response to Invited Papers." In *Translation Research and Interpreting Research,* Christina Schäffner (ed.), 124–127. Clevedon: Multilingual Matters.

Gile, Daniel, Gyde Hansen and Nike Pokorn (ed.) 2010. *Why Translation Studies Matter.* Amsterdam-Philadelphia: Benjamins. doi:10.1075/btl.88

Gläser, Rosemarie. 1990. *Fachtextsorten im Englischen.* Tübingen: Narr.

Gómez Hurtado, Mª Isabel. 2006. *Traducir, ¿capacidad innata o destreza adquirida? [Translating. Innate ability or acquired skill?].* PhD Thesis. University of Granada, Spain.

González Davies, Maria. 2004. *Multiple Voices in the Translation Classroom.* Amsterdam-Philadelphia: John Benjamins. doi:10.1075/btl.54

Gonçalves, Jorge *et al.* 2015. "Workshop on Mobile and Situated Crowdsourcing." *Proceedings of UbiComp/ISWC '15 Adjunct*, September 07–11, 2015, Osaka, Japan. doi:10.1145/2800835.2800966

Google. 2008. "Google in Your Language." https://googleblog.blogspot.com.au/2008/08/google-in-your-language.html

Göpferich, Susanne and Ritta Jääskelainen. 2009. "Process Research into the Development of Translation Competence: Where are We, and Where do we Need to Go?" *Across Languages and Cultures* 10: 169–191. doi:10.1556/Acr.10.2009.2.1

Göpferich, Ssusanne. 1995. *Textsorten in Naturwissenschaften und Technik, Pragmatische Typologie- Kontrastierung-Translation*. Tubinga: Gunter Narr.

Göpferich, Susanne. 2008. *Translationsprozessforschung: Stand – Methoden – Perspektiven*. Tübingen: Gunter Narr.

Göpferich, Susanne. 2009. "Towards a Model of Translation Competence and its Acquisition: the Longusitudial Study TransComp." In *Behind the Mind*, Susanne Gopferich, Arnt. L. Jakobsen and Inger M. Mees (eds.), 11–37. Copenhage: Samfundslitterature.

Göpferich, Susane and Ritta Jääskelainen. 2010. "Process Research into the Development of Translation Competence: Where are We, and where do We Need to Go?" *Across Languages and Cultures* 10: 169–191.

Göpferich, Susanne *et al.* 2011. "Exploring Translation Competence Acquisition: Criteria of Analysis Put to the Test." In *Cognitive Explorations in Translation*, Shannon O'Brien (ed.), 57–85. London: Continuum 2011.

Gorm Hansen, Inge and Barbara Dragsted. 2007. "Speaking your Translation: Exploiting Synergies between Translation and Interpreting." In *Interpreting Studies and Beyond: A Tribute to Miriam Shlesinger*, Fran. Pöchhacker, Arnt L. Jakobsen and Inger M. Mees (eds.), 251–274. Frederiksberg: Copenhagen Business School Press.

Göroj, Attila. 2014a. "Quantification and Comparative Evaluation of Quality: the TAUS Dynamic Quality Framework." *Tradumatica* 12: 443–454. Accessed March 2, 2016. http://revistes.uab.cat/tradumatica/article/view/n12-gorog2/pdf

Göroj, Attila. 2014b. "Translation and Quality: Editorial." *Tradumatica* 12: 388–391. Accessed March 2, 2016. http://revistes.uab.cat/tradumatica/article/view/n12-gorog/pdf_2

Goto, Shinsuke, Donghui Lin, and Toru Ishida. 2014. "Crowdsourcing for Evaluating Machine Translation Quality." *LREC* 2014: 3456–3463

Gouadec, Daniel. 1981. "Paramètres de l'évaluation des traductions." *META* 26(2): 99–116. doi:10.7202/002949ar

Gouadec, Daniel. 1989. "Comprendre, évaluer, prévenir." *TTR* 2: 35–54. Accessed March 2, 2016. http://www.lrec-conf.org/proceedings/lrec2014/pdf/756_Paper.pdf.

Gouadec, Daniel. 2007. *Translation as a Profession*. Amsterdam-Philadelphia: John Benjamins. doi:10.1075/btl.73

Gouadec, Daniel. 2010. "Quality in Translation." In *Handbook of Translation Studies*, Vol I, Yves Gambier and Luc van Doorslaer (eds.), 270–275. Amsterdam-Philadelphia: John Benjamins. doi:10.1075/hts.1.qua1

Gouanvic, Jean M. 1999. *Sociologie de la traduction*. Artois Presses Université.

Gouanvic, Jean M. 2005. "A Bourdieusian Theory of Translation, or the Coincidence of Practicual Field, 'Habitus', Capital and 'Illusio'." *The Translator* 11: 147–166.

Grunwald, David. 2011. "Website Translation Using Post-Edited Machine Translation and Crowdsourcing." *W3C Workshop 2011*. Accessed March 2, 2016. http://videolectures.net/w3cworkshop2011_grunwald_translation/

Guerberof, Anna. 2009. *Productivity and Quality in Post-Editing of Outputs from Translation Memories and Machine Translation*. PhD Dissertation, Universitat Rovira i Virgili, Spain.

Guerberof, Anna. 2009. "Productivity and Quality in MT Post-editing." *Proceedings of MT Summit XII*, Ontario, Canada. Accessed March 2, 2016. http://www.l2f.inesc-id.pt/~fmmb/wiki/uploads/Work/dict.ref6.pdf

Gulati, Asheesh, Pierrette Bouillon, Johanna Gerlach, Victoria Porro and Violeta Seretan. 2015. "The ACCEPT Academic Portal: A User-Centred Online Platform for Pre-editing and Post-editing." *In Proceedings of the 7th International Conference of the Iberian Association of Translation and Interpreting Studies AIETI*, Malaga, Spain, January 23–25. Accessed March 2, 2016. http://www.accept.unige.ch/Products/AIETI-Gulati-al-2015.pdf

Hernandez Guerrero, Maria José. 2014. "Prosumidoras de traducciones: Aproximación al fenómeno de la traducción fan de novela romántica." *Revista Española de Lingüística Aplicada* 29: 88–114.

Gupta, Aakar *et al.* 2012. "mClerk: Enabling Mobile Crowdsourcing in Developing Regions." *Proceedings of CHI'12*, May 5–10, 2012, Austin, Texas, USA. Accessed July 23, 2016. http://www.cs.toronto.edu/~aakar/Publications/mClerk-CHI12.pdf doi:10.1145/2207676.2208320

Halliday, Michael. A. K. and Ruqaiya Hasan. 1976. *Cohesion in English*. London: Longman.

Halverson, Sandra. 1998. "Theory, Method and Object in Descriptive Translation Studies: Establishing a Link between Theoretical/Descriptive Categories, Corpora and a Conception of the Object of Study." *META* 43 (4): 494–514. doi:10.7202/003000ar

Halverson, Sandra. 2010. "Translation." In *Handbook of Translation Studies*, Vol I. Yves Gambier and Luc van Doorslaer (eds.), 378–384. Amsterdam-Philadelphia: John Benjamins. doi:10.1075/hts.1.tra2

Hanes, William F. 2011. "A Cultura do Fansubs sob o Olhar dos Estudos da Traduçao." *In-Traduçoes: revista do programa de pós-graduaçao em estudos da traduçao da UFSC* 11. Accessed March 2, 2016. http://periodicos.ufpb.br/ojs/index.php/ct/article/view/13022/7534

Harari, Yuval. 2015. *Sapiens: A Brief History of Humankind*. London: Harvill Secker.

Harris, Brian and Bianca Sherwood. 1978. "Translating as an Innate Skill." In *Language Interpretation and Communication*, David Gerber and H. Wallace Sinaiko (eds.), 155–170. Plenum: Oxford and New York 1978. doi:10.1007/978-1-4615-9077-4_15

Hatano, Giyoo and Kayoko Inagaki. 1986. "Two courses of expertise." In *Child development and education in Japan*, Harold Stevenson, Hiroshi Azuma and Kenji Hakuta (eds.), 262–272. New York: Freeman.

Hatim, Basil and Ian Mason. 1990. *Discourse and the Translator*. London – New York: Longman.

Hatim, Basil and Ian Mason. 1997. *The Translator as Communicator*. London: Routledge.

Hemmungs Wirtén, Eva. 2012. "Swedish Fansubbers Call Off Strike! Fan-to-Fan Piracy, Translation, and the Primacy of Authorization." In *Amateur Media: Social, Cultural and Legal Perspectives*, Dan Hunter, Ramon Lobato, Megan Richardson and Julian Thomas (eds.), 127–136. New York-London: Routledge.

Hermans, Theo. 1999. *Translation in Systems: Descriptive and Systemic Approaches Explained*. Manchester, England: St. Jerome.

Hermans, Theo. 2007. *The Conference of the Tongues*. Manchester: St. Jerome.

Hermans, Theo. 2013a. "What is not Translation?" In *Routledge Handbook of Translation Studies*, Carmen Millán-Varela and Federica Bartrina (ed.), 75–87. London: Routledge.

Hermans, Theo. 2013b. "Norms of Translation." *The Encyclopedia of Applied Linguistics*. Cambridge: Wiley. doi:10.1002/9781405198431.wbeal0873

Hernandez Guerrero, Maria Jose. 2014. "La traducción de letras de canciones en la web de aficionados Lyrics Translate.com." *Babel* 60: 91–108. doi:10.1075/babel.60.1.06her

Hertog, Erik. 2010 "Community Interpreting." In *Hanbook of Translation Studies*, vol. I, Yves Gambier and Luc van Doorslaer (eds.), 49–54. Amsterdam-Philadelphia: John Benjamins. doi:10.1075/hts.1.comm4

Heydel, Magda and Rybicki, Jan. 2012. "The Stylometry of Collaborative translation." *Digital Humanities 2012: Conference Abstracts*, 212–14. Hamburg: Hamburg University Press. Accessed March 2, 2016. http://www.dh2012.uni-hamburg.de/conference/programme/abstracts/the-stylometry-of-collaborative-translation/

Heyn, Maias. 1998. "Translation Memories: Insights and Prospects." In *Unity in Diversity? Current Trends in Translation Studies*, Lynne Bowker *et al.* (eds.), 123–136. Manchester: St. Jerome Publishing.

Hills, Matt. 2002. *Fan Cultures*. London: Routledge. doi:10.4324/9780203361337

Hodson, 2012. "Why Google Ingress is a data goldmine." *New Scientist*. Accessed March 2, 2016. https://www.newscientist.com/article/mg21628936-200-why-googles-ingress-game-is-a-data-gold-mine/

Hoey, Michael. 2005. *Lexical Priming. A New Theory of Words and Language*. London: Routledge.

Hokkanen, Sari. 2012. "Simultaneous Church Interpreting as Service." *The Translator* 182: 291–309. doi:10.1080/13556509.2012.10799512

Hollan, James, Edwin Hutchins and David Kirsh. 2000. "Distributed Cognition: Toward a New Foundation for Human-Computer Interaction Research." *ACM Transactions on Computer-Human Interaction TOCHI 72*, 174–196. Accessed March 2, 2016. https://www.lri.fr/~mbl/Stanford/CS477/papers/DistributedCognition-TOCHI.pdf

Holz-Mänttäri, Justa. 1984. *Translatorisches Handeln. Theorie und Methode*. Helsinki: Suomalainen Tiedeakatemia.

Hönig, Hans G. 1995. *Konstruktives Übersetzen. Studien zur Translation 1*. Tübingen: Stauffenburg.

Hönig, Hans G. 1998. "Positions, Power and Practice: Functionalist Approaches and Translation Quality Assessment." In *Translation and Quality*, Christina Schäffner (ed.), 6–34. Clevedon: Multilingual Matters.

Hönig, Hans G. 1990. "Sagen, was man nicht weiß – wissen was man nicht sagt. Überlegungen zur übersetzerischen Intuition." In *Übersetzungswissenschaft, Ergebnisse und Perspektiven, Festschrift für Wolfram Wilsszum 65*, Reiner Arntz and Gisela Thome (eds.), 152–161. Tübingen: Narr.

Horvath, Ildikó. 2016. "Volunteer Translation and Interpreting." In *The Modern Translator and Interpreter*, Ildikó Horvath (eds.), 139–150. Budapest: Eövös University Press.

House, Juliane. 1988. "Talking to Oneself or Thinking with Others? On Using Different Thinking Aloud Methods in Translation." *Fremdsprachen lehren und lernen* 17: 84–98.

House, Juliane. 1997. *Translation Quality Assessment: A Model Revisited*. Tübingen: Gunter Narr.

House, Juliane. 2001. "Translation Quality Assessment: Linguistic Description versus Social Evaluation." *META* 46(2): 243–257. doi:10.7202/003141ar

House, Juliane. 2013. "Quality in Translation Studies." In *Routledge Handbook of Translation Studies*, Carmen Millan and Franchesca Batrina (eds), 534–547. New York-London: Routledge.

House, Juliane. 2014. *Translation Quality Assessment: Past and Present*. London: Routledge. doi:10.1057/9781137025487.0017

Howe, Jeff. 2006. *Crowdsourcing: A Definition. Crowdsourcing: Tracking the Rise of the Amateur*. Accessed March 2, 2016. http://crowdsourcing.typepad.com/cs/2006/06/crowdsourcing_a.html

Howe, Jeff. 2008. *Crowdsourcing: Why the Power of the Crowd Is Driving the Future of Business.* New York: Crown Publishing Group.

Hsiao, Chi-Hua, 2014. *The Cultural Translation of US Television Programs and Movies: Subtitle Groups as Cultural Brokers in China.* Master's Dissertation, UCLA. Accessed March 2. 2016. http://escholarship.org/uc/item/9qt39009#page-2

Hu, Chang *et al.* 2011. " The Value of Monolingual Crowdsourcing in a Real-World Translation Scenario: Simulation using Haitian Creole Emergency SMS Messages." *Proceedings of the Sixth Workshop on Statistical Machine Translation.* Accessed March 2 2016. http://www. cs.umd.edu/hcil/monotrans/publications/wmt11monotrans.pdf

Hung, Eva. 1999. "The Role of the Foreign Translator in the Chinese Translation Tradition, 2nd to 19th Century." *Target* 11(2): 223–243. doi:10.1075/target.11.2.03hun

Hung, Eva 2006. "And the Translator Is __' Translators in Chinese History." In *Translating Others*, vol 1, Theo Hermans (ed.), 145–162. Manchester, St. Jerome Press.

Hung Eva and Pollard David. 1997. "The Chinese Tradition." In *The Routledge Encyclopedia of Translation Studies*, Mona Baker (ed.), 365–74. London and New York: Routledge.

Hurtado Albir, Amparo. 1999. *Enseñar a traducir : metodología en la formación de traductores e intérpretes.* Madrid: Edelsa.

Hurtado Albir, Amparo. 2001. *Traduccion y Traductología. Introducción a la traductología.* Madrid: Cátedra.

Hurtado Albir, Amparo *et al.* 2015. "A Retrospective and Prospective View of Translation Research from an Empirical, Experimental, and Cognitive Perspective: the TREC Network." *Translation and Interpreting* 7: 5–25. Accessed March 2, 2016. http://www.trans-int.org/ index.php/transint/article/view/343/181.

Hurtado Albir, A. (ed.) (forthcoming). *Researchig Translation Competence by PACTE Group.* Amsterdam: John Benjamins.

Hutchins, Edwin. 1995a. *Cognition in the Wild.* MIT press.

Hutchins, Edwin. 1995b. "How a Cockpit Remembers its Speeds." *Cognitive Science* 193: 265–288. doi:10.1207/s15516709cog1903_1

Hutchins, Edwin. 2010. "Cognitive Ecology." *Topics in Cognitive Science* 2 (4): 705–715. doi:10.1111/j.1756-8765.2010.01089.x

Hutchins, W. John. 1998. "The Origins of the Computer Workstation." *Machine Translation* 13: 287–307.

Hutchins, W. John. 2014. "Machine Translation: History and Applications." In *Routledge Encyclopedia of Translation Technology*, Sin-Wai Chan (ed.), 120–135. London: Routledge.

Inghilleri, Moira. 2005. "The Sociology of Bourdieu and the Construction of the 'Object' in Translation and Interpreting Studies." *The Translator: Special Issue. Bourdieu and the Sociology of Translation and Interpreting* 11: 125–145. doi:10.1080/13556509.2005.10799195

Inghilleri, Moira. 2009. "Sociological Approaches." In *Encyclopedia of Translation Studies*, Mona Baker and Gabriella Saldanha (eds.), 279–282. New York-London: Routledge.

Innocenti, Veronica and Alessandro Maestri. 2010. "Il lavoro dei fan. Il fansubbing come alternativa al doppiaggio ufficiale in The Big Bang Theory." In *Proceedings of MM2010. Le frontiere del "popolare" tra vecchi e nuovi media. Media Mutations. Convegno internazionale di studi sull'audiovisivo.* Accessed March 2, 2016. http://amsacta.unibo.it/3036/

Internetwoldstats. 2015. *World Internet Users and 2015 Population Stats.* Accessed March 2, 2016. http://www.internetworldstats.com/stats.htm

Ito, Mizuko *et al.* 2009. *Hanging Out, Messing Around and Geeking Out: Living and Learning with New Media.* Cambridge: MIT Press.

Izwaini, Sattar. 2014. "Amateur Translation in Arabic-Speaking Cyberspace." *Perspectives: Studies in Translatology* 22(1): 96–112. doi:10.1080/0907676X.2012.721378

Jääskeläinen, Riitta. 1989. "Translation Assignment in Professional vs. Non-professional Translation: A Think-aloud Protocol Study." In *The Translation Process*, Candace Seguinot (ed.), 87–98. Toronto: H.G. Publications.

Jääskeläinen, Riitta. 2010. "Are All Professionals Experts?: Definitions of Expertise and Reinterpretation of Research Evidence in Process Studies." In *Translation and Cognition*, Gregory Shreve and Erik Angelone (eds.), 213–227. Amsterdam-Philadelphia: John Benjamins. doi:10.1075/ata.xv.12jaa

Jääskeläinen, Riitta. 2011. "Studying the Translation Process." In *Oxford Handbook of Translation Studies*, Kirsten Malmkjaer and Kevin Windle (eds.), 123–135. Oxford: Oxford University Press.

Jääskeläinen, Riitta, Peka Kujamäki, and Mika Jukka. 2011. "Towards Professionalism – or against it?: Dealing with the Changing World in Translation Research and Translation Education." *Across Languages and Cultures* 12 (2): 143–156. doi:10.1556/Acr.12.2011.2.1

Jääskeläinen, Riitta, and Sonja Tirkkonen-Condit. 1991. "Automatised Processes in Professional vs. Non-professional Translation: A Think-aloud Protocol Study." In *Empirical Research in Translation and Intercultural Studies: Selected Papers of the TRANSIF Seminar, Savonnlinna 1988*, Sonja Tirkkonen-Condit (ed.), 89–110. Tubingen: Narr.

Jakab, František, Jozef Janitor, Ján Genči, Karol Kniewald, Michal Nagy, and Vladimir Sidimak. 2008. "Communit-Based Translation of eLearning Materials." *Acta Electrotechnica et Informatica* 8: 64–71.

Jakobsen, Arnt Lykke. 2003. "Effects of Think Aloud on Translation Speed, Revision and Segmentation." In *Looking at eyes. Eye-tracking Studies of Reading and Translation Processing*, Fabio Alves (ed.), 69–95. Amsterdam/Philadelphia: Benjamins.

Jakobsen, Arnt Lykke. 2005 "Investigating Expert Translators' Processing Knowledge." In *Knowledge Systems and Translation*, Hell V. Dam, Jan Engberg and Heidrum Gerzymisch-Arbogast (eds.), 173–189. Berlin-New York: Mouton de Gruyter. doi:10.1515/9783110924305.173

Jansen, Dean, Aleli Alcala and Francisco Guzman. 2014. "Amara: A Sustainable, Global Solution for Accessibility, Powered by Communities of Volunteers." *Universal Access in Human-Computer Interaction. Design for All and Accessibility Practice Lecture Notes in Computer Science* 8516: 401–411. Accessed March 2, 2016. doi:10.1007/978-3-319-07509-9_38

Jenkins, Henry. 1992. *Textual Poachers: Television Fans and Participatory Culture*. New York: Routledge.

Jenkins, Henry. 2002. "*Interactive Audiences*." In *The New Media Book*, Dan Harries (ed.), 151–170. London: BFI.

Jenkins, Henry. 2006a. *Convergence Culture: Where Old and New Media Collide*. New York: New York University Press.

Jenkins, Henry. 2006b. *Fans, Bloggers, and Gamers: Exploring Participatory Culture*. New York: NYU Press.

Jenkins, Henry *et al.* 2006. "Confronting the Challenges of Participatory Cultures." *The John D. and MacArthur Foundation Reports on Digital Media and Learning*. MIT. Accesed March 2, 2016. https://mitpress.mit.edu/sites/default/files/titles/free_download/9780262513623_Confronting_the_Challenges.pdf

Jensen, Anne. 1999. "Time pressure in translation." In *Probing the Process in Translation. Methods and Results*, Gyde Hansen (ed.), 103–119. Copenhagen: Samfundslitteratur.

Jiménez-Crespo, Miguel A. 2009. "Conventions in Localisation: A Corpus Study of Original vs. Translated Web Texts." *Jostrans: The Journal of Specialized Translation* 12: 79–102. Accessed March 2, 2016. http://www.jostrans.org/issue12/art_jimenez.pdf.

Jiménez-Crespo, Miguel A. 2010. "The Intersection of Localization and Translation: A Corpus Study of Spanish Original and Localized Web Forms." *TIS:Translation and Interpreting Studies* 52: 186–207. doi:10.1075/tis.5.2.03jim

Jiménez-Crespo, Miguel A. 2011. "To Adapt or not to Adapt in Web Localization: A Contrastive Genre-based Study of Original and Localized Legal Sections in Corporate Websites." *Jostrans: The Journal of Specialized Translation* 15: 2–27.

Jiménez-Crespo, Miguel A. 2013a. *Translation and Web Localization*. New York-London: Routledge.

Jiménez-Crespo, Miguel A. 2013b. "Crowdsourcing, Corpus Use, and the Search for Translation Naturalness: A Comparable Corpus Study of Facebook and Non-Translated Social Networking Sites." *TIS: Translation and Interpreting Studies* 8: 23–49. doi:10.1075/tis.8.1.02jim

Jiménez-Crespo, Miguel A. 2014. "Beyond Prescription: What Empirical Studies are Telling us about Localization Crowdsourcing." In *Proceedings of Translation and the Computer 36*, 27–35. Accessed March 2, 2016. http://www.mt-archive.info/10/Asling-2014-Jiménez-Crespo.pdf.

Jiménez-Crespo, Miguel A. 2015a. "Volunteer and Collaborative Translation." In *Researching Translation and Interpreting*, Claudia Angelelli and Brian Baer (eds.), 58–70. London-New York: Routledge.

Jiménez-Crespo, Miguel A. 2015b. "The Internet in Translation Education: Two Decades Later." *TIS: Translation and Interpreting Studies* 10: 33–57. doi:10.1075/tis.10.1.03jim

Jiménez-Crespo, Miguel A. 2016. "Testing Explicitation in Translation: Triangulating Corpus and Experimental Studies." *Across Languages and Cultures* 16(2): 257–283. doi:10.1556/084.2015.16.2.6

Jiménez-Crespo, Miguel A. and Maribel Tercedor. 2012. "Applying Corpus Data to Define Needs in Localization Training." *META* 58 (2): 998–1021.

Jiménez-Crespo, Miguel A. and Nitish Singh (2016). "Translation Studies and the Web: TS and International Business and Marketing." In *Border Crossing: Transdiciplinarity in Translation Studies*, Yves Gambier (ed.), 245–262. Amsterdam-Philadelphia: John Benjamins.

Kageura, Kyo, Takeshi Abekawa, Masao Utiyama, Miori Sagara, and Sumita Eiichiro. 2011. "Has Translation Gone Online and Collaborative?: An Experience from Minna no Hon'yaku." *Linguistica Antverpiensia* 10: 45–74.

Kaminka, Ika and Anna Zelinska-Elliot. 2014. "All Together Now: Collaboration between European Translation of Haruki Murakami." *Paper presented at Conference La Traduction Collaborative de L'Antiqueté à Internet*, Paris, France, 5th, 6th, 7th June, 2014.

Kaptelinin, Viktor and Bonnie A. Nardi. 2006. *Acting with Technology: Activity Theory and Interaction Design*. Cambridge: MIT Press.

Kaptelinin, Viktor and Bonnie A. Nardi. 2012. *Activity Theory in HCI: Fundamentals and Reflections*. San Francisco, CA: Morgan and Claypool.

Karamitroglou, Fotios. 2000. *Towards a Methodoolgy for the Investigation of Norms in Audiovisual Translation*. Amsterdam: Rodopi.

Katan, David. 2015. "Overcoming Cultural Barriers to Access through Abusive Subtitling and Transcreation." Paper presented at *6th International Conference Media for All*, University of Western Sydney, Sydney, Australia, 16th-18th, July, 2015.

Kay, Martin. 1980. " The Proper place of Men and Machines in Language Translation." *Research Report CSL-80–11, Xerox PARC, Palo Alto, USA. Reprinted in Machine Translation* 12 (1997): 3–23.

Kelly, Dorothy. 2005. *Handbook for Translation Trainers*. Manchester: St. Jerome.

Kelly, Natalie and Jost Zetzsche. 2012. *Found in Translation*. New York: Perigee Books.

Kelly, Natalie. 2009. *Freelance Translators Clash with LinkedIn over Crowdsourced translators*. Accessed March 2, 2016. At http://www.commonsenseadvisory.com/Default. aspx?Contenttype=ArticleDetAD&tabID=63&Aid=591&moduleId=391

Kelly, Nataly, Rebeca Ray and Donald DePalma. 2011. "From Crawling to Sprinting: Community Translation goes Mainstream." *Linguistica Antverpiensia* 10:45–76.

Kenny, Dorothy. 2009. "Unit of Translation." In *Routledge Encyclopedia of Translation Studies*, Mona Baker and Gabriela Saldanha (eds.), 304–306. New York-London: Routledge.

Kenny, Dorothy. 2011a. "Translation Units and Corpora." In *Corpus-based Translation Studies: Research and Applications*, Alet Kruger, Kim Wallmach and Jeremy Munday, (eds.), 76–102. London: Continuum.

Kenny, Dorothy. 2011b. "The Ethics of Machine Translation." Paper presented at the *New Zealand Society of Translators and Interpreters Annual Conference* 2011, 4–5. Accessed March 20, 2016. http://doras.dcu.ie/17606/1/The_Ethics_of_Machine_Translation_pre-final_version.pdf

Khalaf, Abed Shahooth, Sabariah Md Rashid, Muhd Fauzi Jumingan, and Muhd Suki Othman. 2015. "Problems in amateur subtitling of English movies into Arabic." *Malaysian Journal of Languages and Linguistics* 3: 38–55.

Kim, Mia. 2008. "Readability Analysis of Community Translation: A Systemic Functional approach." *Forum: International Journal of Interpretation and Translation* 6: 105–135. Accessed March 2, 2016. http://www.journals.mymla.org/index.php/MJLL/article/view/21/21.

Kinnunen, Tuija and Kaisa Koskinen (eds.). 2010. *Translators' Agency*. Tampere: Tampere University Press.

Kiraly, Donald. 1995. *Pathways to Translation. Pedagogy and Process*. Kent, London: Kent State University Press.

Kiraly, Don. 2000. *A Social Constructivist Approach to Translator Education – Empowerment from Theory to Practice*. Manchester: St Jerome.

Kiraly, Don. 2012. "Growing a Project-Based Translation Pedagogy: A Fractal Perspective." *META* 57: 82–95. doi:10.7202/1012742ar

Kiraly, Don. 2015. "Occasioning Translator Competence: Moving beyond Social Constructivism toward a Postmodern Alternative to Instructionism." *TIS: Translation and Interpreting Studies* 10:8–32. doi:10.1075/tis.10.1.02kir

Koehn, Philipp. 2010. "Enabling Monolingual Translators: Post-editing vs. Options." In *Proceedings of NAACL HLT 2010: Human Language Technologies: The 2010 Annual Conference of the North American Chapter of the Association for Computational Linguistics*, 537–545. Accessed March 2, 2016. http://aclweb.org/anthologynew/N/N10/N10-1078.pdf

Koponen, Marit and Leena Salmi. 2015. "On the Correctness of Machine Translation: A Machine Translation Post-Editing Task." *Jostrans* 23: 118–136. Accessed March 2, 2016. http://www.jostrans.org/issue23/art_koponen.pdf.

Koskinen, Kaisa. 2004. "Shared Culture? Reflections on Recent Trends in Translation Studies." *Target* 16: 143–156.

Kozinets, Robert V. 2010. *Netnography: Doing Ethnographic Research Online*. London: SAGE.

Krings, Hans P. 1986. "Translation Problems and Translation Strategies of Advanced German learners of French." In *Interlingual and intercultural communication*, Julianne House and Shoshana Blum-Kulka (eds.), 263–75. Tubingen: Gunter Narr.

Krings, Hans P. 1995. *Texte reparieren. Empirische Untersuchungen zum Prozeß der Nachredaktion von Maschinenübersetzungen. Habilitationsschrift.* Hildesheim: Universität Hildesheim.

Kumaran, A K Saravanan and Sandor Maurice. 2008. "WikiBABEL: Community Creation of Multilingual Data." In *Proceedings of the 4th International Symposium on Wikis*. ACM, New York. Accessed March 2, 2016. http://dl.acm.org/citation.cfm?id=1822277 doi:10.1145/1822258.1822277

Kussmal, Paul. 1995. *Training the Translator.* Amsterdam: John Benjamins. doi:10.1075/btl.10

Lachat Leal, Cristina. 2003. *Estrategias y problemas de traducción.* PhD Thesis. University of Granada, Spain.

Lacruz, Isabel. 2014. "Cognates as a Window into the Translator's Mind." In *The Development of Translation Competence: Theories and Methodologies from Psycholinguistics and Cognitive Science*, John Schwieter and Aline Ferreira (eds.), 287–314. Newcastle: Cambridge Scholars Publishing.

Lafeber, Anne. 2012. "Translation Skills and Knowledge – Preliminary Findings of a Survey of Translators and Revisers Working at Inter-governmental Organizations." *META* 57: 108–131. doi:10.7202/1012744ar

Lakhani, Karim R. and Robert G. Wolf. 2005. "Why Hackers do what They do: Understanding Motivation and Effort in Free/Open Source Software Projects." In *Perspectives in Free and Open Source Software*, Joseph Feller, Brian Fitzgerald, Scott Hissam, and Karim Lakhani (eds.), 3–22. Cambridge: MIT.

Larose, Robert. 1998. "Méthodologie de l'évaluation des traductions." *META* 43: 163–186. doi:10.7202/003410ar

Laukanen, Johanna. 1997. "Affective and Attitudinal Factors in Translation Processes." *Target* 82: 257–274.

Lave, Jean. 1988. *Cognition in Practice.* Cambridge: Cambridge University Press. doi:10.1017/CBO9780511609268

Laviosa, Sara. 2002. *Corpus-based Translation Studies.* Amsterdam: Rodopi.

Leadbeater, Charles and Paul Miller. 2004. *The Pro-Am Revolution: How Enthusiasts are Changing Our Society and Economy.* New York: USA Demos. Accessed August 16, 2006. https://www.demos.co.uk/files/proamrevolutionfinal.pdf

Lee, Hye-Kyung. 2010. "Cultural Consumers and Copyright: A Case Study of Anime Fansubbing." *Creative Industries Journal* 33: 235–250.

Lee, Hye-Kyung. 2011. "Participatory Media Fandom: A Case Study of Anime Fansubbing." *Media, Culture & Society* 338: 1131–1147. doi:10.1177/0163443711418271

Lee, Mimi M., Lin Meng-Feng and Curtis J. Bonk 2007. "OOPS, Turning MIT OpenCourseWare into Chinese: An Analysis of a Community of Practice of Global Translators." *International Review of Research in Open and Distance Learning*, 83. Accessed March 2, 2016. http://www.irrodl.org/index.php/irrodl/article/view/463/982

Leonard, Sean. 2005. "Progress Against the Law: Anime and Fandom, with the Key to the Globalization of Culture." *International Journal of Cultural Studies* 3: 281–305. doi:10.1177/1367877905055679

Leontiev, Aleksej. 1978/1987. *Activity, Consiousness, and Personality.* Englewood Cliffs: Prentice Hall.

Letawe, Celine. 2014. "Günter Gras et ses Traducteurs: de la Dynamique collaborative au Dispositif de Controle?" Paper presented at *Conference La Traduction Collaborative de L'Antiqueté à Internet*, Paris, France, 5th-7th June, 2014.

Levy, Pierre. 1997. *Collective Intelligence*. New York: Basic Books.

LISA. 2007. *LISA Globalization Industry Primer*. Romainmôtier, Switzerland: Localization Industry Standards Association.

Lewis, David. 1969. *Convention. A Philosophical Study*. Cambridge, MA: Harvard University Press.

Liu, Xiao. 2014. *Apprentissage dans une communauté de pratique : fansubbing et compétence linguistique*. Masters Thesis, Universite de Montreal, Canada.

Liu, Yefeng, Lehdonvirta, Vili, Alexandrova, Todorka and Tatsuo Nakajima. 2012. "Drawing on Mobile Crowds via Social Media. Case UbiAsk: Image Based Mobile Social Search across Languages." *Multimedia Systems* 18 (1): 53–67. doi:10.1007/s00530-011-0242-0

Lommel, Arle *et al.* 2014. "Multidimensional Quality Metrics MQM: A Framework for Declaring and Describing Translation Quality Metrics." *Tradumatica* 12: 455–463. Accessed March 2, 2016. http://revistes.uab.cat/tradumatica/article/view/n12-lommel-uzskoreit-burchardt/pdf.

Lommel *et al.* 2015. "Quality Translation 21 D3.1: Harmonised Metric." *QT 21 Consortium*. Accessed July 30, 2016. http://www.qt21.eu/wp-content/uploads/2015/11/QT21-D3-1.pdf

Long, Lynne. 2013. –The Translation of Sacred Texts." In *The Routledge Handbook of Translation Studies*, Carmen Millan and Francesca Batrina (eds.), 464–476. New York-London: Routledge.

Lopez, Clara Ines and Maribel Tercedor. 2009. "Corpora and Students' Autonomy in Scientific and Technical Translation Trainin." *Jostrans: The Journal of Specialized Translation* 9: 2–19. Accessed March 2, 2016. http://jostrans.org/issue09/art_lopez_tercedor.pdf.

Lörcher, Wolfgang, 1991. *Translation Performance, Translation Process, and Translation Strategies Investigation*. Tübingen: Gunter Narr.

Lorenz, Jan *et al.* (2011). "How Social Influence Can Undermine the Wisdom of the Crowd." *Proceedings of the National Academy of the Sciences* 108: 9020–9025. doi:10.1073/pnas.1008636108

Luczaj, Kamil, Magdalena Holy-Luczaj and Karolina Cwiek-Rogalska. 2014. "Fansubbers. The case of the Czech Republic and Poland." *COMPASO* 52: 175–198. Accessed March 2, 2016. http://compaso.eu/wpd/wp-content/uploads/2015/02/Compaso2014-52-Luczaj-et-al.pdf

Ludewild, Kathleen. 2014. "Crowdsourcing Video Translations for a Global Network for Health Education." *Poster Presentation, Medical Education Day*, 2014. Accessed March 2, 2016. http://open.umich.edu/sites/default/files/2014_04-mededday-poster-translation-final.pdf

Lyons, Erin. "Far from the Maddening Crowd: Integrating Collaborative Translation Technologies into Healthcare Services in the Developing World." In *Proceedings from Translation and the Computer 36*. Accessed March 2, 2016. http://www.mt-archive.info/10/Asling-2014-Lyons.pdf

Macklovitch, Elliot and Graham Russell. 2002. "What's Been Forgotten in Translation Memory." In *Envisioning Translation Memory in the Information Future: Proceedings of the AMTA 2000*, John S. White (ed.), 137–146. Berlin: Springer Verlang.

Maher, Brigid. 2014. "The Mysterious Case of Theory and Practice: Crime Fiction and Collaborative Translation." *JosTrans – The Journal of Specialised Translation* 22: 132–146. Accessed March 2, 2016. http://www.jostrans.org/issue22/art_maher.pdf.

Mahmud, Farahidayah and Hazleen Aris. 2015. "State of Mobile Crowdsourcing Applications: A Review." *Proceedings of the Software Engineering and Computer Systems ICSECS*, 2015, 27–32. doi:10.1109/ICSECS.2015.7333118

Malmkjaer, Kirsten. 2013. "Where are We? From Holmes Map until Now." In *Routledge Handbook of Translation Studies*, Carmen Millán-Varela and Federica Bartrina (eds.), 31–44. London: Routledge.

Mangiron, Carme. 2013. "Subtitling in Game Localisation: a Descriptive Study." *Perspectives* 211: 42–56. doi:10.1080/0907676X.2012.722653

Mareschal, Geneviève. 2005. "L'enseignement de la traduction au Canada." *META: journal des traducteurs / Meta: Translators' Journal* 50 (1): 250–262. doi:10.7202/010672ar

Martín de León, Celia. 2008. "Translation in the Wild: Traductología y cognición situada." In *La traducción del futuro: mediación lingüística y cultural en el siglo XXI. Vol II. La traducción y su entorno*, Luis Pegenaute, Janet DeCesaris, Merce Tricás y Elisenda Bernal (eds.), 55–64. Barcelona: PPU.

Martin, James R. 1995. "Text and Clause: Fractal Resonance." *Text* 15: 5–42.

Martínez-Gómez, Aída. 2015. "Non-Professional Interpreters." In *The Routledge Handbook of Interpreting*, Holy Mikkelson and Renee Jourdenais (Eds.), 417–431. New York: Routledge.

Martínez Melis, Nicole and Amparo Hurtado Albir. 2001. "Assessment in Translation Studies: Research Needs." *META* 46 (2): 272–287. doi:10.7202/003624ar

Massey, Gary. 2005. "Process-Oriented Translator Training and the Challenge for E-Learning." *META* 50 2: 626–633. doi:10.7202/011006ar

Massey, Gary and Maureen Ehrensberger-Dow. 2011. "Investigating Information Literacy: A Growing Priority in Translation Studies." *Across Languages and Cultures* 12 (2): 193–211. doi:10.1556/Acr.12.2011.2.4

Massey, Gary and Barbara Brändli. 2016. "Collaborative Feedback Flows and How we Can Learn from them: Investigating a Synergetic Learning Experience in Translator Education." In *Towards authentic experiential learning in translator education*, Don Kiraly et al. (eds.), 177–199. Göttingen: V&R unipress/Mainz University Press.

Massidda, Serenella. 2015. *Audiovisual Translation in the Digital Age: The Italian Fansubbing Phenomenon*. London: Palgrave McMillan. doi:10.1057/9781137470379

Matielo, Raquel and Elaine Espindola. 2011 "Domestication and Foreignization: an Analysis of Culture-Specific Items in Official and Non-Official Subtitles of the TV Series Heroes." *Cadernos de Tradução* 271: 71–93.

McClarty, Rebecca. 2012. "Towards a Multidisciplinary Approach in Creative Subtitling." *MonTI* 4 2012: 133–153. http://rua.ua.es/dspace/bitstream/10045/26944/1/MonTI_04_07.pdf

McConnel, Brian. 2008. "Accidental Translation: Creating A Global Translation Community." *Worldwide Lexicon Blog*, July 26, 2008. Accessed March 2, 2016. http://blog.dermundo.com/original/9468.html

McDonough-Dolmaya, Julie. 2007. "How Do Language Professionals Organize Themselves? An Overview of Translation Networks." *META* 52 4: 793–815. doi:10.7202/017697ar

McDonough-Dolmaya, Julie. 2011a. "The Ethics of Crowdsourcing." *Linguistica Antverpiensia* 10: 97–111.

McDonough-Dolmaya, Julie. 2011b. "Moral Ambiguity: Some Shortcomings of Professional Codes of Ethics for Translators." *Jostrans* 15: 28–49.

McDonough-Dolmaya, Julie. 2012. "Analyzing the Crowdsourcing Model and its Impact on Public Perceptions of Translation." *The Translator* 182: 167–191. doi:10.1080/13556509.2012.10799507

McDonough-Dolmaya, Julie. 2015 "Revision history: Translation trends in Wikipedia." *Translation Studies* 8 (1): 16–34. doi:10.1080/14781700.2014.943279

Meier, Patricia and Robert Munro. 2010. "The Unprecedented Role of SMS in Disaster Response: Learning from Haiti." *SAIS Review of International Affairs* 30 2: 91–103. Accessed March 2, 2016. https://courses.cs.washington.edu/courses/cse490d/13wi/ClassMaterials/papers/meier_munro.pdf.

Melby, Alan. 1995. *The Possibility of Language: a Discussion of the Nature of Language.* Amsterdam-Philadelphia: John Benjamins. doi:10.1075/btl.14

Melby, Alan. 1981. "Translators and Machines: Can they Cooperate?" *META* 26: 23–34. doi:10.7202/003619ar

Mellinger, Christopher. 2014. *Computer-Assisted Translation: An Empirical Investigation of Cognitive Effort.* PhD Thesis. University of Kent, USA.

Mellinger, Christopher. 2015. "On the Applicability of Internet-mediated Research Methods to Investigate Translators' Cognitive Behaviour." *Translation and Interpreting* 71: 59–71.

Mesipuu, Maarit. 2012. "Translation Crowdsourcing and User-Translator Motivation at Facebook and Skype." *Translation Spaces* 1: 33–53. doi:10.1075/ts.1.03mes

Metz, Cade 2007. "Web 3.0." *PC magazine.* Accessed July 24, 2016, http://www.academia.edu/download/3467947/web_3.pdf

Meylaerts, Reine. 2008. "Translators and (Their) Norms: Towards a Sociological Construction of the Individual." In Anthony Pym, Miriam Shlesinger and Daniel Simeoni (eds.), *Beyond Descriptive Translation Studies*, 91–102. Amsterdam-Philadelphia: John Benjamins. doi:10.1075/btl.75.08mey

Mikkelson, Holy. 2013. "Community Interpreting." In *Routledge Handbook of Translation Studies*, Carmen Millán-Varela and Francesca Bartrina (ed.), 389–401. London: Routledge.

Miloševski, Tanja. 2013. "Habla oral en los subtítulos televisivos y los subtítulos de aficionados: el caso de la traducción de la serie Los Serrano del español al serbio." *Sendebar* 24: 73–88.

Mitchell, Linda, Johann Roturier and Sharon O'Brien 2013. "Community-Based Post-editing of Machine-Translated Content: Monolingual vs. Bilingual." *Workshop Proceedings: Workshop on Post-editing Technology and Practice WPTP-2*, 35–44. Accessed March 2, 2016. http://www.accept.unige.ch/Products/2013_wptp2_wp7.pdf.

Mitchell, Linda, Sharon O'Brien and Johann Roturier. 2014. "Quality Evaluation in Community Post-editing." *Machine Translation* 28:237–262 doi:10.1007/s10590-014-9160-1

Mitchell, Linda. 2015. *Community Post-Editing of Machine-Translated User-Generated Content.* PhD thesis, Dublin City University, Ireland.

Moorkens, Joss, Stephen Doherty, Dorothy Kenny and Sharon O'Brien. 2013. "A Virtuous Circle: Laundering Translation Memory Data Using Statistical Machine Translation." *Perspectives: Studies in Translatology* 22(3): 291–303. doi:10.1080/0907676X.2013.811275

Morera-Mesa, Aram. 2014. *Crowdsourced Translation Practices from the Process Flow Perspective.* Phd Dissertation. University of Limerick, Ireland.

Morera-Mesa, Aram, John J. Collins and David Filip. 2014. "Selected Crowdsourced Translation Practices." *Proceedings of ASLIB Translating and the Computer 35.* Accessed March 2, 2016. http://www.mt-archive.info/10/Aslib-2013-Morera-Mesa.pdf.

Morera-Mesa, Aram, Lamine Aoudad and J.J. Collins. 2012. "Assessing Support for Community Workflows in Localisation." *Business Process Management Workshops, Series Lecture Notes in Business Information Processing* 99: 195–206. doi:10.1007/978-3-642-28108-2_20

Mossop, Brian. 2005. "What Practitioners Can Bring to Theory? – The Good and the Bad." In *On the Relationships between Translation Theory and Translation Practice*, Peeters (ed.) 23-28. Frankfurt am Mein: Peter Lang.

Mossop, Brian. 2006 "How computerization has changed translation." *META* 51: 777–793. doi:10.7202/014342ar

Mossop, Brian. 2007. *Revising and Editing for Translators*. Manchester: St. Jerome.

Mossop, Brian. 2012. "Revision." In *Handbook of Translation Studies, Volume 2*, Yves Gambier and Luc van Doorslaer (eds.), 135–139. Amsterdam-Philadelphia: John Benjamins.

Muchnik, Lev, Sinan Aral, and Sean Taylor. 2013. "Social Influence Bias: A Randomized Experiment." *Science* 341: 647–651. doi:10.1126/science.1240466

Müller-Birn, Claudia, Leonhard Dobusch and Jim Herbsleb. 2015. "Work-to-Rule: The Emergence of Algorithmic Governance in Wikipedia." In *Proceedings of C&T '13. Munich, Germany*, 80–89. Accessed March 2, 2016. http://www.iisi.de/fileadmin/IISI/upload/C_T/2013/ct2013_proceedings_S3-1_Mueller_Dobusch_Herbsleb.pdf.

Munday, Jeremy. 2008. *Introducing Translation Studies*. New York-London: Routledge.

Muñoz, Ricardo. 2009. "Expertise and Environment in Translation." *Mutatis Mutandis* 2: 24–37.

Muñoz, Ricardo. 2010a. "On Paradigms and Cognitive Translatology." In *Translation and Cognition*, Gregory M. Shreve, and Erik Angelone (eds.), 169–187. Amsterdam-Philadelphia: John Benjamins. doi:10.1075/ata.xv.10mun

Muñoz, Ricardo. 2010b. "Leave no Stone Unturned. On the Development of Cognitive Translatoloy." *TIS Translation and Interpreting Studies* 5 (2):145–162. doi:10.1075/tis.5.2.01mun

Muñoz, Ricardo. 2013 "More than a Way with Words: The Interface between Cognitive Linguistics and Cognitive Translatology." In *Cognitive Linguistics and Translation. Advances in Some Theoretical Models and Applications*, Ana M. Rojo López and Iraide Ibarretxe-Antuñano (eds.), 75–94. Berlin: Mouton de Gruyter. doi:10.1515/9783110302943.75

Muñoz, Ricardo. 2014a. "A Blurred Snapshot of Advances in Translation Process Research." *MonTI Special Issue – Minding Translation* 2014: 49–84.

Muñoz, Ricardo. 2014b. "Situating Translation Expertise: A Review with a Sketch of a Construct." In *The Development of Translation Competence: Theories and Methodologies from Psycholinguistics and Cognitive Science*, Jonh Schwieter and Aline Ferreira (eds.), 2–22. Cambridge: Cambridge Scholars Publishing.

Muñoz Sánchez, Pablo. 2008. "En torno a la localización de videojuegos clásicos mediante técnicas de romhacking: particularidades, calidad y aspectos legales." *Jostrans* 9: 80–95. Accessed March 2, 2016. http://www.jostrans.org/issue09/art_munoz_sanchez.pdf.

Muñoz Sánchez, Pablo. 2009. "Video Game Localisation for Fans by Fans: the Case of Romhacking." *Journal of Internationalization and Localization* 1: 168–185. doi:10.1075/jial.1.07mun

Munro, Rob. 2010. "Crowdsourced Translation for Emergency Response in Haiti: the Global Collaboration of Local Knowledge." *AMTA Workshop on Collaborative Crowdsourcing for Translation*. Accessed March 2, 2016. http://www.mt-archive.info/AMTA-2010-Munro.pdf.

Munro, Rob. 2013. "Translation and Crowdsourcing." Accessed March 2, 2016. http://idibon.com/translation-and-crowdsourcing/

Murata, Toshiki, Mihoko Kitamura, Fukui Tsuyoshi and Tatsuya Sukehiro 2003. "Implementation of Collaborative Translation Environment 'Yakushite Net'." *MT Summit, IX*, 479–482. Accessed March 4, 2016. http://www.mt-archive.info/MTS-2003-Murata.pdf.

Muzii, Luigi. 2009. "Community, Collaborative, Social: will the Language Industry Survive Crowdsourcing?" *IALB-ASTTI XXXIV Annual Conference*. Accessed March 4, 2016. http://www.slideshare.net/muzii/surviving-crowdsourcing-2473146.

Muzii, Luigi. 2013. "Is Quality Under Pressure? Or Is Translation?" *TMT Conference*. 2013. Accessed March 4, 2016. http://www.slideshare.net/muzii/pressure-text.

Mychalak, Krzyzstof. 2015. "Online Localization of Zoouniverse Citizen Science Project: on the Use of Translation Platforms as Tools for Translation Education." *Teaching English with Technology* 15: 61–70. Accessed March 4, 2016. http://yadda.icm.edu.pl/yadda/element/bwmeta1.element.desklight-32a1582e-2f8d-412c-80c6-d6d03086424d.

Narula, Prayag, Gutheim, Philipp, Rolnitzky, David, Kulkarni, Anand and Bjoern Hartmann. 2011. "MobileWorks: A Mobile Crowdsourcing Platform for Workers at the Bottom of the Pyramid." In *Proceedings of the AAAI Workshop on Human Computation (HCOMP '11)*, 121–123. Accessed July 23, 2016. https://www.aaai.org/ocs/index.php/WS/AAAIW11/paper/download/3962/4263.

Neather, Robert. 2015. "Modes of Collaboration and Learning in a Buddhist Volunteer Translation Community: the Buddhist Texts Translation Society as a Community of Practice." Paper presented at the *5th IATIS Conference*, Bello Horizonte, Brazil, 6th-10th, July, 2015.

Neubert, Albert. 1997. "Textlinguistics of Translation: the Textual Approach to Translation". In *Translation Perspectives*, Mary Gladdis Rose (ed.), 87–106. Binghamton: State University of New York.

Neubert, Albert. 2000. "Competence in Language, Languages, and in Translation." In *Developing Translation Competence*, Christina Schäffner and Beverly Adab (eds.), 3–18. Amsterdam-Philadelphia: John Benjamins.

Neubert, Albrecht and Gregory M. Shreve. 1992. *Translation as Text*. Kent: Kent State University Press.

Neunzig, Wilhelm and Helena Tanqueiro. 2005. "Teacher Feedback in Online Education for Trainee Translators." *META* 50 (4): doi:10.7202/019873ar

Newmark, Peter. 1998. *More Paragraphs on Translation*. Buffalo: Multilingual Matters.

Newmark, Peter. 2003. "No Global Communication without Translation." In *Translation Today: Trends and Perspectives*, Gunilla Anderman and Michael Rogers (eds.), 55–68. Translation Buffalo: Multilingual Matters.

Nida, Eugene. 1964. *Towards a Science of Translation*. Leiden: Brill.

Nida, Eugene and Charles R. Taber. 1969. *The Theory and Practice of Translation*. Leiden: Brill.

Nielsen, Jakob. 1999. "Top ten mistakes revisited." *Alertbox by the Norman Nielsen Group*. Accessed July 20, 2016. http://www.useit.com/alertbox/990502.html.

Nielsen, Jakob. 2006. "The 90-9-1 Rule for Participation Inequality in Social Media and Online Communities". *Alertbox by the Norman Nielsen Group*. Accessed July 20th, 2016. https://www.nngroup.com/articles/participation-inequality/

Nobs, Marie L. 2006. *La traducción de folletos turísticos: ¿Qué calidad demandan los turistas*. Granada: Comares.

Nord, Christiane. 1991. *Text Analysis in Translation: Theory, Methodology and Didactic Application of a Model for Translation-Oriented Text Analysis*. Amsterdam-Atlanta: Rodopi.

Nord, Chistiane. 1997. *Functionalist Approaches Explained*. Manchester: St. Jerome.

Nord, Christiane *et al.* 2015. "Socio Cultural and Technical Issues in Non-Expert Dubbing: A Case Study." *International Journal of Society, Culture & Language* 32: 1–16. Accessed March 4, 2016. http://www.ijscl.net/article_11734_1980.html.

Nornes, Abe Mark. 1999. "For an Abusive Subtitling." *Film Quarterly* 523: 7–33.

Nornes, Abe Mark. 2007. *Cinema Babel: Translating Global Cinema*. Minneapolis: University of Minnesota Press.

O'Brien, Sharon. 2006. *Machine Translatability and Post-Editing Effort: An Empirical Study Using Translog and Choice Network Analysis*. PhD Thesis. Dublin City University, Ireland.

O'Brien, Sharon. 2007. "Pauses as Indicators of Cognitive Effort in Post-Editing Machine Translation Output." *Across Languages and Cultures* 7:1–21 doi:10.1556/Acr.7.2006.1.1

O'Brien, Sharon. 2008. "Processing fuzzy matches in translation memory tools: an eye-track-inganalysis." In *Looking at eyes. Eye-tracking Studies of Reading and Translation Processing*, Susanne Göpferich, Arnt Lykke Jakobsen, Inger M. Mees (eds.), 79–102. Copenhagen: Samfundslitteratur.

O'Brien, Sharon. 2011a. "Collaborative Translation." In *Routledge Handbook of Translation Studies*, Vol 2. Carmen Millán Verela and Francesca Bartrina (eds.), 17–20. London: Routledge. doi:10.1075/hts.2.col1

O'Brien, Sharon. 2011b. "Towards Predicting Post Editing Productivity." *Machine Translation* 25: 197–215. doi:10.1007/s1059001190967

O'Brien, Sharon. 2012a. "Towards a Dynamic Quality Evaluation Model for Translation." *Jostrans* 17: 55–77. Accessed March 4th, 2016. http://www.jostrans.org/issue17/art_obrien.pdf.

O'Brien, Sharon. 2012b. "Translation as Human-Computer Interaction." *Translation Spaces* 1: 101–122. doi:10.1075/ts.1.05obr

O'Brien, Sharon. 2016. "Training Translators for Crisis Communication: Translators Without Borders as an Example." In *Mediating Emergencies and Conflicts*, Federico M. Federici (ed.), 85–111. London: Palgrave McMillan.

O'Brien, Sharon and Reinhard Schäler. 2010. "Next Generation Translation and Localization. Users are Taking Charge." In *Proceedings from Translating and the Computer Conference*, 17–18 November 2010, London. Accessed March 4th, 2016. http://doras.dcu.ie/16695/1/Paper_6.pdf.

O'Brien, Sharon and Gabriela Saldanha. 2013. *Research Methodologies in Translation Studies.* New York-London: Routledge.

O'Hagan, Minako. 1996. *The Coming of Age of Teletranslation.* Clevendon-Philadelphia: Multilingual Matters.

O'Hagan, Minako. 2006. "Manga, Anime and Video Games: Globalizing Japanese Cultural Pro-duction." *Perspectives – Studies In Translatology* 14 (4): 243–247.

O'Hagan, Minako. 2008 "Fan Translation Networks: an Accidental Translator Training Environment?" In *Translator and Interpreter Training: Issues, Methods and Debates*, John Kearns (ed.), 159–183. London, New York: Continuum.

O'Hagan, Minako. 2009 "Evolution of User-Generated Translation: Fansubs, Translation Hacking and Crowdsourcing." *The Journal of Internationalization and Localization* 1: 94–121. doi:10.1075/jial.1.04hag

O'Hagan, Minako. 2011. "Introduction: Community Translation: Translation as a Social Activity and its Possible Consequences in the Advent of Web 2.0 and beyond." *Linguistica Antver-piensia* 10: 1–10.

O'Hagan, Minako. 2013. "The Impact of New Technologies on Translation Studies: A Technological Turn?" In *Routledge Handbook of Translation Studies*, Carmen Millán-Varela and Francesca Bartrina (ed.), 503–518. London: Routledge.

O'Hagan, Minako. 2016. "Massively Open Translation: Unpacking the Relationship Between Technology and Translation in the 21st Century." *International Journal of Communication* 10 (2016): 929–946.

O'Hagan, Minako and Carme Mangiron. 2013. *Videogame Localization.* Amsterdam/Philadelphia: John Benjamins. doi:10.1075/btl.106

O'Hagan, Minako and David Ashworth. 2003. *Translation-Mediated Communication in a Digital World.* Clevendon: Multilingual Matters.

Okyayuz, Sirin. 2016. "Translating Humor: A Case of Censorship vs. Social Translation." *European Scientific Journal March* 12 (8): 204–225.

Olohan, Maeve. 2004. *Introducing Corpora in Translation Studies.* London-New York: Routledge.

Olohan, Maeve. 2014. "Why do you Translate? Motivation to Volunteer and TED translation." *Perspectives: Studies in Translatology* 7 (1): 17–33.

Olvera-Lobo, María D. *et al.* 2005. "Translator Training and Modern Market Demands." *Perspectives: Studies in Translatology* 13(2): 132–142. doi:10.1080/09076760508668982

Olvera-Lobo, María D. *et al.* 2009. "Teleworking and Collaborative Work Environments in Translation Training." *Babel* 55 (2): 165–180. doi:10.1075/babel.55.2.05olv

O'Reilly, Tim. 2005. "What is Web 2.0?" *O'Reilly Media.* Accessed July 24, 2016. http://www.oreilly.com/pub/a/web2/archive/what-is-web-20.html

Orrego-Carmona, David. 2012. "Internal Structures and Workflows in Collaborative Subtitling." Paper at the *First International Conference on Non-professional Interpreting and Translation.* Università di Bologna, May 17–19. Accessed March 4th, 2016. http://isg.urv.es/publicity/doctorate/research/documents/Orrego/Orrego-Carmona_Structures-Workflows_NPIT1.pdf

Orrego-Carmona, David. 2014a. "Subtitling, video consumption and viewers: the impact of the young audience." *Translation Spaces* 3: 51–70. doi:10.1075/ts.3.03orr

Orrego-Carmona, David. 2014b "Using Non-Professional Subtitling Platforms for Translator Training." *Rivista internazionale di tecnica della traduzione = International Journal of Translation* 15: 129–144. Accessed March 4, 2016. http://www.openstarts.units.it/dspace/handle/10077/10611.

Orrego-Carmona, David. 2015. *The Reception of Non Professional Subtitling.* PhD Thesis. University Rovira I Virgili, Spain.

PACTE. 2003 "Building a Translation Competence Model." In *Triangulating Translation: Perspectives in Process Oriented Research*, Fabio Alves (ed.), 43–66. Amsterdam: John Benjamins. doi:10.1075/btl.45

PACTE. 2005. "Investigating Translation Competence: Conceptual and Methodological Issues." *META* 50: 609–619. doi:10.7202/011004ar

PACTE. 2008. "First Results of a Translation Competence Experiment: 'Knowledge of Translation' and 'Efficacy of the Translation Process'." In *Translator and Interpreter Training. Issues, Methods and Debates*, John Kearns (ed.), 104–126. London: Continuum.

PACTE. 2011. "Results of the Validation of the PACTE Translation Competence Model: Translation Project and Dynamic Translation Index." In *IATIS Yearbook* 2010, Sharon O'Brien (ed.), 317–343. London: Continuum.

PACTE. 2014. "First Results of PACTE Group's Experimental Research on Translation Competence Acquisition: The Acquisition of Declarative Knowledge of Translation." *MonTI. Monografías de Traducción e Interpretación, Special Issue* 1: 85–115. Accessed March 20, 2016. http://rua.ua.es/dspace/bitstream/10045/43722/1/MonTI_2014_Special_Issue_03.pdf

PACTE. 2015. "Results of PACTE's Experimental Research on the Acquisition of Translation Competence: the Acquisition of Declarative and Procedural Knowledge in Translation. The Dynamic Translation Index." *Translation Spaces* 4(1): 29–53. doi:10.1075/ts.4.1.02bee

Papineni, Kishore *et al.* 2002. "BLEU: a Method for Automatic Evaluation of Machine Translation." In *Proceedings of the 40th Annual Meeting of the Association for Computational Linguistics ACL, Philadelphia*, July 2002, 311–318. Accessed March 4, 2016. http://www.aclweb.org/anthology/P02-1040.pdf.

Paulin, Drew and Caroline Haythornthwaite. 2016. "Crowdsourcing the Curriculum: Redefining E-learning Practices through Peer-Generated Approaches." *The Information Society* 32(2): 130–142.

Pavlović, Natasha. 2007. *Directionality in Collaborative Translation Processes.* PhD Thesis. Universitat Rovira i Virgili, Tarragona.

Pavlović, Tanja. 2013. "The Role of Collaborative Translation Protocols CTPs in Translation Studies." *Jezikoslovlje* 14: 549–563. Accessed March 4, 2016. http://hrcak.srce.hr/file/165567.

Pedersen, Jan. 2011. *Subtitling Norms for Television.* Amsterdam-Philadelphia: John Benjamins. doi:10.1075/btl.98

Perego, Elisa. 2008. "Evidence of Explicitation in Subtitling: Towards a Categorisation." *Across Languages and Cultures* 4(1): 63–88. doi:10.1556/Acr.4.2003.1.4

Pérez-González, Luis and Susam Sebnem – Saraeva. 2012. "Non-professionals Translating and Interpreting: Participatory and Engaged Perspectives." *Special issue of The Translator* 182. Manchester: St. Jerome. doi:10.1080/13556509.2012.10799506

Pérez-González, Luis. 2006. "Fansubbing Anime: Insights into the 'Butterfly Effect' of Globalisation on Audiovisual Translation." *Perspectives* 144: 260–277.

Pérez-González, Luis. 2007. "Intervention in New Amateur Subtitling Cultures: a Multimodal Account." *Linguistica Antverpiensia, New Series-Themes in Translation Studies* 6: 67–80.

Pérez-González, Luis. 2012. "Amateur Subtitling and the Pragmatics of Spectatorial Subjectivity." *Language and Intercultural Communication* 124: 335–352. doi:10.1080/14708477.2012.722100

Pérez-González, Luis. 2013. "Amateur Subtitling as Immaterial Labour in the Digital Media Culture." *Convergence* 19 2: 157–175.

Pérez-González, Luis. 2014. *Audiovisual Translation: Theories, Methods and Issues.* New York-London: Routledge.

Pérez, Estefania and Oliver Carreira. 2011. "Evaluación del Modelo de Crowdsourcing Aplicado a la Traducción de Contenidos en Redes Sociales: Facebook." In *La Traductología Actual: Nueva Vías de Investigación en la Disciplina*, Elisa Calvo Encinas *et al.* (eds.), 99–118. Granada: Comares.

Perrino, Saverio. 2009. "User-Generated Translation: the Future of Translation in a Web 2.0 Environment." *Jostrans* 11:55–78.

Petras, Rebeca. 2011. "Localizing with Community Translation." *Multilingual*, October-November: 40–41.

Plassard, Freddie. 2007. "La traduction face aux nouvelles pratiques en réseaux." *META* 52 (4): 643–657. doi:10.7202/017690ar

Plitt, Mirko and François Masselot. 2010. "A Productivity Test of Statistical Machine Translation Post-Editing in a Typical Localization Context." *Prague Bull Math Linguist* 93: 7–16. doi:10.2478/v10108-010-0010-x

Presas, Marisa. 1996. *Problemas de traducció i competencia traductora.* PhD Thesis. Universitat Autonoma de Barcelona, Spain.

Price, John and Lisa Price 2002. *Hot text. Web Writing that Works.* Berkeley, CA: News Riders.

Pym, Anthony. 2001. "Introduction: The Return to Ethics in Translation Studies." *The Translator, Special Issue The Return to Ethics* 7:129–138.

Pym, Anthony. 2003. "Redefining Translation Competence in an Electronic Age. In Defence of a Minimalist Approach." *META* 48: 481–97. doi:10.7202/008533ar

Pym, Anthony. 2004. *The Moving Text: Localization, Translation and Distribution.* Amsterdam-Philadelphia: John Benjamins. doi:10.1075/btl.49

Pym, Anthony. 2010. *Translation Theories Explained.* London-New York: Routledge.

Pym, Anthony. 2011a. "Translation Research Terms: a Tentative Glossary for Moments of Perplexity and Dispute." In *Translation Research Projects* 3, Anthony Pym (ed.), 75–110. Tarragona: Intercultural Studies Group.

Pym, Anthony. 2011b. "What Technology does to Translating." *Translation and Interpreting*, 3: 1–9.

Pym, Anthony. 2012. *On Translator Ethics: Principles for Mediation Between Cultures.* Amsterdam-Philadelphia: John Benjamins. doi:10.1075/btl.104

Pym, Anthony. 2015a. Review of "Translation as a Social Activity. Community Translation 2.0. Special Issue of Lingustica Antverpiensia New Series / Themes in Translation Studies 10." *Target* 27: 145–153. doi:10.1075/target.27.1.14pym

Pym, Anthony. 2015b. "Translation as Risk Management." *Journal of Pragmatics* 85: 67–80. doi:10.1016/j.pragma.2015.06.010

Pym, Anthony, Miriam Shlesinger, and Zuzana Jettmarová, (eds). 2006. *Sociological Apects of Translating and Interpreting.* Amsterdam-Philadelphia: John Benjamins. doi:10.1075/btl.67

Pym, Anthony, Alexander Perekrestenko and Bram Starink (eds.). 2006. *Translation Technology and its Teaching.* Intercultural Studies Group. Tarragona: Universitat Rovira i Virgili.

Pym, Anthony and Kevin Windle. 2011. "Training translators." In *The Oxford Handbook of Translation Studies*, Kirsten Malmkjaer and Kevin Windle (eds.), Oxford and New York: Oxford University Press. doi::10.1093/oxfordhb/9780199239306.013.0032

Pym, Anthony, David Orrego-Carmona and Olga Torres-Simon. 2016. "Status And Technology in the Professionalization of Translators: Market Disorder and the Return of Hierarchy." *Jostrans: the Journal of Specialized Translation* 25: 33–53. Accessed March 4, 2016. http://www.jostrans.org/issue25/art_pym.pdf

Quah, Chew Kin. 2006. *Translation and Technology.* London: Palgrave Macmillan. doi:10.1057/9780230287105

Rabadán, Rosa. 2008. "Refining the Idea of 'Applied Extensions'." In *Beyond Descriptive Translation Studies*, Anthony Pym, Miriam Shlesinger and David Simeoni (eds.), 103–117. Amsterdam-Philadelphia, John Benjamins. doi:10.1075/btl.75.09rab

Raffel, Burton. 1988. *The Art of Translating Poetry.* Philadelphia: Penn State Press.

Ramírez Polo, Laura and Hang Ferrer Mora. 2010. "Aplicación de las TIC en Traducción e Interpretación en la Universidad de Valencia: experiencias y reflexiones." *Redit: Revista Electrónica de Didáctica de la Traducción y la Interpretación* 4: 23–41.

Ray, Rebeca and Natalie Kelly. 2011. *Crowdsourced Translation: Best Practices for Implementation.* Lowell, Ma: Common Sense Advisory.

Ray, Rebeca. 2011. "HootSuite's Crowdsourced Translation Project." *Multilingual*, 2011. Accessed March 4, 2016. http://dig.multilingual.com/20111011/DEEBC8B850FF305E58D7314914696DFC/20111011.pdf

Raymond, Eric. S. 2001. *The Cathedral and the Bazaar.* Sebastopol: O'Reilly and Associates.

Reiss, Katherina and Jans H. Vermeer. 1984. *Grundlegung einer Allgemeinen Translationstheorie.* Tübingen: Niemeyer. doi:10.1515/9783111351919

Reiss, Katherina. 1971. *Möglichkeiten und Grenzen der übersetungskritik.* München: Hüber.

Remael, Aline. 2010. "Audiovisual translation." In *Handbook of Translation Studies*, Vol 1, Yves Gambier and Luc van Doorslaer (eds.), 12–17. Amsterdam-Philadelphia: John Benjamins. doi:10.1075/hts.1.aud1

Rembert-Lang, LaToya. 2010. "Reinforcing the Tower of Babel: the Impact of Copyright Law on Fansubbing." *Intelectual Property Brief* 2: 21–33. Accessed March 24, 2016. http://digitalcommons.wcl.american.edu/cgi/viewcontent.cgi?article=1051&context=ipbrief

Rickard, Jason. 2009. "Translation in the Community." Paper presented at *LRC XIV Localization in the Cloud Conference*, Limerick, Ireland. 24th, 25th September, 2009. Accessed March 4, 2016. http://slideplayer.com/slide/4099091/

Risku, Hanna. 1998. *Translatorische Kompetenz*. Tübingen: Stauffengurg.

Risku, Hanna. 2002. "Situatedness in Translation Studies." *Cognitive Systems Research* 3: 523–533. doi:10.1016/S1389-0417(02)00055-4

Risku, Hanna. 2014. "Translation Process Research as Interaction Research." *Minding Translation – MonTI Special Issue* 1: 331–353.

Risku, Hanna, and Angela Dickinson. 2009. "Translators as Networkers: The Role of Virtual Communities." *Hermes* 42: 49–70.

Risku, Hanna, and Markus F. Peschl. 2010. "Einführung: Lernen als kooperative Wissens-generierung." [Introduction: Learning as Cooperative Knowledge Generation]. In *Kognition und Technologie im kooperativen Lernen: Vom Wissenstransfer zur Knowledge Creation [Cognition and Technology in Cooperative Learning: From Knowledge Transfer to Knowledge Creation]*, Risku, Hanna and Markus F. Peschl (eds.), 7–14. Göttingen: Vienna Univ. Press.

Risku, Hanna, Florian Windhager and Matthias Apfelthaler. 2013. "A Dynamic Network Model of Translatorial Cognition and Action." *Translation Spaces* 2: 151–182. doi:10.1075/ts.2.08ris

Risku, Hanna and Florian Windhager. 2013 "Extended Translation: A Sociocognitive Research Agenda." *Target* 13: 33–45. doi:10.1075/target.25.1.04ris

Risku, Hanna, Regina Rogl and Christina Pein-Weber. 2016. "Mutual Dependencies: Centrality in Translation Networks." *Jostrans: The Journal of Specialized Translation* 25: 1–22. Accessed July 30, 2016. http://www.jostrans.org/issue25/art_risku.pdf

Rodriguez-Castro, Maria. 2015. "Development and Empirical Validation of a Multifaceted Instrument for Translator Satisfaction." *International Journal of Translation and Interpreting Research* 72, 1–21.

Rogers, Margaret. 2015. *Specialized Translation: Shedding the 'Non-Literary' Tag*. Hampshire: Palgrave McMillan. doi:10.1057/9781137478412

Rojo López, Ana María. 2014. "The Emotional Impact of Translation: a Heart Rate Study." *The Journal of Pragmatics* 7: 31–44.

Rojo, Ana M. and Marina Ramos. Forthcoming-a. "Can Emotion Stir Translation Skill? Defining the Impact of Positive and Negative Emotions on Translation Performance." In *Reembedding Translation Process Research*, Ricardo Muñoz Martín (ed.). Amsterdam and Philadelphia: John Benjamins.

Rojo, Ana M. and Marina Ramos. Forthcoming-b. "The Role of Expertise in Emotion Regulation: Exploring the Effect of Expertise on Translation Performance under emotional stir." In *New Directions in Cognitive and Empirical Translation Process Research*, Isabel La Cruz and Riitta Jääskeläinen (eds.). Amsterdam and Philadelphia: John Benjamins.

Rong, Zongxiao. 2015. "Hybridity within Peer Production: The Power Negotiation of Chinese Fansub Groups." *Media@LSE MS Dissertation Series*. Accessed March 4, 2016. http://www.lse.ac.uk/media@lse/research/mediaWorkingPapers/MScDissertationSeries/2014/Zongxiao-Rong-proofread-by-NK.pdf

Rossum, Joyce van. 2015. *Honorifics in Korean Drama. A Comparison of Translation Procedures between Amateur and Professional Subtitlers*. MA Thesis. Leiden University, Holland.

Rothe-Neves, Rui. 2002. "Translation Quality Assessment for Research Purposes: An Empirical Approach." *Cadernos de Tradução: O processo de Tradução* 2 (10): 113–131.

Roturier, Johann. 2015. *Localizing Apps: A Practical Guide for Translators and Translation Students*. New York-London: Routledge.

Rumelhart, David E. 1980. "Schemata: the Building Blocks of Cognition." In *Theoretical Issues in Reading Comprehension*, Rand J. Spiro, Bertram C. Bruce and William E. Brewer (eds.), 33–58. Hillsdale, NJ: Lawrence Erlbaum Associates.

Sajna, Mateusz. 2013. "Amateur Subtitling – Selected Problems and Solutions." *T21N Translation in Transition* 3:1–17. Accessed March 4, 2016. http://www.t21n.com/homepage/articles/T21N-2013-03-Sajna.pdf

Salmons, Janet (ed.) 2008. *Handbook of Reseacrch on Electronic Collaboration and Organizational Synergy*. Hersey: Information Science Reference.

Sandrini, Peter and Maria García Gonzalez (eds.). 2015. *Translation and Openess*. Insbruck: Innsbruck University Press. doi:10.15203/2936-88-2

Santini, Laura. 2015. "Online Edutainment Videos: Recontextualizing and Reconceptualizing Expert Discourse in a Participatory Web-culture." *Journalism and Mass Communication* 52: 51–63.

Schäffner, Christina. 2010. "Norms of translation." In *Handbook of Translation Studies*, Vol 1, Yves Gambier and Luc Van Doorslaer (eds), 235–244. Amsterdam-Philadelphia: John Benjamins. doi:10.1075/hts.1.nor1

Schotlz, Trebor. 2013. *Digital Labour: the Internet as Playground and Factory*. New York: Routledge.

Secara, Alina. 2011. "R U Ready 4 New Subtitles? Investigating the Potential of Social Translation Practices." *Linguistica Antverpiensia* 10: 153–174.

Séguinot, Candence. 1996. "Some Thoughts about Think-Aloud Protocols." *Target* 8(1): 75–95. doi:10.1075/target.8.1.05seg

Shachaf, Pnina and Noriko Hara, 2010. "Beyond Vandalism: Wikipedia Trolls." *Journal of Information Science* 36(3): 357–370.http://dx.doi.org/10.1177/0165551510365390

Shapiro, Lawrence (ed.). 2014. *The Routledge Handbook of Embodied Cognition*. New York-London: Routledge.

Shimohata, Sayori *et al.* 2001. "Collaborative Translation Environment on the Web." In *Proceedings from Machine MT Summit 8*, 331–334. Accessed March 4, 2016. www.mt-archive.info/MTS-2001-Shimohata.pdf.

Shirky, Clay. 2010. *Cognitive Surplus: Creativity and Generosity in a Connected Age*. New York: Penguin Press.

Shreve, Gregory M. 1997. "Cognition and the Evolution of Translation Competence." In *Cognitive Processes in Translation and Interpreting*, John H. Danks *et al.* (eds.), 120–136. Thousand Oaks, Sage.

Shreve, Gregory. M. 2006a. "Translation and Expertise: the Deliberate Practice." *Journal of Translation Studies* 9: 27–42.

Shreve, Gregory M. 2006b. "Corpus Enhancement and Localization." In *Perspectives on Localization*, Keiran Dunne (ed.), 309–331. Amsterdam-Philadelphia: John Benjamins. doi:10.1075/ata.xiii.22shr

Shreve, Gregory M. and Bruce Diamond. 1997. "Cognitive Processes in Translation and Interpreting: Critical Issues." In *Cognitive Processes in Translation and Interpreting*, John H. Danks *et al.* (eds.), 233–251. Thousand Oaks: Sage.

Shreve, Gregory M. and Eric Angelone. (Eds). 2009. *Translation and Cognition*. Amsterdam-Philadelphia: John Benjamins.

Siddique, Haroon. 2011. "Mob Rule: Iceland Crowdsources its Next Constitution." *The Guardian*, Thursday 9 June 2011. Accessed March 4, 2016. http://www.theguardian.com/world/2011/jun/09/iceland-crowdsourcing-constitution-facebook

Simeoni, Daniel. 1998. "The Pivotal Status of the Translator's Habitus." *Target* 10: 1–39. doi:10.1075/target.10.1.02sim

Singh, Nitish and Arun Pereira. 2005. *The Culturally Customized Website: Customizing Websites for the Global Marketplace*. Oxford: Elsevier.

Sin-Wai, Chan. 2014. "Computer-Aided Translation." In *The Routledge Encyclopedia of Translation Technology*, Chan Sin-Wai (ed.), 32–67. New York-London: Routledge.

Siren, Seija and Kai Hakkarainen. 2002. "The Cognitive Concept of Expertise Applied to Expertise in Translation." *Across Languages and Cultures* 31: 71–82.

Smart, Paul R. 2014. "Embodiment, Cognition and the World Wide Web." In *The Routledge Handbook of Embodied Cognition*, Lawrence Shapiro (ed.), 336–334. New York: Routledge.

Snell-Hornby, Marie. 1988. *Translation Studies. An Integrated Approach*. Amsterdam and Philadelphia: John Benjamins. doi:10.1075/z.38

Snell-Hornby, Marie. 1996. *Translation und Text Ausgewahlte Vortrage*. Vienna: Vienna University Press.

Snell-Hornby, Marie. 2010. "The Turns in Translation Studies." In *Handbook of Translation Studies*. Vol. I, Yves Gambier and Luc van Doorslaer (eds), 366–370. Amsterdam/Philadelphia: Benjamins. doi:10.1075/hts.1.the1

Sommers, Harold. 2003. "The Translator's Workstation." In *Computers and Translation: A Translators Guide*, Harold Sommers (ed.), 13–30. Amsterdam-Philadelphia: John Benjamins. doi:10.1075/btl.35.05som

Sorby, Stella. 2015. "Translating Musical Libreto: a Dynamic Collaboration." *META* 60: 371. doi:10.7202/1032922ar

Spence, Michael. 1973. "Job Market Signalling." *Quarterly Journal of Economics* 87: 355–374. doi:10.2307/1882010

Spies, Carla-Marie and Ilse Feinauer. 2014. "Literary Translation as Collaboration: the Interaction Between Agents in the Production Process of Literary Translations in a South African Publishing House." Paper presented at *Conference La Traduction Collaborative de L'Antiqueté à Internet*, Paris, France, 5th, 6th, 7th June, 2014.

Sprung, Robert C. (ed.). 2000. *Translating into Success. Cutting-edge Strategies for Going Multilingual in a Global Age*. Amsterdam-Philadelphia: John Benjamins. doi:10.1075/ata.xi

St. André, James. 2010. "Lessons from Chinese History: Translation as a Collaborative and Multi-stage Process." *TTR: Traduction, Terminologie, Rédaction* 23 (1): 71–94. doi:10.7202/044929ar

Šubert, Eduard and Ondrej Bojar. 2014. "Twitter Crowd Translation – Design and Objectives." In *Proceedings from Translation and the Computer* 36, 217–227. Accessed March 4, 2016. http://www.mt-archive.info/10/Asling-2014-Subert.pdf

Suojanen, Tytti, Kaisa Koskinen and Tiina Yuominen. 2015. *User Centered Translation*. Manchester: St. Jerome.

Surowiecki, James. 2004. *The Wisdom of Crowds*. New York, NY: W. W. Norton & Company, Inc.

Taibi, Mustapha and Uldis Ozolin. 2016. *Community Translation*. London: Bloomsbury.

Tang, Jun. 2014. "Translating Kung Fu Panda's Kung Fu-related Elements: Cultural Representation in Dubbing and Subtitling." *Perspectives* 22 (3): 437–456. doi:10.1080/0907676X.2013.864686

Tatsumi, Midori *et al*. 2012. "How good is Crowd Post-Editing: its Potential and Limitations." In *Proceedings of AMTA-2012*. Accessed March 4th, 2016. http://www.mt-archive.info/AMTA-2012-Tatsumi.pdf

Tatsuya Sukehiro, Mihoko Kitamura, and Toshiki Murata. 2001. "Collaborative translation environment 'Yakushite.Net'." In *Proceedings of the Sixth Natural Language Processing Pacific Rim Symposium: NLPRS-2001*, 769– 770. Accessed March 4, 2016. http://www.afnlp.org/archives/nlprs2001/pdf/exh-05-01.pdf.

TAUS. 2010. *Post-Editing Guidelines.* Accessed March 4, 2016. https://www.taus.net/academy/best-practices/postedit-best-practices/machine-translation-post-editing-guidelines

TAUS. 2014. *Community Evaluation Best Practices.* Accessed March 4, 2016. https://www.taus.net/academy/best-practices/evaluate-best-practices/community-evaluation-best-practices

Teich, Elke. 2003. *Cross-Linguistic Variation in System and Text: A Methodology for the Investigation of Translations and Comparable Texts.* Berlin: Mouton de Gruyter. doi:10.1515/9783110896541

Tesseur, Wine. 2014a. "Institutional multilingualism in NGOs: Amnesty International's strategic understanding of multilingualism." *META* 59(3): 557–577. doi:10.7202/1028657ar

Tesseur, Wine. 2014b. *Transformation through translation: translation policies at Amnesty International.* PhD thesis, Aston University, UK.

Tirkkonen Condit, Sonja. 1996. "What Is in the Black Box? Professionality in Translational Decisions in the Light of TAP Research." In *Übersetzungswissenschaft im Umbruch. Festschrift für Wolfram Wilss zum 70,* Erich Steiner (eds.), 251–257. Tübingen, Narr.

Tirkkonen-Condit, Sonja. 2005. "The Monitor Model Revisited: Evidence from Process Research." *META* 50 2: 405–414 doi:10.7202/010990ar

Tiselius, Elisabet. 2013. "Expertise without Deliberate Practice? The Case of Simultaneous Interpreters." *The Interpreters' Newsletter* 18.

Toffler, Alvin. 1980. The Third Wave. London: Pan Books.

Tognini Bonelli, Elena. 1996. *Corpus Theory and Practice.* Pescia: Tuscan Word Centre.

Trosborg, Anna. 1997. "Text Typology: Register, Genre and Text Type." In *Text Typology and Translation,* Anna Trosborg (ed.), 3–23. Amsterdam-Philadelphia: John Benjamins. doi:10.1075/btl.26.03tro

Toury, Gideon. 1995. *Descriptive Translation Studies and Beyond.* Amsterdam-Philadelphia: John Benjamins.

Toury, Gideon, 1998. "A Handful of Paragraphs on 'Translation' and 'Norms.'" In *Translation and Norms,* Christina Schäffner (ed.) 10–32. Clevedon: Multilingual Matters.

Toury, Guideon. 2012. *Translation Studies and Beyond. Revised Edition.* Amsterdam-Philadelphia: John Benjamins. doi:10.1075/btl.100

Twitter. 2011. "Translating Twitter into more Languages." *Twitter Blog.* Accessed March 4, 2016. https://blog.twitter.com/2011/translating-twitter-into-more-languages

Tymoczko, Maria. 2000. "Translation and Political Engagement." *The Translator* 6 1: 23–47. doi:10.1080/13556509.2000.10799054

Tymoczko, Maria. 2007. *Enlarging Translation, Empowering Translators.* Manchester: St. Jerome Publishing.

Tyulenev, Sergey. 2009. *Applying Luhmann to Translation Studies: Translation in Society.* New York-London: Routledge.

Tyulenev, Sergey. 2014. *Translation and Society.* New York-London: Routledge.

Tyulenev, Sergey. 2015. "Towards Theorising Translation as an Occupation." *Asia Pacific Translation and Intercultural Studies* 2: 15–29. doi:10.1080/23306343.2015.1013206

Utiyama, Masao and Hitoshi Isahara. 2003. "Reliable measures for aligning Japanese-English news articles and sentences." In *Proceedings of the 41st Annual Meeting of the Association for Computational Linguistics,* 72–79. Accessed March 4, 2016. http://www.aclweb.org/anthology/P03-1010

Utiyama, Masao, Takesi Abekawa, Eiichiro Sumita and Kyo Kageura. 2009. "Minna no Hon'yaku: A Website for Hosting, Archiving, and Promoting Translations." In *Proceedings of Translating and the Computer 31.* London, UK. Accessed March 4, 2016. http://www.mt-archive.info/05/Aslib-2009-Utiyama.pdf

Valli, Paola. 2015. "Disrupt me not." *Keynotes 2015 A Review of the TAUS October Events*, 46–54. Accessed March 4, 2016. https://www.taus.net/blog/disrupt-me-not.

Van de Meer, Jaap. 2010. "Where are Facebook, Google, IBM and Microsoft Taking us?" *TAUS articles*. Accessed March 4, 2016. https://www.taus.net/think-tank/articles/translate-articles/where-are-facebook-google-ibm-and-microsoft-taking-us

Van Dijk, Teun A. 1988. *News as Discourse*. Hillsdale, N.J.: Lawrence Erlbaum Associates.

Van Dijk, Teun A. and Walter Kintsch. 1983. *Strategies of Discourse to Comprehension*. New York: New York Academic Press.

Van Wyke, Ben. 2013. "Translation and Ethics." In *Routledge Handbook of Translation Studies*, Carmen Millan and Franchesca Batrina (eds), 548–560. New York-London: Routledge.

Vandepitte, Sonia. 2008. "Remapping Translation Studies: Towards a Translation Studies Ontology." *META* 533: 569–588. doi:10.7202/019240ar

Vashee, Kirti. 2009. "MT Technology in the Cloud: An Evolving Model." LRC Conference 2009, Limerick, Ireland. Accessed March 4, 2016. https://www.localisation.ie/oldwebsite/resources/conferences/2009/presentations/LRC09-KV.pdf.

Vázquez Áyora, Gerardo. 1977. *Introducción a la Traductología*. Georgetown University Press.

Venuti, Lawrence. 1995. *The Translator Invisibility: a History of Translation*. New York-London: Routledge. doi:10.4324/9780203360064

Venuti, Lawrence. 2009. "American Tradition." In *Encyclopedia of Translation Studies*, Mona Baker and Gabriela Saldanha (eds.), 320–327. New York-London: Routledge.

Verbruggen, Nakita. 2010. *The Translation of Wordplay in Fansubs and Original Subtitles: a Comparative Study*. MA Thesis. Universiteits Ghent, Belgium.

Vinay, Jean P. and Jean L. Darbelnet. 1958. *Stylistique comparée du français et de l'anglais. Méthode de traduction*. París: Didier.

Volk, Martin and Søren Harder. 2007. "Evaluating MT with translations or translators. What is the difference?" In *Proceedings of MT Summit XI, Copenhagen*, 499 – 506. Accessed July 23, 2016. http://www.zora.uzh.ch/20406/2/Volk_Harder_2007V.pdf

Vorderobermeier, Gisella M. (ed.). 2014. *Remapping Habitus in Translation Studies*. Amsterdam-New York: Rodopi/Brill.

Waddington, Christopher. 2001. "Different Methods of Evaluating Student Translation: The Question of Validity." *META* 46: 312–325. doi:10.7202/004583ar

Wang, Fang. 2014. "Similarities and Differences between Fansub Translation and Traditional Paper-based Translation." *Theory and Practice in Language Studies* 4 (9): 1904–1911. Accessed March 4, 2016. http://www.ojs.academypublisher.com/index.php/tpls/article/view/tpls040919041911

Wang, Kenny and Chong Han. 2013. "Accomplishment in the Multitude of Counselors: Peer feedback in Translation Training." *Translation & Interpreting* 5(2): 62–75.

Warren, Robert H., Edoardo Airoldi and David Banks. 2008. "Network Analysis of Wikipedia." In *Statistical Methods in E-Commerce Research*, Wolfgan Jank, and Galit Shmueli (eds.) 81–102. New York: Wiley. doi:10.1002/9780470315262.ch5

Wasala, Asanka, Reinhard Schäler, Jim Buckley, Ruvan Weerasinghe and Chris Exton. 2013. "Collaboratively Building Language Resources while Localising the Web." In *Proceedings of the 3rd Workshop on the People's Web Meets NLP*, ACL 2012, 15–19. Accessed March 4, 2016. http://www.aclweb.org/anthology/W12-4003. doi:10.1007/978-3-642-35085-6_3

Washbourne, Kelly. 2014. "Beyond Error Marking: Written Corrective Feedback for a Dialogic Pedagogy in Translator Training." *The Translator and Interpreter Trainer* 8 (2): 240–256. doi:10.1080/1750399X.2014.908554

Whitaker, Robert, Martin Chorley and Stuart Allen. 2015. "New Frontiers for Crowdsourcing: the Extended Mind." In *Proceedings of the System Sciences HICSS, 2015 48th Hawaii International Conference on System Sciencies*, 1635–1644. doi::10.1109/HICSS.2015.197. Accessed March 4, 2016. http://orca.cf.ac.uk/70239/1/7367b635.pdf.

Wikipedia. 2016. "History of Wikipedia", *Wikipedia*, last modified March 13, 2016. https://en.wikipedia.org/wiki/History_of_Wikipedia

Wilcox, Simone. 2013. *A Comparative Analysis of Fansubbing and Professional DVD Subtitling*. MA Thesis. University of Johannesburg.

Williams, Malcolm. 2003. *Translation Quality Assessment*. Ottawa: Ottawa University Press.

Wilss, Wolfgang. 1994. "A Framework for Decision-Making in Translation." *Target* 6 (2): 131–150. doi:10.1075/target.6.2.02wil

Wittman, Emily. 2013. "Literary Narrative Prose and Translation Studies." In *Routledge Handbook of Translation Studies*, Carmen Millán-Varela and Francesca Bartrina (eds.), 443–444. London: Routledge.

Wolf, Michaela. 2007. "Introduction: the Emergence of a Sociology of Translation." In *Constructing a Sociology of Translation*, Michaela Wolf and Alexandra Fukari (eds.), 1–36. Amsterdam-Philadelphia: John Benjamins. doi:10.1075/btl.74.01wol

Wolf, Michaela. 2010. "Translation 'Going Social'? Challenges to the Ivory Tower of Babel." *MonTI* 2: 29–46. doi:10.6035/MonTI.2010.2.2

Wolf, Michaela. 2012. "The Sociology of Translation and its 'Activist Turn'." *Translation and Interpreting Studies* 7 (2): 129–143. doi:10.1075/tis.7.2.02wol

Wolf, Michaela and Alexandra Fukari (eds.). 2007. *Constructing a Sociology of Translation*. Amsterdam-Philadelphia: John Benjamins. doi:10.1075/btl.74

Wright, Sue E. 2006. "Language Industry Standards." In *Perspectives on Localization*, Keiran Dunne (ed.), 241–278. Amsterdam-Philadelphia: John Benjamins. doi:10.1075/ata.xiii.19wri

Wu, Xianwei. 2010. "Recreation through Translation: Examining China's Online Volunteer Translators." Paper presented at *Conference Shifting Paradigms: How Translation Transforms the Humanities*, University of Illinois at Urbana-Champaign, Oct 14–16, 2010.

Xiao Liu. 2014. *Apprentissage dans une communauté de pratique : fansubbing et compétence linguistique*. MA Thesis, Universite de Montreal, Canada.

Yamada, Masaru. 2015. "Can College Students be Post Editors? An Investigation into Employing Language Learners in Machine Translation plus Post-Editing." *Journal of Machine Translation* 29: 49–67. doi:10.1007/s10590-014-9167-7

Yan, Joshua *et al.* 2014. "Are Two Heads Better than One? Crowdsourced Translations via a Two Step Collaboration of Non-Professional Translators and Editors." In *Proceedings of the 52nd Annual Meeting of the Association for Computational Linguistics*, 1134–1144. Baltimore, Maryland, USA, June 23–25. Accessed March 4, 2016. http://www.aclweb.org/anthology/P14-1107.pdf

Yan, Joshua *et al.* 2015. "Opportunities or Risks to Reduce Labor in Crowdsourcing Translation? Characterizing Cost Versus Quality via a PageRank-HITS Hybrid Model." In *Proceedings of the Twenty-Fourth International Joint Conference on Artificial Intelligence IJCAI 2015*, 1025–1032. Accessed March 4, 2016. http://www.aaai.org/ocs/index.php/IJCAI/IJCAI15/paper/view/10901/10805.

Yin, Xu, Wenjie Liu, Yafang Wang, Cheglei Yang and Lin Lu. 2014. "What? How? Where? A Survey of Crowdsourcing." *Frontier and Future Development of Information Technology in Medicine and Education, Lecture Notes in Electrical Engineering* 269: 221–232. doi:10.1007/978-94-007-7618-0_22

Zaidan, Omar F. and Chris Calliston-Burch. 2011. "Crowdsourcing Translation: Professional Quality from Non-Professionals." In *Proceedings of the 49th Annual Meeting of the Association of Computational Linguistics*, 1120–1129. Accessed March 4, 2016. http://www.cs.jhu.edu/%7Eozaidan/AOC/turk-trans_Zaidan-CCB_acl2011.pdf.

Zanettin, Federico. 1998. "Bilingual Comparable Corpora and the Training of Translators." *META* 43(4): 616–630. doi:10.7202/004638ar

Zanettin, Federico. 2001. "Swimming in Words: Corpora, Translation, and Language Learning." In *Learning with Corpora*, Guy Aston (ed.), 177–197. Houston, TX: Athelstan.

Zhao, Xijing and Jie Gu. 2015. "Legal Regulation or Self-regulation? Copyright Disputes of Chinese Online Video Industries: Case Studies of 'De-piratization' of QVOD, Fansub Group and 'Xunlei'." Paper presented at the *International Conference on Communication/Culture and the Sustainable Development Goals (CCSDG): Challenges for a New Generation*, Chiang Mai University, Thailand. Accessed March 24, 2016. http://rcsd.soc.cmu.ac.th/web/CCSDG/download.php?filename=xijing%20zhao%20and%20jie%20gu%20CCSDG2015.pdf

Zatlin, Phyllis. 2005. *Theatrical Translation and Film Adaptation*. Clevendon: Multilingual Matters.

Zbib, Rahib *et al.* 2013. "Systematic Comparison of Professional and Crowdsourced Reference Translations for Machine Translation." In *Proceedings of NAACL-HLT 2013*, 612–616. Accessed March 1, 2016. http://clair.eecs.umich.edu/aan/paper.php?paper_id=N13-1069#pdf

Zhang, Florence. 2014. "Langue et Plume: la traduction collaboraitve en Chine au seuil du Xxe siecle." Paper presented at the *Conference La Traduction Collaborative de L'Antiqueté à Internet*, Paris, France, 5th, 6th, 7th June, 2014.

Index

A

Abusive subtitling   180–182
Activity theory   104, 201, 219
Actor-Network theory   101, 199
Agency, translator   6, 61, 107,
    197, 199–200, 234–235
Amara   22–23, 32, 35, 56, 65,
    69–70, 73, 79–80, 84, 135,
    143–144, 168, 171, 225
Amazon Mechanical Turks
    13, 83
Anime   29, 35, 47–48, 136, 181,
    185–186, 188, 193, 214–215
App localization   30, 86, 235,
    259
Audiovisual translation   8, 35,
    56–57, 62, 79–80, 84, 179,
    186–188, 231

B

Best practices, crowdsourcing
    64, 91–95, 132
Bible Translation   37–40
Bourdieu, Pierre   195, 197–199,
    202
Bowker, Lynn   1, 4, 52, 146–147,
    151–153, 157–162, 169, 172, 229,
    245
Brabham, Daren   13–18, 20–21,
    25–26, 28, 37, 108, 116, 159,
    175, 212
Buzelin, Hélène   41, 103, 172,
    195–200

C

Camara, Lidia   19–20, 30, 80,
    94, 132–133, 195–196, 217,
    220–221, 223–225, 241
Chesterman, Andrew   24, 61,
    104, 142, 176, 182–185, 195–
    196, 203–207, 220, 262–263

Co-creative user   46
Cognitive approaches   142, 166,
    172–173, 241, 263
    Cognitive Translation Studies
        97–120
    Cognitive Translatology
        2, 97, 98, 99–100, 109–113,
        117–118, 241–250
    Distributed cognition   98,
        101–103, 117, 200
        Embodied cognition   7, 98,
        100–101
    Extended cognition   18, 97,
        99–100, 103, 106, 120
    Situated cognition   100, 263
Cognitive surplus   222, 257
Coherence   67, 117, 140, 154,
    157–158, 162–163, 166–167,
    169–170, 175
Collaborative translation
    protocols   118–120
Collective intelligence   12–15,
    18, 46, 50, 60, 69–70, 108,
    138–139, 166–167
Common Sense Advisory
    45, 55, 92–93, 255, 260
Community translation
    18, 23–28, 54, 241, 255
Community managers   72, 81,
    103, 132–134, 209
Comparable corpus   75, 152–155,
    175
Content Management Systems
    63
Content prioritization   3, 65,
    123, 130, 261
Copyright   49, 209, 213–216
Corpus-based Translation Studies
    2, 154–155, 172, 175–176, 263
    Quality evaluation and
        corpora   151–153

Cronin, Michael   1, 4–5, 23, 25,
    47, 72, 161, 201, 212, 259–260,
    263
CrowdIn   32, 65–67, 69, 72–73,
    78–79, 83, 171–172
Crowdsourcing typologies
    15–17, 31–32
Crowdsourcing platforms
    31, 33, 42, 51, 62, 64, 66, 73,
    76–77, 82–86, 134, 163, 171–
    172, 212, 263

D

Deliberate practice   6, 110–111,
    227, 231–232, 243, 254
DePalma, Don   2, 30–31, 45, 52,
    54–55, 57, 59, 62–64, 72, 78, 85,
    91–94, 133–134, 160, 211, 230,
    257–258, 260
Díaz Cintas, Jorge   29, 48–49,
    75, 158, 179, 182, 186, 188–192,
    213, 215
Digisubbing   20, 79
Dotsub   56, 65, 69–70, 73, 79,
    84, 143–144
Drugan, Johanna   7–8, 121,
    123–125, 130, 143–145, 186,
    204, 209–210
Duolingo   19, 31, 33–34, 84, 154,
    168, 217, 219–220, 227

E

Estellés, Enrique   11–16, 18, 21,
    108, 263
Ethics   8, 49, 61, 181, 185–186,
    195–197, 203–213, 263
    Ethical codes   211
    MT and translation ethics
        207–209
    Professional ethics   212
Experienced non-experts   111

Expertise   6–7, 9, 17, 24, 31,
    3–34, 67–68, 97–100, 109–117,
    129–130, 163, 170–171, 224, 228,
    231, 236, 239, 249, 254, 257
    Absolute and relative experts
        111–112
    Routine and adaptative
        experts   111
    Translation expertise   6, 31,
        99–100, 110–117, 130, 163,
        170, 228, 231, 236, 257

F
Facebook   18, 21–22, 27, 30, 32,
    35, 37–38, 44, 46–47, 52–54, 59,
    65–76, 83–84, 102, 108, 116–117,
    122, 133–137, 140–141, 146–149,
    151, 153–155, 166–167, 170–172,
    176–177, 201, 208, 217–220,
    224–225, 239–240, 254, 257–258
Fandubbing   22, 28–29, 183,
    189–190
Fansubbing   2, 4, 28–29, 46–49,
    81–82, 154, 179–194, 212–216,
    222–224, 234, 260
    Fansubbing and copyright
        213–216
    Fansubbing process   81–82,
        193
Feedback   55, 68–69, 73–78, 80,
    88, 93–94, 108, 110, 116–118,
    132–134, 139, 143–146, 219–
    220, 222, 227–228, 231–232,
    235–241, 248–249, 254
    Feedback classification
        336–241
    Peer feedback   236–240
Fitness for purpose   58, 122, 132
Free and Open Machine
    Translation (FOMT)   2–3,
    86–87
Functionalism   18, 137, 140, 147,
    149–151, 165, 184, 229, 233
Fundubbing   183, 190
Funsubtitling   189

G
Gambier, Yves   2–6, 11, 17,
    22–25, 33, 39, 40–41, 57, 185,
    187–190, 195, 201, 212, 231–232,
    260–262

García, Ignacio   2, 24–25, 31, 38,
    50, 58, 61, 86–87, 90, 123–128,
    130, 161, 228–229, 239, 251,
    260–261
Gengo   7–8, 34, 58, 65, 128–129,
    227
Glosses   180, 186–188, 190–191
Göpferich, Susanne   9, 109–111,
    114–116, 120, 149–151, 158,
    165–168, 235–236, 242,
    246–248
Gouadec, Daniel   6, 18–19,
    62–64, 70–71, 111, 123, 125–127,
    140–142, 228–230, 233,
    235–236, 259

H
Habitus   197–199, 212, 228,
    231–232
Hermans, Theo   12, 61, 182,
    184–186, 196–197
Hurtado Albir, Amparo   33, 117,
    130, 137–139, 144, 158, 166, 229,
    243, 245, 249, 251

I
Interdisciplinarity   4–7, 203,
    230, 261–262
Iterative translation models
    68–70, 89, 132, 135, 141, 146–
    151, 172–174, 176–177, 239–240,
    248, 254

J
Jääskeläinen, Rita   97, 108–109,
    111, 114–115, 119–120, 162,
    228–229, 259

K
Kanjingo   22–23, 77, 84–85
Kiraly, Don   109–110, 227,
    229–233, 237, 242–244, 246,
    248–249, 251, 253–254, 259
Kiva   16, 18, 21–22, 30–32, 36,
    52, 55, 66–67, 73, 76–77, 84,
    103, 132–133, 138, 144–145, 171,
    176, 235

L
Language Industry perspectives
    62–63, 73–81, 91–96, 129–131,
    258–261
Literary translation   6, 18–19,
    26, 33, 37, 40–41, 127–128, 136,
    139, 196, 198–199, 213, 250–251

M
Machine Translation (MT)   1–3,
    5–6, 7–8, 26–27, 29, 31–32,
    35–38, 45, 48, 50–51, 59,
    61–64, 66–68, 70, 72–74, 77–79,
    82–91, 113, 117–118, 121–124,
    126–129, 131–132, 134–141,
    144–146, 154, 159–160, 163,
    176–177, 195–196, 207–209,
    211–213, 217, 229–230, 238–
    239, 240, 252, 258–261
    Statistical MT   3, 50, 66–68,
        78, 85, 88–89, 146, 207–208
    Google Translate   2, 27, 36,
        66, 78, 85–88, 118, 126, 146,
        238–239
    Microsoft Bing   66,
        78–79, 85–87, 118, 136–137,
        207–208, 238–239
Manga   29, 35, 47–48, 214, 225,
    244, 257
"Many eyes" principle   132, 135–
    136, 138–139
Massidda, Serenella   4, 48–49,
    79, 81, 154, 179–181, 185,
    187–193, 212–214, 260–261
MateCat   42, 82, 85–88, 212–213,
    258
MNH-TT   30–31, 76–77, 83–84,
    134, 227, 234–235, 252
Mobile translation   29, 58–59,
    70, 85, 120, 230, 257, 259
Modding   29
MOOCs   34, 133, 253–254
Motivation   8, 17, 25, 33, 36,
    48, 53–54, 58, 64–65, 67–69,
    71–72, 74, 88–89, 91–95, 110,
    118, 131, 136, 195–197, 200–204,
    208–210, 216–224, 236, 245–
    246, 256–257, 262–263
Multidimensional quality
    metrics (MQM)   124–125,
    141

Munday, Jeremy 4, 24, 41, 47,
    175, 261–262
Muñoz, Ricardo 97–99, 101,
    103–104, 107–108, 110–112, 114,
    200, 228, 243, 249

N
Netnography 216, 218–219
Non-professional translation
    4, 12, 19–20, 22–23, 26–28, 58,
    65, 72, 90, 99–100, 108–109,
    111–117, 122–124, 126, 129,
    131–132, 135–136, 144–145, 148,
    154, 161–165, 169–170, 177, 179,
    182–183, 185–193, 196, 198–199,
    205–212, 220, 222, 224–225,
    227–228, 231–232, 235, 241–
    242, 254
Non-profit organizations (NGO)
    13–18, 21–22, 28, 33–36, 52–57,
    62, 67, 71, 73, 76–77, 79–80,
    83–85, 93–94, 122, 127–128,
    132–134, 144–145, 205, 208,
    211–212, 217, 219, 224, 236,
    240–241, 257
Nord, Christiane 18, 54, 137,
    140, 144, 146–150, 159, 167–
    168, 183–184, 189, 229–230, 233

O
O'Brien, Sharon 1, 4–5, 8, 17,
    26–27, 33, 36, 38–40, 42, 45, 55,
    65, 86–87, 94, 97–98, 106, 113,
    117–118, 122–125, 129, 132–133,
    139, 158, 163, 195–196, 203,
    216–217, 219–223, 236, 245
O'Hagan, Minako 1, 4–6, 8–9,
    19–21, 23–25, 27–29, 31, 35,
    42–43, 48–49, 51–52, 54, 59, 61,
    78, 91, 112, 145–146, 150, 160,
    168, 170, 195, 200–201, 213–214,
    225, 227, 229–232, 234, 244
Olohan, Maeve 1, 27, 56–57, 118,
    176, 187, 195, 217, 220–223
Open source software 66, 70,
    83, 216, 235, 252
    Open source software
        localization 12, 13–14,
        19, 28
Open translation 50, 52, 67–69,
    79–80, 132–133, 217

Orrego-Carmona, David 3–4,
    8–9, 22, 30, 35, 81, 134, 136, 181,
    185–189, 196–197, 203, 216, 227,
    231, 234, 241, 251–252

P
PACTE 9, 89–91, 109–110,
    114–115, 228, 231, 241–254
    PACTE competence model
        9, 241, 243–248, 251–254
Paid crowdsourcing 3, 17,
    27–28, 31, 36, 38, 57–60,
    67–68, 113, 123, 128–131, 133,
    144, 170, 176, 203, 229–230,
    257, 260–261
Participatory cultures 19–20,
    37, 45–48, 181
Pérez-González, Luis 8, 19, 35,
    180, 181, 186–188, 190, 193
Post-anime fansubbing 136, 193
Post editing 1–3, 5–8, 27–29,
    35–36, 45, 50, 59, 62, 66, 68,
    73, 77–79, 84–91, 117–118,
    121–123, 126–128, 134–136,
    140, 145–146, 167–168, 170,
    176–177, 206–209, 227–230,
    238–239, 240, 252, 259–261
    Monolingual post editing
        87–90
    Crowd post editing 27–28,
        78, 84–85, 87–90, 117–118,
        167–168, 208, 227–228, 252
Professionalism 6, 109–110, 112,
    197, 199, 204, 220, 241–242
Prosumer 19, 35, 46, 184
Pym, Anthony 1, 7, 23, 26–27,
    93, 107–108, 114, 137–138, 148,
    158, 160–166, 196–210, 214,
    219–220, 228–230, 239–240,
    242–243, 245–246, 251–252,
    258–259, 262

R
Risku, Hanna 18, 26, 97–101,
    103–107, 116, 199–200, 217,
    229–230, 233, 235–236, 263
Romhacking 29, 47–48, 213
Rosetta Foundation 21–23, 31,
    36, 65, 67, 73, 76–77, 84, 94,
    133, 139, 217, 219–220, 224,
    235–236

S
Scanlations 22, 28–29, 47–50,
    213
Segmentation 63, 66, 77, 135,
    140–141, 157, 159–165, 172,
    174–175, 193, 252–253
Shreve, Gregory 9, 19, 97,
    106–107, 110–111, 151, 153,
    158–159, 161, 174, 231, 235–236,
    242–243, 248–249, 252–254
SMS translation 16, 36, 55–56,
    83, 171
Social networking site 2–3, 23–
    24, 33–35, 37–38, 44, 46–47,
    52–57, 62, 65, 67, 71–76, 83–84,
    86, 98, 103–105, 112–113, 128,
    134, 140, 142, 147, 153–155, 168,
    171, 207–210, 233, 258
Socio-constructivism 227–235,
    238
Software localization 1, 19, 28,
    48–50, 55, 70, 72, 133, 135, 165,
    209–210, 216, 252
    Open source software
        (FLOSS) localization
        19, 28, 48–50, 70, 133, 135,
        165, 209–210
Source text 26, 40, 53, 59,
    61–63, 67–68, 77, 89–90,
    112–113, 119–120, 122, 126–127,
    130, 135, 142, 147–150, 153, 157–
    162, 166–169, 172–173, 180,
    182–183, 188–189, 205–206,
    239–240, 246–247, 252–253
Speaklike 33–34, 58, 65,
    128–129
Stepes 5–6, 29, 58–59, 70,
    84–86, 133–134, 230, 257
Subtitling 19, 21–23, 29, 35, 48,
    56–57, 65, 79–84, 171, 179–194,
    214–217, 225, 240–241, 251–
    252, 260–261
Summative evaluation 144, 236

T
Task-based approaches to
    education 238–239, 248–249
TAUS 57, 89–90, 92–93, 123–
    127, 132–135, 255
TAUS dynamic quality
    framework 123–125

TED Open Translation Initiative 16, 20–21, 30, 35, 70, 73, 79–80, 132, 145, 165, 171, 186, 187, 216, 217, 220–221, 239, 241

Text types   33–34, 111, 150–153, 225, 243–244, 249–251

Textual genres   33–36, 150, 152–153, 225, 234, 243–244, 249–253

Toury, Gideon   103–104, 124, 158, 174, 182–183, 242, 248

TRANSCOMP   228, 242–248, 253–254

Transifex   5–6, 22–23, 30–33, 42, 72–73, 83, 134, 234–235

Translation competence   7–9, 89–90, 99–100, 109–110, 176, 210, 227–228, 230–236, 239–254

Translation competence models   228, 233–234, 242–248, 251–253

Translation competence acquisition   8–9, 89–90, 109–110, 176, 231–234, 243, 248–250, 254

Translation crowdsourcing 2, 8, 11–12, 15–18, 21–25, 29–32, 46–48, 64–73, 84–85, 95, 100–109, 155, 225, 230–231, 251, 255, 257–258

Micro task crowdsourcing 83, 113–114, 169–170, 175, 207, 259

Translation management 22–23, 70, 76–77, 86–87, 104, 164–165

Translation memory (TM) 42, 51–52, 59, 61–63, 65–66, 74, 76–79, 82, 85–87, 101–102, 116–118, 134, 140, 142, 157, 159, 160–165, 169, 172, 176, 212, 230, 245, 251–252

Translation memory and segmentation   135, 140, 159–164, 172

Translation networks   31–32, 47–48, 97–98, 101, 103, 105–107, 197, 199–200, 208–209, 222, 234–235, 263

Translation norms   8, 39, 42–43, 62–63, 69, 107, 112, 121,

123–126, 130–132, 134–136, 146–147, 151, 160, 164, 174, 179–194, 198, 206, 209–210, 239, 243, 246–248, 252–253

AVT norms   8, 179–194

Expectancy and professional norms   62–63, 69, 107, 124, 160, 179–190, 193, 209–210

Subtitling norms   180–194

Translation paradigms   4–5, 7–8, 11–17, 38–39, 42–45, 63–64, 68–70, 84–87, 91, 98–99, 101, 107–108, 113, 121, 124, 127, 130, 135. 141, 148–150, 158, 160–161, 165–166, 168–170, 175, 185, 200–201, 206–208, 213, 216–217, 229–232, 242, 247–248, 261–263

Translation quality   3, 36, 70, 80, 93, 97, 118, 121–155, 162, 195–196, 202, 217, 237

External quality   140–141

Internal quality   140–141

Quality tiers   7–8, 126–129, 136–137, 202–203, 258–259

Quality evaluation   7–8, 74–75, 89, 122–124, 126–127, 129, 131–132, 135–139, 141, 146, 148–151, 154, 158

Translation technology   4, 7, 22, 42, 50–52, 61–62, 77, 108, 112, 117–118, 125, 159, 199–200, 229–230, 245

Translation training   1–2, 6, 83, 97, 110–111, 144–145, 158, 218, 227–254

Translation Turns   5–6, 8, 47, 195–197, 200–204, 261–263

Activist Turn   47, 203–204

Economic turn   6, 195, 201–203, 261–263

Sociological turn   5, 8, 195–197, 200–201, 203, 262

Technological turn   5, 8, 195, 200–201, 262

Translation unit   32, 65–67, 71, 114, 172–174, 245

Cognitive approaches   104, 141–142, 165–166, 172–174, 241, 263

Comparative linguistic approaches   174

Natural language processing 63, 172

Translation universals   176

Trommons   22–23, 36, 73, 76–77, 83–84, 134, 139, 234–235, 251–252

TxtEagle   67–68, 83

U

Unbabel   6, 29, 58–59, 66, 71, 78, 84–85, 87, 122, 134, 230, 259

User-generated content   24, 35–36, 44, 87–88, 127–128, 164

User-generated translation 23–24, 28, 54–55, 185

V

Videogame localization   1, 19, 163–164, 170

Viki   35, 56, 79, 84, 191

Volunteer motivation   17, 33, 60, 64–65, 72, 74, 92–95, 118, 132–133, 195–196, 202–204, 216–223, 236

Volunteer profiles   195–196, 216–217, 223–225

W

Web localization   1, 4, 33, 103, 148, 154, 158, 164–165, 176, 229–230, 252, 257

Wikipedia   14–15, 32–34, 44, 52–57, 65, 67–70, 72, 78, 85, 88–89, 134–136, 138–139, 143–144, 167–172, 217, 219–220, 223–224, 236

Wisdom of the crowd   13–15, 18, 51–52, 57–58, 60, 70, 72–73, 82, 113, 123, 169–170, 238–240

Workflow approaches   83–85, 140–141

Crowdsourcing workflows 5, 29–30, 32, 38, 50–53, 55–91, 104–105, 113–114, 116–117, 131–132, 134–136, 140–141, 164–167, 170–172, 174–177, 181, 185–186, 195–196, 202, 206, 257–258